DR. STAN COFFEY

The Return

A Close Look at Revelation and the Magnificent Return of Christ

---

Unless otherwise noted, all Scripture quotations are taken from *A READER'S GUIDE TO THE HOLY BIBLE: KINGS JAMES VERSION,* Thomas Nelson Inc. Publishers, Inc.

Library of Congress Control Number: 2005901045
ISBN: 0-9763742-0-X

Printed in the United States by Morris Publishing
3212 East Highway 30
Kearney, NE 68847
1-800-650-7888

CONTENTS

FOREWARD

I have known Dr. Stan Coffey for many, many years. He has faithfully preached God's Word for all the years of his ministry. I am glad to say that he has been a faithful expositor of God's Word. This is certainly rare today. He has taken books of the Bible and gone through them systematically resulting in real growth and spiritual maturity in the lives of those who have heard him.

This book is a beautiful approach to the book of Revelation. Perhaps all of us are well acquainted with many good volumes dealing with the prophetic, end-time events so graphically portrayed. The reader will certainly get this in Dr. Coffey's helpful volume.

Dr. Coffey has written a book with an unusual, exciting approach. While there is much judgment and wrath in the book of Revelation, for the believer, it is a tremendous book of hope. His title gives us an immediate interest. This book will be a great encouragement to God's children. I really do believe we are coming to the end of the age. Apostasy is all around us. Believers are falling into sin and indifference. Many of God's people are discouraged. Dr. Coffey's book will be helpful for believers at whatever stage they might be.

This book is helpfully arranged in six parts. Each one of these parts has number of chapters. The reader will be assisted in his or her study of Revelation by this helpful arrangement. I am filled with joy to recommend this volume to you. I believe it is going to make a unique contribution to our understanding of and appreciation for God's wonderful revelation of His Son, our Savior, the Lord Jesus Christ.

Dr. Jerry Vines, Pastor
First Baptist Church
Jacksonville, Florida

ACKNOWLEDGEMENTS

The partnership in ministry that I have enjoyed with the San Jacinto Baptist family has been the dream of every pastor. Their loving hearts and evangelistic spirits have motivated me to pursue God's best for me as a pastor and to lead the church to make a difference in the kingdom. I am also grateful to my administrative assistants Geneva Bagwell and Myra Vaughn for their diligent attention to details and for helping me maintain some semblance of sanity. I want to offer a special thanks to David Sylvester, my collaborator on this project, who labored over the laptop to help me arrange words and phrases that would best communicate the prophetic message of Revelation in easily understood language.

Without the love, support, and encouragement of the Pastor's Class, this book would not have been possible. Thanks to all of you for your faithfulness.

A special word of thanks to the following individuals: Bernie Thomas, Jack and Bobbie Hart, Chris and LaVonne Scharbauer, and Wayne and Mary Alice Hedrick.

DEDICATION

To the dearest person on earth to me:

My wife, Glenda Coffey

She has been the ultimate mate, pastor's wife, confident, friend, and partner in my ministry for thirty-eight years. Her outward beauty is exceeded only by her beauty within. Because of her love, I am the most blessed of men.

Stan Coffey

ABOUT THE AUTHOR

Dr. Stan Coffey has served as Senior Pastor of San Jacinto Baptist Church in Amarillo, Texas for more than twenty-four years in two tenures at the church. Originally from Oklahoma, he is the author of several books and audiotape series and a frequent speaker at state and national gatherings and church crusades.

Dr. Coffey is also a former president of the Southern Baptist Convention Pastors' Conference and a former president of the Southern Baptists of Texas Convention. He is also the recipient of the W. A. Criswell Lifetime Achievement Award in pastoral evangelism given by the Southern Baptists of Texas Convention. He lives with his wife, Glenda in Amarillo, Texas. They have two married children, Scott and Natalie.

PART 1

THE GLORY OF THE RISEN JESUS

Chapter 1

WHY STUDY THE REVELATION?
Revelation 1: 1-3

The book of Revelation is packed with lessons for today's reader and brimming with prophecies concerning the future as well. A thorough study is a worthy endeavor and full of blessings for those willing to pursue a studious investigation. To understand the entirety of the book in light of current world events requires an exhaustive and expository study of the book and it is to that end that this effort will precede. This snapshot review of the twenty-two chapters of the book will take the reader on a stimulating journey intended to whet the appetite of any curious bible student.

The apostle John, the scribe and writer of the vision, was a prophet and traditionally has been identified as John the apostle, the son of Zebedee. During his day, Rome made debilitating demands against Christians to recant their faith and accept the cult of emperor worship. Theologians propose that the height of this intense persecution occurred during the reign of the emotionally warped Domitian who ruled from A. D. 81-96. This position regarding the dating of the events is consistent with the one held by the renowned church father Irenaeus and other early Christian writers as well.

Furthermore, this era of time in church history is known for its loss of vitality and for spiritual complacency in the churches. Such spiritual lethargy is revealed in the descriptions of and warnings to the seven churches to which John referred in chapters two and three of the Revelation.

Virtually everyone is concerned about the future and what it holds for each of us. Our human curiosity is piqued as we consider the future in light of current events unfolding on the world scene. Those who write concerning the future and those who claim to have predictive powers attract hungry and eager audiences. The prediction of the future has become a marketable commodity that is subject to abuse.

Many people consult the horoscope longing for comfort. Others pursue the signs of the zodiac and astrological predictions to give meaning and hope. Cold comfort is the unfulfilling result. Discovering the realities of the future and personal hope for the present does not lie in the stars, but rather is to be found in the last book of the Bible that authoritatively and accurately reveals the future and points us to the Lord Jesus, the hope of glory. The book reveals the great climatic events that will bring the world to the brink of the close of human history when time shall be no more.

No book is as important in light of the days in which we live as the Revelation. In this prophetic and inspired work, we see light and darkness opposing one another. We read and envision God and the Lamb, Christ Jesus. We are literary witnesses to the greatest bloodbath and the greatest carnage the world has ever known. We read of the fire as it falls from heaven consuming all of which stands in its path. We witness the supernatural power of the Holy Spirit who moves us toward the personal revival that will come in the last days.

The book also contains the graphic description of a river of blood extending two hundred feet in breadth and measuring six feet in depth and ten miles in length. In the Revelation, we will be witnesses to the climactic and victorious return of Christ in person to the earth gloriously predicted within these prophetic pages.

For what reason should we study this literary biblical masterpiece? The Church as a whole simply disregards the book as too vague and therefore not worthy of a serious look.

The first three verses reveal the reason for a contemplative study. Revelation 1:3 promises, "*Blessed is he that readeth, and they that hear the words of this prophecy.*" Those who desire the blessing must take heed.

The Prophecy That is Reported

Four primary views concerning the appropriate method of interpretation have emerged in the Christian community. The *preterist* view purports that the events of Revelation are now past tense and therefore are not to occur in the future. The events of the book are seen as a reporting of the past persecution of the early church under the oppressive hand of the Roman Empire. Lessons abide within the book but one is to assume that no predictive component is to be found.

Others prefer the *panoramic* view of the Revelation, also known as the continuous historical view and suggest that Revelation is a mere summary of secular and church history in total. The primary downfall of this perspective is that it is too inclusive and attempts to include all historical events, a virtually impossible task and one that certainly does not and will not fall into the logical pattern of the Revelation.

Third, the parabolic or *allegorical* viewpoint maintains that the Revelation is written in symbolic language, a claim that is certainly true, and that the book does not necessarily depict actual and literal events. Further, as the Bible speaks of the stars falling from heaven or refers to the moon turning to blood and the sun to darkness, it is not recording literal occurrences but rather symbolic events as representative of spiritual truths. This view further maintains that the writings are primarily representative of the struggle between good and evil. Few serious conservative scholars, if any, hold to this view.

A fourth view is that the Revelation is to read as *prophetic,* the view from which we will proceed. First, the writings of the book primarily deal with the future as God has so ordered it. Multiple times in the first chapter, the book is referred to as prophecy. As an interpretive rule of thumb, prophecy often includes a double meaning that involves current and futuristic events. For example, as Isaiah the prophet spoke to the nation of Israel concerning the coming of Jesus Christ and His incarnation in Isaiah 9 and 53, he referred to the One coming who would be the *"wonderful counselor, the mighty God, the everlasting Father, and the Prince of Peace."* He came and He is coming! Further, Isaiah stated that Jesus would sit upon the throne of his father David and that He would reign forever, a message of encouragement packed with future implications as well referencing His time on earth as the God-man and a future appearance as well. Jesus came - but will come.

A second reason to recognize the prophetic nature of the book is that many events predicted therein are yet to occur. Countless events foretold in the book are unprecedented in human history. Revelation speaks of a time when a third of the earth's vegetation will be consumed by fire. It refers to a future time when the oceans become so polluted that sea life will not exist, and to a time during which the fresh waters we know and enjoy will be contaminated and without practical use. The sad conditions of our modern ecology and the destructive effects of modern industry on the environment make such prophecies even more believable.

Third, the prophetic nature of the Revelation is further underscored by the claim that the consummation of the events must occur for the prophecies of the Old Testament to be fulfilled. Jesus boldly said, "*Heaven and earth shall pass away*", and further said, "*But My word shall never pass away.*" Obviously, such a dramatic event as the passing of the heavens and earth from the scene has yet to occur but is clearly predicted in the book. To view the scriptures as the infallible and inerrant word of God requires of the honest interpreter that he or she see the Revelation as prophetic in nature in order to be consistent with the revelatory nature of our Lord.

The Promise to be Received

Verse three of the first chapter clearly promises that a *blessing* is in store for the believer who reads, hears, and obeys the words of the prophecy. What *blessings* are in mind, one might ask? To be blessed in this context means to experience high favor, to be congratulated, or to experience true happiness. The benefit for the faithful readers of these profound words is the encouragement of our faith, the deepening of our prayer life, and the unique ability to interpret all of life in light of the current and coming victory that is ours as fully devoted followers of Jesus Christ. Our perspective changes as God adds to our lives that which cannot be received other than supernaturally.

To activate this blessing as we read and obey, we must apply the truths found in the pages so that the accumulation of knowledge is behavioral in its impact rather than merely academic. Truth, fully received, penetrates the heart and leads to behavioral change. Little profit is received from a mere cognitive understanding of the beast of chapter thirteen, the great harlot of chapter eighteen, or the four horsemen of chapter six. Faith requires feet and is intended to impact our lives.

The prophecy opens with these words, "*The revelation of Jesus Christ, which God gave unto him, to shew unto his servants things which must shortly come to pass; and he sent and signified it by his angel unto his servant John*" (1:1). The word *revelation* is derived from the Greek compound *"apa-kalupto"* meaning to take away the cover. Revelation is essentially the unveiling of Jesus for the faithful reader.

Knowledge is progressing at breakneck speed. Interestingly, Daniel 12:4 records that in the last days many will run to and fro upon the earth and knowledge will be increased. I firmly believe that this reference is to the knowledge of Jesus Christ that will be fully unveiled and revealed at the time of His second coming.

The Revelation is packed with picturesque symbols such as beasts, locusts, a rainbow wrapped around the throne of God, and the twenty-four elders who are vividly displayed. Why the extensive use of symbolism, one might inquire? Symbols carry unchanging meaning whereas mere words alter in meaning over time. The word for love in I Corinthians thirteen, *charity,* previously understood to be synonymous with love, is viewed very differently today. Symbols carry consistent meaning, a benefit that at least partially explains their extensive use in the book. Second, the code language of the book was also an effective tool in preventing the Roman authorities from discovering its meanings and consequently increasing the brutal persecution on those in the faith community. Scholars estimate the date of the writing by John as near 95 A.D., a time of intense intimidation, physical harm, and retaliation against God's people who were regarded as cultic. To estimate, in approximately fifty percent of the instances of the use of symbols, the book itself interprets the symbolic mysteries for the reader.

The promise for the faithful reader is one of enlightenment as to what God says concerning the last days and an ongoing promise of refreshing encouragement and sustaining hope. Believers are encouraged as the destruction of evil is boldly predicted and accomplished. Encouragement fills our souls as we look to the day when the current injustice, corruption, greed, hatred, and other atrocities such as starving children one day will be no more. God will right the wrong, settle the score, balance the scales of justice, obliterate the evil and replace it with the eternal reign of Jesus Christ.

The faithful reader of the book also is blessed to realize that the redemption of mankind finally will be consummated. A proper understanding of Revelation leads to a more complete understanding of other passages of scripture, particularly Genesis. The creation that is initiated in Genesis is consummated in Revelation. The story of the creation of the heavens and earth is depicted in Genesis – the story of the re-creation is magnified in Revelation. Genesis portrays the story of the tree of life abused by Adam and Eve - in Revelation man is again invited to take part in the tree of life. In Genesis, man lost paradise but regains it in Revelation. Satan is introduced in Genesis and is unceremoniously destroyed in Revelation. In Genesis, one reads of the first death in history in the murder of Abel by his angry brother Cain – in Revelation we are promised that death will be no more. In Genesis, Eve is the first bride - in Revelation we read of the last bride, the Church, as she is beautifully presented to Jesus the bridegroom. Stimulating and fulfilling is the experience to be received by the diligent reader of these prophetic words.

The Person Who is Revealed

The Revelation centrally concerns Jesus the Christ. To attempt to remove Jesus from center focus is akin to removing the heat from the fire, or the blood from the cross. While physically existing on earth, Jesus was fully God and simultaneously fully man.

His deity was veiled in His humanity. Once only in his earthly ministry while on the mount of transfiguration did God allow his cohorts Peter, James and John to see Him in full glory. As they saw Him, they fell face down as though dead. In Revelation, the veil of Jesus is finally lifted and we will see Christ in His glorified body.

We look to the day when we as believers will be joint heirs and will reign with Him for all of eternity with bodies like His. His long-awaited appearance will be the grand consummation of our faith.

The Preparation That is Required

Verse one reminds the reader that God gave the revelation *"to shew his servants things which must shortly come to pass."* As we believers begin to understand what is to come we are more effectively motivated to make spiritual preparations for that climactic day. The result of such awareness is to increase our love for others, to pray as never before, to share Christ's message of eternal life with passion, and to study His word with more determination. The word *"shortly"* in this Greek context is derived for the word *tachos,* English for tachometer referring to the speed of rotation. The implication of John's foreboding words is that the events herein described will occur speedily when they begin to unfold. For example, the raising of the dead will occur in the *twinkling of an eye,* or in the fraction of a second, referring to the brevity of time required to accomplish such a supernatural feat.

Consider the rapid and historical fall of the Berlin Wall. Who would have predicted that the events of 1990 would have touched off a chain reaction resulting in the demise of communism in Eastern Europe? It has been said that God's sovereignty moves the hand of time. As the events on the prophetic calendar begin to unfold they will transpire with blinding speed.

Revelation 1:3 also states that *"the time is at hand".* The apostle is again reminding the reader of the imminent return of Christ. Such a reminder is to spur the believer to take action and make diligent preparations for His return. The book of Revelation was written to prepare churches in existence in that day for the coming events, and to provide encouragement that Christ could come at any moment and remove the persecution from their battered lives. His coming will be unexpected but not unpredicted. Readers, be alert!

The time has been at hand for two thousand years, one might comment, and yet the return of Jesus has yet to occur. The majority of the predicted events of the book do not require fulfillment for the rapture of the church to occur. Many events described in the book, such as ecological calamities, will occur *after* believers have been vacated from the earth. Some bible students today propose that the Church will experience three and a half years of tribulation, be purified by persecution, and then the return of Christ and the rapture will occur. This interpretation is widely known as the mid-tribulationist view. Such a notion seems to deny the imminent nature of His return and is therefore invalid. The believer must live as though Jesus died yesterday, rose again this morning, and is coming back today!

As Jesus breaks open the eastern sky in a dramatic reappearance, He is coming not to suffer but rather to reign. He is coming not to be mistreated but to reign in majesty. As He is unveiled in the manner described in the book of Revelation, we will see Him not as He was but rather as He is. The last time that our world saw Christ with the naked eye was on the cross; we will see Him the second time wearing a crown.

Such magnificent words must have been soothing grace to the early Christians as many of their fellow believers were thrown to the lions as mere sporting events, doused with torches, and burned alive at the stake. It is within these prophetic words that readers today as well may find hope.

Chapter 2

COURAGE IN THE MIDST OF DIFFICULTY
Revelation 1: 4-8

The writer John makes crystal clear his intention of dedicating the revelation that was given to him to Jesus Christ. Using words in adoration of his Lord such as *"unto him who loved us"*, John the apostle lovingly dedicated his writings to Jesus as would a writer to his or her spouse in an effort to express honor. John dedicated these apocalyptic and revealing words to Jesus who is the One progressively unveiled in this biblical drama.

The scribe who recorded these inspired words and the identity of the recipients are clearly delineated in the opening words of verse four, *"John to the seven churches which are in Asia"*. He reminded the reader that the message of the book is primarily to the churches that were in existence in the first century.

Bearing a common name in that day, John was an *honored man* and is consistently identified as an apostle of the Lord Jesus and the recipient of this final book in the biblical cannon written in approximately A.D. 95. He is also the writer of the brief letters of I, II, and III John, and the Gospel of John. John was further identified as the *"disciple whom Jesus loved"*. Scholars have dubbed him the beloved apostle for it is John who by deed and word has given us a beautiful portrayal of the beloved nature of our Lord.

John's fame was such that the mention of his name immediately identified him in the seven churches about which he wrote. Scholars remind us that he was the sole remaining apostle alive at the writing of the Revelation. According to church history and tradition, the other apostles had met their demise or had been mercilessly martyred for the cause of Christ.

In A.D. 69-70, the city of Jerusalem was viciously ransacked and destroyed in fulfillment of the prophecy of Jesus in Matthew 24. The result was a massive dispersion of the Christian Jews who resided there. John was among those who rapidly dispersed and relocated in the city of Ephesus in Asia Minor. I have visited the area of Ephesus and have witnessed the marvelous statues and breathtaking sculptures that highlight the landscape. It is an amazing reminder of the sights and sounds of the New Testament world. John became pastor of the believers in Ephesus and functioned in that role until his forced exile to the Isle of Patmos at the hands of the ruling Roman authorities.

John was a *humble man* as well. He writes, "*John, who also am your brother, and your companion in tribulation*" (1:9). John took care not to position himself as spiritually superior to his readers. What an accurate portrayal of the Church, as God intended it to be, is revealed in these tender words. Dictatorial lordship over others exercised by some leaders in our day is not the plan of God for His people. God has identified spiritual leaders in the church, to be sure, yet spiritual equality in the family of God and in the eyes of God is implied here. Spiritual leaders such as the apostle John are not immune to the trials and difficulties of the man in the pew. He identifies by personal experience with the lives of those whom he serves. Spiritual leaders in our day must do likewise.

Due to his unwavering stand for his Lord, John was also a *hated man.* The scripture points to the Word of God, to John's adherence to the Word and to the testimony of Jesus as reasons for his forced exile to a neighboring island. The Roman authorities attempted to silence his witness and thus curtail the growth of the Christian church that found itself in direct competition and in an adversarial relationship with Rome. The first massive persecution of the Church occurred under the neurotic emperor Nero. The second wave of hatred from the government came at the hands of the emperor Domitian. Persecution is not an option for the fully devoted believer. Believers are twice-born people in a once-born world whose ethical code based upon the words of Jesus often comes into sharp conflict with the dominant worldview. America has her faults, but as of this writing, owning a copy of the scriptures is not an illegal act as it once was in the nation of Russia.

John's new home on the Isle of Patmos was located in the Aegean Sea. It was small in size and rocky terrain jutted from the landscape. The island had little vegetation. Scholars believe that a cave tucked away in the island is the location where John sat as he penned the vision of the Revelation he received from God.

Reasons for Persecution

John suffered persecution but not without cause. Had God in His sovereignty not allowed for the exile of the beloved apostle He might have chosen another method for the recording of these prophetic words. Secluded and alone, John wrote profound words that continue to impact our society and world today. Sales of prophetic literature soar to inconceivable levels as world tension increases. The terrorist attacks on America in September 2001 mushroomed the sale of prophetic literature by a whopping eighty percent!

Why are believers persecuted today? Why did God allow persecution of such fierce intensity in John's day? In part, early believers were persecuted because they were *evangelistic.* Hundreds of thousands of citizens had turned to Christ and their allegiance to the Roman emperor became suspect. Conversions to Christ irritated the authorities and spurred Satan to rise up against the Church. Churches today who do not realize the conversion of people to faith in Christ are very little threat to anyone.

Early believers experienced intimidation because they were also *exclusive* in their refusal to bow to Caesar as lord. Roman authorities insisted that citizens of conquered countries verbalize the mantra, *Caesar is lord.* Rejecting the mantra and choosing not to offer a pinch of incense to Caesar resulted in intense governmental retaliation and often imprisonment or death. Believers were often subjected to killer animals in the arenas of Rome as sporting events meant to entertain the masses and force future believers to recant their faith and worship Caesar. The emperor Domitian was bent upon destroying every believer on the face of the earth.

Believers were also harassed because they were *enthusiastic* in the practice of their faith. The fire of the Holy Spirit burned brightly in their hearts further irritating Caesar and his henchmen. Enthusiasm is derived from the two root words *en* and *theos,* signifying "in God". True heartfelt and outwardly expressed enthusiasm is not contrived or manufactured by human emotion but rather is rooted in the work of God in our hearts. Believers today are often depicted by the media as lacking in intellect and duped into emotional frenzy. Our faith is not founded on groundless truths nor is it simply the emotional expressions of a simplistic and gullible mind. The truth of God rightly understood produces an emotional response guided by the Holy Spirit. Knowledge and zeal rightly practiced complement one another.

A Message for the Church

The message received by John in a vision and recorded for posterity and instruction essentially is not merely generic to the general population but rather a specific one for the Church then and now. The location of the seven churches to which his words are addressed is our modern day Greek Islands and portions of Turkey. These seven churches are accurate representations of the churches of today as well. Scholars remind us that each of these unique seven churches represents a particular aspect of the church age. The church age refers to the era ranging from the Day of Pentecost described in Acts chapter two to the time when Christ comes to remove the Church from the world. John writes these words to many in the faith community who had become doctrinally corrupt, spiritually lax and complacent in their practice. The early church, as well as the church of today, was in need of a loving but direct rebuke and John delivered the rebuke pointedly, indeed.

In this prophetic book, Jesus' *representation is revealed.* In Revelation 1: 5-6, Jesus is herein identified as the *"faithful witness"*. Human beings, in contrast to Jesus, are prone to failure. Abraham was God's faithful witness yet faltered when in Egypt. Israel was faithful for a season yet turned to idols as replacements for God. Churches often fail in their mission yet Jesus has never and will never fail. Events promised in the Revelation will come to pass and burst upon the world scene to the startling amazement and sheer terror of the skeptical world. No man will be unaware that it is Jesus the Messiah who has arrived.

In these verses we see also that His *resurrection is revealed.* He is herein referred to as the "*first begotten of the dead*" meaning that Jesus was the first to be raised from the dead never to die again (1:5). Lazarus, a colorful character in the gospels, died and was resurrected – but later died a second death. Jesus Christ rose to stay risen and to usher His Church into the glorious millennial reign and into eternity with Him.

His *royalty is revealed* as well in that He is crowned the "*prince of the kings of the earth*" (1:5) No president or monarch compares in authority with our risen Lord. His authority is unmatched and His splendor is inconceivable to the human mind. He is coming to rule and to initiate His rule with the millennial reign that will be established at His second coming. Further, his *redemption is revealed* in that the blood of Jesus shed at the cross and revealed in the scarlet thread of redemption permeates the entire Bible from Genesis to Revelation. Believers today have not been cleansed from the ravages of sin by the waters of baptism but rather by the blood of Jesus who *"cleanses us from all sin".* Notice that Jesus loves us and then washes us clean from the effects of our sin. Scriptures record that He *"loved us and washed us"* (1:5). There are some today who may choose to love us only if God's *washing* has already done its complete work. Most of us prefer clean sheep as friends. The father of the prodigal son whose story is recorded in the gospels loved his rebellious son even in the midst of his rebellion and did not require a *washing* before he would display that pure love to his wayward son. What a beautiful portrayal of the unconditional love of God. John points to the Jesus of this revelation who incarnates and communicates the love of His Father.

In the cleansing and saving work of God in the lives of believers His *regeneration is revealed* as well. Scriptures teach that God has made us to be a kingdom of priests. Early believers understood this truth to mean that they no longer needed a priest to communicate with God. In the Jewish system, the priest was required to intercede with God for the sins of the people once each year on the Day of Atonement. Since the time of the cleansing and atonement act on the cross, believers may experience the atoning of their sins without a human priest to act on their behalf because the cleansing blood of Jesus atones for all sin. Human mediation is therefore unnecessary.

John further reminds the reader that Jesus is coming soon, and as He does *"every eye shall see him"*, a quotation taken from Zechariah 1:7. The Bible does not indicate that every eye will see Him simultaneously or in the same manner. Scriptures mention the second coming of Jesus an astounding three hundred eighteen times underscoring the validity and importance of this coming event. The Church will see Him as He removes believers from the world in the rapture or in the *snatching away* while the rest of faithless humanity will see Him come in judgment. When He comes in the Battle of Armageddon as described in chapter nineteen, the masses will wail and cry in distress due to their failure to believe the claims of Jesus and follow Him.

The Coronation of Jesus

Verses seven and eight prophesy concerning His coronation. Here Jesus is identified as the *"Alpha and Omega"*, the beginning and the end referenced by the first and last letters of the Greek alphabet. The implication is that Jesus is the sum total of the person of God and the beginning and end of human history. He defies and transcends human history. He occupies history but initiated it as well. He is indeed the dominating character within the purview of human history – but in reality, He *is* history as well.

As a kingdom of priests, our Lord has given us the ability by His Spirit to endure and conquer the difficulties we may encounter as aliens on this earth. This world is truly not our home.

Take courage!

Chapter 3

THE ONLY PHOTOGRAPH OF JESUS
Revelation 1: 9-18

Most of us have seen a rendering by an artist of Jesus decorating the walls of the church of our childhood. Many of these artistic depictions often portray Jesus as effeminate with long flowing hair, silky smooth skin, and lacking in authority. He is often portrayed as a man of slight build and physical weakness. Paintings also depict him as a pale Galilean and nothing more than a Jewish peasant struggling for credibility. Others claimed that His contribution on earth was limited to his work as a great teacher with unusual insight yet was less than divine. Many claimed that He lacked real power although He deserved commendation for worthy intentions.

The word *revelation* refers to the unveiling or uncovering of Jesus Christ for others to see and worship. Due to the intensity of the persecution to which believers living in the first century were subjected, God offers in Revelation the gradual but sure unveiling of Jesus as a means of encouraging believers and motivating us to keep the faith.

The writer John, exiled to the Isle of Patmos received a specific vision from God while imprisoned on the island. His exile was due in part to his faithful and effective proclamation of God's word, a powerful word that served as an irritant to the Roman emperor Domitian who wanted to obliterate its message. Absolute rule by the Roman authorities was enforced by any and all means necessary. John's claim that Jesus was the only Lord sent shock waves throughout the Roman political system. John proclaimed that the true Lord was not Caesar nor the mythological Zeus or Apollo but was Jesus and Jesus alone. Such public rhetoric bought John an unceremonious transfer to the remote island located southwest of Ephesus as a means to silence his influence.

The message of the cross of Jesus Christ and its accompanying ethical and behavioral implications will forever run counter to the prevailing worldview of the day and will result in volatile conflict. The cross is a message of offense, the scriptures claim, and is often a stumbling block to those who refuse to receive it. Believers should experience no surprise when the cultural tide washes over them in an act of retaliation. Jesus said, *"Woe unto you when all men shall speak well of you"* (Luke 6: 26). John was subjected to the full brunt of the prevailing Roman worldview and was tossed onto an abandoned island as a result. He was exiled there as well due to the testimony of Christ and the fact that he bore no shame to be called a follower of Jesus Christ. Alone in exile, he was away from friends, family, and the flock of God to which he had been assigned. In that solitude he received the most breathtaking and influential vision man has ever received.

One Man-Two Locations

God does not forsake His people. John was no exception. John described the circumstances surrounding reception of the vision, *"I was in the Spirit on the Lord's day"* (1:10). Theologians have long debated the experience of living *"in the Spirit."* Essentially, John was caught up in an experience of spiritual ecstasy in which the cares of this world diminished in their ability to control his emotions, and he began to live and flourish in another world, as it were. Theologically, this state of being is known as *walking in the Spirit.* Christians are citizens of two worlds – alive in the flesh on planet earth and spiritual residents of heaven. Believers live with a sense of alienation from this temporary earthly residence. A careful balance of these two spheres of existence leads to spiritual health.

The long-used phrase, "some people are so heavenly minded that they are no earthly good" has a ring of truth. Some people think in spiritual terms to the extent of ignoring the needs of the body of Christ while others become materialistic and therefore miss the life of the Spirit. A life of worship and a life of work may not interconnect and therefore our lives become dangerously *compartmentalized,* to use the modern vernacular. John lived in the natural world but was caught up in the supernatural, a realm that provided the setting for him to hear and record God's magnificent vision.

Life in the Spirit

John is a fitting illustration that believers have the privilege to know the Spirit and to be led into all truth, a concept that John claimed in the gospel that he authored. In solitude on the island, John was transported in the Spirit from earth into the portals of heaven. He was informed during the midst of the vision concerning details and predictions of the future. Revelation concerns a first century man who envisioned twenty-first century events such as thermonuclear war, global mass destruction, and massive starvation. His recorded vision is breathtaking to readers as we investigate the accuracy of the prophecy and its implications for the future of our planetary system.

John was in the Spirit *"on the Lord's day"* (1:10). Scriptures give priority to the Lord's Day. People who choose to treat the day of worship as any other day of the week find that failure to prioritize their lives and provide times for spiritual rejuvenation have a high price to pay. The channel of communication with God becomes muddled and our hearts degenerate toward life in the natural, void of spiritual vitality.

Some years ago a man who faithfully watched our television broadcast wrote to me insisting that hell was in our path because we failed to worship on Saturday. He failed to realize that under the law, the Sabbath was to commemorate God's work of creation and to honor God because He is the maker of all things. God commanded the Jews to honor Him on the seventh day. After the resurrection, however, the Old Testament requirement of the Sabbath was fulfilled. Jesus said, *"I came to fulfill the law."* Christians after the resurrection gathered to worship on the first day of the week to underscore the day of resurrection. John is seen in Revelation worshipping alone on the Lord's Day meaning Sunday, interestingly the day on which God chose to give this incredible vision to him.

It was on the Lord's Day at a Sunday evening service, recorded in John 20:19, that the Lord appeared to his disciples who claimed that they had seen the Lord. Doubting Thomas, who required a thoughtful apologetic before believing, threw doubt on their astonishing claims. John listened well as God lifted him into the realm of the Spirit and revealed things to him most of which had not been previously known.

Life in the Spirit is available for any believer and is possible for all. No vision of the magnitude of John's vision is required to accompany that experience in order to claim a close relationship with the Spirit.

Jesus Revealed

Verse ten records that the voice John heard behind him was *"as of a trumpet."* The writer Paul claims in I Thessalonians chapter four that as Jesus comes again to claim and remove the Church, the experience will be accompanied by the sound of the trumpet. John was instructed that the prophetic revelation of Jesus was to be recorded and sent to the seven churches in existence in Asia Minor. John must have gasped as he saw the vision of Jesus unfold before his startled eyes. Scripture records in 1: 14-16,

> *His head and his hairs were white like wool, as white as snow; and his eyes were as a flame of fire; and his feet like unto fine brass, as if they burned in a furnace, and his voice as the sound of many waters. And he had in his right hand seven stars: and out of his mouth went a sharp two-edged sword: and his countenance was as the sun shineth in his strength.*

This amazing passage is one of the clearest enunciations of the concept of the triune God in all of scripture. Critics today often claim that Jesus never claimed to be God. Jesus' claim as the *Alpha* and the *Omega* implies that God has always existed as the self-existent One, and that Jesus has forever existed as well. Jesus existed before His birth in Bethlehem. As renowned preacher

Shadrack Lockridge quipped, "He is older than His mother and the same age as His father!" No question about it, Jesus is timeless!

Jesus is herein pictured as the *reigning Christ.* The clothing adorning Jesus is indication of His undeniable reign. His garment is shown flowing downward to His feet and around His chest is draped a golden girdle. While walking on earth as the God-man, the deity of Jesus was veiled by His humanity though the full nature of His existence was His all the while. In this *apokalypsis,* or more full exposure, Jesus is here seen dressed as the God that He is, the Lord of Lords.

Christ Jesus is also the *righteous Christ.* The prophet Isaiah in chapter six repeats the word *holy* three times in rapid succession to underscore His essential nature. Revelation 1:14 describes his features, *"his head and his hairs were white like wool."* The color of white signified His holiness. In Daniel chapter seven, the Ancient of Days, the Almighty God is presented in precisely the same manner as the risen Christ is revealed here in the revelation.

He is also the *revealing Christ.* Revelation 1:14 reminds us that *"His eyes were as a flame of fire,"* a significant use of a metaphor that speaks of His omniscience or His ability to know all things. He possesses the unprecedented ability to see beyond the human façade, and with breathtaking and searing ability, peer into the hearts of man and reveal his or her thoughts. God is to be feared, the scriptures remind us, because all things are "*naked and opened unto the eyes of him with whom we have to do*" (Hebrews 4:13). God knows our actions and more – He knows the motives that drive those actions as well.

Our Lord is also seen here as the *relentless Christ.* Revelation 1:15 records, *"His feet like unto fine brass, as if they burned in a furnace"* (1:15). What significance should one attribute to His feet? The nineteenth chapter of Revelation records in the judgment scene that Christ will tread the winepress of the wrath of Almighty God. The feet like fine brass speak of certain judgment because brass is a familiar symbol of judgment in the Bible. In a related episode, the book of Numbers records that poisonous snakes infiltrated the camp of the Israelites and killed many of the people with lethal bites. God instructed the leader Moses to raise a serpent of brass in the middle of the camp and to inform the people that those who looked upon the serpent would live. That brass serpent was a type of Christ in that it represented the future means whereby man could truly live because the sins of mankind would be laid upon Jesus. Such an act would atone for the sins of man and give to him eternal life. Jesus is pictured here as relentless in His desire to bring swift and sure judgment upon the earth.

The *regal Christ* Jesus is graphically portrayed as having a voice as the *"sound of many waters"* (1:15). To illustrate, the heavy waters of the famed Niagara Falls crash to the rocks and waters below with such force the noise is deafening. The picture of the voice of Jesus as similar to the sound of roaring waters is of One who is majestic and glorious. With similarity, Ezekiel 43 and Psalm 29 describe the glory of God as the sound of many rushing waters. The guttural roar of fast moving water creates a distinct awareness of His awesome power.

The rule of Jesus is further described in the graphic picture of *"seven stars"* (1:16). The stars are representative of the angels or pastoral messengers of the seven churches to which the words of the revelation are addressed. The right hand signifies the hand of authority or the hand of power. The pastoral leaders of the seven churches were in the hand of our authoritative God. God has a unique way of directing the affairs of His pastors. His rule is providential and sovereign.

As the *revenging Christ*, Jesus is pictured as taking seriously the matter of settling the score and righting the wrongs that have been perpetrated against His people. John saw Jesus as having a *"sharp two-edged sword"* protruding out of His mouth (1:16). Liberal theologians who doubt the total veracity of the scriptures and liberal politicians who either deny the existence of Christ or who reject the concept of the wrath of God strongly object at this juncture. God is a God of love and would not inflict harmful judgment on mankind, they insist. In prophetic reality, the sword cuts in order to heal. As a surgeon who applies the sharp scalpel on the wounded area, the Lord Jesus will perform a surgery of justice to balance the scales of justice and further exemplify His righteous character.

Jesus is vividly portrayed as the *resplendent Christ* as well. John saw in the vision of Jesus, *"His countenance was as the sun shineth in his strength"* (1:16). To look into the radiant face of Jesus was akin to gazing into the face of the sun. In 1:17, John turned his eyes toward Jesus and fell *"as dead"*. The glory was so magnificent that John dropped to his knees in a weakened and submitted position. On the mount of transfiguration recorded in the gospels, the threesome of Peter, James, and John reacted in a similar manner as the veil of humanity was lifted from the person of Jesus Christ. One day as we are in heaven, believers will gaze into the glorious face of Jesus without recoiling, yet we will recognize His full authority and reign.

Jesus is also pictured here as displaying kind and loving compassion to the frightened John. He says, *"Fear not…........I am he that liveth, and was dead; and, behold, I am alive for evermore, Amen; and have the keys of hell and of death"* (1:18). The assuring promise of our life with Christ is He comes to us in moments of despair and speaks peace.

Jesus herein reminds us of His eternal presence. The *"keys"* that He possesses remind us that Christ is able to open to us the door of eternal life of which death attempts to deprive us. Death deprives us of physical life – but Christ opens the door of death and thereby presents us with eternal life. To know Jesus as Lord is to experience no permanent death. The physical death of the believer merely ushers in a new era of eternal life. Jesus robbed death of its sting and the grave of its goal. As John was nearing one hundred years old at the time of his writing, he must have found these loving words of Jesus to be words of sustaining grace.

Truly Jesus is the One who removes all fear.

Chapter 4

DISCOVERING THE SECRET OF REVELATION
Revelation 1: 19-20

To the occasional or causal reader of the Revelation, a prophetic book of this magnitude written with heavy use of symbols and in coded language can be a daunting task indeed. The challenging task of understanding its meaning may motivate the reader to set aside the Bible from frustration or confusion. Furthermore, the multitude of interpretations that decorate the theological landscape often cause the reader to eliminate from his or her mind any desire to discover the truth because the truth appears forever elusive.

Attempts to outline the book of Revelation are as numerous as the pebbles of sand on the seashore. The most helpful outline, however, is the one as presented by the writer John in Revelation 1:19. As Jesus is speaking to John he says these words, "*Write the things which thou hast seen, and the things which are, and the things which shall be hereafter.*" In one smooth stroke, God outlined in simple terms the entire book of Revelation for the reader. Essentially, the contents of the prophecy are given in three time frames of God's work in terms of the past, the present, and the future.

The Things That John Had Seen

John was eyewitness to the things that he had *seen,* referring to the words that have been recorded in chapter one that we have discussed previously. The things that *are* relate to the stern words written in Revelation 2-3 that relate to the seven churches that were the recipients of the entire prophecy. These bold words relate to the Church Age that is commonly defined as the time from the ascension of Jesus to heaven and continuing to the time in the future when Jesus will come and dramatically remove the Church from the world.

The third era of time related in the book deals with events that occur *hereafter*. The bulk of the prophecy of the book falls into this category and is recorded in chapter four to the end of the book. Again, I believe the appropriate hermeneutic for the book is to see it as prophetic since the bulk of its message has yet to occur.

The movement in Europe to consolidate powers and create one great European government and economic power, the unrest in the Middle East, and the continuing saga of the collapse of Communism and the reconfiguration of the Soviet Union are all paving the way for the fulfillment of what we read in these prophetic pages. For example, we read that an army of two hundred million men will be fielded and will cross the River Euphrates into the land of Israel.

Today, jutting into the sky is a great dam on the Euphrates River located in the country of Turkey. The Bible says that the waters of that river will become dry and allow this huge army to march across its bed.

Further, to understand the meaning of the book, it is important to realize a critical rule of biblical interpretation. As symbols appear in the scriptures, it is wise to trace their meanings as given throughout the entire Bible. For example, Leviticus speaks of the tabernacle in the wilderness and the lampstand that was present in that holy place. The lampstand was to shine and thereby reflect the glory of God. The lampstand symbolized the glory of God in Leviticus – and in Revelation symbolizes the churches that received the written vision. When Jesus came, He claimed to be the light of the world yet also said to the disciples, *"ye are the light of the world."* Is there a contradiction within these two claims? Perhaps the analogy of the sun and moon is appropriate. The sun is light to the world in the day as is the moon at night. The moon has no light of its own but rather receives it from the sun.

Similarly, the Church is the light of the world in that she receives light from the Son of God. Like the moon, we as believers merely reflect what we have received. Consequently, He is in the midst of His churches, symbolized in the Revelation as lampstands. We are also reminded that He performs His works through the medium of the Church. The Church is Christ's presence with His people and in the world.

The Number Seven

We read as well in these verses that Christ is vitally interested in the protection of His pastors. Here, He is pictured as holding seven stars in His right hand. Words written to actual churches addressed seven such congregations in existence in John's day. The number seven often has both symbolic as well as literal implications. Seven is the number of completion and biblically refers to completion and perfection. Seven notes on the musical scale are necessary, for to play the scale and stop without striking the final tone leaves for the listener a sense of incompletion and emotional void. All of the vivid colors in the spectrum of the rainbow are needed to paint the sky in full splendor.

The *"stars",* mentioned in 1:20 referring to the angels of the seven churches, are translated *angellos* in Greek writings or messengers to readers today. Scholars often agree that the pastors of the seven churches are viewed here as the primary messengers of God to His Church. God is fully capable of protecting His pastors but at times sees the need to rebuke and chastise them as well for the protection of His bride, the Church. The ultimate chastening or rebuke of the pastor is an act that God reserves for Himself although human mediation may play a role as well in preserving accountability. Essentially, the word John received was complete and not lacking in any regard.

The Things That Are

The message to the seven churches recorded in blunt terms in chapters two and three have a primary, prophetic and practical meaning for today's believers. Contrary to popular assumption, the last word to the Church given by our Lord was not the Great Commission recorded in Matthew 28, but rather the stern words given to the seven churches of this revelation.

For what reasons would the vision of God given to His scribe John be directed to the churches? First, John wrote to *commend the churches* for their efforts to continue the gospel in the midst of the hotbed of persecution. Like our Lord Jesus, John writes to compliment the church but also proceeds to warn and correct as well as would a loving father. Second, he writes to *condemn the churches* for lazy spiritual commitments that skew the message of the Church and hamper its witness. The two-edged sword previously mentioned serves to cut as well as to heal. Third, the purpose of the direct words to the churches was to *counsel the churches.* These visionary words were insightful and diagnostic in assessing the needed changes in the Church. The basis of any diagnosis a church of today may need may be found in the pages of God's word.

The church at Ephesus received a warning for its propensity toward formality that served to douse the fires of excitement and passion in the church. They had truly lost their first love and were operating on the basis of human ingenuity rather than passion.

The church at Smyrna endured great bouts with fear because of the fierce intensity of their persecution. Concerning their suffering, John wrote that they should *"fear not"*. John encouraged them their ability to endure heinous acts of retaliation would assure them that they would receive an appropriate reward in the end.

The congregation at Pergamos faltered because of their lack of attention to doctrinal purity. The demand of repentance on their part, insisted upon by our Lord, was stern and replete with special attention given to the false teachers who had infiltrated the church and wreaked havoc.

Thyatira was home to a church that was false and hypocritical in that the members gave external evidence of credibility as a church but were shallow in the spiritual commitment of their hearts. John's words to the few faithful members motivated them to remain true and loyal to the Lord.

The church at Sardis was dying. God communicated to this church that its role had not been completed and that their floundering ministry should be strengthened and preserved. They were furthermore warned that a failure to *wake up* would result in the Lord's rod of correction that would strike as quickly and unexpectedly as a thief.

The church at Philadelphia was feeble in that it was blessed with tremendous opportunity in spite of its human weaknesses. Seen as faithful to the Word and refusing to deny the name of Jesus in favor of political or cultural approval, this band of believers was destined to see God use its weaknesses as displays of His power.

The fellowship at Laodicea, the final church to which John directed the vision, was known as fashionable and culturally astute. Perhaps the facilities in which the members gathered were adorned with the finest of decor yet their hearts were described by John as neither hot nor cold, a condition irritating our Lord. In need of nothing material, they failed to realize their need for God. This seventh church is amazingly accurate in its representation of the condition of the modern Church. In our day, churches are often financially prosperous yet spiritually cold. Jesus often lingers outside the walls of the modern church longing to be allowed in.

I recall the story of the man who was one of few residents of a mountain community. He decided to move into the city to be near medical facilities. He attended a well-respected church in his new community but found it significantly different than the one in his mountain community. Stark, cold, and predictable in its style, no altar call or opportunity to officially unite with the fellowship was given. He prayed to the Lord and complained about his dilemma. The Lord replied, "Please don't worry, my son; I have been trying to get in that church for more than forty years!" Sadly, the presence of the Lord seems to be absent from many of the churches of our day.

The Things That Shall be Hereafter

The word *hereafter* utilized in this passage is an important key to interpreting the remainder of the vision commencing in chapter four. The use of this word denotes an era of time and is an obvious fallacy in the argument of those who would have us believe that the writings of the Revelation are merely symbolic and not referencing actual events in the present as well as in the future. The word is a compound usage of the Greek words *meta and tauta* meaning "after these things". Simply put, the words of chapter four and beyond refer to that which is to occur after what has been described in the preceding three chapters. A definite time line begins to surface when the words are interpreted literally, the most natural way to understand scripture.

Interestingly, no mention whatsoever of the Church is to be found from chapter four to the conclusion of the revelation. Why so, the curious student might inquire? No stronger proof that the Church will be raptured and absent during the time of tribulation may be found in holy scripture. After mentioning the Church in nineteen instances in the first three chapters, it vanishes from the pages from chapter four and beyond. The Church is simply not present on the earth during this era of God's activity. At the *snatching away* or removal of the Church, God will commence His plan for the seven-year tribulation. The Church Age will have come to an abrupt end. God will then begin dealing with the world under the auspices of a new dispensation. His primary dealings will be with the Jewish people. The tribulation will occur in part as a means to motivate the Jewish people to receive Jesus as Messiah and Lord.

Believers ought to rejoice as the loving plan of God begins to unfold and as we realize that the pain of the tribulation experience will have no effect upon His bride whom He will have tucked away in safety.

Believers – take courage!

PART 2

WISE WORDS TO TODAY'S CHURCH

Chapter 5

EPHESUS: HONEYMOON LOVE
Revelation 2: 1-7

Someone quipped that marriage is defined as two becoming one – and after the honeymoon the newlyweds discover which one! The church in Ephesus was a fellowship that experienced the familiar phenomenon of waning love. God's corrective words to this church serve as a needed admonition to today's church as well.

The vision received by John beginning in chapter two turns our attention to *the things which are*, referencing the time line previously discussed and detailed in Revelation 1:19. This era refers to the Church Age that chronologically concludes at the end of Revelation 3.

A quick review of these profound words to the seven churches located in Asia Minor, with specific attention to the words directed to the seventh church in Laodicea, leads the reader to recognize that the stage is set for the soon return of Jesus Christ to the earth.

The City of Ephesus

This notable city was located in present day Turkey. Its political clout was significant and had resulted in the Roman government making the unusual decision to grant freedom to the city to govern itself as a *free* city. As a seaport, its commercial and merchant business was an important facet of its identity and economy. Merchants from all parts of the known world traded there and wealth was in abundance.

The apostle Paul ventured into the city and confronted the idol worshippers of the Greek goddess Diana. The resulting riot led to the gathering of a majority of the entire city population in a local stadium to discuss the turmoil instigated by Paul's clear denunciation of their pagan practices. Silversmiths who labored in the city making pagan trinkets used in worship saw their net profits plummet. Pagans were turning to Christ and were suddenly losing their taste for paganism.

Paul stayed in the city for two years and was used by God to build an influential church. The letter to the Ephesians is replete with proof of the spiritual depth and maturity of this fellowship. It was in that great piece of biblical literature that Paul wrote, *"For by grace are ye saved through faith, and that not of yourselves; it is the gift of God; Not of works lest any man should boast"* (Ephesians 2:8-9). The grace of God at work in the lives of men made the news in Ephesus.

Young Timothy became pastor of the fellowship in Ephesus after the departure of Paul. Following closely on the heels of Timothy's ministry among the Ephesians was John the apostle and writer of Revelation. John was met with severe criticism, intimidation, and finally banishment to the Isle of Patmos due to his bold proclamation of the truths of Jesus Christ.

Ephesus has also produced some of the most significant archeological artifacts discovered to date. The great stadium has now been excavated and is similar in size and scope to American sports stadiums in existence today. I have visited the remains of Ephesus and continue to be amazed at its breathtaking architecture.

Concerning the church in Ephesus John wrote, *"These things sayeth he that holdeth the seven stars in his right hand, who walketh in the midst of the seven golden candlesticks"* (2:1). Jesus herein reveals something of Himself. He is seen holding the seven stars in his right hand. Essentially, He reveals to the reader and to the people of Ephesus that He is no distant God removed from their experience but rather lovingly supervises the pastors and walks in and among the activities of the church. Having eyes as a flame of fire, Jesus has the unprecedented ability to peer beyond outward appearances and into the deepest needs and passions of the human heart.

A Word of Commendation

Displaying His consistent characteristic of love and showing a true desire to commend His children, God said to the Ephesians in 2: 2-3,

> *I know thy works, and thy labor, and thy patience, and how thou canst not bear them which are evil; and thou has tried them which say they are apostles, and are not, and hast found them liars: And hast borne, and hast patience, and for my name's sake hast laboured, and hast not fainted.*

He commends the members of the fellowship because He *knows,* in an intimate way, the intense dedication of their efforts. In this context, w*ork* signifies a full measure of activity that does not lack in diligent effort and that shows no slothfulness regarding the effort of the church to do ministry. The danger of our efforts to work in the church is that we may be tempted to work on the basis of human ingenuity and intelligence and thereby fail to realize our need for the power of the Holy Spirit. God often chooses to work through the medium of His people to accomplish His purposes in the world yet He wants us to resist the temptation to claim personal credit for the fruit that may result. The scriptures chart a careful balance between the efforts of the people of God and the empowerment of the Holy Spirit in accomplishing the ultimate will of God in His Church.

In a similar thought, God commended the Ephesian fellowship for its *labor,* referring to an extra measure of effort that involves true sacrifice on their part. The familiar phrase of modern churches, "not equal gifts but equal sacrifice", is an accurate portrayal of the kind of effort to which the apostle refers. Believers today often are hesitant to part with material possessions and to rearrange priorities but must do so to effectively communicate the heart of Jesus and avoid the modern spirit of self-absorption.

The believers in Ephesus are further commended for their patience. In 2:2, the Greek word *patience* translates "to remain under." John takes note of their unique commitment to remain faithful to the things of God in spite of the intensity of their persecution. Maturity may be measured as we observe the level of pressure it takes to cause a man to shrink back from serving Christ.

The steady discipline and moral fortitude of the Ephesian believers is also noted in this passage. John was well aware that they had no real taste for evil or evildoers. The late bible teacher and revivalist Vance Havner once commented that some churches appear so worldly-minded in their behavior that new believers must *backslide* to feel at home in the fellowship. To take a firm stand on the moral and behavioral implications of our faith in Christ is to invite certain criticism. The story is told of a country preacher whose church had recently concluded a series of revival meetings. A friend asked whether additions had come into the membership during the meetings. The wise preacher shot back, " Yes, we had a few additions, but the subtractions were a real blessing."

The Ephesian church was commended for its faithful attention to doctrine as well. John wrote, *"Thou hatest the deeds of the Nicolaitanes, which I also hate"* (2:6). The Nicolaitanes were a band of people originally led by Nicolas of Antioch. Their name is derived from the compound Greek words *nekeo-laos,* or "to conquer the people." This cult that surfaced within the early church was fed a false doctrine claiming that for one to truly know and experience grace, he or she must first experience sin. They were led to believe that the more they sinned, the greater magnitude of God's grace they would experience. They assumed that lurid sexual deviations and other sins merely invited a greater dose of grace. The Ephesians refused to tolerate such foolish heresy and gained the approval of the Lord in doing so. We must realize that grace is not a license to sin!

The fellowship in Ephesus also carefully scrutinized some in their rank who claimed to be apostles yet were found to be imposters. Apostles, by biblical definition, were those of special spiritual identity who had walked and talked with Jesus in person and who had been chosen by Him for the special assignment of taking the gospel into uncharted territories. Scripture reminds us that the Church is built upon the foundation of the apostles.

Differentiating between a true apostle and an imposter was of critical importance. In our day as well, this gift of discernment is desperately needed.

A Word of Complaint

Said in a loving yet firm tone of correction, John wrote that the church in Ephesus was guilty as charged in that it had long left its first love. He said, *"Nevertheless I have somewhat against thee, because thou hast left thy first love"* (2:4). The endearing and passionate love of a couple recently married is pleasing to observe. Couples in love give full attention to one another apparently unaware of others in their midst. They drip with love – fervent love. John is herein attempting to remind the believers that passionate love for the Lord is the force that drives the church and earns credibility within the community. Pure doctrine, worthy morals, and personal discipline are noteworthy goals and traits to desire, yet are unacceptable substitutes for an unquenchable love for God as it is expressed to others. With that brand of love alive within the church of today, evangelistic fruit will be the natural result.

A Word of Counsel

John unfolded for the Ephesians and for believers today a three-fold remedy for rekindling the fires of passionate love within the church. John wrote, *"Remember therefore from whence thou art fallen, and repent and do the first work"* (2:5). Essentially, John counseled the people of Ephesus to repent of their lazy spiritual commitments and to renew their first love.

True repentance requires change or it is no real repentance at all. John's further admonition to do the *"first works"* was a vivid reminder to them to recapture their original sense of mission. They had been commended for their notable love for others thirty years earlier (Ephesians 1:15-16). Such a remarkable spirit of love within the fellowship was solidified with solid biblical doctrine and behavioral change. It had affected the institution of marriage and had a positive impact on interpersonal relationships with their peers and employers as well. The gospel of grace also had converted the unconverted; lives were eternally changed. John once again pled with them to recover their original mission as instruments of God's grace.

A Word of Consequence

John reminded the Ephesian believers that failure to pursue their mission assignment received from God would lead to their demise. John warns in 2:5, *"I will come unto thee quickly, and will remove thy candlestick out of his place, except thou repent."* Visit the ruins of Ephesus and you will quickly see that no church exists there today. The failure to maintain passionate love for Jesus leads to the sure demise of any church. When love wanes, the ability of a church to influence the community that surrounds the church dies like an abandoned ember in a campfire. The importance of maintaining fervency and a passion to impact the lives of men and women with the grace of our Lord will never be overstated.

John wrote to him who *"hath an ear"*, referring to those with sufficient spiritual awareness to hear a specific message from God. I believe that John is referring to those who listen with attentive hearts. Consequently, those who listen with spiritual ears will have the Spirit-given ability to avoid the dreadful demise of their church. These faithful listeners also will be blessed to experience intimate fellowship with our Lord by eating *"of the tree of life"* (2:7).

The internal deterioration of a church is a fate met by hundreds of churches in America each year. Many lose focus. Others lose passion. Some neglect to give attention to the salvation of souls in favor of social improvement or other less eternal endeavors.

This sad prophecy concerning of the demise of lifeless churches came to further fruition near the year 300 A.D. when the emperor Constantine became the ruler of Rome. With self-serving fanfare, he issued a ruling that all citizens would be Christians. Mass baptisms resulted. Pagans were baptized and rose from the waters still pagans. As a result, the world was plunged into a period of spiritual and moral darkness that was void of the true light of Jesus Christ.

As the love of Jesus fills our hearts, we will serve Him passionately. We will be motivated by that love rather than merely striving on the basis of sheer duty.

Honeymoon love is great. Love for a lifetime is greater.

Chapter 6

SMYRNA: WHY CHRISTIANS SUFFER
Revelation 2: 8-11

The issue of suffering among Christians is a volatile one that results in the endless publication of theological materials debating the subject. The core of the debate centers on the question as to whether a loving God, who desires to give blessings to His children, would allow heartache to afflict the ones He loves. To watch them suffer and choose not to intervene is inconsistent with His character, some claim.

The experience of the believers in the early church of Smyrna took suffering to new heights. Discovering the potential reasons for their difficult dilemma captures the attention of the reader in this interesting passage of scripture.

The City of Smyrna

Located forty miles north of the city of Ephesus, Smyrna rested on a plot of land that is today called Izmir in the country of Turkey. It derived its name from the production of myrrh that served as its chief industry. Myrrh was one of the three exquisite gifts given to the Christ child by the wise men near the end of the second year after His birth. Myrrh also found effective use in embalming the bodies of the deceased, a procedure applied to Jesus before His burial. The economy of Smyrna depended greatly upon this valuable commodity.

Smyrna was the crown city of Asia Minor, a center of emperor worship. This unique city was renowned for the worship of Caesar. Prophetically, the city was known for suffering continual and intense persecution. This era of persecution spanned from 100 A.D to approximately 300 A.D. Scholars inform us that ten intense periods of persecution afflicted the early church at the hands of the fierce Roman Empire. To this group of bewildered believers, John wrote these words in 2:8 on behalf of Jesus who identified Himself as, *"the first and the last, which was dead, and is alive."* With these consoling words, Jesus reminded the believers of His continual presence with them in the midst of their distress. Describing Himself as the *"One who was dead and is alive"*, Jesus gave to them and to us as well the assurance that He is a God of saving grace and a conqueror of the sting of death. In that regard, take courage my friend!

A Message of Trouble

John wrote these words to the Smyrnian believers, *"I know thy works and tribulation"* (2:9). The Greek word *thlipsis,* denoting tribulation or trials, is a familiar word in our experience that refers to the personal pressure or distress that we often sense. Believers at Smyrna suffered fierce persecution to a degree not even imaginable to Christians today.

Today's believers are distressed to a degree but such stress is often self-imposed as we pursue the American dream with all its accompanied demands for material accumulation. To the contrary, these early church believers knew little of materialism but rather were severely harassed by the Roman authorities. *Thlipsis* was the word commonly used to describe the pressing upon or the treading of grapes to produce wine and for the grinding of wheat resulting in flour. More than common aches and pains, the believers in Smyrna were constantly persecuted for their stand for Christ – an experience to which few American believers are able to relate.

John further wrote that God was aware of their *"poverty"*. Two Greek words are commonly used to describe poverty. One refers to a person who labors for a living but earns no more than is necessary to meet the basic material requirements of daily life. He or she lives hand to mouth, as it were. The graphic word employed by John in this passage suggests more severity and describes the awful condition of abject poverty experienced by the Smyrnian Christians who had nothing at all. Many were deprived of the privilege of holding employment in the midst of a booming economy. The affluent may have flaunted their financial status in the faces of these believers adding insult to injury.

Jesus further extended His comfort due to the *"blasphemy"* to which they were subjected. The word here employed by John refers to slander. A wicked and slanderous campaign was being waged against these precious believers at the hands of imposters within the fellowship. I believe these soothing words of comfort are directed to the *true Jews*, those whose hearts had been converted regardless of ethnic identity, and about which Paul wrote in the letter to the Romans. In condemning terms, John referred to the evil-hearted men who were motivated by Satan himself to harass God's people. In a real sense, they comprised a false religion and a false faith and were masquerading as angels of light.

As believers, we may rest assured that our Lord is attentive to our every distress as well. He reminded the church at Smyrna that He is the One who *knows* (from the Greek term *eido)* their pain and anguish from His own personal experience.

A Message of Treasure

Noting their poverty, John further wrote that God was aware of their position as *"rich"* (2:9). Is such a claim inconsistent or contradictory?

John intended for the believers and for us as well to recognize that true wealth is not measured by the size of our financial portfolios. This faithful band was rich in prayer and was rich in the promises of God they were destined to receive. They experienced a supernatural wealth of power originating far beyond the realm of human ingenuity or ability.

John exhorted the believers of Smyrna that they should not succumb to the temptation to walk in fear. Such an admonition must have been a difficult pill for some to swallow as we read of the persecution they encountered. John predicted that many of these believers were to be unceremoniously tossed into prison for *"ten days"* (2:10). The number ten is symbolic for human completion. Humans possess ten fingers and ten toes. We commonly use multiples of ten to quickly count our currency. I believe that God is saying that He will allow Satan to test the believers in Smyrna to the limits of human endurance, a complete testing. Scholars also suggest that this reference may be to the ten significant periods of persecution inflicted by Roman emperors. Some have speculated that these ten eras of time may refer to the series of Roman administrations dating from the time of Nero to the time of Diocletian.

John encouraged these weary followers to continue their faithfulness *"unto death"* (2:10). I believe that the message God intended to convey was that they should remain true to God by experiencing death to self. His desire is for us as believers to be alive only to the things of God. The question as to their ultimate allegiance was forcefully put to the church at Smyrna – and it begs for an answer from us as well. As folk singer Bob Dylan sang, *You Gotta' Serve Somebody.*

A Message of Triumph

Those who were faithful would receive the *"crown of life"* (2:10). The scriptures often speak of the crown of life as a reward. Believers who are steadfast and true to their faith will receive the blessing of kingly glory and a full measure of the pleasure of God.

It is important to note that faithfulness is not the trait that earns the right of the believer to avoid the second death or eternal separation. However, faithfulness is the primary proof of the authenticity of his or her claim to be a true believer. Revelation 2:11 reads, "H*e that hath an ear, let him hear what the Spirit saith unto the churches; He that overcometh shall not be hurt of the second death."* Revelation 20 reminds us that the second death is eternity in the lake of fire and eternal separation from God. Those who *overcome* by their faithfulness will not be subjected to this dreaded and real experience to come.

One writer quipped, "The faith that fizzles before the finish was faulty from the first." He was correct. Faithfulness on our part does not earn the prize of eternal life nor does it insulate us from suffering. On the contrary, it suggests that our hearts have been so revolutionized by the grace of our Lord that we possess the needed motivation to endure any and all things that come our way.

Reason Christians Suffer

Contrary to the notions of the theological movement commonly known as *health and wealth*, believers are afflicted with difficulties, distress, money worries, and health problems and often endure these trials with benefit. Satan can and does inflict distress yet the scriptures also indicate that certain difficulties and disappointments often come at the hand of God who has a greater good in mind.

As Christians, we suffer the effects of living in a fallen world. Death, and its lesser accompanying distresses and various forms of earthly deterioration, originated in the Garden of Eden as Adam and Eve sinned by choice. In the popular motion picture series *Jurassic Park,* we are reminded of the second law of thermodynamics that indicates that what we see in the universe is moving from a state of complexity and organization toward a state of chaos and disorder. The Garden of Eden had no hurricanes yet after the *Fall* they have become quite common. Sin by choice has impacted the world. It is not a fully safe place to live.

Believers also experience heartache due to the normal operation of God's moral law of sowing and reaping. Those who sow wild oats do not reap peace. Forgiveness from the heart of God may be experienced yet the consequences of a decision to live a life unchecked by moral standards will still hit, often hard. A skydiver with a faulty parachute who plummets toward his death may receive forgiveness for the sin of negligence – but the ground is still hard.

Followers of Christ may also suffer because of the work of Satan. The gospels depict the story of a woman who had been bound in torment by Satan. Just as God gave permission for Job to be afflicted by Satan, this woman also experienced trauma at the hands of the Evil One. Satan does attack God's children yet He does his dastardly deeds on a divine leash.

Suffering may also occur in the life of a believer as a method of discipline used by the Lord. Events, however unpleasant and unpredicted, may serve to achieve a greater goal by motivating us toward greater faith. They may also serve to clear the path for a career change so that we may more effectively accomplish God's will for our lives.

Events in our lives may serve to mature us to be more like Jesus in our manner and behavior. The friction and turmoil within the distress serves to melt away our human imperfections and lead us to a greater level of holiness. The suffering itself is not good yet the work of God in us within the experience is beneficial and enduring.

Suffering builds belief as well. Paul wrote in Romans 5:3 that we *"glory in tribulations."* To maintain a posture of faithfulness under intense scrutiny or amidst trouble causes the Christian to build spiritual muscle. The bodybuilder who refuses to endure the pressure created by the weight receives no benefit. His muscular growth is stunted. The believer who fails to stand strong while in the heat of persecution experiences the halting of his spiritual growth as well. Spiritual atrophy sets in. Psalms 119:71 teaches us that affliction causes us to learn the *"statutes"* of God. Affliction, rightly received, produces holiness.

Further, suffering stabilizes our strength. The apostle Peter wrote that the experience of suffering serves to make us *"perfect"* (I Peter 5:10). In this context, to be perfect is to be mature or complete. Mature believers are marked by a history of much heartache. Suffering also is an effective means to capture our attention. God is often communicating yet believers are seldom listening. John wrote that those with ears, spiritual ears that are alert, should hear well what the Spirit is saying.

Ministry is also multiplied and enhanced through suffering. Paul wrote in his letter to the Corinthians, *"Who comforteth us in all our tribulation, that we may be able to comfort them which are in any trouble…* (II Corinthians 1:4). Those who endure specific trouble are imminently qualified to hold the hands of others with similar pain.

Last, suffering glorifies God. In a way not completely explainable, suffering may point the spotlight of attention toward God. Paul wrote these direct words concerning suffering, *"For unto you it is given in the behalf of Christ, not only to believe on him, but also to suffer for his sake"* (Philippians 1:29). In addition to a life of joy and peace for the believer a measure of suffering may be added to his or her experience. This notion is irritating to those who propose that all sickness and calamity is the ugly work of Satan and is never within God's plan for His children. I remember the experience of one of the members of our fellowship who was badly injured in an automobile accident while on vacation. With broken arms and in great pain, he led his attending nurse to accept the claims of Christ. In a real way, his pain led to her gain.

God does heal, however. We should and must pray for healing, yet if our sovereign Lord chooses to delay the healing even until the time of His second coming, He is still worthy of our trust. There is a diamond within the darkness of our suffering and a pot of gold blessings at the end of the rainbow.

Into every life some rain must fall.

Chapter 7

PERGAMUM: A BAD MARRIAGE
Revelation 2: 12-17

One brave wag wrote, "*All men are born free – but then some get married.*" After his wife read his words, I am sure that the weather was a bit cool in his home that particular evening. The writer John penned penetrating words to the church at Pergamum concerning a different kind of marriage, however. He wrote concerning the marriage between church and state, an issue that dominates the headlines and talk shows of our day but is certainly not a new issue to the Christian community.

Church and State

The freedom of the Spirit to move and to perform His work in the hearts of men in the city of Pergamum and beyond was hampered by governmental rulings that attempted to popularize faith in Christ and offer it free of charge and without its accompanying behavioral implications.

The city of Pergamum was the first of the cities of the Roman Empire to enforce emperor worship. Dominating the landscape of this pagan city was the Temple of Zeus, one of the seven wonders of the ancient world. This wicked city was filled with idolatry and a plethora of demonic activity. Pergamum rested on the site of modern day Bergama and located twenty miles inland from the Aegean Sea. The city was constructed on a hill arching one thousand feet into the air and rested on a broad fertile plain. Pergamum was the first city in all of Asia to erect a temple to Caesar, the Roman emperor.

The church of Pergamum existed during the period of history dating from approximately 312 A.D. to near 500 A.D. In 312 A.D., the emperor Constantine declared a marriage between church and state with the result that tens of thousands of non-believers experienced the rite of believers' baptism. They walked into the waters as pagans and emerged from the baptismal pool still as pagan in mindset as before. The distinctive identity of the church rapidly eroded as Constantine proposed a new definition of the word Christian, one that was void of the act of regeneration within the hearts of men. These new Christians were not real Christians!

Such a marriage of church and state also led to an escalation of wealth within the church. Social acceptance and this new wealth stagnated the Church and began to dilute its message. Constantine had a vision in which he saw a cross and the words, "*in this sign, conquer.*" As a result, the powerful leader began to conquer the world and utilized as his banner the cross of Jesus Christ. In the final analysis, the state began to encroach upon the freedom and message of the church, and to a large degree, turned the Church into a political structure that served the interests of the state. Such a marriage punished both partners. Government is not to be void of the dictates of God and the church is not be governed by any other than by the One who gave His life for her.

Sharp Words

John wrote pointed words to the church at Pergamum and identified Jesus as the One who *"hath the sharp sword with two edges"* (2:12). Earlier, the Romans introduced into warfare a new breed of sword with two edges. Sabers and similar weapons of war existed for centuries yet the sword with two sharp edges was a new concept. This particular sword was short in length and quite broad and provided for its user an effective way to attack from behind and plunge it into the heart of an unsuspecting opponent. It cut as it entered – and cut again as it exited. Few victims survived.

The Word of God is herein described as having the ability to cut in both directions. It has the capability to convict as we feel its sharp edges yet also has the ability to heal like the scalpel of a skilled surgeon. The ultimate goal of the Word is to lead to redemption and restoration of fallen men. John's words were sharp and cutting.

The Faith of This Church

In 2:13, the vision records, *"I know thy works, and where thou dwellest, even where Satan's seat is."* The word "*seat*" is derived from the common Greek word *thronos* meaning throne. John identified the throne of Satan as a major center of power and authority in Pergamum. Satanic influence had infiltrated the city. This was no Bible Belt area but rather the headquarters of much of Satan's evil activity. God purposefully placed His church within a stone's throw of hell so that the believers might turn on the light of the gospel and dispel the darkness of evil all around it. As believers today, we may find ourselves in careers or corporate offices that appear to be bastions of darkness and centers of corrupt morality. Such a position, however, may be a grand opportunity for the believer to shine the Light and dispel the darkness.

The city fathers of Pergamum were dedicated to the worship of Zeus and to the Roman emperor. The altar of Zeus rested prominently on the Acropolis and was central to the practice of pagan worship. This faithful band of believers in Pergamum lived in a very dark world that was held hostage by Satan himself. The light of the Holy Spirit illuminating from their hearts dispelled the darkness.

John commended them for the *person of their faith.* He complimented the believers because they had held strong and fast to the *"Name"* of Jesus the Christ. Refusing to deny the name of Jesus, they called to Him in prayer and looked to Him and to Him only as their means of salvation. Political and military pressure mounted, yet they refused to relegate Jesus to a role less than divine. Mohammed was never the name whereby men gain salvation; Buddha has no regeneration to offer the hearts of man; only Jesus saves from the ravages of human sin and offers eternal life.

Our hymnals are filled with songs concerning the name of Jesus. I love the hymns. They speak of Jesus in simple yet profound terms and describe His essential character and nature – concepts that could fade away with each passing generation if we fail to emphasize them.

The amazing *power of their faith* serves as a fitting prototype to us as believers today. The words of chapter 2:13 make reference to an early victim of the persecution. John wrote, "*Thou holdest fast my name, and hast not denied my faith, even in those days wherein Antipas was my faithful martyr, who was slain among you.*" Modern believers know little of the pressures early Christians faced in the practice of their faith. I remember hearing of Christians in China who packed one hundred and fifty believers into a home for worship. Fearing arrest and even death, they sang softly in small groups only for fear the volume might alert the authorities. Today, we have the privilege of singing without restriction and yet some of us refuse to sound a single note of praise!

Historians claim that Antipas may have met his fate by incineration inside a brass bull. Theologians further claim that Antipas may have ministered as a local pastor and suffered because of it. The Roman authorities evidently assumed that with the annihilation of Antipas, the worship of Jesus might subside or disappear. No such flimsy faith was evident within the hearts of these faithful followers. The gospel message continued to spread.

The Failings of This Church

As is common with believers of every generation, the church at Pergamum had its faults as well. John wrote in 2:14, "*I have a few things against thee, because thou hast there them that hold the doctrine of Balaam, who taught Balac to cast a stumblingblock before the children of Israel, to eat things sacrificed unto idols, and to commit fornication.*" The story of the prophet Balaam is recorded in Numbers 22-24. Balak, King of Moab, offered a handsome sum of money to the prophet Balaam to curse the children of Israel. Balaam responded that he was unable to effectively curse the Israelites because God had chosen to bless them. Perhaps hungry for money, Balaam offered instead to tempt them to adopt idol worship practices and entice them with sexual opportunities.

Balaam prostituted his remarkable gift of prophecy and arranged for the beautiful and sensual girls of Moab to proposition the men of Israel (Numbers 25:1). The disastrous result was the intermarriage of God's people with the pagan Moabites. Their faith in the One true God began to deteriorate. Not desiring His name to be tarnished, God responded by taking the lives of twenty-four thousand Israelites.

Temptations to abandon the practices of our faith in Christ abound on every hand and are available at any moment. The ever-present doctrine of Balaam might be defined as assuming that our secure faith in Christ is forever accompanied by an immediate act of forgiveness. The truth is, we are indeed free in Christ yet we are not free to abandon the morality of our faith. To do so calls into question the authenticity of the very faith we claim to possess. The late evangelist Billy Sunday referred to those who practice such unrestricted license as *heavenly devils*. To sing the words of the hymn, *"My Jesus I love the"* also requires the genuine believer to sing the phrase, *"For thee all the follies of sin I resign."* Some of us want to love Jesus while we sin!

A second failing of this church in Pergamum was due to their unfortunate agreement with and practice of the ways of the Nicolaitans. As previously explained in our discussion of the Ephesian church, the root meaning of the word Nicolaitanes refers to ruling of the people. As Constantine institutionalized the church under state control, a hierarchy comprised of bishops and cardinals began to appear. It was assumed that the masses were simply not capable of understanding the faith and governing authorities were therefore necessary. They failed to realize that every believer in Christ is described by the apostle Peter as a priest and a member of the royal priesthood of our Lord. Each believer has experienced Spirit baptism and therefore may be led into all truth by the interpretive powers of the Holy Spirit.

John wrote that if the church in Pergamum failed to destroy this doctrine and its damaging effects, He would *"fight against them with the sword of my mouth"* (2:16). Such a bold promise came to fruition in the sixteenth century as God raised up men such as Martin Luther and John Calvin to boldly restate that each and every man has an equal capability before God to know and communicate with God. The Church has never been the same since the reformers made this bold scriptural claim for the world to hear and understand.

In addition to the false notion that only certain classes of people could truly know and understand God, Nicolas also led people to replace liberty in Christ with license. Tempting them with a variety of vices and sexual experiences, Nicolas made inroads into the church to disintegrate its distinctive message. It was a clever ploy that some could not resist.

We must remember that churches are known not by their steeples but rather by the behavior of its members. Our lives verify our claims.

The Future of the Church

John closed his words to the church at Pergamum with a three-fold promise. Three gifts are in focus here as John comforted the church with promises and blessings. John wrote, *"To him that overcometh will I give to eat of the hidden manna, and will give him a white stone, and in the stone a new name written, which no one knoweth saving him who receiveth it"* (2:17).

One promise from our Lord to those who overcome by their faith is to give us this *"hidden manna"*. In Old Testament usage, manna was the food that came from heaven and found on the ground each day as sustenance for the Israelite people as they wandered. Manna is also a type of Christ in the scriptures in that Christ is our ultimate sustenance. White in color, it symbolized the purity of Jesus. Its small size symbolized the humility of Jesus; its taste was sweet signifying sweet aroma of Christ within the believer. *"Hidden"* manna was that which was placed inside a golden pot and put into the Ark of the Covenant carried by the wandering Jewish people. John's penetrating words here refer to a promise that believers one day will see the real manna in the unveiling of Jesus Christ in person as He returns.

The *"white stone"* was utilized in the early church as a hospitality card of a sort and a means of identification. It identified personal credibility and standing in the community. Winning athletes were given a white stone as a ticket into the award ceremony after sporting events. God's word to the Pergamum church suggests that one day we will have full access to and have full knowledge of Jesus as we reign with Him.

The third promise referred to by John is that of a *"new name"* (2:17). God promised that believers will be given a new name that speaks of God's special love. The name will be one of endearment. This new name is of such a personal and intimate nature that only the recipient will know what it is. This name will serve as another loving illustration of God's care for His children.

As believers, we need no human intermediary to call upon the Lord. We have direct line to the throne room. Jesus has paved the way.

Chapter 8

THYATIRA: WOMEN IN THE MINISTRY
Revelation 2: 18-29

Few issues ignite debate in the church of today like the role of women. The writer John does not avoid this volatile issue that had raised its ugly head in the church at Thyatira but rather attacked it with direct and scathing words.

A proper understanding of the role of the sexes in the church of our Lord is absolutely vital in maintaining health in the church. This incredibly divisive issue has led to the demise of a countless number of churches when handled incorrectly and without biblical guidance. To sort through the teachings of the Bible without undue influence from the culture mores of our day is a challenge indeed.

The Contributions of Women

Women have played an undeniably important and significant role in the history of the church and in the advancement of the gospel. In Acts 16, the woman Lydia was known as a seller of fine purple garments, and served as a leader in the church at Philippi. As a convert to Jesus Christ, she gladly opened the doors of her home for the gatherings of the local church. She encouraged the apostle Paul and was an ardent supporter of the work of God in her region.

Women were the last to leave the scene of the cross after the death of Jesus and were the first to arrive at the tomb of Jesus with the hope that He was alive. Ruth and Esther, books of the Bible in the Old Testament, are named in honor of women. Our Lord makes no effort to denigrate women in the least but rather expects great respect be given to them. The revolutionary nature of the gospel served to lift the status of women to an unprecedented level as cultural and political norms of the day tended to deny women the most basic elements of human respect. Paul wrote in his letter to the Galatians, *"in Christ there is neither male nor female,"* a claim that was certainly not welcomed news to the guardians of the cultural status quo (Galatians 2:28).

In the scriptures, women symbolize both good and evil. In Revelation, we read of the *"great harlot"* that personifies false religion and the false church. In contrast, God chose the symbolism of the *"bride"* to describe the love of His life, the bride of Christ comprised of true believers in the faith who have entered into a relationship of spiritual matrimony with Him. His love and respect for the gifts and value of women decorate the pages of scripture.

Jesus and the Church at Thyatira

The church that gathered in the city of Thyatira read the words of John herein identifying Jesus in a three-fold manner. Jesus identifies Himself as the Son of God and consequently, Lord of the Church. Further, He is seen as with *"eyes like unto a flame of fire, and his feet are like fine brass"* (2:18). With flaming eyes, He possesses the uncanny ability to peer beyond outward appearance and into the inner thoughts and motives of the human heart. His feet pictured as feet like fine brass symbolize the certainty of His future arrival to judge the earth. The brass altar in the Old Testament tabernacle was the location where sacrifice for sin was continually offered – the place where sin was judged.

Thyatira was renown for its numerous trade guilds and for its wool and dye industries. It rested on a plot of land located approximately thirty-miles southeast of Pergamum. The city had existed under the heavy controlling hand of the Romans for almost three centuries. Situated in a long valley, it had no natural defenses and was known for being rebuilt numerous times. Essentially, it was a military outpost for the city of Pergamum.

The church at Thyatira was a *working church.* John wrote that God was well aware of the work of the church in the proclamation of the gospel. Their efforts had not gone unnoticed.

Further, the Thyatiran church was a *loving church* that reached beyond the boundaries of its own desires and needs and into the lives of the masses that surrounded them. John chose the common Greek word *agape* to describe the unconditional love in the heart of God that found expression in the church at Thyatira.

The people were members of a *ministering church* as well. Their acts of service described by John in 2:19 ministered to the immediate tangible needs of others. They willingly functioned as the hands of God and as people who touched the lives of others in a meaningful way.

As an *enduring church,* John complimented them for their patience and perseverance under distress. Last, John wrote to commend them as a *growing church.* John wrote of them in 2:19, *"and thy works, and the last to be more than the first."* Always looking to improve their effectiveness for God, John took note of their worthy efforts.

Honest and genuine in the giving of compliments, John quickly turned to the major issue at hand that had stirred the righteous anger of the Lord.

The Wicked Woman

A heinous abomination had arisen within the fellowship at Thyatira. With pointed words, John wrote in 2:20,

> *Notwithstanding I have a few things against thee, because thou sufferest that woman Jezebel, which calleth herself a prophetess, to teach and to seduce my servants to commit fornication, and to eat things sacrificed unto idols.*

With one brief stroke of a writer's quill, John exposed an awful sin that was tolerated in the church. The source of the sin was found in the person of Jezebel. Theologians propose that her name was symbolic and a reference to the wicked and immoral deeds of the woman by the same name who was married to King Ahab. Her wicked exploits are graphically displayed in I Kings 21: 25-26.

To slander the character of another person reaches the pinnacle when the name of Jezebel is hurled. The spirit of Jezebel refers to a spirit of domination that tends to relegate any man involved in a given scenario to secondary status. When introduced as leaders of the nation, this wicked couple might be presented as *Jezebel and her husband*, reminding us of a certain governmental administration in recent days, if you know what I mean! She dominated the land of Israel by her iron-fisted and immoral rule.

Essentially, the Bible clearly and vigorously acknowledges the value of women in the church. Equally important and often overlooked is the scriptural injunction that the role of women is not to include serving in positions of spiritual authority over men. Large bodies of believers in our day are forced to deal with that very issue.

I was a featured speaker at the gathering of California Southern Baptists several years ago and watched with interest as that body made the bold move to exclude from participation in the convention an individual church that was served by a female pastor. Not bigoted or narrow-minded, that brave group simply reflected the teachings of the scripture in the face of cultural pressure to do otherwise. They are to be commended for such a courageous stand.

The Role of Women

In a penetrating and direct manner, the apostle Paul wrote in I Timothy 2: 12, *"I suffer not a woman to teach, nor to usurp authority over the man, but to be in silence. For Adam was first formed, then Eve. And Adam was not deceived, but the woman being deceived was in the transgression."* The application of these words is as critical in our day as it was in the first century. Or course, critics surface at this juncture and claim that Paul's words were of value only to the culture of the first century or that he was restricted by his own limited understanding. Other similar arguments attempt to diffuse this teaching and prevent it from influencing the church of today. To propose that the meaning of scripture *evolves* over time is to deny the very essence of the Bible and of Jesus Himself. Scripture is timeless and is not bound by the cultural tides.

Paul's words in I Timothy 2:12 have application within the home as well as the church. The husband is to be the spiritual leader and wife is to serve as one who completes and supports his role and is to provide personal care and attention to the atmosphere of the home in a manner for which she only has been uniquely gifted. What complicates and irritates this arrangement is the failure of a husband to provide unrestricted love in the home. Men are not to abuse their wives either physically or by means of neglect. Neither are they to behave in an insensitive manner displaying little or no care concerning her personal needs or desires. As Christ laid down His life for the Church, men are to do likewise for their wives. To do less irritates life in the home and leads to marital ruin.

Women are often wonderful and gifted teachers. Yet in this biblical admonition, Paul warned that no usurping of authority in an act of dominance over the man is to be permitted. As women teach, they are to do so under the authority of the pastor and in a manner that does not relegate the role of their husbands to lesser importance. In I Timothy 3:1 and in the following verses, Paul wrote of the office of bishop and its qualifications. One significant qualification is that the bishop or pastor be *"husband of one wife."* To my knowledge, it appears to be a biological impossibility for a woman to fulfill that function!

Paul's words in I Corinthians 14:33-35 deal with the volatile issue of the silence of women in the church. May women utter a word within the doors of the church building? May they teach a class or ask a question? To summarize, Paul commands that it is God's perfect plan that husbands are to speak and to be the lead spokesmen in the gatherings of the church. As if anticipating an unending firestorm of controversy, Paul wrote in 14:33, *"God is not the author of confusion, but of peace, as in all churches of the saints. Let your women keep silence in the churches; for it is not permitted unto them to speak."* It must be noted that the words to the Corinthian church spanning chapters twelve through fourteen primarily deal with the matter of the public use of the spiritual gifts, specifically tongues. (A brief scan of the controversies that have erupted in the Church will reveal that often the root of the conflict often lies at the feet of women who have insisted in the public display of their alleged gift of tongues. Many may choose to challenge me on that observation, yet more than thirty years of pastoral ministry has led me to that conclusion). Further, the best of conservative commentaries agree that Paul's words concerning the silence of women must be read in light of the divisive problem that had arisen with the abuse of the gift of tongues.

The wicked woman Jezebel in the church at Thyatira was a prophetess and claimed that her alleged message from God was authoritative. In no uncertain terms in Revelation 2:20, God charged that she had willingly *"seduced my servants."* The Old Testament character Jezebel had introduced the worship of the pagan god Baal to the nation of Israel. Baal worship was cruel and warped in its mindset in that it included the sacrifice of babies to the pagan god Molech. Further, Jezebel convinced her husband Ahab to falsely accuse a man named Naboth in order that Ahab might steal his vineyard. Jezebel also designed another plot to kill the prophet Elijah because of his opposition to her.

In the church at Thyatira, Jezebel introduced fornication. Meaning unfaithfulness to a vow, this brand of fornication could have surfaced in the form of spiritual fornication as well as moral fornication. In any regard, a spirit that led to the breaking of vows began to strangle the ministry of the church. She also convinced the people to eat things sacrificed to idols. To do so violated the consciences of believers who had come to assume that evil spirits often infiltrated the meat that remained unused in pagan worship rituals. To eat it was to expose the recipient to demons, some assumed. Spiritual damage and stunted spiritual growth resulted in the lives of those who believed in such a notion.

The Judicious Mercy of our Lord

John wrote in 2:21, *"I gave her space to repent of her fornication, and she repented not. Behold, I will cast her into a bed, and them that commit adultery with her into great tribulation…….. and I will kill her children."* In spite of her heinous sin, Jezebel was offered the incredible forgiving grace of our Lord yet evidently brushed it aside in an act of arrogance. The promise here is that she would begin to reap certain judgment.

The judgment inflicted upon the Jezebel of the book of I Kings included her being flung to the ground by the guards from the palace. In a bloody scene, scripture records that her body was devoured by dogs. To seduce and afflict the bride of Christ will lead to certain retribution from her husband, the Lord Himself.

I firmly believe that one aspect of this promised judgment upon Jezebel and her followers refers to the events of the Great Tribulation after the Church has departed the earth. False believers will miss the Rapture of the Church and will consequently endure the pain of the tribulation. In 2:23 John wrote, *"I will kill her children with death; and all the churches shall know that I am he which searcheth the reins and hearts; and I will give unto every one of you according to your works."* The deceived children of Jezebel who comprise the false church will be the victims of a horrifying judgment still to come.

The concluding words in 2:25 to the Thyatiran church include the admonition, *"That which ye have already hold fast till I come."* John herein encouraged the church to avoid the sinful ways of Jezebel and any and all of her partners in sin, and to hold the Word of God in their hearts as the only rule of practice.

Faithfulness to God is not the means to achieve salvation but rather the proof that salvation in Christ has genuinely occurred in the heart. God further said to the church at Thyatira, *"…to Him will I give power over the nations"* (2:26). These words are a reference to the millennial reign of Christ with His people after His second return to the earth. We as believers will function as kings and priests in the millennial kingdom of our Lord. Believers will also receive the "*morning star*", a reference to the ultimate Star, Jesus Himself (2:28). The star that shines with the greatest illumination before dawn is also a harbinger of the dawn that is to come. Jesus will shine His prophetic light and bring a swift end to the darkness of our world.

Whether uniquely designed by God as women or men, we must shine the light of Jesus until He comes.

Chapter 9

SARDIS: AUTOPSY OF A DEAD CHURCH
Revelation 3: 1-6

Churches, like people, pass through significant phases in their lives. Spiritual rites of passage leave both blessings and disappointments for those who experience them. Each of us has been born with a full measure of human depravity and the people in the church at Sardis were no exception.

In this section of Revelation, the writer John took aim at the church in Sardis and pointedly diagnosed the atmospheric conditions of a church that was void of spiritual life. The condition described herein was not terminal and the solutions God proposed through John have modern application as well for any church whose strength has been drained, vision lost, or that has opted for the greener pastures of personal comfort. Living at ease in Zion does not lend itself to fulfilling the divine mission of the church. When churches become institutionalized and adopt as their mission the perpetuation of the status quo and the preservation of their histories, spiritual rigor mortis sets it. In its basic definition, tradition itself is not unwise to follow or sinful yet the worship of the past is another matter.

The Church at Sardis

The city of Sardis was located about thirty miles south of Thyatira. This city was perched more than fifteen hundred feet above the valley floor on the Acropolis and was practically impregnable due to its natural defensive design. It was renowned for its industries of harvesting and for dying of wool for exquisite garments. Aesop, renowned as a writer of fables, hailed from Sardis. Tradition informs us that Mileto, another resident and author from Sardis, was said to have produced the first commentary on Revelation.

The imperial cult of emperor worship operating in full force in Sardis was a direct challenge to the faith of this church. Sadly, the church to which John directed these pointed words was essentially dead, devoid of spiritual life and power. They gathered for worship yet none occurred.

The church at Sardis is representative of the condition of the church that spanned the era from the first century to the mid-1800's. When I refer to the *church* in this context, I have in mind the Roman church that dominated the religious scene at that time. The church suffered for a long period of time in the grip of spiritual darkness. With the emergence of the Age of Reason and the Renaissance in Europe, the social acceptability of atheism dramatically increased. The ability of man to employ human logic as opposed to and in preference to the wisdom of God began to dominate the scene. This spirit of human reasoning and ingenuity infiltrated the church at Sardis. This same spirit of arrogant independence is alive and well in the church of today.

To the Sardis church John wrote in 3:1, *"And unto the angel of the church in Sardis write; 'These things saith he that hath the seven Spirits of God, and the seven stars."* The reference to the number seven is indicative of John's intention to remind the church that Jesus was fully divine, complete in every dimension of His existence, and indwelt by the Holy Spirit. To be full of the Holy Spirit is to enjoy the complete submission of our lives to the Spirit. I believe that a further reason that Jesus identifies Himself as the holder of the Spirits is that the life of a church is solely dependent upon the freedom of the Holy Spirit to indwell any church fellowship. Possessing the *"seven Spirits"* is a claim by Jesus that should serve to assure all readers that the Lord whom we worship is not lacking in any dimension. He can be trusted. He was and is the God-man.

A Message to the Dead

John wrote in 3:1, *"I know thy works, that thou hast a name that thou livest, and art dead."* Claiming to *"know"* their works and activities as a church indicates personal knowledge rather than mere hearsay or assumption. The public recognition that the church had acquired refers to its socially respectable reputation in which the members evidently took great pride. To the degree that a church desires social respectability in the community and relegates its biblical mission as light in the darkness to secondary status, that church will be a dead church.

As a whole, the church of the seventeenth and eighteenth centuries was institutionalized in the sense that it abandoned its distinctive mission to challenge and therefore transform the culture. Its tendency to blend with the cultural mores of the day and its failure to confront the sinful heart of man led to the loss of its distinctive influence. Yet in the midst of this sad state of affairs, God began to raise a holy remnant of believers full of the Holy Spirit. During the time of the Reformation came the great awakenings in Europe sweeping in the masses like prairie fires and subsequently impacting America as well.

John continued God's words to Sardis in 3:2 – 5a,

> *Be watchful, and strengthen the things which remain, that are ready to die: for I have not found thy works perfect before God. Remember therefore how thou hast received and heard, and hold fast, and repent. If therefore thou shalt not watch, I will come on thee as a thief, and thou shalt not know what hour I will come upon thee. Thou hast a few names even in Sardis which have not defiled their garments; and they shall walk with me in white: for they are worthy. He that overcometh, the same shall be clothed in white raiment.*

The church in Sardis had yet to complete its assigned mission. They settled for less than a full effort and had lost sight of the goal of the church. In that sense, they were less than perfect. As a church, their work for God lay incomplete and lagged due to inattention. I have learned in more than thirty years of pastoral ministry that the life of a church may not be determined from reading a church publication or accurately assessed merely by its organizational structure. Furthermore, some churches exist primarily on the basis of their past successes or reputation. When the prayer life of a church is perfunctory and mechanical at best and the Spirit of God seems distant or uninvolved, what remains to drive the church is mere human ingenuity. The wheels of church activity roll on yet no real progress is realized.

When the Bible speaks of physical death, it is not referring to the death of the spirit but to the death of the body. The scriptures indicate that the death of the body is analogous to sleep. Our bodies are dead yet our spirits have departed. In contrast, churches often maintain their physical existence yet the presence of the Holy Spirit is nowhere to be found. These lifeless churches are spiritually dead although physically alive. Churches with real life drip with the presence of the Spirit.

In the pages of the Old Testament we read of the difficult yet thrilling ministry of Ezekiel. God desired to give an assignment to the prophet as He does to young preachers today who have heard that clarion call. I remember the story of the single seminary student who prayed that God would one day grant him his wish of a big church and a beautiful wife. Six months after graduation and after arriving at his first church, an old friend called to inquire about him and whether his prayer had been answered. The young preacher sheepishly replied, *"Almost I guess - I got a beautiful church and a big wife!"*

Elijah must have flinched as he was informed of this curious assignment. God escorted Elijah to a perch in view of the wilderness. Gazing into the valley, Elijah was startled to lay his eyes upon a valley of dry bones. Scriptures record, *"Lo, they were very dry"* (Ezekiel 37:2). God commanded His startled prophet to assume the role of prophesying or preaching to the dry bones in order to cause them to experience new life. As the faithful prophet spoke, the Spirit of God swept over the bones causing their spontaneous gathering into skeletons and finally into flesh and sinew. The Spirit breathed resuscitating life into those lifeless bones, representative of the people of Israel who had neglected God.

Dead churches may rise again as well. As the Holy Spirit was poured into the people of Jerusalem on the Day of Pentecost, they began speaking the words of our Lord with a holy boldness. Life was restored. Without the Spirit, no church has life. Structure, order and decorum are no substitutes for that which gives real life and breathes vitality into the veins of a church. Without the Spirit, the church is dead.

Further, dead churches have no ability to feel. Like a corpse with no sense of or response to touch, churches without the Spirit are insensitive to the things of the Lord. I have preached in dead churches. Few experiences are more dreaded than preaching the words of life to listeners in the pew who are generally unaware of their dead condition. As one fellow quipped, "It would be a blessing if someone would just come forward to make an announcement!" When the Spirit is not present, nothing else matters.

A Message to the Dying

To the church in Sardis in which the embers of the Spirit were smoldering at best, John wrote in 3:2, *"Be watchful, and strengthen the things which remain, that are ready to die."* John wrote to encourage the believers that they must live with a continual sense of expectancy that their Lord was soon to return. The commandment of our Lord to share the way to salvation is as critical in our day as it was in Sardis. We must be about the fulfilling of His commission to us to introduce people to faith in Christ.

The flames of the Spirit in the church at Sardis were flickering and almost extinguished. Jesus is herein spurring the church to action and insisting that they quickly evaluate their effectiveness and passion for Christ and take immediate action to correct the problem. In a similar way, the apostle told his young protégé Timothy to *"stir up the gift of God which is in thee"* (II Timothy 1:6). John is here directing the church at Sardis to give ultimate priority to their mission and to enjoy the revitalizing work of the Spirit who will spur them to appropriate action.

Encouraging them to remind themselves of the manner by which they had received the gospel, John wrote that they ought to relive the moment as motivation to experience the ongoing work of the Spirit in personal renewal. Spiritual growth, personal revival and inner restoration are activated in the same manner that we initially receive eternal life – by means of faith. It is not in our effort to "*hold fast and repent*" that we achieve eternal life (3:3). John is reminding the believers in Sardis to allow the faith of Jesus within their souls to propel them toward true sacrificial service. It is the faith received at salvation that serves our protection from eternal punishment for our personal failures. Some of us fail in marriage; others stumble and fall in careers or in the task of parenting, yet our failure is never meant to be fatal. God's grace offers a second chance.

The repentance about which John wrote was meant to instigate a change of mind for the Sardis believers. The origin of the term *repent* refers to a military command to abruptly turn in the opposite direction at the command of the officer. Likewise, the soldier of Christ must change his mind and replace his thoughts and passions with those of Christ. God works effectively as he invades our thoughts and attitudes. Satan works in the shadows to infiltrate our thinking and emotions with thoughts of depression, discouragement and defeat. His ultimate weapon is to rob the believer of a sense of worth and value as a believer and to convince us to live our lives apart from the power and presence of God. Sadly, the pews of churches are decorated with people who have been duped by Satan's lie.

Jesus changes the hearts of people and changed people change communities. John insisted upon an act of repentance knowing that until sorrow and remorse filled their hearts, little change would be realized.

A Message to the Dedicated

Have you ever concluded that the entire world is rotten to the core and all is hopeless? Greed in the business world, ethical and moral dishonesty in the church, and temporary commitments in every arena of life tend to discourage weary believers. Yet God always has a remnant. He preserves His church and maintains a perpetual witness in the world. He searches the hearts and minds of His people and adds His incredible blessing where He finds faith. He always has and always will.

The prophet Elijah reached such a point of despair that he concluded that he only remained as the sole true servant of his Lord. God quickly reminded him of the error of his thinking by providing seven thousand unbending believers who had not sold their souls to Baal in abandonment of their faith in God. Elijah got the message.

The church in Sardis experienced spiritual deadness yet a few members still remained in the fellowship and had *"not defiled their garments"* (3:4). They had refused to adopt the ways of the world and allow them to capture their passions. The garments of their souls remained white with purity and these faithful believers would be granted the privilege of walking with God, *"in white: for they are worthy"* (3:4). The color white here symbolizes the purity and holiness of God and the holy character of truly committed followers of Christ. Personal effort does not gain for us the gift of salvation but rather it is the gift of faith dwelling within our hearts and minds that establishes our position as righteous in His eyes. We are not saved because we are faithful – we are faithful because we have been saved. True believers with a full dose of Jesus act like it!

All believers fail at one time or another. Some make the mistake of inflicting themselves with a sense of false condemnation by claiming their perpetual unworthiness. In the core of our hearts we are all unworthy, yet the death of Jesus gives us the privilege of being the recipients of His love and the promise of life forever.

Salvation is provided to us in three tenses: *we have been saved* from the punishment that sin would inflict; *we are being saved* from the ongoing destructive power of sin; and, *we will be saved* one day from the damning nature of sin at His second coming. Clothed not in our own goodness but rather in the goodness of Jesus, we will be presented as faultless before the throne of Jesus Christ.

John concluded his words to the church at Sardis in 3:5, *"I will not blot out his name out of the book of life"*. Evidently, a heavenly book of life records the names of every individual who has ever existed. Such a monumental task is foreign to our human minds yet well within unlimited powers of our Lord. As people die, those who have failed to receive Christ see their names blotted from the pages of the book of life. On the contrary, true believers whose names remain in this book will be presented to God as worthy of joining His eternal fellowship. John wrote in 3:5, *"I will confess his name before my Father and before his angels."* God will claim His children as His and His alone.

Until that time, dead churches may repent, experience new life, be revitalized, and live again – dead believers may do the same.

Chapter 10

PHILADELPHIA: SURVIVING THE END-TIME CRISIS
Revelation 3: 7-13

What a wonderful privilege we have been granted to serve a God who is loving and just. The words that fell from the pen of the apostle John to the church in the cultured city of Philadelphia serve to remind all believers that we will be spared from the coming wrath of the period known as the tribulation. In love, He will remove us from the earth; in justice He will deal with those left behind. In which group are you?

In a gentle yet direct manner, the aging John wrote to a church that is representative of the church as it existed in the era of the eighteenth and nineteenth centuries. It was during that era that God ushered in one the greatest movements of revival, renewal, and missions expansion that the world has ever known.

The Church at Philadelphia

Located on the site of the modern city of Alashetir, Philadelphia was founded near 190 B.C by King Attalus II, the king of Pergamum. His unusual devotion to his brother led to the selection of the name for the city – the city of brotherly love. The city was located on an important commercial route known as the Imperial Post Road.

Philadelphia housed some of the great institutions of academia and was a major center for education. Interestingly, the church in this city received no word of rebuke from the pen of the apostle John. Scholars speculate that this church may be a model for the ideal church in the mind of our Lord.

Prophetically, this church is partly representative of those in the era of church history extending beyond the missions movement of the eighteenth and nineteenth centuries to include the Church Age of our day as well. Our era is best represented by the characteristics of the church at Laodicea that was neither *hot nor cold.* However, shades of the Philadelphian church may be observed in the church of today as well. The church of today has drifted toward moral and spiritual middle ground and generally refusing to become distinctive in the world. The loving Philadelphian church had a holy remnant within its membership that I believe has a modern offspring of like mind and heart. That fellowship of genuine believers continues to exist as the Lord's remnant in the world before He comes.

The Character of Christ

To the church at Philadelphia John wrote in 3:7-8,

> *These things saith he that is holy, he that is true, he that hath the key of David, he that openeth, and no man shutteth; and shutteth, and no man openeth; I know thy works: behold, I have set before thee an open door, and no man can shut it: for thou hast a little strength,and has kept my word, and hast not denied my name.*

Jesus is here described as the One who is holy. This claim is stated to serve as an encouragement to the church at Philadelphia that the Holy One is righteous and just. As the high priest in Hebrews 7:26, Jesus is pictured as the One who is "*holy, harmless, undefiled, separate from sinners, and made higher than the heavens.*" Some critics today attempt to convince a skeptical public that Jesus was not God and that He never made such a bold claim. This passage clearly and convincingly destroys that argument in that God, and God alone, is holy. Jesus, fully God, is herein described as holy and consequently identical in nature with God the Father.

Jesus is further described in this passage as One who is "*true*" (3:7). Holiness emphasizes what and who Jesus is – His description as true is an accurate portrayal of what Jesus does. Jesus was no mere teacher with unusual gifts of communication or a mere prophet who declared truth as a man among men. He *is* truth and apart from Him no truth exists. Religious charlatans of our day appear on the airwaves and have within their ranks those who preach the truth of Christ while living in such as way as to deny that very truth. The messenger often dilutes or distorts the message. In contrast, Jesus preaches truth – and He *is* the truth.

Jesus is the One in possession of the *"key of David"* (3:7). The Bible teaches that God entered into a covenant with David in which He promised that One was on the way who would rule the world and whose kingdom would never end. Holding this key, Jesus will unlock the secrets of that promise at His return.

Further, Jesus is pictured here as the One who opens what no other will ever shut and who shuts what no man will ever open. This passage concerning Christ is a clear indication of His sovereignty or His ability to do what He well pleases in His time. His full and complete deity is vital to realize and acknowledge in a day such as ours when cults claim erroneous views about Jesus and attempt to strip Him of His deity.

To this persecuted and harassed church, John's words must have served to solidify their confidence in the ability of our Lord to direct their affairs. Soothing words such as these were assuredly welcome news to weary travelers.

The Commendation of Christ

In characteristic fashion, John wrote that Jesus was well aware of their *"works"* or efforts to serve Him. He knew them well as He walked within their midst. Rest assured that no difficult experience or dark day that you may be enduring escapes the notice or loving eyes of our Lord.

This unique church had been granted an open door of opportunity to advance the gospel. They stared a grand opportunity in the face. Jesus desired to motivate them to greater levels of service than ever. The opening of ministry doors was a sovereign act of God that no man was capable of closing. All of us as believers today have open doors of service yet often fail to walk through the doors and allow His hand to operate through us as channels of His grace.

One motivating factor that prepared the way for significant ministry opportunities was the church's *"little strength"* (3:8). John complimented the church for its ability to accomplish a variety of tasks even though their human ingenuity and raw power was limited. It is with the realization of our limited human ability that we may experience the strength of our Lord. For God to work in and through His followers does not require of us great personal charisma, power, or wealth. On the contrary, He is scanning the horizon for the warm hearts of available people. God often does a great work through a church with limited opportunities and meager means in order to claim the glory for Himself.

John continued his words to the church by acknowledging in, *"(Thou) hast kept my word, and hast not denied my name"* (3:8). Herein lies the primary key to experiencing the blessing of God in ministry as an individual or church family. The pews and people of the Philadelphian church had been saturated with the Word of God. In faithfully keeping the Word, they gave authenticity to their faith by obedience to its commands. To believe is good – to obey is better. Their obedience to Jesus was fleshed out in the face of the Roman demand to declare Caesar as the only lord. In a similar vein, people left behind in the tribulation will be pressured to give allegiance to the one-world ruler. As believers today, we are tempted to declare our allegiance to a variety of other gods who vie for the control of our hearts. The gods of perpetual pleasure and materialism beat at the door of our hearts demanding attention.

In the face of unrelenting pressure, this band of Philadelphian believers kept His word and received commendation as a result.

The Commitment of Christ to His Church

John continued his communication to the church and in so doing gave insight into the details concerning the rapture of the Church and its timing. He wrote in 3:9-10,

> *Behold, I will make them of the synagogue of Satan, which say they are Jews, and are not, but do lie; behold, I will make them to come and worship before thy feet, and to know that I have loved thee. Because thou hast kept the word of my patience, I also will keep thee*

> *from the hour of temptation, which shall come upon all the world, to try them that dwell upon the earth.*

I believe that John's reference to the synagogue of Satan points to a group of Judaizers. This group of deceivers is identified numerous times in the writings of Paul in the New Testament as those who preached the name of Christ yet insisted on simultaneous adherence to the dictates of Old Testament law. Jesus herein indicates that this group was composed of false believers who intended to distort the core message of the gospel. Simple devotion to Christ was less than acceptable to this group of Jewish traditionalists who also insisted on adherence to various restrictions of the Law.

The vision given to John records these words in 3:10, *"I also will keep thee from the hour of temptation."* In this context, the promise of Jesus to *"keep"* believers from an approaching hour of testing refers to His ability to protect or preserve them from its harm and from the *"hour"* of testing as well. The *"hour"* of this dreaded experience refers to a period or era of time. Essentially, believers will be free from the pain and harassment of the tribulation and mercifully spared from the entire painful era. This period of intense testing was also noted by Daniel and by the weeping prophet Jeremiah who described it as the time of *Jacob's trouble.* Further, Jesus taught of this coming terror in Matthew 24:21 and described it as unprecedented, "*…….such as was not since the beginning of the world to this time, no, nor ever shall be.*"

The Church will not be found on the earth during this period. People left behind will endure a multitude of catastrophic events. John indicated for the readers that this time of tribulation will inflict punishment upon *"them that dwell upon the earth,"* referring to those who remain as earth dwellers and who are not numbered among believers (3:10).

As believers, we are citizens of a heavenly kingdom who temporarily reside as aliens on this earth. Truly, we are simply passing through with our treasures all laid up somewhere beyond the blue, the old hymn reminds us.

This global judgment during the painful seven years of tribulation will not involve or afflict us as followers of Jesus Christ. In 3:11, John motivated his readers and the church of Philadelphia to take heart that Jesus would come *"quickly"* (3:11).

His sudden return to the earth to claim His bride will be unexpected. Readers, look up!

On Crowns and Rewards

Scripture identifies five crowns that are available for believers to receive as rewards. John wrote that we are to hold fast to the faith that we have and to allow *"that no man take thy crown"* (3:11).

This biblical concept regarding rewards for believers is interesting. Are awards available to be stolen? In what manner could a reward be lost? In I Corinthians 3 Paul wrote that the deeds of men will be tested by fire. If the deeds of man are composed of that which is lasting, they will remain and his reward will be assured. To the contrary, works that are identified as temporary and void of that which is eternal will be burned in this moment of evaluation.

Further, there are those who receive salvation *"so as by fire"* (I Corinthians 3:15). Saved, but less than fruitful, their faulty deeds will be consumed by the fires of evaluation. Consequently, these believers maintain the security of their salvation yet lose their reward due to poor efforts to serve God. A second manner one might lose his or her reward is to succumb to the clever temptations of Satan to hamper the life of the believer and thereby stunt spiritual growth. Third, the cares of this world often serve to discourage and distract believers from our ultimate purpose in life. Satan takes great delight in removing joy and service from the life of the believer and stealing his potential reward in so doing. These crowns from our Lord will be generously rewarded to those faithful to the cause. In short, serve Him and serve Him well!

The Comfort We Have in Christ

In 3:12 John wrote, *"Him that overcometh will I make a pillar in the temple of my God."* In the pagan temples that dotted the landscape of that day, pillars were erected featuring the inscribed names of individuals who had given funds for the construction of the temples. Recognition was given to those whose sacrifice had paved the way for the temples to exist. In a similar vein, John is here saying that believers who have been spiritual pillars in the church and who faithfully continue in their faith will receive eternal commendation for so doing. Loyalty and perseverance as *overcomers* will result in a payday. As the great preacher R.G. Lee put it, *payday some day.*

Recording the vision of Jesus, John continued in 3:12, *"I will write upon him the name of my God, and the name of the city of my God, which is the new Jerusalem."* As faithful believers, we will be granted the privilege of living as residents of the new heavenly city, the dwelling place of Christ and His followers. The *"new name"* that will be presented to believers refers to the fact that we as mortal humans are unable to fully understand God or the depths of His wisdom. At His coming, we will know Him in heaven in a manner that causes our former relationship with Him to pale in comparison. The fullness of His presence will be available to us as believers to a degree not previously imagined. With *"new"* names, we will know Him in His fullness. Our ability to understand and know Him will have no limit.

Those with the spiritual ears to hear God's message are synonymous with those who are true followers of Jesus Christ. John wrote that we must hear Him clearly – and be ready!

Chapter 11

LAODICEA: CHURCHES IN THE TRIBULATION
Revelation 3: 14-22

The unprecedented wealth of Microsoft Chairman Bill Gates has served as a talking point for journalists and business pundits. One report detailed the exquisite features of his home located near Seattle, Washington. It features over fifty-five thousand square feet of living space, a dining hall for two hundred guests, a movie theater, and climate control in each room that is activated by voice command. Downturns in the stock market often reduce his portfolio by billions of dollars yet appear to have little impact upon his financial clout. In a material sense, he has need of nothing. The members of the church at Laodicea thought that they needed nothing as well.

The scriptures are quite clear that there are individuals in the churches of today who are generally unaware that they will experience the travails of the seven-year tribulation. In Revelation 3:10 we are informed that true believers will be kept from the painful afflictions of the tribulation because the Church will have vanished. Those left behind will wail in agony and scurry about in an effort to escape this coming pain.

In Matthew 25, Jesus related the story of the ten virgins of which five were wise and five were portrayed as foolish. Those described as foolish were seen as such due to their failure to have oil for their lamps to provide light for the wedding party as it arrived. After they made a quick purchase of oil, they were too late to be received at the wedding. Jesus responded that He did not know them. As the rapture and tribulation days approach, there are many who assume that they will be spared from the tribulation yet will be sadly mistaken. Jesus said much about the eternal demise of those who *profess* Christ yet do not *possess* Him in their hearts. To summarize, a large segment of the members of the church of today will endure the fires of the tribulation period because they have never been truly converted.

A recent article in *Newsweek* magazine reported that the number of self-proclaimed Christians in America is at an all-time high. Yet the sin of immorality is increasing at an alarming rate and lawlessness and mayhem continue to dominate the news and spread like a prairie fire. Interestingly, the number of those who claim to attend church is far less than the actual count of those who do. A casual glance at today's brand of Christianity reveals that in many cases it fails to change the heart and the behavior of its adherents.

If the large contingency of Americans who claim to be Christian were genuinely distinctive in deed and in word, the heart of our nation would dramatically change. Like the members of the Laodicean church, many people today do not truly know Christ and will suffer the consequences of the tribulation and judgment to come.

The Church at Laodicea

To the church at Laodicea John wrote in 3: 14-17,

> *And unto the angel of the church of the Laodiceans write; 'These things saith the Amen, the faithful and true witness, the beginning of the creation of God; I know thy works, that thou art neither cold nor hot: I would thou wert cold or hot. So then because thou art lukewarm, and neither cold nor hot, I will spew thee out of my mouth. Because thou sayest, I am rich, and increased with goods, and have need of nothing; and knowest not that thou art wretched, and miserable, and poor, and blind, and naked:'*

In contrast to the church in Philadelphia, this church saw itself as independent, strong, and in need of essentially nothing to continue to exist. The city was renowned as a banking center. Wealth was in abundance. Laodicea was also known for the production of an eye salve effective in treating eye infections. This thriving city also constructed an underground aqueduct due to its inadequate water supply. Their water was unpleasing to the taste and was often spat on the ground in disgust.

These characteristics of the city are reflected in John's stern words of warning and condemnation to the church located there. The wealth that they possessed was false wealth. Eye salve cured sight problems yet failed to deal with spiritual blindness. They were clothed in the finest of fabric yet spiritually threadbare.

A Word of Revelation

Jesus identified Himself as *"The Amen, the faithful and true witness, the beginning of the creation of God"* (3:14). The word *amen* is a word of confirmation and when offered at the end of a prayer suggests agreement. In the Greek language, it translates "I agree, let it be so, or let it be confirmed". Jesus Himself is the *amen* of confirmation and agreement with God the Father as they are One in divine essence. In contrast to Jesus, this wayward church was certainly not faithful and true.

The cults of today attempt to point to this verse in an effort to disclaim and disprove the deity of Christ. An old heresy claims that Christ was the first creation of God and therefore not God. Essentially, the verse indicates that all of creation began with Christ. In John 1:1, the Bible says, *"In the beginning was the Word, and the Word was with God, and the Word was God."* Christ was the very origin of creation. He was not created in the creation but rather already existed at the outset of the creation experience. The scriptures claim *all things were made by Him.*

A Word of Rebuke

John wrote to reveal to the church the core of its very nature. He exposed their carnality and pointed to the remedy. Hiding the truth about themselves was no longer possible. Their lives and behavior were laid bare for the readers and for public scrutiny. The hearing of a message from God whether in writing or in a public worship gathering should reveal the needs of the heart and should lead to inner change. Sadly, some hearers never truly hear and consequently never respond. The church at Laodicea never fully heard the message.

In biting words, John wrote, *"I know thy works, that thou art neither cold nor hot: I would thou wert cold or hot"* (3:15). The nearby city of Hierapolis was famous for its hot springs and the city of Colossae for its cold mountain waters. John's readers knew well the meaning of the analogy. Residents of Laodicea often spat city water from their mouths due to its putrid taste. These church members were lukewarm in spiritual temperature, content with status quo, and not genuinely committed to the claims of Christ. In short, they were religious yet spiritually lost.

Tepid, lukewarm church members do great harm to the cause of Christ because they impede the gospel by falsely portraying the image of a genuine Christian. Lacking in true spiritual fire and emotional zeal, these institutionalized church members prohibit the effective spread of the claims of Christ in their respective churches.

Further, a tepid faith is an insult to Christ Himself. Jesus, referring to Himself, once said in John 2:17, "*the zeal of thine house hath eaten me up.*" Authentic believers who are consumed with fiery zeal live and breathe the ministry of our Lord. Unfortunately in our day, fanatical zeal is frowned upon as excessive. Mediocrity is applauded as fully adequate.

Concerning those who had deceived themselves, John wrote in 3:17, *"Thou sayest, I am rich, and increased with goods."* Simply stated, these foolish fellows were not true believers. The story is told of a fellow who never thought the sermon of the day was intended for his benefit. On a cold, snowy day this fellow was the sole person in attendance at Sunday worship other than the pastor. In convicting eloquence, the preacher took aim and fired. On the way out the door, the fellow commented, "Pastor, it's so sad that those who needed this message were not here today." Some people never get it.

The church at Laodicea never got it. They were incredibly rich with worldly goods yet spiritually poverty stricken. Tepid in spiritual temperature, they were spiritually useless. As long-time

Texas evangelist Freddie Gage quipped, "You can't thaw them out – and you can't heat them up!"

Further, the members of the Laodicean church were *"wretched"* or characterized by a spirit of mediocrity. In their minds, nothing else was needed. Emotional expressions of worship to God were seen as unnecessary and the product of uncultured people who were psychologically unbalanced.

"Miserable, poor and blind" in heart, the members of this church were the recipients of the pity of Jesus. They appeared numb to their own unrepentant state. They were rich in a worldly sense yet poverty-stricken to the things of God. They were blind and unable to see God for whom really He was. Although the city was renowned for the healing of eye ailments, the eyes of their hearts were blinded (3:17).

Jesus counseled them to buy a *"white raiment"* indicating that their only remedy for sin was the purity and untarnished nature of the Lamb of God (3:18). In so doing, they would be adorned with the robe of righteousness, the only garment that truly matters.

A Word of Repentance

In an attempt to pave a pathway to repentance for this rebellious church, John wrote in 3:19, *"As many as I love, I rebuke and chasten."* Only those with the spiritual sensitivity to recognize the rebuke of the Lord will be granted passage to heaven. True believers recognize sin and sense true conviction when we engage in sin. To feel no remorse and fail to agree with God in acknowledging the presence of sin is to underscore one's own spiritual lostness. In love for His children, Jesus is more than willing to *"chasten"* us for the purpose of correction.

I say with experience and authority that few churches in our day hear messages on the chastening hand of the Lord but they ought to. Few pastors want to risk the retaliation of influential members in the pew who may not welcome any hint of correction. Yet the voice of the Holy Spirit speaks to the believer with a desire to correct us. As the correction of a child with a voice command fails to succeed, we often revoke privileges as a means of discipline.

A sense of joy and freedom is temporarily suspended in order to capture the undivided attention of the child. Our Lord also allows His hand of discipline to be applied and does so in a variety of ways in order to mold us into His image.

These words of John should serve as a warning to those who never sense the chastening of the Lord. To never experience His hand of correction is an indication of spiritual lostness. The children of Satan do not receive the loving discipline of the Lord – they simply slide into hell for an eternity.

A Word of Reconciliation

John wrote in 3:20, *"Behold, I stand at the door, and knock."* These words were directed to a church. It was a sad scene indeed to imagine the Lord on the outskirts of a church not allowed to venture in. Their sense of self-sufficiency served to quench their desire to truly know Him. I often utilize this passage to illustrate to a non-believer that God wants us to accept Him by responding to the knock of the Spirit on the door of our hearts. We receive Him by prayer. However, the primary intention of these words of Jesus to the church of today is to remind us that He desires to be the central focus and passion of our hearts and churches. The structures and perfunctory functions of the church often persuade its members that Jesus is less than the primary focus and that His power is unnecessary.

I believe that Billy Graham was correct in his assumption and observation that sixty to eighty percent of church members today are unregenerate and have never met the Savior. This accounts for the obvious discrepancy between the verbal claims of those who say they are followers of Christ and their behavior that suggests otherwise.

Jesus invited the Laodicean false believers and invites us today as well to be reconciled to Him. His invitation includes a sweet promise from a loving God who is full of grace, *"If any man hear my voice, and open the door, I will come in to him, and will sup with him and he with me"* (3:20). Churches who have failed to welcome Jesus into their midst still have an open invitation to respond to the gentle knocking of our Lord. Individuals who have adopted the ways of the world as their lord may still come to know the true Lord in all of His grace and love. He stands waiting and ready to walk into the heart of anyone who repents. The knock of the Lord may come in a variety of ways; sorrow, death, blessings, and unexpected circumstances may serve to open the door of the heart to the work of the Spirit.

To those willing to hear and heed His voice, He promises to offer sweet fellowship at His table. As we welcome and dote over a special guest received into our homes, our Lord is waiting with open arms to receive us.

Many people know the church. Fewer people truly know the Lord of the Church.

PART THREE

THE RAPTURE AND SEVEN-YEAR TRIBULATION PERIOD

Chapter 12

THE FIRST CHRISTIAN TO DISAPPEAR
Revelation 4: 1-2

Not in a single instance do we read of the seven churches from the end of chapter three until their reappearance at the Battle of Armageddon in chapter nineteen. The reason is that the Church is no longer on the earth during this horrifying era of prophetic fulfillment.

Revelation 4:1 begins, *"After this I looked.........."* The Greek words, *"after this"* are of critical importance in understanding the chronological time to which John is referring. This phrase is identical to the one used in 1:19 in which John provided for all readers a simple and concise outline for the entire book. These two words are derived from the Greek *meta tauta* and translated to indicate what will occur after the events of Revelation 2-3. A specific sequence of events is in mind. Chapter four begins the third and final sequence of these end-time events that were revealed to the writer John who had been forcibly banished to the Isle of Patmos.

The words and prophetic visions of chapter four and beyond mark the end of the Church Age and the commencement of the heavenly age for believers and the tribulation for unbelievers left behind. Future events herein predicted and described in detail chart two distinct pathways for those who believe in Christ and those who do not.

John writes in 4:1,

> *After this I looked, and behold, a door was opened in heaven; and the first voice which I heard was as it were of a trumpet talking with me; which said, Come up hither, and I will shew thee things which must be hereafter.*

The seventh church located in Laodicea to which John wrote this stinging indictment typifies and pictures for us of the condition of Christianity at the time of Christ's future return. As the Church Age closes, the last public invitation to receive Christ will have been given, the last presentation of the gospel will have been given, and the last sinner will be converted. The body of Christ will be complete. Christ will snatch away His children to usher in the coming era that is graphically described in chapter four and beyond.

Why do I believe that 4:1-2 describes the rapture or vanishing of the Church? The scripture says that a door was opened in heaven. God spoke to the startled John and His voice is described as like a trumpet. The voice John heard commanded Him to *"come up hither."*

As the angel spoke to the shepherds concerning the birth of Jesus he said, "...*Fear not: for, behold, I bring you good tidings of great joy, which shall be to all people. For unto you is born this day in the city of David a Saviour which is Christ the Lord*" (Luke 2: 10b-11). When God makes a dramatic entrance into world history with a startling announcement, it is truly good news. Human history is forever altered when God fulfills a promise to His people.

The fulfillment of His previous promise to return some day is symbolically fulfilled in the vision recorded here in 4:1-2. The passage is not describing the first coming of Christ at His birth but rather the announcement of the dramatic end of the Church Age and the sudden rapture of the Church from the earth.

The Destiny of the Church

The Church is mentioned twenty times in the vision of John in the first three chapters of Revelation. Not a single mention may be found from 4:1 until the events in chapter nineteen. The Church will have vacated the earth in a dramatic removal. Journalists will struggle to write the headlines. News anchormen will be at a loss for words.

John was suddenly caught up in the Spirit and was swept away into the very throne room of God. Revelation 4:2 records, "*Behold, a throne was set in heaven.*" Through supernatural conveyance,

John was transferred to the throne of God. In his vision, John saw Christ standing before him. Earlier Jesus had placed His hand on the shoulder of John and encouraged him to live without fear. John found himself in the very presence of God. What occurred to John in the spiritual realm is representative of what is to occur supernaturally for all believers when Jesus breaks open the eastern skies.

The opening of the door in the throne room of heaven is significant. In Genesis 7:11, a door was opened in judgment. In Malachi 3:10, God promised the opening of the windows of heaven from which will pour blessings to those who faithfully tithe their earnings. In Luke 10:18, Jesus spoke of a door being opened and Satan tossed out of heaven. In Acts 7:56, the martyred deacon Stephen met his death by stoning. As he lay dying he muttered, "*Behold, I see the heavens opened, and the Son of man standing on the right hand of God.*" Doors open when God speaks.

The opening of the door of the throne room for John is a vivid picture of the opening of heaven's door for the rapture of the Church. The scriptures record other disappearances of believers that serve as precursors of the coming rapture. In Hebrews 11:5, we read of the sudden disappearance of the Old Testament character Enoch.

> *By faith Enoch was translated that he should not see death; and was not found, because God had translated him: for before his translation he had this testimony, that he pleased God.*

Enoch's disappearance caused quite a stir. Enoch lived before the Great Flood. Due to wicked behavior on earth, God made the decision to judge the world with a flood. Before the heavens poured onto the earth, Enoch was snatched away. He was a man of incredible faith and God spared him. In a similar manner, those of us with faith in God at the time of the rapture will suddenly be translated into the realm of God's presence.

Some of the believers in Thessalonica evidently assumed that they had missed the departure of the Church and were greatly distressed over it. Further, they believed that their loved ones who had passed away would miss the rapture. Paul wrote to correct these two erroneous ideas. He explained to these weary pilgrims that those who had died were merely *"asleep"*, a term common in New Testament language for the death of the body.

The soul or spirit of dead believers is translated into the presence of Jesus at the moment of physical death. Paul also taught the Thessalonicans that dead believers would return with Christ to the earth. In I Thessalonians 4:15-16 Paul wrote,

> *For this we say unto you by the word of the Lord, that we which are alive and remain unto the coming of the Lord shall not prevent (precede) them which are asleep. For the Lord himself shall descend from heaven with a shout, with the voice of the archangel, and with the trump of God: and the dead in Christ shall rise first.*

These verses serve as a consoling promise that our dead loved ones who were believers have been in the Lord's presence since the time of their death and will return with Him to claim His children. The spirits and the physical bodies of believers who have passed away will be supernaturally reunited and transformed into a permanent glorified state. The *"clouds"* to which Paul refers in I Thessalonians 4:17 are those of the *shekinah* glory that will surround Jesus as He comes. Paul's words *"caught up"* are identical to those in Revelation 4:1-2.

Our destiny is heaven and the abrupt nature of our departure is assured.

The Disappearance of the Church

The dramatic transportation of John into the throne room of God is symbolic and descriptive of the coming experience of the Church at the outset of the tribulation period. As John saw a door supernaturally open for him to ascend into heaven, believers one day will see the clouds open and Jesus will return in full triumph. When Jesus ascended into heaven from the Mount of Olives as recorded in Acts 1, gravity was temporarily suspended and He began to rise into the air. The clouds of glory received him into their heavenly arms. One day from those glorious clouds, Jesus will personally descend.

John heard a sound like a trumpet that was the voice of God speaking to him. In ancient Israel, the trumpet was useful in assembling the people for gatherings such as worship. The trumpet was also instrumental in announcing a call to battle. In the story of Gideon recorded in Judges 6-7, Gideon blew the trumpet assembling 32,000 people. In I Corinthians 15:51-52, the apostle Paul referred to the sound of the trumpet to announce the coming of Christ. Paul wrote,

> *Behold, I show you a mystery; We shall not all sleep, but we shall all be changed. In a moment, in the twinkling of an eye, at the last trump: for the trumpet shall sound, and the dead shall be raised incorruptible, and we shall be changed.*

Not all believers will be dead at the coming of Christ to the earth, yet all of us will be *"changed"*. This change to occur refers to our future with bodies that will no longer groan and deteriorate. The most rapid movement of the human body is that of the twinkling of the eye. The coming of Jesus and His dramatic gift to us of a perpetually healthy body will occur in an instant. The Church will be swept away with lightning speed.

The Deliverance of the Church

One primary benefit of the rapture of the Church is the ability to *escape* the terrors of the tribulation period as God unleashes His just wrath with full fury. The judgment of the tribulation period will be enacted upon Israel. This judgment will also include God's retribution and the demonstration of His wrath inflicted upon an unbelieving world.

The second benefit of the rapture for believers is the privilege of *entrance* into heaven. As Jesus told John to come into heaven to receive the remainder of the vision, believers one day will be granted the privilege of a reunion with the saints who have preceded us in heaven. This second gathering of separated believers will be the mother of all family reunions and a sight to behold. Christmas is a warm and loving time of reunion for those who love one another yet the reunion of Christmas for families will pale in comparison to the reunion of the saints in heaven.

The rapture of the Church will also include a *revival* at the throne of God. In 4:2, Jesus is pictured as sitting on the throne. John must have seen this unbelievable sight with an open mouth and aghast in astonishment. With the assurance that Christ is seated on the throne, believers should take heart and cast off all of our fears.

As God said to the shepherds and to Mary and Joseph, we must not succumb to fear. Since sin made its rude entrance into the world, fear has gripped the heart of every man. We fear personal failure, career disappointment, crippling illness and sudden death. The command to live without fear is one of the most often repeated admonitions in all of scripture. With Christ on the throne, why fear? Perhaps poet Henry Wadsworth Longfellow captured the essence of the promises of Jesus with the composition of that great hymn, *I Heard the Bells on Christmas Day.*

And in despair I bowed my head;
'There is no peace on earth,' I said
'For hate is strong, and mocks the song
Of peace on earth, good will to men.'

Then pealed the bells more loud and deep:
'God is not dead, nor doth He sleep;
The wrong shall fail, the right prevail
With peace on earth, good will to men.'

The sudden snatching away of the Church will also provide a means of divine *retribution* upon the world. With the Church having vanished from the earth, our loving yet just God will pour out retribution as He graphically depicted in Revelation 6-19. Yet we are to live without fear and allow God's promises to spare us from the travails to come and to serve as soothing grace for our needy souls.

God knows our need. He is just and fair. His coming will be sudden and sure. As John was swept into heaven, we will soon follow.

Take heart!

Chapter 13

THE FIRST FIVE MINUTES IN HEAVEN
Revelation 4: 2b-11

To clarify the sequence of coming events, it is critical to realize that the Church will have vanished from the earth as the events of chapter four and beyond begin to unfold. The transporting of John into the throne room of heaven during the vision he received while on Patmos is a precursor of the rapture of believers still to come.

As believers are raptured into the presence of our Lord, the judgment seat of Christ will be held. Contrary to public opinion, the destinies of heaven or hell will not be determined by evaluating the quality of our behavior or our level of inner goodness. Eternal destiny will be determined by whether we truly have believed in Christ and committed our lives to Him.

The judgment seat of Christ will specifically evaluate the deeds of the believer for the purpose of doling out rewards. I believe that the concept of degrees of reward in heaven is a doctrine often ignored by today's church. The New Testament details five crowns that believers may earn on the basis of our personal efforts in ministry.

In the twinkling of an eye, John was catapulted from the sandy shores of Patmos into the presence of God in the throne room. The description of that scene beginning at 4:3 informs us of what will occur at the judgment seat.

It is important to note that our loved ones who have passed from this life have yet to receive their rewards. We often comment that they have *gone on to their reward* yet the reward has not been granted. In this life, we applaud our loved ones for their unconditional love for us, for their influence in leading others to faith in Christ, and for the contributions to the kingdom they provided. Their sacrificial and compassionate investments in others continue to accrue eternal interest.

The Person of the Throne

Revelation might also be known as the *Throne Book* because the vision given to John continually refers to events related to the throne of God. As a monarch or leader of a country sits on the throne, he does so in sovereignty and authority. Yet no sovereign leader begins to compare with the ultimate authority of the One who sits on the throne of eternal authority. In this vision, John saw the *stability of God.* In a time such as ours when what was once nailed down is coming up, a reminder of the ultimate authority and stability of our God is welcomed and needed.

I read an article in *Newsweek* magazine concerning nuclear proliferation. The writer warned readers that the world is not a safer and secure place since the demise of the Soviet Union. At the time of writing, the author of the article noted that no fewer than twenty-five countries had the capability of using nuclear weapons. The scriptures remind us that peace is often assumed but in reality will be forever elusive. The Bible says, *"For when they say Peace and safety; then sudden destruction cometh upon them"* (I Thessalonians 5:3). In an unstable world in which John lived, it must have been soothing grace to read of the One who is truly stable and who will provide perfect peace for His children when He comes.

The image of Jesus seated upon the throne must have also reminded John of the *sovereignty of God.* The kingdoms of men will come and go but the reign of our Lord will never meet its demise. America is in its infancy compared to the age-old kingdoms of Europe and China, yet America and all other nations will cease to exist as the kingdom of God assumes eternal reign. John caught a breathtaking glimpse of the throne and His coming reign.

John must have stared in silent wonder as he saw the *splendor of God.* Revelation 4:3 records, *"He that sat upon the throne was to look upon like a jasper and a sardius stone and there was a rainbow round about the throne, in sight like unto an emerald."* The jasper stone was crystal clear and speaks of the transparency of our Lord. He is faultless and without guile or flaw. He is perpetually holy. Men often hide themselves in shame from the eyes of the world yet God has no reason to hide His nature from us. The sardius stone in

John's vision was blood red and reminds us of the cross of Calvary at which Jesus shed His blood for mankind. As we read of the city of God at the end of Revelation, we will note that these two stones are embedded in the foundation of the holy city, the new Jerusalem. The holiness and blood of Jesus are foundational doctrines of our faith.

The rainbow that surrounded the throne was like an emerald. Emeralds are green in color. The color green often reminds of the evergreen tree that never sheds its leaves. Through the changing of the seasons and the fluctuating temperatures and seasons that the earth endures, its leaves remain intact. God's character and holiness remain forever secure and consistent as well.

This rainbow seen by John encompassing the throne of God was a vivid reminder of the promises of our Lord that will never fail. Interestingly, this rainbow completely encircles the throne. I believe that the completed arch of the rainbow speaks of the completion of knowledge upon our arrival in heaven. In his letter to the Corinthians, Paul taught that in our current state we have a limited understanding with limitations much like as a person who peers into a mirror sees his image *darkly* or incompletely. Unexplained tragedies occur and I often shrug my shoulders with the victims and admit my lack of understanding. Yet in the rapture and reign of our Lord, that which is now lacking in clarity and explanation will be fully revealed. Jesus is and will always be seated securely on His throne!

The People Around the Throne

Revelation 4:4 reads, *"Round about the throne were four and twenty seats, and upon the seats I saw four and twenty elders sitting."* I believe that these twenty-four elders are representative. In Old Testament history, King David chose twenty-four priests to represent all of the priests of Israel. The elders seated on the throne and seen by John represent the twelve patriarchs of the Old Testament and the twelve apostles of the New Testament. As the imposter, Judas will not be included among this number because he was a *devil from the beginning*, the scriptures claim. I believe that the apostle Paul may fill his vacancy. The saints from all the ages are here represented in this scene.

Notice the *position* of the elders. These elders pictured in 4:4 are *"clothed in white raiment; and they had on their heads crowns of gold."* In the words to the seven churches in Asia recorded in chapters two and three, we are reminded that those who overcome as true believers will be granted the privilege of sitting on the throne with the Lord. Here in the throne scene, John caught a glimpse of that promise to come. The privilege of sitting with Christ on His throne will result in ecstatic glory for every believer.

The *perfection* of the elders is revealed in the clothing of white raiment and golden crowns. The whiteness of the clothing is a vivid picture of the righteousness of Jesus. The robes of the elders have been made white by the red blood of the Lamb who died for us. What a gift to know that we will not stand before God on the basis of our inherent goodness. Our personal goodness has the value of filthy rags as indicated in Isaiah 64:6. As the great hymn says, Jesus truly did pay it all and all to Him we owe. He did not make the down payment on our salvation with His death and then assign future payments to us. He paid it all!

As we read of this scene in heaven that John witnessed, we also note the *possession* of the elders. The book of Jude teaches that He is able to keep us and to present us as faultless before the throne. In the possession of the elders on the throne, John saw golden crowns upon their heads. The word *"crown"* is derived from the Greek word *stephanos* referring to the crown of a victor in ancient Olympian games. The *bema* seat was the stand of the judges from which they evaluated the athletes on the basis of their adherence to the rules and their personal effort. A laurel wreath served as a crown upon their heads. Winning athletes often wore the crown and took a victory lap around the stadium for all to see. At this point in John's vision, the resurrection and judgment seat of Christ will have occurred because the crowns of reward will have been distributed.

When will crowns be distributed? We will receive our crowns at the time of the Lord's appearing. Contrary to the teaching of some, the Church will not endure the tribulation or even the first half of it. A clear understanding of this scene in heaven will not allow for a mid-tribulation or post-tribulation view of the coming of Christ.

In an expression of false humility, some believers today claim that their only desire is for a little spot in the land of eternal glory or a cabin in the corner of heaven. Such a statement appears sweet and humble, yet it is entirely lacking in scriptural ground. Our capacity to fully enjoy heaven with a full measure of reward is predicated upon the quality of our service for the Lord while here on earth.

Our deeds are critically important, a truth we will more fully investigate in our review of succeeding verses. The apostle Paul wrote that he was poised to claim his crown of reward, an experience awaiting millions of believers as well. He described this promise in II Timothy 4: 6-8,

> *I am now ready to be offered, and the time of my departure is at hand. I have fought a good fight, I have finished my course, I have kept the faith: henceforth there is laid up for me a crown of righteousness, which the Lord, the righteous judge, shall give me at that day: and not to me only, but unto all them also that love his appearing.*

The Proceedings of the Throne

Included in the sights and sounds that John witnessed in his vision at the throne scene was preview of the coming day of judgment. In 4:5 the Bible says, *"Out of the throne proceeded lightnings and thunderings and voices."* We often hear of a person who has committed an offense of some kind remark in jest, "I thought God would strike me dead." The insinuation of such a remark is that God angrily demands that all sinners be punished with sudden death. However, these scriptures do point to the righteous intentions of our Lord to thoroughly evaluate His children in order to determine appropriate rewards.

The judgment herein predicted will be *fearful* in that our deeds and words will be laid bare for inspection. Wayward sins and other misgivings certainly will not result in the God's approval. We must be aware that our actions are of a critically important nature. Our sins will not simply pass away into oblivion without notice. God will issue a holy and righteous rule of judgment and assign rewards in proportion to the quality of our deeds in life.

Revelation 4:5b records, *"there were seven lamps of fire burning before the throne, which are the seven Spirits of God."* The seven lamps of fire point to the *factual* nature of God's judgment that is on the way. He will evaluate His children by utilizing His full and complete knowledge. Lamps illuminate and clarify the objects of our attention. Similarly, the fullness of the light of God will clarify and accentuate the truth of our lives for all to see.

This judgment to come will also be *final.* Revelation 4:6 reads, *"And before the throne there was a sea of glass like unto crystal: and in the midst of the throne, and round about the throne, were four beasts full of eyes before and behind."* The beautiful lakes and ponds of mountainous Colorado often appear still and glassy. A sudden hush of serenity and beauty captures our attention as we view such magnificent splendor. The serenity that we experience when a glassy lake glistening in a meadow seemingly undisturbed offers a moment of quiet rest for busy lives.

The serenity God will bring to us in heaven will cause any experience of earthly serenity to pale in comparison. Our prayer lives serve as a precursor of this coming peace and serenity awaiting us in heaven.

The judgment to occur at the throne will have a ring of finality. Our lifetime wait for the evaluation of our deeds will come to an end. For the faithful believer, that experience will be bathed in the living serenity of our Lord. Perhaps the hymn writer best captured this concept when he wrote,

There is a place of quiet rest
Near to the heart of God
A place where sin cannot molest

Near to the heart of God.

Praise at the Throne

At our first five minutes in heaven, we will be gloriously caught up in the praises of our Lord. In picturesque language, John described the scene for us in 4: 7-11,

> *And the first beast was like a lion, and the second beast like a calf, and the third beast had the face as a man, and the fourth beast was like a flying eagle. And the four beasts had each of them six wings about him; and they were full of eyes within: and they rest not day and night, saying,'Holy, holy, holy, Lord God Almighty, which was, and is, and is to come. And when those beasts give glory and honour and thanks to him that sat on the throne, who liveth forever and ever, The four and twenty elders fall down before him that sat on the throne, and worship him that liveth for ever and ever, and cast their crowns before the throne, saying,'Thou art worthy, O Lord, to receive glory and honour and power: for thou hast created all things, and for thy pleasure they are and were created.'*

The word employed by the writer John for *"beast"* is derived from the Greek root *zao* translated in English as zoo or zoology, the study of animals. Here John is speaking of four living creatures. The lion represents undomesticated life. The calf points to tame or domesticated wild life. The face of the man is symbolic of intelligent life. The eagle reminds readers of fowl life. The Psalmist wrote, *"Let everything that hath breath praise the Lord"* (Psalm 150:6). John graphically captured the essence of this command in his description of creation offering unending praises to our Lord.

Interestingly, the creatures of our God and King are first seen giving praises to our Lord. Man, represented by the twenty-four elders, then joins the chorus of praise after he has been given his crown of reward. At this incredible scene of praise, believers will lay their crowns of reward at the feet of our Lord and thereby deny any desire for personal acclaim or reward. We will acknowledge that the deeds of our lives will have been motivated solely by the kindness of our Lord at work within us. Negligent believers will have precious little to place at the feet of Jesus while those who served Him faithfully until the very end will lay before Him crowns of extravagant and sacrificial service.

Some years ago, our ministerial staff enjoyed our annual Christmas party. I had forgotten our decision to each draw at random the name of a fellow staff member to whom we would present a gift. I arrived at the party without a gift and was red-faced with embarrassment. I whispered to my wife Glenda that I had forgotten to bring a gift. In characteristic fashion, she muttered that she had brought them and pointed toward a table. The gifts were beautifully wrapped and ready to present. Thank God for wives! She saved my neck. I quietly praised God that I had my gift to give. In the Day of Judgment, I will not have the privilege of claiming a reward based upon the service of Glenda or any other person. My reward will be based solely upon the gifts of service that I personally bring to the throne of our Lord.

His gift to us is life forever – our gift to Him is a lifetime of loving service.

Chapter 14

A BOOK MORE HOLY THAN THE BIBLE
Revelation 5: 1-8

Is it possible that a book might exist that could be described as more holy than the Bible? Since childhood, our Bibles have been a lamp to our feet and a light unto our paths. The Bible is God's revelation of Himself to us. Yet there is a book in heaven that no man is able to open. It is so incredibly holy and sacred that no man is worthy to open its pages.

In the throne scene portrayed in the concluding verses of chapter four, we read of the four living creatures that are caught up in the perpetual praise of our Lord. Representing all living things, these creatures feature six wings. Why six in number? The number six is the number of man. The Bible informs us that when the Antichrist arrives his number will be *666*. The number six is also representative of the creation. God's creative work was completed in six days. The six wings appearing on the four living creatures in this throne scene are representative of the whole of creation.

In his vision, John saw a book appear in the right hand of the One on the throne. He wrote in 5:1-8,

> *And I saw in the right hand of him that sat on the throne a book written within and on the backside, sealed with seven seals. And I saw a strong angel proclaiming with a loud voice, 'Who is worthy to open the book, and to loose the seals thereof?' And no man in heaven, nor in earth, neither under the earth, was able to open the book, neither to look thereon. And I wept much, because no man was found worthy to open and to read the book, neither to look thereon. And one of the elders saith unto me, 'Weep not: behold, the Lion of the tribe of Juda, the root of David, hath prevailed to open the book, and to loose the seven seals thereof.' And I beheld, and lo, in the midst of the throne and of the four beasts, and in the midst of the elders, stood a Lamb as it had been slain, having seven horns*

and seven eyes, which are the seven Spirits of God sent forth into all the earth. And he came and took the book out of the right hand of him that sat upon the throne. And when he had taken the book, the four beasts and four and twenty elders fell down before the Lamb, having every one of them harps, and golden vials(or bowls) full of odours, which are the prayers of the saints.

At this scene to be experienced by all believers after we have been raptured from the earth, we also will see this heavenly book held in the right hand of God. The angelic hosts will be present. The four living creatures representing all of creation will be in attendance. Yet no one in attendance will be worthy to open and reveal the contents of this book for all to see.

The first word of chapter five is *and,* a conjunctive word that connects the thought to that of chapter four. Of course, original manuscripts of the Bible had no chapter and verse divisions featured in our modern copies of the scriptures. One temptation of the modern reader is to assume a break in time sequence or subject matter from one chapter to the next due to chapter divisions. John made no mention whatsoever of a delay in time before the true contents of this book will be revealed. God is on the throne and in His hand is this magnificent book.

A Symbolic Book

This unusual book is sealed seven times. This book will not be heavenly bound in the manner of our Bibles today. This book is a scroll. Scrolls were rolled and sealed. The Romans sealed important documents with seven seals. As each seal was opened, the reader was able to read a portion of the contents. In that day, seals were also utilized as means of identification much like the seals officially utilized today by a notary public. In the days of the early church, the seal was also used for protection. As Jesus was laid in the tomb, the Romans sealed the tomb to protect it from unlawful entry. To break the seal of a Roman tomb was a crime punishable by death.

The scroll seen in the hand of the Lord is a book of redemption. As we proceed through the book of Revelation, we will note that as each seal is opened, prophecy will be fulfilled and judgment will be unleashed on the earth.

In the days of the early church, documents of ownership were used to identify slaves. If a slave owner mortgaged or sold his slave, the slave would then be indentured to another owner. A provision in the law allowed that the slave could be redeemed or reclaimed by the original owner. Reflecting that concept, the apostle Peter wrote that we as believers are not redeemed by things that are corruptible such as silver and gold, but rather by the precious blood of Jesus Christ, our original owner. With the shed blood of Jesus, God paid the price for our freedom. Man's freedom had previously been lost due to his sinfulness. By sinning, we forfeited our freedom and yet regained it by the blood of Jesus on the cross thus assuring the redemption of our souls.

In the Old Testament we read of the redemption of the land. At the time that the children of Israel were given the promised land each family received a parcel. Each parcel was to remain in the family for generations to come yet due to war or high taxes, land was often lost. The law allowed for the redemption of the land, a provision that many exercised.

On the external portions of this scroll John read the terms of redemption. Man was once granted dominion over the earth yet through the sin of Adam, man lost his right of dominion. Consequently, the earth was cursed. As a result, animals were untamed. The environment became hostile toward man. The ecology began to deteriorate. The sin of man brought a curse upon the whole world. The eighth chapter of Romans teaches us that the whole creation will emit continual groanings until the time of its redemption.

At His second coming, our dominion will be regained. As *"priests"* we will reign upon and over the earth (5:10). God originally designed us in the creation to rule and reign in the earth yet Satan tempted man to sin and thwarted this perfect plan. Satan presented a temptation to Jesus and offered Him the kingdoms of this world if Jesus would simply bow down and worship him. Notice in that scene Jesus did not inform Satan that he had no kingdoms to offer. Since the Fall of man, Satan has held control over the earthly kingdoms. He instigated the wickedness of Hitler. He motivated the violence in Bosnia and tempted the terrorists who targeted the Twin Towers of New York and the walls of the Pentagon. He motivates immorality. He loves death.

In the redemption and reclaiming of our dominion, the creation will once again revert to the possession of our Lord who will restore the divine privilege of dominion over the earth to His people. What man once lost will again be found.

Cult leader David Koresh of the Branch Davidians claimed the power to open the seven seals of Revelation. In so doing, he claimed to be Christ. No man is capable of opening these seals. When Christ opens the seals, events will transpire on the earth that will usher in the end of the world as we know it.

The final holocaust against the Jewish people will be unleashed and the magnificence of Christ at the Battle of Armageddon will be revealed to all. Inside this scroll or book, we will read of how man lost dominion over the earth. On its exterior, we will read of the terms for the redemption of our ownership of the earth.

A Sealed Book

The one to open and reveal the contents of this mysterious book must be one who has never sinned. In John's vision, we read of the *quest of the angel* to search and discover someone who might qualify to open the book. John saw the angel searching the corners of heaven and scanning all of the earth itself yet no one capable of opening the book was found. Perhaps he considered the patriarch Abraham, King David, the renowned apostle Paul, the beloved John, or the bold deacon Stephen, yet no one was found who qualified.

John began to weep at the failure to find a man able to open the book. Notice in these verses the incredible *quandary of the apostle.* The word employed here by John to describe his act of weeping describes enormous sorrow accompanied by copious tears. This graphic word was also utilized in the gospels to describe the wailings of Jesus in the Garden of Gethsemane prior to his horrible death. John must have realized that a failure to open the book would prevent further prophecies from being fulfilled.

The world would be doomed in its sin and never see the light of redemption should this book not be opened. John wailed at such a frightening possibility.

A Significant Book

The One to open the book was identified by John as none other than Christ Himself. He is identified in 5:5 as from *"the Lion of the tribe of Juda, the Root of David."* As one of the twelve tribes of Israel, Judah was the tribe from which David had come. This is an obvious reference to Christ as the Messiah. The Bible reminds us that Jesus descended in His earthly lineage from the tribe of the family of David and is consequently known as the Lion of Judah. A lion suggests that which is royal and regal. Jesus is here referred to as the *"Root of David"*. He is both the offspring of David in a human sense and is the ancestor of David as well in a supernatural way. Jesus was seen by John as the One who has *"prevailed to open the book"* as He defeated sin on the cross of Calvary. Jesus is imminently qualified to open the seals of the book and thereby welcome the fulfillment of prophecies ushering in the eternal reign of Christ over the world.

As John turned to see a Lion, he saw a lamb. This Lamb in the vision of John featured seven horns and seven eyes symbolic of the seven spirits of God. The Lamb is the One who had been slain yet is alive and well, and standing tall and with unprecedented power. His posture of standing points to the sure and certain resurrection of Jesus from the clutches of death.

Multiple scriptures utilize the analogy of a lamb to underscore an important doctrinal truth. As leader of the Israelites, Abraham led his son Isaac to the crest of the mountain and was prepared to plunge the dagger into the heart of his son. God stayed the hand of Abraham and instead provided a lamb for sacrifice.

God taught a valuable lesson to the Israelites as He delivered them from the slavery of Egypt. He instructed them to catch an unblemished lamb, slay it and accumulate its blood in a basin. The blood was to be applied on the doorposts of Israelite houses as a sign that the coming angel of death was to allow their eldest child to live.

Throughout history, the Jewish people have practiced the custom of penning a lamb to protect it from injury. They guarded the lamb carefully and allowed the children to establish a loving relationship with it as a pet. As the time came for the sacrifice of the lamb, one can imagine the grief felt by the children as the lamb was led to slaughter. In giving that lamb to God, the families were reminded of the precious sacrifice of God who covered their sins with the blood.

One significant theological question in the Bible regards the true identify of the Lamb. In Matthew, Mark and Luke, we read of no lamb at all. In the Gospel of John, John the Baptist wrote, *"Behold the Lamb of God, which taketh away the sin of the world."* Spotless and without blemish, Jesus is the sacrificial Lamb. No other Lamb can take away the sins of the world.

The Lamb in John's vision is seen with seven horns. The horns speak of His unfathomable authority. The seven horns also speak of perfection. The Lamb has complete and total authority. The seven eyes of the Lamb represent the omniscience of God and His qualification to adjudicate the earth.

John was also vividly aware of the sovereignty of Jesus Christ. Jesus is seen here removing the book from the right hand of God. As He fulfills this promise some day, all of creation will bow in humble adoration of our loving God. John wrote in 5:8, *"And when He had taken the book, the four beasts and four and twenty elders fell down before the Lamb, having every one of them harps, and golden vials full of odours, which are the prayers of saints."* How incredible it is to realize that God stores away in remembrance the prayers of His children. Our unanswered prayers for the end of suffering and for peace in our lives and in the world will one day be fully answered.

God will remove the curse from the world. The right and privilege of our God-given dominion will be gloriously restored. As Jesus breaks the seals and unfolds the scroll, the rest of history will unfold before our very eyes.

Chapter 15

HOPE FOR A WEARY WORLD
Revelation 5: 8-14

Psychologists have observed that all men have three basic needs in this life: something to do, someone to love, and something to hope for. As we read of John's vision in the throne room of God, we are introduced to the ultimate answer to a lifetime of hoping. John was witness to the songs of the saints that will be the most glorious of all expressions of praise when Christ takes us to our eternal home.

The book of all books rested in the right hand of God. In John's vision, Jesus removed it and one day it will be opened by Jesus Himself. It contains the terms and plans to restore to man his dominion over the earth that was lost in the Fall. In order for the earth to be redeemed and for creation to be restored to its intended place in God's economy, the plans and procedures of the book must be executed.

As the book is opened, all of heaven will burst into spontaneous songs of praise to our Lord. John penned these magnificent words in 5: 8-14,

> *And when he had taken the book, the four beasts and four and twenty elders fell down before the Lamb, having every one of them harps, and golden vials full of odours, which are the prayers of the saints. And they sung a new song, saying, 'Thou art worthy to take the book, and to open the seals thereof: for thou wast slain, and hast redeemed us to God by thy blood out of every kindred, and tongue, and people, and nation; And hast made us unto our God kings and priests: and we shall reign on the earth.' And I beheld, and I heard the voice of many angels round about the throne and the beasts and the elders: and the number of them was ten thousand time ten thousand, and thousands of thousands; Saying with a loud voice, ' Worthy is the Lamb that was slain to receive power, and riches, and*

> *wisdom, and strength, and honour, and glory, and blessings.' And every creature which is in heaven, and on the earth, and under the earth, and such as are in the sea, and all that are in them, heard I saying, 'Blessing, and honour, and glory, and power, be unto him that sitteth upon the throne, and unto the Lamb forever and ever. And the four beasts said, 'Amen'. And the four and twenty elders fell down and worshipped him that liveth forever and ever.*

In this passage John wrote of the second instance of vibrant praise since the snatching away of the Church recorded in 4:1. The soothing words that fell from the pen of John were a cause for hope in our weary world. We live in a world of continual tension and distress. We have experienced delicate negotiations with North Korea concerning nuclear capability. We have witnessed the heartbreak of war in Bosnia and shuddered at the loss of our security as terrorists viciously attacked the heart of America forcing us to retaliate against Afghanistan to prevent further loss of life. Christians in Sudan are systematically executed. Hope is often elusive and fleeting but hope ultimately will come in the person of Christ when He returns.

Songs of the Savior's Sacrifice

Upon hearing that the world will be redeemed and returned to the ownership of our Lord and His children, an explosion of praise will occur. As the closed contents of the scroll previously sealed is revealed, praise will erupt from the twenty-four elders who will fall prostrate before the Lamb of God.

This *"new song"* to be sung is one that is new in quality. Rich in meaning and flush with the long-waited promises of the return of Jesus to claim His children, these songs of praise will be an incredible sound to hear. For the first time, many in the Church will see unanswered prayers suddenly answered. The Church also will become vividly aware of the righteous wrath of God that will rain upon all evil men during the seven-year tribulation. We will be thrilled that Satan will lose his fangs and be thrown into the lake of fire. What greater reason to sing could we have?

These songs will have a familiar ring in that they will be songs praising the Savior's sacrifice. Jesus truly is worthy to be praised *because of His sacrifice.* The willingness of God to offer His Son on the cross, resulting in the shedding of His blood and the loss of His life, is a cause to celebrate. We experience the redemption of our sinful souls solely because of the blood of Jesus. Such a concept is difficult for our finite minds to grasp yet it defines the core of the gospel message. Only a sinless Savior could redeem and pay the penalty for sinful man.

In our midst today are those who attempt to omit any and all references to the blood of Jesus claiming that such a barbaric notion indicates a slaughterhouse religion. Some refuse to sing of a *fountain filled with blood drawn from Emmanuel's veins.* Yet the scriptures indicate that Jesus died a substitutionary death – dying in our place. As the hands of Jesus were forcibly nailed to the beams of the cross, He grappled with the all of the forces of hell and won.

Christ is also deserving of our praise *because of His success.* In 5:9 John wrote that Jesus *"redeemed us to God by thy blood out of every kindred, and tongue, and people, and nation."* John is writing in 96 A.D. near the close of the first century. In that day, churches were struggling to maintain their distinctive voice while suffering under the heavy hand of the Roman government. In spite of constant opposition, the message of the cross spread like prairie fire over the globe and continues to do so today. This incredible scene of redemption will involve members of every people group, creed, and color of those who chose to follow Jesus.

Detractors point to the fact that Jesus never authored a book, never attained advanced degrees, never realized significant financial success, and never ventured more than two hundred miles beyond the place of His birth. Such a meager record is not fitting for someone who claimed to be Messiah, some say. Could a person of such limited success make a legitimate claim to success? A poet wrote,

Yet I am well within the mark when I say
That all the armies who ever marched,

And all the navies that were ever built
And all the kings that ever reigned
And all the parliaments that ever sat
Have not affected the life of man on the earth
As that One solitary life.

Songs of the Savior's Sufficiency

If we were to simultaneously scan the congregational gatherings of hundreds of thousands of Christian churches, we would see believers from every tribe, color, and nation gathered to worship the One who is truly worthy of our praise. Some people worship in spacious cathedrals utilizing the elements of formal liturgy while others gather in mud huts employing native chants and songs to express their love for God. In 5:10 John wrote, *"Thou hast made us unto our God kings and priests: and we shall reign on the earth."* This verse reveals an important truth in that the saints are here pictured singing a new song of praise because they see the fulfillment of long-awaited prophecy. Evil kings and kingdoms will meet their demise and the true King will initiate His reign. He truly is sufficient and worthy to be adored!

What an incredible blessing that we as believers, in fact, really are priests. Most of us wear no clerical collars and perhaps never administer the ordinances yet we are priests in the fullest sense! God "*hast made us unto our God kings and priests: and we shall reign on the earth*" (5:10). A more accurate translation of the Greek meaning of his truth is that we are a "kingdom of priests".

Within the Jewish nation was the tribe of Levi from which all priests came. In the system of the Law, it was necessary for a person to be a priest in order to approach God directly. The high priests approached God only once a year on the Day of Atonement by venturing into the Holy of Holies. While there the priest sprinkled blood on the mercy seat of the Ark of the Covenant as atonement or payment for the sins of the people. Assisting priests attended to the daily sacrifices on the altar. The smoke from the sacrifices perpetually rose to the heavens in a continual act of worship and atonement. Those not of the tribe of Levi or who were not priests were required to acquire the services of a priest to offer their animals in sacrifice.

In the New Covenant instituted by Jesus Christ, we as believers have the unique privilege of personally approaching God without the need of a human intermediary. Believers also may interpret the meaning of the scriptures with the guiding hand of the Holy Spirit who dwells in all believers and who promised to *lead us into all truth* (John 16:13). The doctrinal term for such a privilege is the *priesthood of the believer.*

John described the singers who sang these songs of praise around the throne. This scene will become a reality when Christ returns. Those of us who sing poorly and who may have been asked to avoid singing altogether will join this heavenly chorus. We will have *instruments* in our hands to use in praising our Lord. John wrote, *"having every one of them harps, and golden vials of odour"* (5:8). A harp is a stringed instrument capable of producing beautiful tones at the hands of a skilled musician. As King David heard the refreshing and melodious sounds of the harp, his troubled soul found rest. In our day, church orchestras are filled with skilled musicians who use their unique talents for God and for His church. This scene of praise in heaven will be one in which every person eager to offer praise will be able to do so skillfully and with a heart full of passion. King David was the author of more than one thousands songs.

In the praise room of heaven, all believers will have an ability to offer up our praises with an ability considered equally as worthy and acceptable as the skillful praise of the King David. Praise resides in the heart of every true believer yet few of us express it effectively. In heaven, our praise will flow freely.

John wrote also of the *incense* of the singers in heaven described as *"golden vials of odours"* (5:8). A bowl of incense represents the prayers of the saints. I believe that God's intention here is to instruct us concerning the value of prayer. Here on this earth, we often are tempted to conclude that prayer has little or no value whatsoever because so few prayers seem to be answered. Prayers seem to fall on deaf ears and seem to never make their way into heaven. Some requests that we make will have no answer until the prayers of days gone by and stored in God's heart are finally answered. The implication of these words of John is that prayer is so incredibly valuable that God never forgets even one! The saints some day will approach the throne of God carrying bowls full of the prayers of the saints to which our loving God will respond.

John wrote these sobering words as the Roman emperor intensified the pressure upon the Church. Vowing to obliterate Christianity from the face of the earth and thereby destroy his competition, the emperor failed to realize that prayer will never be destroyed. There is victory in prayer, either now or in the future. Think about and visualize the future experience that we will have in standing before the throne of Jesus and offering our sweet aroma of prayers to Him.

Few of us realize the unique privilege that we have as priests to approach Him in prayer. Hebrews 4:16 reminds us that we may approach Him *boldly* and experience His grace as we do.

Songs of the Savior's Supremacy

Beginning at 5:11, John introduced the reader to one of the primary passages in all of Revelation concerning the deity of Jesus Christ. In 5:11-12 John wrote that he heard, *"the voice of many angels round the throne....... saying with a loud voice, 'Worthy is the Lamb that was slain to receive power, and riches, and wisdom, and strength, and honour, and glory, and blessing.'"* This choir of angels appears to perform their duties antiphonally. A clear reading of the verse indicates that its members were *"saying"* the praises to God. Whether they sang or spoke is not a debate worth entering yet suffice to say these angels point to the supremacy of Jesus Christ indicating that no one else even begins to compare with the magnificence of Christ.

This scene of praise to come will capture the attention of the entire earth. Regarding this scene John wrote in 5: 13-14,

> *And every creature which is in heaven, and on the earth, and under the earth, and such as are in the sea, and all that are in them, heard I saying, 'Blessing, and honour, and glory, and power, be unto him*

that sitteth upon the throne, and unto the Lamb for ever and ever'. And the four beasts said, 'Amen'. And the four and twenty elders fell down and worshipped him that liveth for ever and ever.

God has created us to be instruments of praise. It has been said that the crown jewel of the Church is praise. In many churches, the jewel is missing or at least badly tarnished. Praise has the capacity to *redeem the sinner.* Those without Christ often venture into a church that practices deliberate praise and find themselves supernaturally drawn toward Christ. Just as the scripture promises, God does inhabit the praises of His people.

Praise is uniquely able to *refresh the saint* as well. Tired and weary from the pressures of the daily grind, a moment of pure and unobstructed praise injects vigor and restoration into the veins of those who practice it. Praise has a cleansing effect in the life of the believer and motivates us to focus on the goodness of the Lord and away from the distresses we may carry. Christ alone is supreme and worthy of our praise!

Notice that in the scene of praise recorded in 5:13-14 that man is not specifically mentioned in this gathering. I find the omission of man as striking and significant. Could it be that evil men to suffer the pain of the tribulation period will not praise God while the rest of creation looks forward to this time of redemption?

Not only in this passage do we read of the supremacy of the Savior as *proclaimed*, we also read of His supremacy graphically *presented.* John pictured Jesus in this passage as One who is worthy *"to receive power"* (5:12). While on earth as the God-man, Jesus was seen by some to be less than divine. Their views were distorted by their focus on His humanity, by preconceived notions concerning a coming Messiah, or by satanic interference. Yet Jesus is fully divine and is the only One who is worthy to receive all praises that acknowledge His uniqueness. Whatever form our giving may take, He is worthy to receive it and does so lovingly.

John also wrote that the supremacy of Jesus should to be *praised.* This gathered chorus, comprised of the entire creation, will rejoice at what God is preparing to do as the prophetic timetable advances. Jesus will open the seals of the book and reveal the events soon to commence during the tribulation period.

Some praise is boisterous and celebrative in nature. Other forms or expressions are given in quietness and reflection. John wrote that the four beasts, representing all of creation, responded, *"Amen",* indicating full and complete agreement with the expressions of praises in progress.

Perhaps Revelation 4-5 is a *praise and amen school* for all of us who failed to learn the habit of praise while here on earth! In an act of quiet reverence, the twenty-four elders fell face forward in an humble act of homage to our glorious God.

Whether with volume and jubilant physical motion, or offered in humble and silent meditation, our praise must well up and overflow from the purity of our hearts. We must avoid expressions of mere rote of ritual that may tempt us to disengage our hearts from the true purpose in worship.

Hope for weary pilgrims continually comes by means of the grace of our Lord. It will fully and completely be ours with His return! Do you need hope?

Chapter 16

THE HORSES ARE RIDING
Revelation 6: 1-8

The writer John witnessed the opening of the first of seven seals of the scroll that rested in the hand of Jesus. He wrote of these events to come by utilizing the analogy of four horses. These events to come depicted in graphic descriptions of the four horses introduce the reader to the details of the horrifying events of the seven-year tribulation period.

The scroll held securely in the hand of Jesus and sealed seven times contained the forfeited inheritance of man. This forfeiture was of God's rule on earth, a rule once held by man before Satan unleashed his subtle yet effective temptations in the Garden of Eden. The result of the *Fall* in the Garden of Eden has been ongoing painful bouts with imperfection, sickness, sorrow and disease afflicting mankind. Jesus and Jesus alone is deemed worthy to open the seals of the scroll and thereby secure the reestablishment of man's dominion over the earth.

In this magnificent scene to which John was a witness, Jesus took the scroll and proceeded to execute its contents. This epic struggle to be experienced by those left behind will occur during the tribulation period after the Church has vacated the scene. John wrote of these events to come in Revelation 6-19 climaxing with the return of Christ establishing His millennial kingdom. The prize to be won during the course of this terrifying experience is the dominion of the earth. Who will govern the universe? Who will own the world? Will Satan suffer a final defeat? Like many of you, I have read the back of the book – Jesus wins!

Concerning the appearance of the four horses of the apocalypse, John wrote in 6: 1-8,

> *And I saw when the Lamb opened one of the seals, and I heard, as it were the noise of thunder, one of the four beasts saying, 'Come and*

> *see'. And I saw, and behold a white horse: and he that sat on him had a bow and a crown was given unto him: and he went forth conquering, and to conquer. And when he had opened the second seal, I heard the second beast say, 'Come and see'. And there went out another horse that was red: and power was given to him that sat thereon to take peace from the earth, and that they should kill one another: and there was given unto him a great sword. And when he had opened the third seal, I heard the third beast say, 'Come and see', and I beheld, and lo a black horse; and he that sat on him had a pair of balances in his hand. And I heard a voice in the midst of the four beasts say, 'A measure of wheat for a penny, and three measures of barley for a penny; and see thou hurt not the oil and the wine.' And when he had opened the fourth seal, I heard the voice of the fourth beast say, 'Come and see'. And I looked, and behold a pale horse: and his name that sat on him was Death, and Hell followed with him. And Power was given unto them over the fourth part of the earth, to kill with sword, and with hunger, and with death, and with the beasts of the earth.*

The events herein described are a synopsis of what is to come during the tribulation period. The last three and a half years of this intense and painful scenario is commonly known as the *Great Tribulation* due to the intensifying levels of pain and persecution as the tribulation progresses. Readers of the vision are introduced to the seven seals, seven trumpets, and seven bowls of wrath to be unleashed upon mankind remaining on the earth. The portion of the Lord's Prayer requesting, *"thy kingdom come, thy will be done"*, will discover its fulfillment as God's plan is enacted.

The White Horse: A Counterfeit Christ

With the appearance of the white horse, John heard a thunderous voice from one of the four living creatures in the throne scene saying, *"Come and see"* (6:6). In our day, thunder warns of a coming storm accompanied by howling winds and drenching rains yet it often wreaks havoc as well. John saw a coming storm that will severely afflict mankind in the tribulation. Unprecedented havoc upon the earth will result. Terror will fill the hearts of the masses.

Some have viewed this graphic passage as referring to Christ's dramatic appearance riding upon a white horse related in Revelation 19. A closer look at this important picture reveals that this white horse is representative of a false Christ personified by Satan who will deceive the world. Satan has never been blessed with an original thought or plan in all history. He has been nothing more than a deceiver and is described as *"more subtle than any beast of the field"* (Genesis 3: 1a).

A series of false Christs will surface and the Antichrist himself will appear as a man of religion and establish a deceptive system of religious faith. His will claim to be the messiah of the world. The scriptures refer to him as the *man of sin* or *man of perdition.* He is also known as the *beast* as vividly portrayed in Revelation 13. He will position himself as the great world ruler preaching a platform of peace rather than war. His soothing and motivating words will capture the minds and hearts of the unsuspecting masses. The book of Daniel also informs us that this great leader will emerge and will destroy many by employing deceptive political and religious tactics.

Never in history has the prospect for peace been greater than now. The dismantling of nuclear arms continues to be pursued in many countries thus giving a sigh of relief to the world. Several prime ministers of Israel have moved toward peace negotiations with Yasser Arafat of the Palestinian Liberation Organization regarding ownership of certain plots of land in the West Bank and other issues as well. Russian President Putin continues to pursue democratic ideals in the new Common Wealth of States. Terror struck our hearts once again as terrorists unleashed their fury on America on September 11, 2001 yet many Americans have confidence in our military to punish these evil foes and prevent future bloodshed on our soil. Yet as many conclude that peace is imminent, no real peace will be realized. Any semblance of world peace that may be achieved will be short-lived, however.

The one sitting on the white horse is pictured wearing a crown. The crown signifies his position as a ruler with great authority. With a bow in his hand and a crown resting upon his head, he is seen *"conquering"* (6:2). However, his bow has no arrow. Of what value is a gun without a bullet? Bearing no arrows, he will appear harmless but will display ruthless power.

Perhaps this false Christ will be the one who continues the global dismantling of nuclear arms and will gain ongoing authority to supervise that process in the world thereby acquiring worldwide respect. His message will be one of peace yet peace will not be the true desire of his heart. His global coup will be the mother of all deceptions and be bloodless for a time. The masses of the world will be deceived by his charisma and promises of peace and prosperity.

The Red Horse: A Wicked War

The rider perched on the back of the red horse that John envisioned was given extraordinary power to afflict the world with war and death. Essentially, the removal of serenity from the earth will send terror into the hearts of those who remain. Jesus also spoke of these events recorded in Matthew 24: 4-6.

> *Jesus answered and said unto them, 'Take heed that no man deceive you. For many shall come in my name, saying, 'I am Christ', and shall deceive many. And ye shall hear of wars and rumours of wars: see that ye be not troubled: for all these things must come to pass, but the end is not yet.*

The rider of the white horse will come in deception while the evil represented by the rider of the red horse will result in the removal of peace and serenity from the hearts and lives of men. Jesus also addressed these comments to the Jews who will be dealt with during the time also known as Daniel's *seventieth week*. This experience will focus on the final dealings of God with the nation of Israel. A major purpose of the tribulation period will be to convince the Jewish people to recognize and accept the true Messiah.

The red horse, representing the theft of peace and the onslaught of vicious and deadly war, will gallop freely in the earth instigating horrible conflict. As false peace and a system of socialistic government begin to be established, war will break out. The Antichrist will be a man of war and he will be forced to deal with the nation of Israel that he hates with a passion. He will punish them with the most severe holocaust the world has ever known.

As the red horse gallops about the earth, men will slaughter one another. John saw the rider of the horse carrying a sword. In the Greek language, this sword is short in length and capable of being effective at close range and is easily maneuverable. Civil war and strife will pummel mankind.

We have witnessed similar bloodshed in Bosnia in the struggle with Serbia yet that conflict is a minor skirmish compared to the intensity of war to come during the tribulation. Germ warfare may be unleashed upon unsuspecting groups of people. Nuclear weapons may be detonated. The world will believe that all hell has broken loose!

The entire planet will be affected and drawn into war. For those left behind, no place to hide will be found.

The Black Horse: A Fatal Famine

As war devastates the earth, pollution will poison the waters and the earth may be subjected to the scorching heat of thermonuclear weapons. The black horse appearing in John's vision refers primarily to the consequent famine. The economic systems of various nations will begin to collapse and the world will be brought to its knees in utter poverty.

The color black is symbolic of famine. Famine always follows on the heels of warfare. The wars in Bosnia have largely prevented the people from cultivating their crops. Polluted waters resulting from the war have damaged the farming system of the country necessitating a response from the United Nations in giving food and other aid. The devastation is Bosnia will be a picnic in comparison to the coming economic hardship in the tribulation represented by the rider of the black horse.

John saw this rider carrying a *"pair of balances in his hand"* (6:5). Balances were scales originally used to weigh gold. These balances to which John referred are similar to those seen on the emblems of justice with the fulcrum in the middle with the balances positioned on each side. In the tribulation, these balances will measure food that will be more precious than gold. In light of their recent suffering, the people in Somalia or the victims of the war in Afghanistan might choose food rather than a heavy bag of gold. Food will become so scarce in the tribulation that it will be coveted like diamonds in our day.

The *"penny"* in this passage represents a wage for one day of work. In the tribulation, such a wage will provide for only one meal (6:6). Such financial devastation will break the back of families and individuals leading to widespread theft and mayhem. The enormity of the need in the lives of those left behind will serve to solidify the rule of the Antichrist and enhance his system of new world order.

An interesting phrase heard by John and uttered by the third living creature regards oil and wine. John wrote in 6:6, *"hurt not the oil and wine."* I believe the implication is that those who are rich during the tribulation will become richer while those who are poor will slip further into abject poverty. The middle class will disappear and the masses border on starvation while those in authority will live like kings. The world has never known such coming devastation. If you do not know Christ, now is the time!

The Pale Horse: A Permeating Pestilence

John saw the rider on the fourth horse of the apocalypse riding a horse that was pale in color. The word *"pale"* in the Greek language in this passage is translated in English as "chlorophyll". This color is ashen in appearance like that of a decomposing corpse.

As the waters of the earth are polluted and crops are destroyed in war, disease will spread unabated. In our day, much of disease is held in check by advancements in technology and medicine yet in the tribulation medicine will be scarce and generally unavailable. Diseases heretofore thought to be conquered, such as diphtheria, smallpox or malaria, will spread like a prairie fire. Many will also lose their lives in warfare by the sword as well as by pestilence and disease.

In the coming devastation by pestilence, the scripture indicates that the *mission* of the rider will be to see the death of one-fourth of the world's populace, an astounding 1.5 billion people! The reference to *"death"* indicates pestilence or disease. It is striking to note that no cure for AIDS has been discovered to date. Perhaps no cure will ever be found. The deadly plague of the tribulation will involve a multitude of diseases currently without a cure.

The *method* to be employed in this judgment represented by the pale horse will be devastating war, horrendous disease, and gut-wrenching famine. Many nations today are known to have secretly stockpiled germ warfare weapons. In the tribulation, these arsenals potentially may be loosed to obliterate the masses. No one will have a defense.

While this terror is unleashed, the Church will be resting safely in the presence of our Lord.

Chapter 17

SAINTS IN HEAVEN SEE SAINTS ON EARTH
Revelation 6: 9-17

After John had caught a glimpse of the four horsemen of the apocalypse and the events to come on earth when the first four seals of the scroll are broken, the scene at the throne abruptly changes. The opening of the fifth seal shifts our attention to heaven. John wrote in 6:9,

> *And when he had opened the fifth seal, I saw under the altar the souls of them that were slain for the word of God, and for the testimony which they held.*

Such an interesting passage causes a number of questions to surface in our minds. Will the saints in heaven see events on earth as they occur? We will recognize those left behind? How much of the pain inflicting those left behind during the tribulation will we be aware of? Few passages in Revelation feature more graphic and horrifying language than does this one.

John gives us an eyewitness view into the plight and desires of the martyrs who have lost their lives for the cause of Christ and who are residing in heaven.

The Presentation of the Martyrs

These holy martyrs in heaven that John saw in his vision are men and women who were savagely killed for their unwillingness to renounce the name of Christ. Today, such savagery is perpetrated against Christians in countries such as the Sudan and others. John revealed to us the two motivations for their martyrdom: because of the word of God, and because of their unbending testimony as followers of Jesus. The history of Christianity is marked in blood by those who have given their lives so that believers today might worship in freedom and without fear of governmental retaliation.

Such freedom, however, is not allowed in all areas of the earth. In 1973, the ruler of Afghanistan launched an assault on the only existing Christian church in that country and wiped the building off of the face of the earth. To believe in Christ or to proclaim His name in that country is a crime potentially punishable by death.

At the time of John's writing of this vision near 95-99 A. D., the emperor was on a rampage to obliterate followers of Christ. The intensity of this religious holocaust reached its zenith as many believers were killed and John was isolated on a deserted island in an attempt to silence his voice. To fully imagine what believers in the first century endured is difficult for believers today since many of us live in the lap of luxury and nest in our comfortable surroundings.

On a mission trip to Russia, I spoke with a number of faithful Russian pastors who have endured the fires of persecution. One particular pastor had recently been released from prison after serving a seven-year sentence. His crime was the preaching of the gospel. I offered my encouragement realizing that I had experienced nothing akin to his experience. The apostle John offered these words in chapter six as a means to encourage the faithful martyrs he saw residing in heaven who were anxious for justice to be applied to their perpetrators and for the rest of history to unfold.

The Condition of the Martyrs

In 6:9 we read that John saw the *"souls"* of those who had lost their lives for Jesus. The soul is the mind, emotion, and the will of an individual. It is the existence of the soul that distinguishes man from the rest of creation. Animals are not possessed with these three dimensions of personhood. Animals are designed to live merely by instinct. In contrast, man has been designed with the freedom of moral choice, for better or worse.

Although these martyrs have been transported from the grave of their material bodies and into heaven, they are seen here as possessing a conscious existence. In 6:10 we read,

> *And they cried with a loud voice, saying, 'How long, O Lord, holy and true, dost thou not judge and avenge our blood on them that dwell on the earth?*

The scriptures teach that God gives a type of spiritual body to those who die as followers of Jesus Christ. The apostle Paul wrote, *"We know that if our earthly house of this tabernacle were dissolved, we have a building of God, a house not made with hands, eternal in the heavens"* (II Corinthians 5:1). Here Paul is referring to the temporary body that Christians will receive at the time of death. Our resurrected body will be a gift to be received at a later time. Until that time, we *groan* to be the recipients of that body.

Several significant truths may be derived from John's words given here in 6:10. These martyrs are alive, utter words that are recognizable, see clearly with their eyes, and have white robes draped around them. Some form of physical existence or body evidently exists. This passage also informs us concerning the *doctrine of soul sleep.* Essentially, some believe that this theological concept teaches that at death one goes to the grave and awaits the resurrection. Only believers will be raised from the dead. While asleep in the grave they are not cognizant at all. However, there is at least one problem with this notion – it is not true. No scriptural grounds exist for such a faulty conclusion. This passage conclusively destroys that theory.

The scriptures teach that as one dies, he continues to exist. In the story of the death of Lazarus recorded in Luke 16, we read that at his death he was transferred to *"Abraham's bosom."* As the father of the Jewish faith, Abraham's bosom was the term for paradise. The angels carried Lazarus to this location in the presence of God. The story further teaches that the rich man in the scene passed away, *"in hell he lift up his eyes."* After death, those who are believers experience blessedness and maintain the ability to see, feel, think, and are impacted by emotions. The rich man who did not know Christ at the time of death commented, *"Send Lazarus, that he may dip the tip of his finger in water, and cool my tongue, for I am tormented in this flame."* Obviously, his senses were in full operation.

Such a conscious state of existence after death is not the teachings of Garner Ted Armstrong of the World Wide Church of God, the Jehovah Witnesses, nor of a number of other cults. Yet the Bible is crystal clear that the rich man residing in hell in the Lazarus story had a mouth, tongue, memory, and a will.

The thief who positioned on the cross next to Jesus asked, *"Lord, remember me when thou comest into thy kingdom"* (Luke 23: 42). This repentant robber acknowledged the lordship of Jesus Christ and asked for entrance in heaven on that basis. Jesus responded that heaven would be his final destination. This *"paradise"* to which Jesus referred is described in the scriptures as a beautiful palatial garden. It is a place of unprecedented beauty. This word is another term for heaven – not the final heaven to descend at the end of the millennial kingdom but rather the heaven where Jesus now resides. In II Corinthians 5:8, Paul underscored this concept of residing at death in the presence of Jesus. He wrote, *"to be absent from the body and to be present with the Lord."*

The Cry of the Martyrs

The cry of these martyrs in heaven for God to avenge their blood and inflict their killers with severe punishment seems to be a strange request. Regarding the cry of these saints, John wrote in 6:10,

> *They cried with a loud voice, saying, 'How long, O Lord, holy and true, dost thou not judge and avenge our blood on them that dwell on the earth?*

It is critically important to note that their cry is for the act of avengement to come from the Lord Himself. These martyrs are not requesting permission to retaliate personally in like manner and with excessive bloodshed. They are consciously aware that their killers continue on earth in their mischief and rebellion. These heavenly martyrs are anxious for justice to be meted out swiftly and surely. Perhaps God has explained to them what must occur on earth for the reclaiming of the dominion of the earth. The revelation of that plan to the martyrs may fill them with great anticipation. They simply are unable to wait and are seen here pleading for the plan of God to move forward without delay.

These faithful martyrs are crying out for the wrong in the earth to fail and for that which is right ultimately to prevail. They want an end to suffering. They stand waiting and ready for the full execution of the contents of the seven-seal scroll. They eagerly desire that the rest of the promises of eternity come to fruition.

The Comfort of the Martyrs

It is not in the mind of our Lord that any of His children be unhappy in heaven. Pain will not afflict the minds and bodies of God's children. The anguish of this world will have melted away when heaven unfolds. In this life, many of us often wonder whether we will experience concern over the lostness of our loved ones who will remain left behind on earth. Will we experience grief over others? We are not fully capable of comprehending the full nature of our feelings concerning those left behind because our perspective at that time will be heavenly in nature and not restricted by earthly limitations. Yet God will continue to be the God of all comfort to His children who are at home with Him! In our discomfort, He will provide comfort.

The sources of that comfort for those of us in heaven are vividly described in John's words in 6:11,

> *And white robes were given unto every one of them; and it was said unto them, that they should rest yet for a little season, until their fellowservants also and their brethren, that should be killed as they were, should be fulfilled.*

The gift of these white robes adorning believers in heaven is symbolic of divine approval and of the blessed nature of our relationship with God. Second, God will comfort these eager martyrs of the faith by admonishing them to *"rest a little season."* In these words of instruction, John saw in his vision that God will insist that these Christian martyrs allow Him only to administer the justice to be applied to the guilty persecutors. Justice will be swift and sure. Believers must entrust their anxieties to Him. He alone fully knows how to deal with the aggressors on earth.

Revelation 14:13 records, *"Blessed are the dead which die in the Lord…(for) they may rest from their labours."* Martyrs who have faithfully served the Lord and suffered because of it will one day cease to experience pain and will see the anxiety melt away from their lives. These martyrs will simply rest in the promises and protection of our Lord.

The age-old question concerning why a God of love allows both love and evil to co-exist in the world begs for an answer. Perhaps the angels in heaven ask that identical question. As a pastor, I often hear such heart-felt questions emerge from the painful experiences of people I know and love. Why did my mother die of cancer? Why did God allow the Twin Towers in New York City to be decimated? Why do little children die? Adequate answers will be not fully discovered this side of heaven. God simply asks us to trust Him. Things do work together for good for those who love Him, as the scripture indicates, yet that promised good often appears slow in coming (Romans 8:28).

In heaven, time is not measured as we measure by hours and weeks. God's timetable in heaven will commence as He sees fit. The sovereign closing of history and the ushering in of the eternal reign of Christ will appear to unfold rapidly or slowly. It will merely occur as God desires and on His time. The effects of time will not affect the saints in heaven as it now affects on earth. Time in heaven will be meaningless. No sense of rush or delay will ever exist in heaven. Time will fly yet will remain still. We will be unaware of it.

The Panic of the Multitudes

In glaring contrast to this comforting scene involving the martyrs in heaven, John wrote in 6:12-17 of the horrifying fear and desperation that will be unleashed upon the remaining people on the earth.

> *And I beheld when he had opened the sixth seal, and lo, there was a great earthquake; and the sun became black as sackcloth of hair, and the moon became as blood; And the stars of heaven fell unto the earth, even as a fig tree casteth her untimely figs, when she is shaken of a mighty wind. And the heaven departed as a scroll when it is rolled together; and every mountain and island were moved out of their places. And the kings of the earth, and the great men, and the rich men, and the chief captains, and the mighty men, and every bondman, and every free man, hid themselves in the dens and in the rocks of the mountains; And said to the mountains and rocks, 'Fall on us, and hide us from the face of him that sitteth on the throne, and from the wrath of the Lamb: For the great day of his wrath is come; and who shall be able to stand?*

The great *"day"* of God's wrath to be visited upon the earth in the tribulation is not a twenty-four hour period of time in duration but rather refers to the entire experience. Those poor souls on earth who will be the unfortunate victims of this wrath will ask the rhetorical question, *"who shall be able to stand"* (6:17)? No answer is expected, of course, because no one will have the capacity to escape the coming terror to afflict those who are left behind.

The *cause* of this severe panic to be experienced by unconverted men and women will be the cataclysmic events to occur. In his vision, John saw a *"great earthquake."* In the original Greek language, the word *"great"* implies a global earthquake of unprecedented and indescribable proportions. The earthquakes that have rocked California in recent years will be miniscule tremors in comparison to the earthquakes of the tribulation. News reports often point to the *Big One* inevitably to come yet man will never experience the upheaval of the earth like which will shake the world in the tribulation. In the scriptures, earthquakes are often seen as indicative of the judgment of God. Seismologists report that earthquakes have been increasing consistently in quantity and in intensity in recent days. Such activity is described in Matthew as indicative of the second coming of Jesus Christ.

We often refer to the earth as the *terra firma* meaning the solid ground on which we stand. The solid ground of man will shake and rumble during the tribulation. Men will shudder and fall as the ground rocks beneath them. No safe place to hide will be found. Literally, the whole world will shake at the judgment of God.

In this frightening day of terror the sun will experience a total eclipse. Darkness will replace light. The sun will hide its face from the judgment of God. The earth will shiver and rumble. The moon will have an eerie appearance like blood. Astrophysicists have discovered that there is a gradual reddening of the surface of the moon in our day. In the day of tribulation, the entire surface of the moon will appear red as blood. Fear will grip the hearts of men.

Those of us with apple or apricot trees planted on our property are well aware that a gust of wind will snap the branches holding the ripe fruit and blow the trees to the ground. The stars in the heavens will fall to the ground in like manner.

John wrote that he saw global upheaval in the heavens and recorded that scene in 6:14, *"the heaven departed as a scroll when it is rolled together."* There is symbolic as well as literal meaning in John's words. To roll a map or a set of architectural blueprints causes the document to take the shape that we give it. To unroll it at a later date, and then turn loose of it, causes the document to return to the shape in which it had been stored. I believe that John intends to communicate that for a time heaven will be closed for business. The map of heaven will be rolled up and unavailable. The activity of heaven will be temporarily suspended. People may continue to pray at this time yet God will not hear them.

The book of Proverbs promises that God will mock those who are unconverted when their calamity comes because they perpetually refused to respond to His offer of grace during their lives. At this black and dreary moment in the tribulation, the doors of heaven will be closed.

Revelation 6:14 records this horrifying event, *"every mountain and every island were moved out of their places."* Enormous ecological disaster will cause the disfigurement of the world. Mountains and islands will be ripped asunder and no longer recognizable. Nothing will be left in its original form. Panic will grip the throat of mankind.

The Completeness of the Panic

Revelation records seven groups of people that will endure these cataclysmic events. The number seven is the biblical number signifying completion. No class or creed of people left on earth will escape the events to come. The intellectuals and academicians of our day as well as untutored rustics will be equally afflicted by this coming calamity. The masses will compete to claim asylum in the rocks and caves. No person will find safe refuge.

Wealth and academic achievement will be of no use in escaping the wrath and pain to come. The wrath of the tribulation will be no respecter of persons. Cry as they might, there will be no place to hide.

The Consequences of the Panic

As a result of sheer terror and without any other option, those left behind on earth without Christ in their hearts will quickly call for the largest prayer gathering in history. As we watched in amazement the tragic results of the earthquake in California in recent years, we were given a glimpse of what is to come in the tribulation. As Californians gazed in stunned silence when all of their material possessions lay in ruins, a paralyzing sense of defeat seemed to set in. In tragedy, we are stripped of our confidence in human ability. Our human frailty is exposed for all to see. Desperation takes its toll.

In the tribulation, those left behind will plead with the rocks to fall on them and take them out of their misery. In our day, prayer meetings attract meager crowds yet in the day of tribulation, this gathering will assemble multiplied millions. Their cries will be for the age-old rocks of the mountains to crush them and will attempt to hide themselves from the Rock of Ages. Shaking with a fear of the Lord, they will attempt to hide themselves from His presence. They will clamor to end it all yet will be unable to do so.

This terrible *"wrath"* that will pounce on the earth with a vengeance is derived from the Greek word *orge* meaning a violent explosion of wrath. The wrath of God, brewing for all of history, will explode on the face of the earth. His love rejected and his kindness forever scorned, God will unfurl just and sudden punishment upon those who have rejected Him.

The world will be plunged into utter darkness. An eerie sense of finality will encompass the earth. Will any person receive a second chance to know Christ? John received the answer to that question as the vision continued to unfold.

Chapter 18

THE 144,000 IN THE TRIBULATION
Revelation 7: 1-9

John proceeded to inform his readers of the coming upheaval in the earth's ecological system and the accompanying pain to be inflicted upon unconverted men and women left on earth to endure the tribulation. After doing so, John redirected his attention to the appearance of four angels that appeared in his vision.

These four angels were seen by John positioned at the four corners of the globe. This passage is a parenthesis in the prophetic events of Revelation. John wrote in 7:1-4,

> *And after these things I saw four angels standing on the four corners of the earth, holding the four winds of the earth, that the wind should not blow on the earth, nor on the sea, nor on any tree. And I saw another angel ascending from the east, having the seal of the living God: and he cried with a loud voice to the four angels, to whom it was given to hurt the earth and the sea, Saying, 'Hurt not the earth, neither the sea, nor the trees, till we have sealed the servants of our God in their foreheads'. And I heard the number of them which were sealed: and there were sealed an hundred and forty and four thousand of all the tribes of the children of Israel.*

A natural and linear reading of Revelation leads the reader to assume that Revelation 7 will detail the opening of the seventh seal of the scroll coming quickly on the heels of the sixth. However, in this pause in that progression, the reader is taken to a scene depicting angels with a peculiar task. The events of the seventh seal are placed on hold until the activity of 144,000 Jewish evangelists and their effectiveness is fully reported.

The Suspension of Judgment

These angels are seen restricting the winds that blow from the four corners of the earth. The ecological engines of the earth and the movement of the winds are temporarily suspended signifying a divine suspension of judgment upon the remaining inhabitants of the earth.

This passage features a *trinity of fours* as we read of angels, corners of the globe, and the winds being described as numbering four in each category. These angels are special messengers of God who function to propagate the plan of God in the tribulation. In scanning the Old Testament, we read that angels fought valiantly on behalf of Israel. Jesus described angels in these parables as agents of God's judgment. As Jesus spoke of the coming tribulation and judgment to come, he said that angels will separate the wheat from the tares thereby clearly differentiating between those who are lost versus those who will live on in eternity with our Lord.

As these angels return to earth, they will come for the purpose of enabling judgment to proceed. Before that judgment is enacted, John envisioned that one final act of God's mercy will be made known to the earth. This expression of mercy will take form in the protection of a band of evangelists at work in the tribulation.

The claim that the angels are standing at the four corners of the earth is not a scientific statement concerning the flat or round shape of the earth. However, the Old Testament does speak of God sitting on the circle of the earth giving credence to the Bible's scientific accuracy. If the Bible speaks scientifically, it does so accurately.

These angels will operate from the corners of the compass. The suspended winds are winds of judgment. These winds will produce an unprecedented storm to pound the earth into submission. For a time, judgment upon the earth will be held at bay by the four angels. As they release the restraints, the winds of judgment will howl at record levels. No flurry of hurricanes in our day even begins to measure in intensity compared to the upheaval to come.

Judgment will be suspended until the seal of God is placed upon these servants of God. It appears that the judgment of God will allow man to reap the painful consequences of what he has sown. Our mistreatment of the creation with weapons of mass destruction and ecological mismanagement finally will result in divine retaliation against mankind.

The Seal of God

John saw another angel described as *"having the seal of the living God"* (7:2). In biblical days, a seal was often imprinted in wax or another substance and used for identifying *possession.* Homes today often display a family crest that may trace ancestry to England or another country of origin. That family crest is a seal. It identifies what the family possesses and its true identity.

In biblical terminology, a seal also identified a believer in Christ as genuine. The apostle Paul wrote, *"Nevertheless the foundation of God standeth sure, having this seal. The Lord knoweth them that are his"* (II Timothy 2:19a). The seal of salvation is a graphic reminder to Satan of those who do not belong to him. They have another Master.

Another use of the seal in the scriptures is to indicate *protection.* John wrote in 7:3, *"Hurt not the earth, neither the sea, nor the trees, till we have sealed the servants of our God in their foreheads."* The pounding of the earth and the sea in judgment will be suspended until the seal of protection is given to God's servants. In a similar way, the New Testament teaches that a believer in Christ is *"sealed unto the day of redemption"* by the Holy Spirit (Ephesians 4:30).

Seals also imply *preservation.* In the Passover story related in Exodus 12, the children of Israel were preserved from death at the hands of the death angel. The last plague in which the firstborn male of every home was to be slain came because of the outright refusal of Pharaoh to set free the people of God. God preserved the people of Israel by instructing them to wipe the blood of a lamb on the doorpost of their homes. With the blood in full view, the death angel moved on to another home recognizing the seal of protection over that family. Those who submitted themselves to the provision of the blood were preserved. In a similar way, those of us who trust the blood of Christ in our day are rewarded with eternal preservation in heaven.

The Seal of the Holy Spirit

How important for us today is the meaning of the seal of God? God seals the eternal security of every believer by means of the Holy Spirit. We as followers of Jesus Christ are God's possession. We may attempt to turn away from God yet He will never turn away from us. To be eternally lost is not possible for the believer who has truly been found. The act of recreation in the heart of man by the Spirit can never be reversed because the seal is unbreakable.

No failure in our lives as believers will ever result in the breaking of the eternal seal of the Holy Spirit upon our salvation. If our acts of sinfulness lead to the loss of our salvation, then acts of goodness become the means whereby we must regain our salvation. Such a faulty notion places the believer on the slippery slope of performance. Salvation is not a matter of what we do – but rather of what He has done! We are sealed and sealed forever.

In the Abraham story in Genesis, we read that God asked that the Jewish peoples submit to the physical rite of circumcision as a sign that they believed the promise of God to make them a great nation. Circumcision indicated that they were partners in a covenant with God. This seal of circumcision was further indicative of their secure position with God.

The Holy Spirit *is* the seal of God in our lives as believers. Asking questions and experiencing doubt regarding the security of our salvation is unnecessary because our imperfections do not determine or negate our salvation. Once saved, the Holy Spirit affixes His permanence in our hearts.

A Selected People

So who are the 144,000 to be sealed in the tribulation? At this juncture, the Church will have vanished in the rapture and avoided the tribulation. Those to be sealed were seen by John to be 12,000 Jewish people from each of the twelve tribes of Israel.

To take a spiritualist or allegorical view of this passage provides no logical explanation for the sealing of the 144,000. This group is composed of real men and women of the Jewish nation who receive Christ in the tribulation albeit with great pain and anguish. The result of their efforts on earth is a great revival accompanied by the conversion of multitudes.

Who are they not? Seventh-Day Adventists originally believed that the 144,000 are believers on earth who had been faithful to keep the Sabbath Day and would do so until Christ returns. Their perspective is that the Christian faith requires the keeping of the law regarding Saturday worship and necessitates other requirements regarding the eating of meat, etc. Herbert W. Armstrong, founder of the Worldwide Church of God, adopted and taught a system that is essentially a syncretism of Jewish law and belief. Many of them worship on Saturdays as well. They propose that the ten tribes of Israel, or the *lost tribes*, are those who ventured into the area of Great Britain and are the Anglo-Saxons from which most of us descended. To them, the 144,000 are a select group of British people and Americans who comprise the new or spiritual Israel. Such a claim is faulty, of course. To its credit, the Armstrong movement as a whole has disavowed many of these notions and has adopted many biblical positions generally accepted by evangelical scholars.

Others claim that the 144,000 represent the Church yet the Church is not present in this scene. Believers will be resting comfortably in heaven!

I firmly believe that this group is a select group of Jews. Proper biblical hermeneutics dictate that a literal interpretation of the passage is expected unless there is ample cause to approach the passage figuratively or symbolically. For example, in Isaiah 55:12 the *trees clapped their hands*. Figurative language is obviously in mind.

The apostle Paul weighs in on the issue in his theological treatise in Romans 9-11 concerning the future of Israel and the purposes of God for Israel after the Church Age is past. Paul clearly explained to the Roman fellowship that God had not finished with the nation of Israel. Of course, the book of Daniel informs us that God will deal with the Israelite people for *seventy weeks of years* or 490 years. From the time of the edict of the pagan king Cyrus to restore Jerusalem in the 5th century B.C. to the time Christ came in His triumphal entry totals 483 years. Remaining to occur are seven years of unfulfilled history.

Today's Israel is generally secular. The people in the nation know well Jewish and Christian history. They are erudite, intellectual, well informed and academically astute. Yet most of them are in a state of unbelief and many are atheists although from their childhood they are taught the mantra, *"The Lord our God is one."* Since the days of the Old Testament, the Jewish peoples have perpetually slipped into greater unbelief.

Paul wrote that God has a plan for Israel. In Romans 11: 1-2a, he said, *"I say then, hath God cast away his people? God forbid.........God hath not cast away his people which he foreknew."* So what is Paul indicating? We are saved in this age of grace not by our ancestry as Jews or Gentiles but rather by our faith in Jesus Christ. Yet God is not finished with the nation of Israel (Romans 11:25).

In Israel today we see Orthodox Jews who are powerful and zealous in their belief. They faithfully bow at the Wailing Wall and pray. They perpetuate the spiritual heritage of Israel. A Jewish diplomat may be heard denying faith in God yet also claim that God gave the nation to them as a gift. Such inconsistency is a paradox they are unwilling to see.

Paul contends in Romans 11:25a, *"I would not, brethren, that ye should be ignorant of this mystery lest ye should be wise in your own conceits."* He intends the reader to clearly realize that God is not finished in his dealings with Israel. Israel remains special in God's eyes and no anti-Semitic view is ever appropriate. Yet the scriptures teach that the Jewish peoples will be *blinded* to the truth until the end of the Church Age. At that time in prophetic history, the attention of God will turn dramatically toward the Jewish people. As the blinders are removed from their eyes, *"all Israel shall be saved"* (Romans 11:26). Not every Jewish person in history will be saved in an eternal sense but all those who are present at the coming of Christ at the Battle of Armageddon will be preserved and protected. In the Battle, the Jewish nation will be pressured by the armies of the Antichrist yet will be spared.

In the Israeli War of 1948, they recognized that God fought for them and enabled them to win against the Arabs with a small band of Jewish renegades doing battle. Yet many in the nation today do not recognize God or give credit to Him. One day the blinders will fall from their eyes and they will suddenly see Jesus as the Messiah, a truth they have perpetually failed to grasp. I believe that time is very near.

The Work of the 144,000

What will the 144,000 actually do? In 7:3, we read that they are the *"servants"* of God. With the divine seal of protection of God upon them, these Spirit-filled evangelists will preach the gospel, in the land of Israel and across the globe. Their message will not go unheard and multitudes will come to faith in Christ as the Messiah (7:9).

Their evangelistic efforts will not be without terrible persecution, however. The severity of the persecution against Israel will dramatically increase in magnitude. In recent days, the rise of the neo-Nazi party in Germany threatens Israel. Members of the Aryan race and other militant groups in America and other countries continue to spit hatred at the Jews and against people of color. One might assume that the world would have learned the lesson of World War II that God has His hand on the Jews. The Egyptian taskmaster Pharaoh bucked God's plan and paid a high price. King Herod attempted to kill all male Jewish babies under the age of two yet failed. The Jews will forever wear a target on their foreheads.

Yet in the day of tribulation, God will give to them a band of Jewish evangelists whose message will penetrate the hard hearts of the Jews and *"then shall the end come"* (Matthew 24:14b). That *"end"* refers to the end of the activity of the tribulation era. John the Baptist preached a message of repentance to the Jews in the first century. The Jewish people shunned his message and would not receive him. What happened in the days of John will be repeated in the tribulation era. With the evangelistic mandate of John the Baptist, these 144,000 preachers of the gospel will offer a second chance for Israel to repent and turn to Christ. After seven years of tribulation conflict and pain, the blinders will fall from their eyes, and all of Israel will be protected and saved. The prophet Zechariah teaches that as that moment comes, Jesus will touch down on the Mount of Olives (Zechariah 14:4).. The Mount of Olives will split into halves and Jesus will make His way up the Kidron Valley, through the golden gates and onto the temple mount. In that temple, He will declare Himself as truly the God of the world.

These 144,000 Jewish evangelists will move about under the protective seal of God. As believers today, we enjoy the seal of the Holy Spirit ensuring our permanent security in His family!

Chapter 19

EVANGELISM IN THE TRIBULATION
Revelation 7: 9-17

The Christian community has experienced a running debate concerning the possibility of people coming to faith in Christ after the rapture of the Church and during the seven-year tribulation. After the removal of the Church from the world, 144,000 flaming Jewish evangelists will spread the gospel and will do so very effectively. Millions of Bibles will be left on the earth. The gospel preserved on audio tape recordings will remain in the homes of believers who vacate the earth. Opportunities to be exposed to the gospel will abound. Yet the difficulty and persecution accompanying the gospel message will wreak havoc in the lives of those who listen and believe.

I firmly believe that many people will be converted to Christ during the tribulation era. Chapter 7 instructs us that these *"servants of God"* will be sealed in security and boldly share the claims of Christ while on earth.

The scene abruptly shifts once again to heaven where John saw a countless multitude praising God. This crowd of converts is comprised of those who will take the difficult leap of faith in receiving Christ during the events of the tribulation.

As many accept Christ in this painful seven-year era of judgment, special stipulations and circumstances will accompany their conversion experience. In his vision, John saw a magnificent scene recorded in 7:9-13,

> *After this I beheld, and lo, a great multitude, which no man could number, of all nations, and kindreds, and people, and tongues, stood before the throne, and before the Lamb, clothed with white robes, and palms in their hands; And cried with a loud voice, saying, 'Salvation to our God which sitteth upon the throne, and unto the Lamb'. And all the angels stood round about the throne, and about the elders and*

> *the four beasts, and fell before the throne on their faces, and worshipped God, saying, 'Amen: Blessing, and glory, and wisdom, and thanksgiving, and honour, and power, and might, be unto our God for ever and ever. Amen.' and one of the elders answered, saying unto me, 'What are these which are arrayed in white robes? And whence came they?'*

Who are the elders appearing in this heavenly scene? These twenty-four elders are representative of saints from the Old and New Testament eras of the Church. In earlier scenes in John's vision, we read of these elders casting their crowns of worship and service at the feet of Jesus. This *"multitude"* appearing in chapter 7 is another group. This group is not composed of people saved in the Old Testament era nor within the New Testament age of grace but rather an additional group.

One of the elders in the throne scene inquired as to the identity of this other group. Jesus identified them in 7:14,

> A*nd he said unto me, 'These are they which came out of great tribulation, and have washed their robes, and made them white in the blood of the Lamb.*

Whether coming to faith in the age of the Old Testament covenant, in the New Testament age of grace, or during the terrible moments of the tribulation, each of us comes by the blood of Christ and receives the cleansing from sin that the experience provides. This third group of believers is no exception.

A Difficult Conversion

This multitude, previously pagan and having not received Christ prior to the rapture, was seen draped in white robes. The filthiness of their sinful lives will be replaced by the white purity of Christ's sacrifice on the cross.

After being transported into heaven, they will lift up praises to God without restraint. In 7:15-17 we read,

> *Therefore are they before the throne of God, and serve him day and night in his temple: and he that sitteth on the throne shall dwell among them. They shall hunger no more, neither thirst any more: neither shall the sun light on them, nor any heat. For the Lamb which is in the midst of the throne shall feed them and shall lead them unto living fountains of waters: and God shall* **wipe away all tears** *from their eyes.*

A sense of welcomed relief will be evident in the lives of this multitude in heaven as this horrendous experience of suffering during the tribulation will be past. Instigating much of their pain and anguish will be their refusal to receive the *mark of the beast* thereby eliciting the wrath of the Antichrist. Their pains of hunger and thirst and persecution on earth will be alleviated only in heaven.

In heaven, the sun will no longer *"light on them"* suggesting that in the tribulation experience they had no form of shelter (7:16). Such homelessness will be widespread in the tribulation. The pain during the tribulation experience will be most severe in the lives of those who come to faith in Christ.

The Origin of the Multitude

Who comprises this multitude John saw in heaven? We know that they will appear during the tribulation period and will be given white robes indicating their conversion to Christ.

Perhaps John 10:16 will shed light on this question. Some readers will wince at interpretation yet we must be willing to search diligently for the identity of this multitude in heaven.

As Jesus speaks of His sheep, He clearly claims that true sheep *"know"* Him. As the Jews rejected Christ, He opened the door of salvation to all men on the basis of His death on the cross and thus all believers are members of God's flock. Look at these interesting words in John 10:16 also echoed in Isaiah 56:8,

> *"And other sheep I have, which are not of this fold: them also I must bring, and they shall hear my voice; and there shall be one fold, and one shepherd."*

Perhaps the multitude saved during the tribulation era, transferred into heaven, and seen by John in his vision is comprised of these *"other sheep"*. They are not believers who will be gathered during the Church Age prior to the rapture nor are they identified as Old Testament saints. Their salvation will come after the removal of the Church. These *"other sheep"* will join the heavenly throng and unite with the multitudes in worship.

The Redemption of the Multitude

Their standing position in heaven indicates that the process of redemption into God's family has been completed. God is on the throne and Christ is Lord despite the tribulation waging on.

John's prophetic words have practical as well as futuristic implications. Believers during John's lifetime routinely were being slaughtered at the hands of the emperor Caesar. This word of encouragement to believers was desperately needed. The end of hunger and thirst will come soon to the brave converts who will take a courageous leap of faith during the mother of all persecutions.

On our arrival in heaven some day, our physical and emotional needs will fade into non-existence as Jesus will capture our focus and alleviate any sense of need we may have. We will not be left wanting in any dimension of our lives because Jesus will have fully met our deepest needs.

The Nature of the Multitude

This multitude in heaven will be so vast John commented that no man will be capable of numbering it. A plethora of ethnic groups and nationalities will be assembled in the midst of the most momentous revival meeting in history. Wearing the *"white robes"* of conversion to Jesus Christ, this multitude will wave palm branches in honor of the Lord and acknowledge their victory over the forces of the Antichrist (7:9). This magnificent scene in heaven is reminiscent of the triumphant entry of Jesus into Jerusalem recorded in the gospels as the people lined the streets and waved their branches an as act of homage.

In 7:10, we read that they will praise God for His *grace* and shout, *"Salvation to our God."* This group, as well as all believers in history, will well up with gratefulness to our Lord for our eternal salvation and place in heaven. Second, they will praise our Lord for his *government* because He sits upon the throne in unchallenged majesty and rule. His sacrificial *gift* of Jesus as the sacrificial Lamb of God for the sins of mankind will result in more praises offered to our glorious Lord.

Such magnificent praise will motivate the elders, the angels, and the four living creatures representing all of the creation assembled at the throne, to offer even more jubilant praise. Have you noticed the momentum that praise generates? Sterile, lifeless churches serve to repel praise and quench the life of the Spirit in any church. To the contrary, lively praise full of passion and joy causes an emotional reaction in the heart and draws people into sweet communion with the Lord.

The Reward of the Multitude

This multitude, mercilessly harassed during the tribulation, will be given a front row seat in heaven. Revelation 7:15 records, *"therefore are they before the throne of God, and serve him……..day and night."* No greater destiny could one imagine than the one to be given to this faithful band of converts who resists the demands of the Antichrist and profess Jesus Christ as Lord.

God will *"dwell"* among them and among other believers in heaven. In biblical usage, to *"dwell"* indicates God's desire to make a home or place of residence among them. Believers will dwell with God and He with them. We will be at home in His presence and any false assumption that we will be mere guests rather than honored members of God's family will quickly fade away (7:15).

The Folly of Waiting to Accept Christ

Knowing the possibility of conversion to Christ after the rapture has removed the Church, some people today choose to place Christ on hold, as it were, with the thought of becoming a child of God during the tribulation. Some skeptics seem to believe that the actual occurrence of the rapture and tribulation will serve as final proof of the claims of the Bible and therefore choose to wait until that undeniable proof arrives on the scene.

I have a question. Will those not brave enough to make a public claim for Christ during our day actually be willing to make that claim in the face of death threats in the tribulation? Will some be willing to refuse the *mark of the beast* and invite guaranteed physical pain and anguish upon themselves? I doubt it.

II Thessalonians 2:10-12 sheds valuable light on this subject. The writer Paul is herein referring to this day of trouble to come and the activities of the Antichrist. The Church will have been removed and the Holy Spirit one day will step aside and allow Satan to have his way on the earth for a season. The evil of our day will pale in comparison to the evil to come. Paul wrote,

> *And with all deceivableness of unrighteousness in them that perish; because they received not the love of the truth, that they might be saved, And for this cause God shall send them strong delusion, that they should believe a lie: That they all might be damned who believed not the truth, but had pleasure in unrighteousness.*

I believe that the implication of Paul is that those who choose to reject the gospel prior to the rapture will be hoodwinked by the Antichrist. These unsuspecting lost men and women will believe that the Antichrist is the long-awaited Christ and will join forces with him.

With certainty, we may conclude that those who have been *enlightened* by the gospel and had ample opportunity in this life to accept Christ, yet refused Him will not be numbered among this great multitude of converts in heaven. Those who willfully and deliberately reject Christ during our Age of Grace will not be converted after the rapture. God will allow an effective delusion to blind the unconverted to the truth. The apostle wrote of this delusion to come in II Thessalonians 2:9, *"whose coming is after the working of Satan with all power and signs and lying wonders."* The Antichrist will perform signs and wonders and capture the allegiance of the religious community. He will operate as a *white witch* and deceive the nations.

I believe that those to be converted to Christ during the tribulation will be only those who have never rejected Him and who have never heard the message and brushed it aside.

The Sin Against Grace

Hebrews 10:26 must weigh in the matter of rejecting the grace that is offered by our Lord.

> *For if we sin willfully after that we have received the knowledge of the truth, there remaineth no more sacrifice for sins, But a certain fearful looking for of judgment and fiery indignation, which shall devour the adversaries. He that despises Moses' law died without mercy under two or three witnesses: Of how much sorer punishment, suppose ye, shall he be thought worthy, who hath trodden under foot the Son of God, and hath counted the blood of the covenant, wherewith he was sanctified, an unholy thing, and hath done despite unto the Spirit of grace?*

A frightening account or rebellion recorded in Numbers 16 illustrates this matter of willful sin in the rebellion of Korah, a rebel who denied the leadership of God's chosen leader Moses. The wrath of God erupted and Korah and his followers consequently were swallowed by the earth. Their rebellion was against the delegated authority of God and was a sin against the knowledge they had received. Korah and his friends did not act in ignorance. They knew full well that God had appointed Moses to lead yet indignantly challenged him anyway. God was not pleased.

Those who sadly choose the path of rejecting God's grace will reap certain consequences. The writer of Hebrews continues in 10:30-31,

> *For we know him that hath said, 'Vengeance belongeth unto me, I will recompense, saith the Lord.' And again, 'The Lord shall judge his people. It is a fearful thing to fall unto the hands of the living God.'*

Such a fearful moment is descriptive of the coming plight of the world during the tribulation time. Those who have willfully rejected the lordship of Jesus Christ will fall into hands of wrath rather than grace.

After Christ comes for His church, will anyone have another chance to convert? No single individual who has willfully rejected the path to salvation prior to the rapture will be afforded that opportunity. Hebrews 6:4-6 sheds light on the finality of such rejection.

> *For it is impossible for those who were once enlightened, and have tasted of the heavenly gift, and were made partakers of the Holy Ghost, and have tasted the good word of God, and the powers of the world to come, If they shall fall away, to renew them again unto repentance; seeing they crucify to themselves the Son of God afresh, and put him to an open shame.*

Some people have tasted the heavenly gift yet have stopped short of committing themselves to Christ. Those who fail to receive Him yet who have been exposed to the full message of the gospel will not have a further possibility of choosing *"repentance."* A poet once wrote,

> *There is a line by us not seen*
> *That crosses every path,*
> *The boundary between God's mercy and God's wrath.*

Those who have rejected the truth and crossed the point of no return will never have another chance to receive Christ. All hope is lost for the One who rejects Jesus Christ's gift of grace. Eternal destinies will have been set in stone. These verses inform us that this category of people will have been recipients of the conviction of the Holy Spirit yet turned it away. Conviction is not synonymous with conversion. All of us have known individuals who have experienced the conviction of God to come to faith in Christ yet have turned away in unbelief and rejection. As the years fade into history, any remaining residue of the Spirit's work in their lives seems to disappear. Another moment of conviction may never come.

The scriptures do not teach a second chance for salvation during the rapture for those who have previously rejected Him with arrogance. The writer of Hebrews concludes his argument by encouraging men and women, *"harden not your hearts"* (3:18).

For some, the deliberate rejection of God's gift of grace and the hardening of the heart is an inoperable condition.

Receive Christ, now!

Chapter 20

THE COMING HOLOCAUST
Revelation 8: 1-13

The motion picture, *Schindler's List* was a Hollywood blockbuster that stunned audiences with its graphic portrayal of the mistreatment and mass sacrifice of the Jewish peoples in World War II. Mr. Schindler, a Nazi, was less than a religious man yet showed unusual compassion for the Jews who were in confinement. His life is another sterling example of God's choice in utilizing unknowing participants to protect His chosen people. With unusual acts of compassion, Schindler acquired the release of countless numbers of Jews from captivity and cried over his inability to release even more.

Another holocaust yet to come will cause the holocaust of the Jewish people in World War II to pale in comparison. John saw in his vision a prediction of the coming ecological and geographic upheaval to be unleashed upon mankind. Men and women will scurry about to avoid the pain of the tribulation.

Even a casual reading of the eighth chapter will strike fear and trembling into the heart of any reader. Could anyone want to experience destruction such as this? As the seventh seal is broken unveiling the next calamity to come, a silent moment of prelude will occur. John wrote these sobering words.

> *And when he had opened the seventh seal, there was silence in heaven about the space of half an hour. And I saw the seven angels which stood before God; and to them were given seven trumpets. And another angel came and stood at the altar, having a golden censer; and there was given unto him much incense, that he should offer it with the prayers of all saints upon the golden altar which was before the throne. And the smoke of the incense, which came with the prayers of the saints, ascended up before God out of the angel's hand. And the angel took the censer, and filled it with fire of the altar, and*

cast it into the earth: and there were voices, and thunderings, and lightnings, and an earthquake. And the seven angels which had the seven trumpets prepared themselves to sound. The first angel sounded, and there followed hail and fire mingled with blood, and they were cast upon the earth: and the third part of trees was burnt up, and all green grass was burnt up. And the second angel sounded, and as it were a great mountain burning with fire was cast into the sea: and the third part of the sea became blood; And the third part of the creatures which were in the sea, and had life, died; and the third part of the ships were destroyed. And the third angel sounded, and there fell a great star from heaven, burning as it were a lamp, and it fell upon the third part of the rivers, and upon the fountains of waters; And the name of the star is called Wormwood: and the third part of the waters became wormwood; and many men died of the waters, because they were made bitter. And the fourth angel sounded, and the third part of the sun was smitten, and the third pat of the moon, and the third part of the stars; so as the third part of them was darkened, and the day shone not for a third part of it, and the night likewise. And I beheld, and heart an angel flying through the midst of heaven, saying with a loud voice, 'Woe, woe, woe, to the inhabiters of the earth by reason of the other voices of the trumpet of the three angels, which are yet to sound.'

A Silent Prelude to Disaster

In our busy and noisy world, thirty minutes of complete silence is an eternity. As the seventh seal of the scroll is broken, an eerie silence will invade heaven for half an hour. The purpose of this quiet interlude is to prepare heaven for the fierce judgments soon to be inflicted upon earth.

After the resounding praises of the multitudes subside, a hush will invade the halls of heaven. This moment of solitude will underscore the holy and righteous nature of the judgment to come. The judgment will be swift and frightening, to say the least, and no man will question its divine origin. Heavenly choirs will pause in their singing. The heavenly hosts will cease their praise, and the twenty-four elders at the throne will seal their lips as they anticipate the coming nightmare on earth. However, the calm before this storm of judgment will be short-lived.

In the spring of the year, we often have days that are hot and sultry with no breeze at all causing the leaves of the trees to sway. Yet on the horizon, we may simultaneously see thunderheads taking form and reaching thousands of feet into the sky. Such atmospheric movement may indicate severe weather in the forecast. Before the storm pounces upon the earth, an eerie lull in the sky often predicts the fury to come. Stillness and solitude in the skies serves as a warning of things to come.

In this period of lull in the tribulation, all of the hosts of heaven will wait breathlessly in anticipation of the outpouring of God's wrath as the seven trumpets prepare to sound. God's judgment will be unleashed in a mighty display of wrath against the earth and its rebellious inhabitants.

Solemn Preparations

In the book of the Revelation, we read of seven seals, seven trumpets, and seven bowls of wrath to come. Each of these occurrences vividly described in the vision indicate various aspects of the judgment. Many biblical scholars believe that these judgments are listed in chronological order. In any case, we may rest assured that these judgments, numbering *seven* in each category, represent a full and complete judgment.

In 8:2, John wrote of the seven angels that appeared at the breaking of the seventh seal. These seven angels will be prepared by God to blow their trumpets with each indicating a single aspect of God's judgment. The Greek text indicates that these are angels *in the presence* of God. They have existed with God from eternity past and their function is to praise God, to fulfill His wishes, and to minister to Him.

Trumpets have forever had biblical significance. One Jewish feast is commonly known as the Feast of Trumpets. Throughout the history of Israel, trumpets were employed to sound a call to assembly, to gather for worship, and to be used in festivals. The blast of the trumpet also served as a battle cry. These angels will be poised with their trumpets in hand ready to announce the coming wrath of God.

Saintly Prayers

The *"saints"* in heaven that John saw were the saints of all the ages, particularly those of the tribulation who came to Christ amidst severe persecution. Revelation is not often thought of as a book of instruction concerning prayer, yet this passage is rich in its teaching concerning the subject.

In 8:3-4, John wrote of the prayers of intercession at the throne of God. John saw in his vision an additional angel standing at the altar holding a *"golden censer."* This container held in the angel's hand is a vessel used in temple worship. Scholars tell us that this vessel was a golden pan, suspended on a rope or chain and used to carry fiery coals from the brazen altar to the incense altar. The coals served to ignite the incense symbolizing the prayers offered to God. Incense produces a fragrant aroma. God views our prayers as sweet fragrances offered to Him.

John saw the angel of prayer holding this golden censer at the *"golden altar"*. Where is this golden altar located? Further in Revelation we read that the temple of God will be opened in heaven and the Ark of the Covenant will be seen there. During the wilderness wanderings of the Jewish people, the Old Testament tabernacle was a pattern for the temple of the Jews. The pieces of furniture adorning the Old Testament tabernacle represented Jesus and various spiritual truths for New Testament believers. The book of Hebrews reminds us that the tabernacle on earth was patterned after the true temple in heaven. In the heavenly temple resides the Ark of the Covenant located in the Holy of Holies. In the temple is the throne where God dwells.

The Prayer of Intercession

This additional angel will arrive on the scene carrying the prayers of the saints. These prayers will be intermingled with the incense of the altar that represent the intercessory work of Jesus Christ in enabling us to pray. As Jesus gave His life on the cross,

He became our mediator. Our prayers become effective by praying *in Jesus' name.* He is the great priest who stands at the right hand of God and continually intercedes for His children.

Should I ever stand before a judge in a courtroom I want to be absolutely sure that I have a lawyer that the judge already knows well. When we stand in God's courtroom, we may rest assured that Jesus is already faithfully delivering our prayers to the Judge and is our faithful intermediary with the Father.

Whether this additional angel is Jesus Himself, or His viceroy, his function is to deliver the prayers and intercede for the saints. Jesus commingles His prayers with ours and essentially presents a package of prayers to the Father.

The Picture of Retribution

These prayers of the angel are very specific in nature. The angel will take the fire upon the altar and fling it toward the earth. Accompanying this scene will be thunderous displays that will shake the universe. Flashes of lightning will illuminate the skies. This graphic description by John is indicative of a significant truth concerning God's character. Obviously, the world is filled with evil and turmoil that often afflicts God's children. The age-old question remains as to why a God of love allows calamity. We must recognize that Satan is ultimately responsible for every heartache. As Adam and Eve were entangled by Satan and made poor choices in the Garden by disobeying the simple commands of their Lord, the entire human race became perpetually infected with sin. Christ came as the second Adam to redeem sinful man by atoning for the sins of all men. Yet sinfulness still permeates the world. Jesus will come soon and will right every wrong and balance the books of justice and fairness.

No question about it, life is unfair. Yet God will reestablish His system of fairness by judging the evil in our world. He will accomplish this feat in dramatic fashion during the tribulation. God's throne of grace now offered to all men one day will become a throne of divine judgment. The *"fire"* taken from the altar and flung to earth will introduce the first judgment upon mankind.

Rebellious mankind will pay an enormous price for his rejection of Christ in this outpouring of divine wrath.

Sinners' Punishment

The first four of the seven acts of judgment introduced by the blasts of the trumpets will be severe in nature yet not as severe as the remaining three. As the first angel picks up his trumpet and sounds its blast for all to hear, the scriptures introduce us to the initial act of punishment by God.

In 8:7, we read of a *botanical scarcity* that will come. In our day of nuclear capability, it is not unrealistic to envision botanical devastation. John wrote of the coming *"hail and fire mingled with blood."* Incredibly, one-third of the earth's vegetation will be incinerated. Civilization will teeter on the brink of total disaster.

Some years ago, I traveled to Russia on a mission venture and became an eyewitness to some of the people who had been exposed to radiation explosions at Chernobyl. In the hospitals we were eyewitnesses to the hopeless condition of many victims of that explosion. In one of our crusades, a lady rushed down the aisle with tears flowing down her cheeks begging us to take her son to America and seek medical help for his afflictions resulting from the nuclear explosion.

In similar fashion, this devastating fire mingled with bloody hail will scorch the grasses of the earth and many of its inhabitants. In the tribulation earth will not be a place any one will desire to live. The devastation in Nagasaki and Hiroshima during World War II will appear like insignificant forest fires compared to the coming geological and ecological devastation..

The second trumpet blast will result in a *boiling sea.* In 8:8 we read, *"as it were a great mountain burning with fire cast into the sea."* Such language is symbolic and could refer to a meteor on a course to plummet into the sea or to another heavenly body that will fall from the sky creating global havoc. This mountain of burning bloody hail will turn one-third of the seas to blood resulting in the death of one-third of sea life. Trade will be severely curtailed due to the upheaval of the oceans and the destruction of the one-third of the world's ships. Damage to the seas and the food supplies will create further poverty and starvation (8:9).

I read in the news that the coasts of Newfoundland have experienced severe shortages of cod causing the deterioration of the economy in that area. Over one million residents have depended upon the codfish for employment yet cod has become very scarce. People are suffering the effects of unemployment and the economy is withering away. In this coming day of ecological destruction during the tribulation, economic trouble will follow the poisoning of the seas and all men will suffer the severe consequences. Until that time, the nations of the world will move toward a greater dependency upon one another. As this form of international interdependency reaches its zenith, the wrath of God will strike. Food will become scarce and will be valued like gold. Panic will grip the throat of the world.

The third trumpet blast will signify the judgment of a *bitter star*. John wrote that he saw an enormous star fall from heaven and plunge into a third of the rivers on earth. The springs of the waters also will be poisoned as this star reaches the earth. John identified the star as *"Wormwood"*, a term referring to bitterness. A variety of species of wormwood grow in Palestine and all have a strong and bitter taste. The name of the plant is commonly used to suggest bitterness, sorrow, and calamity.

One third of the earth's water supply will be contaminated. Jesus is the water of life yet those who endure the tribulation will have rejected Him as the true water for their lives. The poisoning of the waters will be a stark reminder of their rejection of Jesus Christ as the ultimate means to quench their thirsting souls.

The Old Testament account of the rebellious followers of Moses at Marah is a precursor of this episode to come. Some of the Israelites under the leadership of Moses complained of the bitter water in the wilderness. Moses commanded the people to cast a tree into the waters in order to create pure and clean water. They followed his commands and the waters became pleasing to the taste. Because Jesus gave His life on the tree, life becomes sweet for those or us who accept Him. However, as this enormous star in the tribulation falls to the earth resulting in the contamination of the waters, the opposite will be true. Due to a lifetime of rejection of the Son of God, the waters of the earth will become bitter. With each drink of water, evil men will be reminded of their decision to reject the Lord.

The fourth trumpet will sound a blast ushering in a *blackened sky*. One-third each of the sun, the moon, and the stars will be smitten. The natural light of the skies will diminish by one-third in volume. Perhaps this loss of light will be the result of pollution or due to the destruction of the power systems of the world when power supplies are interrupted. In any regard, God Himself will operate the world's lighting system and no man will question His ability to do so.

A comparison of the coming events of Revelation 8 and the apocalyptic discourse in Luke 21:26 is interesting and reveals insight concerning these tribulation events. Luke wrote of the powers of heaven. The word *power* in Luke 21 is derived from the Greek term *dunamis* or dynamite, suggesting an explosive force. In the coming events of the tribulation, the entire globe will shake. The word *"heaven"* in Luke's writings is a unique word describing heaven and is similar to our English word uranium. In the tribulation, the world will experience an unprecedented explosion. The world will shake and rock and its equilibrium will be affected. No man will be safe.

Nations such as North Korea, Iraq and others are said to be developing nuclear weapons that have the capacity for the destruction of large portions of the earth and for the simultaneous annihilation of millions of people. The explosion to come in the heavens during the tribulation will dwarf any nuclear capability currently known to man.

The cataclysmic events of the first four trumpets will be severe yet the final three judgments to be announced will be much worse. In his vision, John heard the sound of an eagle announcing further holocaust events to come. In 8:13, the eagle said, *"Woe, woe, woe, to the inhabiters of the earth."*

The fury of the tribulation will have only begun.

Chapter 21

WHEN DEMONS RULE THE WORLD
Revelation 9: 1-12

In the late 1970's, the blockbuster movie *The Exorcist* introduced the American public to demonic activity, albeit in a manner less than accurate. The public often appears evenly divided between those who acknowledge the existence and activity of demons and those who do not. A clear reading of John's vision will grip the throat of the reader as he reads of the coming onslaught of demonic activity and devastation during the tribulation era.

Israel will one day forge a treaty with the Antichrist. After a time of false security, Israel will experience a severe testing of the requirements of that treaty spanning a period of three and a half years. The treaty will be violated after the three and a half year period precipitating an escalation of pain and anguish during the Great Tribulation, the final half of the dreadful tribulation. Demons will rear their ugly heads in unprecedented fashion and inflict much pain. Those who once cast aspersions and threw barbs of criticism at those who believe in demons will suddenly stare demons in the face.

Concerning the coming invasion of demonic activity, John wrote in 9: 1-4,

> *And the fifth angel sounded, and I saw a star fall from heaven unto the earth: and to him was given the key of the bottomless pit. And he opened the bottomless pit; and there arose a smoke out of the pit, as the smoke of a great furnace; and the sun and the air were darkened by reason of the smoke of the pit. And there came out of the smoke locusts upon the earth: and unto them was given power, as the scorpions of the earth have power. And it was commanded them that they should not hurt the grass of the earth, neither any green thing, neither any tree; but only those men which have not the seal of God in their foreheads.*

Satan the Destroyer

Who is the *"star"* depicted in 9:1? No literal star is in view here. The *"star"* is symbolic of a person. John employed the personal pronoun *"him"* implying that this star has creature qualities. This star *"had fallen"* from heaven suggesting an occurrence in the past. Perhaps God gave John a historical review of the momentous event in biblical history describing the fall of Satan from his heavenly position. I firmly believe that this unnamed personality is none other than Satan himself, the Destroyer. Other terms for Satan that John used in this passage are the Greek noun *Apollyon* and the Hebrew term *Abaddon*, names employed for book titles by novelists Jerry B. Jenkins and Bob Larson, respectively.

A similar reference to Satan from the lips of Jesus himself is mentioned in Luke 10:17-18. Jesus spoke of the power of God that is available when true believers recognize their power over the Evil One. Jesus sent His disciples in twos into the cities that He would soon visit. He instructed them concerning the source of their power in Luke 10:17, *"The seventy returned again with joy, saying, 'Lord, even the demons are subject unto us through thy name.' And He said unto them, 'I beheld Satan as the lightning fall from heaven.'"* Jesus assured them of their power over Satan. He is a fallen creature and is on a short leash controlled by the Lord. He is powerful indeed, yet less than omnipotent and in full subjection to his God.

In eternity past, Satan fell from his coveted position in the heavenly hosts. God unceremoniously expelled him from heaven and from access to the Holy of Holies. He was tossed out of heaven on the basis of the atoning death of Jesus who was slain on the cross *"before the foundation of the earth"* (Ephesians 1:4). The death of Christ was a future event in the mind of God for all of eternity. In describing Satan, the prophet Isaiah wrote in 14:12-14,

> *How art thou fallen from heaven, O Lucifer, son of the morning! how art thou cut down to the ground, which didst weaken the nations! For thou hast said in thine heart, 'I will ascend into heaven, I will exalt my throne above the stars of God: I will sit also upon the mount of the congregation, in the sides of the north: I will ascend*

> *above the heights of the clouds; I will be like the most High.' Yet thou shalt be brought down to hell, to the sides of the pit.*

Satan made the critical mistake of leading a third of the angels to rebel against God. His thirst to exalt himself and to claim divinity for himself, a privilege he is not intended to have, led to his sudden removal from heaven. He promised to *"ascend"* to the heavenly realm yet God promised quite the opposite. In the Luke 10:17-18 passage, Jesus clearly described this fall of Satan from his claim to exaltation and then proceeded to remind the disciples that they were to exert authority over him without fear.

Satan, then and now, will be defeated not with physical force but with the divine authority Jesus has granted to us. Do not tremble in your encounters with him – he is a defeated foe!

Satan and the Bottomless Pit

As John heard the fifth angel let out a bleat from his trumpet, he saw the key to the bottomless pit given to the *"star"* fallen from heaven (9:1). This notorious pit is mentioned seven times in the book of Revelation. The fact that Satan is presented with the key to the pit suggests that he has not had previous possession of it. The Greek terminology for *"bottomless pit"* may be literally translated, "the well of the abyss." It is a literal rather than a mere figurative location.

Remember that in the Isaiah passage God reminded Satan that he was to be brought down to the *"sides of the pit."* A similar reference to this concept is recorded in Revelation 20:1 where we read that an angel one day will come to the bottomless pit with *"a great chain in his hand."* At the appropriate moment on God's timetable, Satan will be incarcerated in this dark dungeon to have no further influence in this world for a thousand years (20:1-3).

In the story involving demons inhabiting sheep, we read in Luke 8:31 of the demons begging Jesus not to send the *"out into the deep."* Obviously, demons know of this place and fear it greatly. Jude 6 sheds light on this subject as well. Jude 6 records, *"And the angels which kept not their first estate, but left their own habitation; he hath reserved in everlasting chains under darkness unto the judgment of the great day."* Their dwelling place in ages past was the presence of God. In rebellion, these sinful angels who assumed demonic character found a new residence and are now *"chained"* and bound by creature limitations. Their coming demise is certain and will ultimately come at the eternal confinement of Satan in the abyss. This band of fallen angels, who comprise a particular host of demons, will one day be perpetually bound in the eternal dungeon prepared by our Lord. Their evil and lascivious behavior and the havoc they have imposed on the world will meet its just reward.

Considering our current level of oppression at the hand of demons, can the world survive a more severe invasion of demonic activity? This coming demonic holocaust alone ought to be adequate cause for even the casual reader of Revelation to reach out to our living Christ for salvation. The waters of the earth will turn to blood and the heavens will shake violently, yet nothing will compare with the demonic invasion to come.

In II Peter 2:4 we read of the judgment of God to come on these rebellious angels. Peter wrote, *"For if God spared not the angels that sinned, but cast them down to hell and delivered them into chains of darkness, to be reserved unto judgment:....."* Peter employed the Greek word *tartaros* for the place called hell. His graphic description is of a location like that of a dungeon. Like a deep and dark well with no apparent bottom hell is a bottomless and unending chasm of terror. This area of hell also is a place of indescribable darkness.

The temporary release of these confined demons during the tribulation is another reason I do not believe that the Church will be present upon the earth during this terror. These demons will unleash their evil powers on mankind after the *One who now restrains them*, the Holy Spirit, has removed His children from harm's way (II Thessalonians 2:7).

The Terror of the Demons

Demons will wreak havoc and inflict much pain, yet in what manner? These demons will have an appearance like locusts yet will not be real locusts because none of the green grass will be eaten.

They will be instructed that no damage is to be done on the earth except to *"those men which have not the seal of God in their foreheads"* (9:4). All men on the earth will be fair game to the demons with the exception of the 144,000 Jewish evangelists and their converts during the tribulation. This furious activity of pain and anguish will span a period of *"five months"* (9:5a).

The common colloquialism, *hell on earth*, will assume new meaning as these demons attack mankind. The effect of this torment imposed by the demons will be *"as the torment of a scorpion"* (9:5b). Men will not die yet will prefer death to this horrendous physical pain. Historians inform us that Roman soldiers were taught not to cry out in agony when tortured and to be stoic and unresponsive to pain. Grit and determination was a highly valued asset. Yet when the scorpions of the desert injected their venom into the flesh of the soldiers, no such rugged stoicism was to be seen. Like any of us, they screamed in agony!

This demonic pain inflicted upon mankind will be unrelenting. John wrote in 9:6, *"In those days shall men seek death, and shall not find it"*. In their desperate desire to end it all, no end to the pain will come. The victims of such an awful moment will be robbed of any sense of peace, serenity, confidence and security. Men will beg for a funeral.

These demons masquerading as locusts are not ordinary locusts as they will have a king to which they submit. *"Apollyon"*, the Greek name of the demonic king, translated as *the destroyer*, is one of the many names of Satan. These demons are emissaries of Satan and have as their mission the destruction of God's people and all that is holy, and the distribution of pain to unbelievers left behind in the tribulation.

The Power of the Demons

From their description we may glean much concerning this incredible demonic power to be unleashed. In 9:7a John wrote, *"And the shapes of the locusts were like unto horses prepared unto battle."* These demons will be on a warpath looking for a battle. In medieval times, horses were adorned with particular kinds of armament that provided protection for the mount as well as the rider. These demons of the tribulation will be well prepared for battle. They will attack and destroy any remaining vestiges of peace and comfort.

In 9:7b John wrote, *"On their heads were as it were crowns like gold, and their faces were as the faces of men."* Literal crowns or the crowns to be awarded to faithful followers of Christ are not in mind. John wrote here of a counterfeit crown by which Satan will arrogantly display his desire for ultimate control. The demons will possess limited authority imposed by our sovereign Lord, yet they will claim unmitigated authority and ability to spread their pain and anguish. The appearance of human faces upon the demons denotes their intelligence. Satan is an intelligent being but does not compare with the omniscience our Lord possesses!

These demons to roam the earth will also utilize seduction to accomplish their mission. John wrote in 9:8, *"They had hair as the hair of women, and their teeth were as the teeth of lions."* Demons in our day never show their true colors. They come as angels of light presenting sin as truly righteous. Sex is a powerful temptation and demons know that fact very well. Advertisers make fortunes seducing the unsuspecting public. Satan's demons will employ the finest of tactics in seducing men to submit to the demands of Satan himself. Lost men who think they have chosen life will find nothing but death. In Satan's theology, darkness is light. It always has been; it forever will be.

The teeth of the demons, appearing like those of a lion, will be seductive and attractive and will proceed to tear asunder men trapped in the tribulation. Their vicious torment will stop short of death since the demons know full well that delaying death will allow them to increase the amount of pain they inflict. Their insatiable desire will be to inflict as much pain as possible.

Man will find no successful defense against these creatures in Satan's entourage. John wrote in 9:9, *"They had breastplates, as it were breastplates of iron; and the sound of their wings was as the sound of chariots of many horses running to battle."* The breastplates of iron suggest their wicked and intense cruelty. Destruction and pain will be their goal and they will act without remorse or concern for others. In the days of the Old Testament, swarms of locust were described as appearing like black clouds of smoke. As countless numbers of locusts descended upon a crop, the flutter of their wings made a whirring sound. These terrifying demonic creatures of the tribulation will be heard as they travel and will be as swift as leopards pouncing upon their prey.

Their capability to inflict physical pain will be unimaginable. In 9:10 John described their abilities, *"They had tails like unto scorpions, and there were stings in their tails: and their power was to hurt men five months."* The physical pain to be inflicted will cause evil men of the tribulation to plead for death.

The world system presupposes that freedom for man is the ultimate goal in life to be attained. Yet that freedom, seen in man's deliberate choice to reject the grace of Christ, will lead him to a sure and sudden painful destruction. Demonic activity in the world today is a mere sampling of the fury to erupt when these demons are released from the bottomless pit.

If you do not know Christ, the time is now, not later.

Chapter 22

THE QUESTION OF DEMONIC INFLUENCE
Revelation 9: 13-21

Some alleged theological scholars in our day propose that demons are the mere figment of overactive imaginations and do not exist. Sadly, they insist that evil is merely the fruit of the poor choices that men often make.

Jesus was quite clear that demons were active in His day. He spoke to them with authority and barked orders at them to obey His commands. Demons inflicted harm and affected individual behavior yet remained under the watchful and authoritative eye of God who delegated such authority to His disciples.

Demons originated as fallen angels, a band comprised of one-third of the angels of heaven who followed Lucifer as he *fell* from heaven. In essence, demons are spirit beings who do not possess bodies of their own yet are capable of inhabiting the bodies of others. They are quite skilled at infiltrating the minds of men and are adept at altering behavior in so doing. The Bible reminds us that an effective method they employ to accomplish their work is mind control.

The apostle Paul taught that we as believers have available to us the *"weapons of our warfare"* that are capable of demolishing the strongholds of demons. Such evil influence takes our thoughts captive to do Satan's bidding and often convinces men that sin is inconsequential (II Corinthians 10). Satan is as subtle as nerve gas yet powerfully effective. If we do not submit to the controlling influence of the Holy Spirit, we are fair game to demonic oppression and influence.

As the *bottomless pit* full of demons is opened during the tribulation, hordes of demons will rush to the surface of the earth to inflict pain and agony upon mankind left behind after the rapture. After John heard the blast of the sixth trumpet in the hand of the angel, he wrote these chilling words in 9:13-21,

And the sixth angel sounded, and I heard a voice from the four horns of the golden altar which is before God, saying to the sixth angel which had the trumpet, 'Loose the four angels which are bound in the great river Euphrates.' And the four angels were loosed, which were prepared for an hour, and a day, and a month, and a year, for to slay the third part of man. And the number of the army of the horsemen were two hundred thousand thousand: and I heard the number of them. And thus I saw the horses in the vision, and them that sat on them, having breastplates of fire, and of jacinth, and brimstone: and the heads of the horses were as the heads of lions; and out of their mouths issued fire and smoke and brimstone. By these three was the third part of men killed, by the fire, and by the smoke, and by the brimstone, which issued out of their mouths. For their power is in their mouth, and in their tails: for their tails were like unto serpents, and had heads, and with them they do hurt. And the rest of the men which were not killed by these plagues yet repented not of the works of their hands, that they should not worship devils, and idols of gold, and silver, and brass, and stone, and of wood: which neither can see, nor hear, nor walk: Neither repented they of their murders, nor of their sorceries, nor of their fornication, nor of their thefts.

The Sixth Trumpet: Mankind Attacked

As the sixth trumpet blast reverberated, John heard a voice coming from the *"four horns of the golden altar"* (9:13). This graphic scene is one of judgment as the angels who sounded these successive trumpet blasts are pictured residing in heaven.

The imagery of horns in the Bible denotes power. The horns in this scene are four in number signifying the comprehensive four points on the compass. This power of God to judge is universal. The golden altar represents the incomparable royalty and holiness of our Lord.

A key biblical truth concerning the nature of man and his destiny is appropriate to mention at this point. If the judgment of our sinfulness does not fall upon the cross of Jesus Christ, then men will stand alone one day to give an account. In that frightful moment of the tribulation, men will fight for survival and attempt to avoid the judgment of God yet will fail miserably.

Today, we exist in an age of grace with the opportunity to appropriate the grace of God as atonement for our sins. In the day of tribulation, the tide will turn. Those who have lived a graceless and unrepentant life will face sudden judgment at the hands of a holy and righteous God. His wrath in unleashing demonic activity upon the rebellious earth will be just and fair yet horrendous. No man will enjoy the experience.

The judgment of our holy God let loose on earth will be a graphic portrayal of His distaste for sin. God views the dark malady of sin so severely that He gave the life of His son to atone for that sin. In so doing, men who accept that offer of grace have their sin debt *paid in full.*

Spirit Powers and Territorial Demons

Demons previously incarcerated in the bottomless pit and released to attack the earth will torment the minds and souls of men for a span of five months. However, they will not possess the capability to kill.

In John's vision, we read that the four angels are bound in the area of modern Iran and Iraq. Not all demons are confined in an identifiable location as countless legions continue to run loose wreaking havoc in our world. These specific four demons described perhaps rank at the top of their class in wickedness. I often refer to them as *The Filthy Four.*

God has sovereignly chosen to preserve these particular four demons in a bound condition until the time of the tribulation. Satan has certain latitudes upon the earth yet also has divine boundaries imposed upon his freedoms. I believe that these demons will rule over empires. Satan has ranks of demons. Specific demons are assigned to influence political leaders into lapses in moral and ethical judgment resulting in suffering and heartache in the world.

These four wicked demons rule and influence four great empires in the areas of the Middle East. Their targeted area is near the River Euphrates, the area where the prophet Daniel stood strong in the face of evil.

Daniel also has provided for us a prophecy of the tribulation from the Jewish perspective. In Daniel 10: 12-13 he wrote,

> *Then said he unto me, 'Fear not, Daniel: for from the first day that thou didst set thine heart to understand, and to chasten thyself before thy God, thy words were heard, and I am come for thy words'. But the prince of the kingdom of Persia withstood me one and twenty days: but, lo, Michael, one of the chief princes, came to help me: and I remained there with the kings of Persia.*

This evil angel attempted to restrain God's answer to Daniel's prayer. This angel was assigned to the *"kingdom of Persia"*, modern Iraq. Demonic angels are at work in random fashion yet also in specific locations.

In Genesis, we read of the River Euphrates. On the banks of that river, Nimrod attempted to construct a tower that would reach God. This river is historic and is the cradle as well as the grave for the kingdom of Satan.

John saw in his vision the future release of the four angels near the Euphrates River for a specific purpose and in a specific era of time. The time of their activity will be *"for an hour, and a day, and a month, and a year, for to slay the third part of men"* (9:15).

A quick glance leads the reader to conclude that thirteen months of attack are in view here, yet a closer look reveals a different interpretation. The New American Standard version of the scriptures and the Revised Standard Version translates the word *"a"* as *"this"*, indicating a specific moment in history, an era of activity. This loosing of the demons will occur as God desires and on His prophetic schedule.

No Panic in Heaven

One fellow quipped that God is not in heaven wringing his sweaty palms wondering what to do next. Our loving Lord is in full control. No panic permeates the hallways of heaven. When the Antichrist unleashes his demonic forces in the tribulation, the earth will shake and tremble yet heaven and the Church will be untouched.

As the great destruction on earth is unfurled, an additional one-third of mankind will be annihilated. We have read in John's vision that twenty-five percent of mankind will have already been lost (6:8). This additional loss of a third of mankind will leave only half of the population of the tribulation era alive. To many, death will be the preferred option.

Two Hundred Million Soldiers

No nation in the days of the apostle John in the first century was capable of fielding a massive army of two hundred million recruits. In the 1960's, Communist China alone boasted of the capability of doing so.

This massive force will cross the Euphrates River that will one day be *"dried up"* (16:12). This army will arrive from the east. Red China will one day awaken like a sleeping giant and burst upon the prophetic scene.

Much of the world is breathing easier these days at the demise of the former Soviet Union yet this sense of peace is temporary at best if we understand the role that China will one day occupy. Their weapons of mass destruction are not in existence for no purpose.

This fierce battle to come will commence as the armies from the east march into Palestine. I believe that John is describing in his vision the modern mechanics of warfare to be employed in this battle. He wrote in 9: 17-18,

> *And thus I saw the horses in the vision, and them that sat on them, having breastplates of fire, and of jacinth, and brimstone, and the heads of the horses were as the heads of lions; and out of their*

> *mouths issued fire, and smoke and brimstone. By these three was the third part of the men killed....*

Perhaps John envisioned the coming use of napalm and germ warfare in a battle so fierce that a third of mankind will perish.

In recent days, the government of Turkey constructed an enormous dam to control the massive waters of the Euphrates River. It is now possible for its raging waters to be contained within the boundaries of Turkey. Some of the waters are being gradually released yet a struggle between Turkey and Iraq has erupted. Turkey controls the flow of the river and therefore wields great power.

In the tribulation conflict, water will become a precious commodity and exceptionally scarce. Prophetic commentators believe that Turkey one day will cause the drying of the riverbed allowing the massive tribulation army to sweep into the land of Palestine unabated.

No Last Chance to Receive Christ

Those who lived a lifetime of rejection of the grace that Christ offers will reap a whirlwind of embattlement and judgment. As the end-time battle progresses, these four wicked angels described by John will target the areas of Iran, Iraq, and Turkey for their assault. The result of this demonic activity will open the path for the armies of the east to invade Palestine.

Even in the midst of such carnage, the remaining inhabitants on the earth will further harden their hearts to the things of God. John wrote in 9:20, *"Yet (they) repented not of the works of their hands."* In spite of repeated opportunities to receive Christ before the rapture and the pain of the tribulation, those left behind still refuse to repent.

Why such hardness of the heart? I believe that those remaining on the earth at this time, with the exception of the 144,000 sealed by God and their converts, will have committed the *unpardonable sin.* Essentially, this fatal sin is the rejection of the witness of the Holy Spirit to the claims of Christ and of His offer of grace. No matter how dramatic the witness of God before the eyes of these perpetual rebels, they will not turn to Christ.

Six Sins in the Tribulation

John continues the record of his vision by providing a graphic portrayal of this state of perpetual rebellion by listing six sins that are the fruit of demonic influence. It has been said that sin will keep us from the Bible; and the Bible will keep us from sin!

First, the worship of devils will characterize these tribulation rebels. In our area of West Texas, the buckle of the *Bible Belt*, many assume that the worship of demons simply does not exist. It does! The worshippers of Satan are ardent evangelists selling their brand of perversion to any and all who will listen. Their passion is to counter the works of Jesus Christ.

During a massive crusade effort in our church that resulted in hundreds of conversions to Christ, I witnessed an older teenage girl share with a counselor concerning her entrapment in devil worship. She had performed sacrifices to Satan and had concluded that she could never be a follower of Christ. Demonic strongholds in her life were strong indeed. After attending three crusades services, she took a leap of faith and came to Christ. Quiet and unnoticed, many Satan worshippers often come to church worship services with the intention of disrupting the work of the Spirit in leading people to Christ. Devil worshippers often target specific individuals within the ranks of spiritual leadership in order to neuter the effectiveness of their work and tarnish their witness.

In our day, those who do not worship Jesus Christ have inadvertently joined ranks with Satan. There is no middle ground.

Second, tribulation rebels will be guilty of the sin of idolatry or the worship of material things, *"the idols of gold and silver, and brass, and of wood"* (9:20). Even more than in our day of secular materialism, those in the tribulation will live for the god of pleasure. These rebels will have no desire for the world to come or for heaven as it unfolds in the millennial kingdom for believers to enjoy. Materialism will have gripped their hearts like a vice.

People who are biblically illiterate and self-absorbed often turn to the promises of materialism to meet their inner needs. Their interest in the things of God is mere lip service. Some people venture into the church for the social status it offers. Others are involved in the church for the sense of emotional security it may offer or for the hope of financial blessings for those *claiming the promises.* Yet the promises of materialism are empty and void.

The third sin to which men in the tribulation will hold is murder. Violence will escalate in the world for reasons of self-preservation and the growing corruption of the heart of man. The killing of the innocent will continue with no signs of remorse.

Another sin of the tribulation will be an increased use of drugs. The *"sorceries"* to which John referred in his vision have their etymological derivation in our English word for pharmacy, or the Greek *pharmakeia.* The deterioration of the family, loss of respect for others, and a desire to escape reality will serve to escalate the use of drugs during the tribulation. It has been my observation that those with this craving need are void of the Holy Spirit in their lives leaving an emptiness crying to be filled.

A fifth sin prevalent in the tribulation is the proliferation of fornication. Sexuality immorality is as old as the world itself, yet this brand of deviation and permissiveness will be the mother of all lascivious behaviors. Previous administrations in Washington have promoted the fatal myth of *safe sex.* Past Surgeon General Jocelyn Elders, thankfully terminated from her position, once commented that she would wear a condom on her head as a crown if such an act would promote the widespread use of the device. It is interesting that our currency carries the phrase *In God We Trust,* yet many political leaders ignore the commands of the One in whom we say we trust. In the tribulation, sexual ethics will be no more. Chaos will escalate to unimaginable proportions.

The last sin to which John referred is theft. Any person and any thing of value will be fair game during the tribulation. The thirst for survival and an unquenchable appetite for self-gratification will drive the crime rate to its highest level.

Satan will have his heyday as his demonic emissaries are unleashed to run amuck. But his time is limited. His ultimate authority, the Lord God Himself, will soon display His power.

Chapter 23

WHEN TIME SHALL BE NO MORE
Revelation 10: 1-13

On the heels of the opening of the sixth seal of the scroll and the massive loss of human life during the tribulation, God allows for an interlude in the continuation of His judgment on earth. In this temporary pause, His compassionate character will be experienced even in the midst of frightening retribution.

This interlude or pause in the outpouring of judgment will be for the purpose of comforting the people of God. In the midst of this tribulation fury, those who will have come to Christ against all odds will welcome this lull in the storm. Second, this interlude will serve to confirm the sovereignty of God as still in tact and Jesus Christ as in full control. In the midst of such carnage and destruction, many may question the whereabouts of a loving God. Is He asleep? Does He care? We may rest assured that He is and forever will be at the helm of eternal destiny.

Coming on the heels of the *"star"* or Satan discussed in chapter nine, John wrote of *"another mighty angel"* to descend carrying a book in his hand. In 10:1-13 John wrote,

> *And I saw another mighty angel come down from heaven, clothed with a cloud and a rainbow was upon his head, and his face was as it were the sun, and his feet as pillars of fire: And he had in his hand a little book open: and he set his right foot upon the sea, and his left foot on the earth, And cried with a loud voice, as when a lion roareth: and when he had cried, seven thunders uttered their voices. And when the seven thunders had uttered their voices, I was about to write: And I heard a voice from heaven saying unto me, 'Seal up those things which the seven thunders uttered, and write them not.' And the angel which I saw stand upon the sea and upon the earth lifted up his hand to heaven, and sware by him that liveth for ever and ever, who created heaven, and the things that therein are, and*

the earth, and the things that therein are, and the sea, and the things which are therein, that there should be time no longer: But in the days of the voice of the seventh angel, when he shall begin to sound, the mystery of God should be finished, as he hath declared to his servants the prophets. And the voice which I heard from heaven spake unto me again, and said, 'Go and take the little book which is open in the hand of the angel which standeth upon the sea and upon the earth'. And I went unto the angel, and said unto him, 'Give me the little book.' And he said unto me, 'Take it, and eat it up; and it shall make thy belly bitter, but it shall be in they mouth sweet as honey.' And I took the little book out of the angel's hand, and ate it up; and it was in my mouth sweet as honey: and as soon as I had eaten it, my belly was bitter. And he said unto me, 'Thou must prophesy again before many peoples, and nations, and tongues, and kings.

The Descent of Jesus

I believe that the *"mighty angel"* descending from heaven in this passage is none other than Jesus Christ himself. The Old Testament is replete with passages depicting the appearances of Jesus to the saints of old prior to His incarnation on earth. For example, an angel of the Lord appeared to Joshua as he contemplated his strategy to confront and overcome Jericho. Joshua bowed to the angel signifying that the angel, described as the captain of the hosts of the Lord, was Jesus Himself. A pre-incarnation appearance such as this is known as a *theophany.*

As we read of the *descent* of this angel, other reasons to identify the angel as Jesus Christ must be mentioned. The purpose of Revelation is to reveal Christ as well as to provide a glimpse into God's prophetic timetable. To not allow Christ to remain the center focus of the vision is to miss the central purpose of the book.

Some years ago, scientists were experiencing a bit of trauma in harmonizing the laws of astronomy. They had assumed that the earth was located at the center of the universe, an assumption resulting in many gnawing and unanswered questions. Copernicus burst upon the scene and proposed that the sun rested at the center of the universe. This dramatic shift in focus allowed the rest of astronomy to develop along logical and scientifically verifiable lines. As readers of Revelation allow the *Son* to be the focus of our study and passion, John's vision will begin to unfold and more clearly communicate its eternal purpose.

Further, this angel to descend from heaven must certainly be Jesus due to his place of *dwelling*. His origin prior to descent is heaven. The scriptures describe Jesus as now sitting at the *right hand of God*. Further, I believe that this angel is Jesus Himself because of His *description*. John employed graphic terms in describing Him as *"clothed with a cloud"* (10:1). Biblically, clouds are the attire of deity and often refer to the glory of God. As the children of Israel wandered in the desert, God appeared to them in a pillar of cloud in the day and in a pillar of fire at night. Such a cloud clothed Him in deity. The Israelites recognized Him as their divine guide. In addition, when Jesus returns some day to claim His bride, He will come with the clouds, the scriptures promise.

This angel to descend was also portrayed as having a rainbow about His head. A rainbow speaks of a covenant or promise. The first biblical mention of a rainbow occurred when God promised to Noah never again to destroy the earth by flooding. The rainbow of Revelation 4 speaks of the perpetual covenant that God made with His people. This rainbow is a vivid reminder of the promises of God and of His covenant of grace and mercy with those who accept His offer.

This mighty angel to descend after the sounds of the sixth trumpet have subsided will have a *"face…as it were the sun"* (10:1). John saw a remarkably bright and shining light as he gazed into the face of the angel. In other passages, bright lights often accompanied the appearances of God to His people. As the disciples Peter, James, and John were on the *mount of transfiguration* with our Lord, the deity of Jesus suddenly began to shine as His humanity became less noticeable. His face became as bright as the sun at high noon in the desert (Matthew 17). The apostle Paul was struck by God's presence on the road to Damascus and was immobilized by a blinding light.

No doubt, this angel of Revelation 10 must be the Lord Jesus Himself. His feet were like *"pillars of fire"* signifying judgment. In Revelation 1, we read of the face of Jesus described as like the sun and His feet like brass burned in the fire. Jesus is the One from whom the acts of judgment will originate. This angel with the little book in his hand is the Lord Himself.

The Dominion of Jesus

John saw this angel holding a little book with his right hand extended. This book, identical with the one described in chapter five, is the title deed to the earth and contains terms for the redemption of the world. He has a *charge* to keep in redeeming the world for God's children.

This angel also has a *claim.* John watched in rapt attention as the angel planted one foot on the waters of the sea and the other on dry land. Such a bold act clearly stakes the claim of our Lord to the entire earth. As Columbus searched for America and set foot on dry land, he placed one foot on the land and the other on the waters of the sea. He planted the *standard* of Spain and claimed possession of the land on behalf of King Ferdinand and Queen Isabella. In John's incredible vision, the angel planted his feet in a bold declaration. God owns it all and will do with it as He wishes. God spoke of His divine claim to all that exists in Psalm 2:8, *"Ask of Me, and I shall give thee the heathen for thine inheritance."* In Colossians, we read that Christ has spoiled the demonic powers and principalities by means of His death and resurrection. All of the earth will be placed under his feet in a show of dominion. He is the *lord of the land* and the *lord of the sea* as well!

In 10:3 we also read of His *cry.* The cry of this angel was like a lion roaring at full pitch. Such a vivid description speaks of His majesty and royalty. As lions roar in the jungle, the rest of its inhabitants pause to acknowledge his presence and authority. This roaring angelic Lord that John envisioned is fully in charge of destiny and all of the earth will know it well.

John Stops Writing

As the angel cried out with His *voice*, seven peels of thunder ripped across the skies. In 1:19, Jesus gave careful instructions to John to write what he saw. In 10:4, God commanded the apostle to lay his pen aside for a time. As the seven claps of thunder reverberated, the writer John quickly prepared to record their meanings but was forbidden by God to do so. Revelation 10:4 reads, *"Seal up those things which the seven thunders uttered, and write them not."* John laid his pen in his lap in an act of obedience.

The *"seven thunders"* refer to the complete and comprehensive nature of the judgment to come. The command to John to not record the meanings of these claps of thunder may refer to God's choice to conceal from us some of the details of His divine plan for the ages.

Gnawing questions linger in our minds and certain mysterious elements of prophecy may remain just that – mysterious. God is God and His choice to reveal His ways will occur on His timetable alone regardless of how desperately we desire to know and understand.

In 10: 6-7 we read of the *vow* of the angel *"that time should be no longer"*. What does this phrase mean? In the Greek language, the phrase refers to the fact that no delay will remain. The delay of God's judgment will cease and it will proceed without restriction.

In the days of John, the saints of God were longing for the return of Jesus. They reached their limit of suffering and ridicule and wanted Christ to remove them from the earth. Yet God's calendar is not identical with our own. His timing is perfect yet often appears confusing to us as mortals who are limited by our finite understanding.

In our day, God has delayed His coming to allow countless others to come to faith in Christ and to be ready for His coming. This delay in our lives will reach its end as this Divine angel will cancel all delays. The window of opportunity for mankind to establish a relationship with God will abruptly close.

The Mystery Will Be Solved

The Bible continually speaks of the mysteries of God. The Church is one of these mysteries and is comprised of people who have chosen to commit their lives to Christ and now live as *aliens* in this world. This segmentation of society based upon a deliberate choice or refusal to accept Christ is mysterious indeed.

The mystery to which John refers concerns the question of the continual presence of evil in the world and why a loving God would allow such heartache. This mysterious dimension of our Lord's plan will be revealed as He cancels the delay of His judgment and fully reveals Himself in the millennial reign to come.

Sweet Words

As John watched this scene unfold in his vision, he was careful to be obedient to the Word of God. The voice of this Heavenly angel instructed John to take the book from the angel and *"eat it up"* (10:9). The weeping prophet Jeremiah had a similar encounter with God. He wrote in Jeremiah 15:16, *"Thy words were found, and I did eat them; and thy word was unto me the joy and rejoicing of mine heart."* The apostle Peter wrote that believers should desire the *"sincere milk of the word"* (I Peter 2:2).

Historians tell us that Jewish boys often learned the Hebrew alphabet with motivation provided by the eating of the letters. In the early days of Judaism, people wrote on slate. A mixture of honey and flour was utilized as ink. As they learned the letters successfully, their teacher allowed the children to eat them. Such a treat delighted the young learners and whetted their appetites for more learning. What they learned was ingested into their bodies. As the saying goes, *you are what you eat.* Our character is formed by what we eat from the Word.

In the first Passover, the Jews were to take the blood of the perfect lamb and wipe it on their doorposts. They also prepared the flesh of the lamb from which the blood had been taken in order to eat it as the family meal. Such a scene is a vivid reminder that we as believers must continually partake of the Lamb of God as our sustenance. As blood gives life to the cells of our bodies, the Word of God injects life into our spiritual cells.

As John took this little book of redemption from the hand of the divine angel, he informed us that the Word must be *personally received.* God wants us to get into the Bible – and wants the Bible to get into us! As we digest it, it ministers life and allows for our growth.

As this angel exemplifies, the Word alive and at work in us will have two effects. First, the promises of God and the revelation of His compassionate character are sweet to the taste. Some portions of the Word, however, are difficult to digest. The judgment and wrath of God are dimensions of the biblical meal many would prefer to ignore and refuse to eat. The effects of these less than desirable and often traumatic portions of our lives are bitter to the taste. Yet the just character of our Lord must be balanced with His compassion in order to achieve optimum spiritual health. His nutritional plan is without fault. His ways and His words are perfect.

The Word must also be *publicly proclaimed.* John wrote in 10:11, *"Thou must prophesy again before many peoples, and nations, and tongues, and kings."* While recording the words of this magnificent vision on the Island of Patmos, John was approximately one hundred years of age. His ministry was nearing an end. Scholars believe that he experienced no further public ministry after his banishment to the island. His remaining ministry occurred through the written word. His words traveled where he would never go. The divine words of Revelation have survived the ages and continue to enthrall and capture the attention of the world.

John wrote clearly of the coming judgment. The divine angel will one day cancel the delay of that judgment and just recompense will be dispensed upon the earth.

In that day, time *will be no more.* Now is the day to receive our Lord while there is still time.

Chapter 24

THE TEMPLE WILL RISE AGAIN
Revelation 11: 1-2

After three and a half years of pain and anguish in the tribulation, the reign of the Antichrist will be fully established as he displays his charisma and skill to hoodwink the nations into acceptance of his solution to the world's unrest. This gifted deceiver will assume full control of the nations of the world and will secure a peace pact with Israel and Arabia in the process.

The Allure of the Antichrist

One explanation for the success of the Antichrist in securing a pact with Israel will be his unique ability to acknowledge and endorse Israel's ongoing political aspirations and desire for independence. Second, the Antichrist will experience success at the negotiating table because of his false promise to assist strict Orthodox Jews in the rebuilding of the temple, a project that has burned in their hearts since its destruction in the first century.

In recent years, we read of the tragic massacre of Arab worshippers in Hebron at the hand of a radical Orthodox Jewish leader. Hebron is located on the West Bank, identified as Palestinian territory and inhabited by many Palestinians as well as Jews. Radical Jewish leaders and others will rush to support the Antichrist due to his offer to assist in rebuilding the temple. Orthodox Jews firmly believe that for their Messiah to come and their belief system to be confirmed, a temple must exist to house their sacrificial system of worship as practiced in Old Testament days. The Antichrist will gladly agree to grant their longstanding desires.

Israeli Prime Minister Rabin caught the wrath of a group of strict Orthodox Jews in recent years due to his willingness to negotiate and accept concessions regarding the ownership of Israel's coveted lands. This group of Jewish protestors strongly believes that the land of Israel was a gift from God. They are more than willing to die to guard their treasured possession. In allowing for the revival and rebuilding of the temple and the reestablishment of Mosaic ritual, the Antichrist will gain wide appeal and support. His political skills will be unmatched.

Concerning the promised rebuilding of the temple in Jerusalem, John wrote these words in 11: 1-2,

> *And there was given me a reed like unto a rod: and the angel stood, saying, 'Rise, and measure the temple of God, and the altar, and them that worship therein. But the court which is without the temple leave out, and measure it not; for it is given unto the Gentiles: and the holy city shall they tread under foot forty and two months.*

Temples in the Past

The temple project will commence during the tribulation. Amazingly, when the Holy Spirit spoke to John to measure the temple with a *reed like unto a rod,* no temple existed to measure. John's words were penned in 95 A.D. The temple in Jerusalem had been viciously ransacked and destroyed in 70 A.D. by the Roman general Titus. The temple of this passage is yet to be rebuilt. Since the time of the destruction of Herod's temple in the first century, no temple has existed. Synagogues are in operation, yet no temple may be found in Israel.

I Kings 8 details the dedication of the original temple built under the command of Solomon. During construction, the stones were measured and cut in a remote quarry so that the sounds of hammers and chisels would not reverberate in the temple and thereby dishonor it. I believe that this policy signified reverence for a holy God in allowing the temple to remain undisturbed by such material functions. The temple was built as a testimony to the nations of the holiness and righteous character of God. At the dedication, the glory of God filled the temple overwhelming the people of God with emotion. The *cloud* of God's glory caused the priest to be unable to stand to minister (I Kings 8: 10-11). Solomon's temple met its demise in 583 B.C. as King

Nebuchadnezzar plundered the city taking the Israelites into captivity. He struck a debilitating blow into the heart of Israel by attacking and demolishing her temple.

A second temple was built by Zerubbabel in 490 B. C. near the time the Jews returned from their years of exile in Babylon. The scribe and teacher Ezra motivated the Jewish people to build the temple. As the people released from captivity began to arrive, they constructed homes for themselves yet allowed God's house to *lie desolate*, the scriptures indicate. The prophet Haggai also assisted in motivating the people to begin the building process of the temple. These poverty-stricken Jews rallied and miraculously rebuilt the structure. Those of the younger generation marveled in wonder at its completion while the older generation bemoaned the fact that the glory of the second temple paled in comparison to that of Solomon's temple. Later, Antiochus Epiphanes obliterated the temple in 168 B.C.

Herod's temple is identified in the New Testament and was present during the time of Jesus. Today in Israel an exact model of Jerusalem is present and occupies an acre of land. Sightseers are welcomed to visit the replica.

Herod's great temple was incredibly beautiful and was constructed by Herod in 6 B.C with ulterior motives in mind. Herod was not fully Jewish but rather only half Jewish eliciting the suspicions of the Jewish people. Herod desperately wanted credibility with the Jews yet never achieved his goal. The visit to the temple by the young boy Jesus is recorded in Luke 2:21-22.

> *When the eight days were accomplished for the circumcising of the child, his name was called JESUS, which was so named of the angel before he was conceived in the womb. And when the days of her purification according to the law of Moses were accomplished, they brought him to Jerusalem, to present him to the Lord.*

Jesus was taken by his parents into the temple according to the customs of the law (Luke 2:27). Located next to the temple was the Antonio Fortress where the Roman governor lived and held court.

Next to the temple mound today is the famous Wailing Wall where Jews arrive daily to pray. Approximately ten feet of the wall, the western or retaining wall, is the same wall that existed in the days of Jesus. Jesus was tried by Pontius Pilot in the Antonio Fortress located adjacent to the temple.

Only the high priest was allowed into the Holy of Holies in the temple of Herod. Inside the Holy of Holies was the mercy seat that rested above the Ark of the Covenant, the place where blood was annually sprinkled as an act of intercession on behalf of Israel and her sins. As the high priest entered, he would utter the word of Jesus on the cross, *tetelestai,* translated "it is finished." As the high priest uttered that historical word it was understood that the sins of Israel had been atoned and forgiven. That event was known as the Day of Atonement. Yet when Jesus whispered that word of completion on the cross, His death became our means of atonement. Such an act of forgiveness was established *"before the foundation of the world"* and is the means of salvation today for all who respond (Ephesians 1:4).

When Jesus cried out on the cross, he *"yielded up the ghost"* signifying the release of His spirit (Matthew 27:50). Jesus was in full control of His spirit and died at the precise moment that had been predetermined in heaven. At His death, the veil of the temple was torn asunder from top to bottom accompanied by a tremendous earthquake rattling the environment. This event was a dramatic message to the Jews that they no longer were required to commune with God by means of a high priest or by the practice of altar sacrifice and ritual. Their intermediary in communicating with the Father became the Messiah Himself and continues to be so today.

To believers then and now, the tearing of the veil was significant and rich in meaning. Tearing from top to bottom, this event was the work of God in obliterating the barriers between God and man. No high priest is needed for us to meet with the Father. Jesus Himself is the one and only necessary mediator.

Another temple, the millennial temple described in Ezekiel 40-44, will be constructed and occupied by our Lord Himself during the one thousand year millennium. This temple will become a graphic reminder of the finished work of Christ on the cross of Calvary.

Last, the New Testament clearly teaches that we as believers are identified as the temple of the Holy Spirit. God now has no temple for His people, conversely indicating that God has a people for His temple. As opposed to a physical building, we are the dwelling place of the Lord. Our bodies are the residence of the Holy Spirit.

The temple of Jerusalem featured three rooms: the outer court, also described as the court *"which is without"*, the inner court, and the Holy of Holies (11:2). In a similar way, man is tri-dimensional in being as we possess a body, mind, and soul or spirit. The body corresponds to the outer court; the mind to the inner court; and the spirit or soul to the Holy of Holies where we commune with God. To damage any of the three dimensions of personhood is to damage the temple of God. None of the aforementioned temples refers to the future temple depicted in Revelation 11: 1-2.

Rebuilding the Jerusalem Temple

When will the temple of Jerusalem be rebuilt? This passage indicates that construction will be completed during the first part of the tribulation. In the second half of the tribulation, the Antichrist will violate his treaty of peace with Israel by entering the temple in a defiant proclamation of himself as God. He will brazenly corrupt the Holy of Holies by entering its domain and announcing himself as God.

The construction site will be in the Holy City. The site of the original temple in Jerusalem once again will feature the crown jewel of all structures for the nation of Israel, the temple.

Obstacles to Rebuilding

Our generation is the only one that has witnessed several specific signs and events previously predicted in the Bible indicating the soon return of Christ to the earth. Israel did not exist as a nation until May 14, 1948. Jews did not reside in their homeland at that time yet have begun to return in record number. Second, the Jews did not possess control of the old city of Jerusalem yet reclaimed ownership in the Six Day War commencing on June 7, 1967 when Moshe Dayan and the Israeli army drove the Arabs out of the city. They staked a claim to Jerusalem and promised to defend it to the end of time. For the prophecy to be fulfilled concerning reconstruction of the temple, this new temple must be erected on the exact location of Solomon's temple.

Second, the Mosque of Omar, commonly known as the Dome of the Rock, is an exquisite and beautiful Moslem dome that serves as the third most holy site to the Moslems. It is hollow in the center and features a giant rock jutting out of the mountain inside the mosque. Countless Moslems worship in this location each year. It was previously assumed that the location of the dome would require its removal to make way for the Jewish temple to be rebuilt. Further study and excavation since the middle 1980's have indicated that the original site of the Jewish temple was adjacent to the Dome of the Rock. A rebuilt temple could be erected without disturbing the revered Moslem mosque.

The move toward one world religion continues to gain momentum. Such false unity will please the Antichrist. False peace will come largely due to his deceptive offer to resolve religious conflict.

Much conflict in the world is instigated by religious conflict. Arabs often participate in *jihad,* or holy war. The vast majority of problems in the Middle East are religious rather than political in nature. Politicians will never solve religious conflict. What I foresee occurring on the temple mound in the tribulation is the peaceful convergence of the three great world religions in a demonstration of false unity in spite of the fact that Islam, Christianity, and Judaism lack theological agreement.

Perhaps one facet of the peace treaty secured by the Antichrist with the Arab world will allow Israel to build her temple next to the Mosque of Omar. Perhaps Christians will construct a structure on that holy site as well. The world may rejoice at such a magnificent show of unity yet false unity is no unity at all. Such a travesty to the cause of Christ will be further indication of the *New World Order* already en vogue in our day. The desire for world unity in our day is driven by an emphasis on a unified economic policy, a common currency, and by disarmament. False euphoria will medicate the masses and men will be enthralled with the Antichrist.

The peace treaty to be signed at the urging of the Antichrist is detailed in Daniel 9:27. He will confirm this covenant with the Jews. Without a conscience to restrict him, he will proceed to violate it forty-two months later.

The Need for Another Temple

In Revelation 11:1, John wrote that he was instructed to measure the temple with a *"reed like unto a rod."* Biblically, the rod was an instrument of chastisement. For example, in the days of the Old Testament, God used the rod of the Assyrians to discipline Israel for her rebellious ways.

This tribulation temple will serve as a judgment against the Jewish people. As they assume that they have become the recipients of blessings due to the rebuilding of their holy temple, the Antichrist will burst into the temple and make his arrogant claim to be God.

Jesus spoke of the severing of this covenant with Israel in Matthew 24: 15. Paul wrote of it in II Thessalonians 2: 3-4. God will use the Gentiles to trod underfoot and desecrate the Holy City resulting in the severe chastisement of the Jewish people.

The rebuilding of the temple will also serve as a total repudiation of the Jews' perpetual rejection of Jesus as the Messiah. The continual movement toward one world religion presupposes that all roads lead to heaven. Today, a multitude of denominations and religious groups readily believe in the concept of *universal salvation.* This false doctrine proposes many paths to salvation. Little talk of hell or judgment is ever heard in these circles. Particularly distasteful to these religious pluralists is the notion that Jesus is the only way.

By the way, Jesus is the only way!

As the preparations for the rebuilding of the temple continue to be made, the signs of the times continue to appear

Jesus is coming. Be ready!

Chapter 25

THE TWO WITNESSES INVADE THE EARTH
Revelation 11: 3-13

The rebuilding of the Jewish temple in Jerusalem in the tribulation era will actually occur. Plans for reconstruction are currently underway. In our day, many Jews stipulate in their wills that a portion of their estates be given to this future rebuilding project. All indications point to the area east of the Dome of the Rock as the rebuilding site. That location will leave the revered Moslem mosque untouched by Jewish hands although the battle over property rights continues.

The ongoing attempt at negotiating peace between the Israelis and the Palestinians continuing in our today is a forerunner of the pact that the Antichrist will sign with the nation of Israel in the tribulation. Who would have dreamed that the Iron Curtain between East and West Berlin would collapse and fall to the ground? Who could have predicted the demise of communism in the former Soviet Union? These events, and others, miraculously occurred clearing the way for the preaching of the gospel into all the earth in fulfillment of the prophecy that global exposure to the gospel must first occur, and *"then shall the end come"* (Matthew 24:14).

After an official procurement of peace and security is secured for Israel in the tribulation, the temple will be constructed. Perhaps its construction will occur prior to the appearance of the Antichrist or after his arrival. In either case, it will be built. Presently, a rabbinical school is in operation in Jerusalem in which priests are receiving training to minister in this future temple.

The reestablishment of the temple will be the ultimate repudiation of Christ as the Messiah since His death obliterated the necessity for the Old Testament sacrificial system, a truth that the Jews reject to this day. Yet the Jewish system of altar sacrifice and other Old Testament practices will be reinstated. The Jews will heap lavish praise upon and endorse the Antichrist due to his self-proclaimed support of the rebuilding of the temple.

During that era, two unique witnesses will appear that will proclaim a message from God primarily related to Israel. Their influence will be widespread. John wrote of this event in 11: 3-13,

> *And I will give power unto my two witnesses, and they shall prophesy a thousand two hundred and threescore days, clothed in sackcloth. These are the two olive trees, and the two candlesticks standing before the God of the earth. And if any man will hurt them, fire proceedeth out of their mouth, and devoureth their enemies: and if any man will hurt them, he must in this manner be killed. These have power to shut heaven, that it rain not in the days of their prophecy: and have power over waters to turn them to blood, and to smite the earth with all plagues, as often as they will. And when they shall have finished their testimony, the beast that ascendeth out of the bottomless pit shall make war against them, and shall overcome them, and kill them. And their dead bodies shall lie in the street of the great city, which spiritually is called Sodom and Egypt, where also our Lord was crucified. And they of the people and kindreds and tongues and nations shall see their dead bodies three days and an half, and shall not suffer their dead bodies to be put in graves. And they that dwell upon the earth shall rejoice over them, and make merry, and shall send gifts one to another; because these two prophets tormented them that dwelt on the earth. And after three days and an half the Spirit of life from God entered into them, and they stood upon their feet; and great fear fell upon them which saw them. And they heard a great voice from heaven saying unto them, 'Come up hither.' And they ascended up to heaven in a cloud; and their enemies beheld them. And the same hour was there a great earthquake, and the tenth part of the city fell, and in the earthquake were slain of men seven thousand: and the remnant were affrighted, and gave glory to the God of heaven.*

Two Witnesses for 1260 Days

No passage in the Revelation is more fascinating than the prediction of the activity of these two unique witnesses to burst upon the scene. The word *"witness"* herein describes real people. Even in this horrible era of tribulation, God will provide a living witness for Himself on the earth. These two individuals will prophesy very effectively. They will be clothed in *sackcloth*. Their clothing will be an indication of mourning at the coming judgment to be unleashed on the remainder of civilization.

In picturesque language, John described these two witnesses as two olive trees and two candlesticks. The prophet Zechariah also referred to the olive trees and candlesticks approximately six hundred years before John penned these words (Zechariah 4: 2-3). Olive trees produce oil, a biblical symbol of the Holy Spirit. Candlesticks illuminate with light. The oil of the Spirit at work in these two witnesses, and in us as well, is required for effective ministry to result.

Their message, however, will ignite enormous protest among the masses as they expose the deception and falsehood of the Antichrist. The masses of the world will heap vitriolic hatred upon these two brave emissaries of our Lord. Their ministry will span three and one half year, 1260 days.

The Power of the Witnesses

These two men will be given incredible power with which to devour those who attempt to kill them (11:5). Of course, those in the tribulation who refuse to wear the *mark of the beast* will be destroyed, including converts to Jesus Christ who took the step of faith at the urging of the 144,000 Jewish evangelists (16:2, 19:20).

The Antichrist will employ any and all means to silence the voices of these witnesses. Their significant power and effectiveness will prevent their demise at the hands of the Antichrist. Until God allows their death, they will continue to flourish and preach to the masses.

Incredibly, they will possess the power to create drought by withholding the rains for three and a half years. They will possess the ability to inflict death, to turn the waters into blood creating further disruption of trade, and to afflict men with disease. Their magnificent show of signs and wonders will be a vivid display of the power of God at work through them.

Who Are They?

Although the Bible does not specifically identify these two witnesses, I believe that they are Elijah and Moses. Consider the similar traits and abilities of these two witnesses and those of Elijah and Moses. The prophet Elijah was granted the ability to close the windows of heaven to prevent rain for a period of three and one half years (I Kings 17:1). The grounds of Israel were crusty and dry for that length of time. These two witnesses of the tribulation will function for that identical length of time with identical abilities.

The patriarch Moses was gifted with the supernatural ability to turn water into blood thus afflicting the Egyptians with an awful plague for disallowing the release of Israel from captivity (Exodus 7:20). The two witnesses will have similar powers regarding plague and disease. Perhaps the most convincing proof that the two witnesses will be Elijah and Moses is to be found in Matthew 17: 1-3.

> *After six days Jesus taketh Peter, James, and John his brother, and bringeth them up into an high mountain apart, and (He) was transfigured before them: and his face did shine as the sun, and his raiment was white as the light. And, behold, there appeared unto them Moses and Elias (Elijah) talking with him.*

In this poignant moment in the gospels, Moses and Elijah had vacated the earth long ago yet they appear alive and well in this scene on the mountain. Their identities are recognizable and they are seen conversing with Jesus. Other passages inform us that they discussed with Jesus His exodus and death. I believe that Moses was chosen to appear due to his authorship of the Pentateuch and that Elijah appeared as a representative of the prophets. They represented two major sections of Old Testament writings, the law and the prophets.

These Old Testament writings continue to carry enormous validity with the Jewish people of today. This discussion between Elijah and Moses and our Lord forces Jewish people to make a definitive decision regarding the authenticity of the Messiah. Sadly, they are yet to be convinced.

Irritated Jews

I believe that these two witnesses will dramatically declare that the rebuilt temple in Jerusalem is not valid and of no use since the Messiah became the ultimate sacrifice for sins. The need for the sacrificial system was thereby eliminated. This controversial message, delivered by the law-giver Moses and by the prophet Elijah, will instigate enormous protest from the Jewish people.

The Jews looked carefully for their Messiah to appear and asked deliberate and penetrating questions to discover the real truth. John 1: 25-27a records this search,

> *They asked him, and said unto him, 'Why baptizest thou then, if thou be not that Christ, nor (Elias), neither that prophet?' John answered them, saying, I baptize with water: but there standeth one among you, whom ye know not. He it is, who coming after me is preferred before me…*

Jesus taught that John the Baptist was a fulfillment of Elijah yet was not Elijah himself. Elijah is still to appear in the chronology of future events. In the fifth century B.C., the prophet Malachi wrote, *"I will send you Elijah the prophet before the coming of the great and dreadful day of the Lord"* (Malachi 4:5). John the Baptist served as the forerunner at the first coming of Jesus; Elijah will occupy that role in the tribulation period preceding the second coming of our Lord.

In the tribulation, the Age of Grace will have vanished and the Age of Law will have been reestablished. God will not appoint new prophets in the tribulation but rather will cause the reappearance of these venerable Old Testament personalities to share a witness to the Jews. This era of ministry yet to come will occur during the *seventieth week*, the seven years of tribulation about which Daniel wrote.

The Persecution of the Two Witnesses

The wicked and furious persecution leveled against them will demonstrate again the sovereignty of God before the eyes of the world. At this time, the Antichrist will wreak havoc in the world and cause the death of any and all who refuse his *mark*. The fate of the two witnesses will rest ultimately in the hands of God. Regarding his vision John wrote in 11:7,

> *When they shall have finished their testimony, the beast that ascendeth out of the bottomless pit shall make war against them, and shall overcome them, and kill them.*

The temporary demise of these witnesses will come only after their divine mission comes to a climax. Even in the tribulation era God will continue to preserve His people in a compassionate manner. Yet the fulfillment of His mission is of paramount importance and should take precedence over our desire for peace and comfort. If life in heaven were our only mission, why live? To miss the gritty experience of living on earth would be to avoid all distress and temptation. Yet God has a purpose for each of us on our journey in life. However, our journeys may be fraught with distress and peril on every hand. As John Blanchard asked, Jesus wore a crown of thorns; should we expect a bed of roses?

Dead Bodies on Display

In a show of arrogant force, the Antichrist will kill the two witnesses and display their lifeless bodies in the city of Jerusalem for the masses of the world to see. John referred to this city as the one *"called Sodom and Egypt"* (11:8). Why Sodom and Egypt? Egypt was renowned for its intense oppression of the people of God; Sodom is synonymous with wickedness.

The Antichrist will function as a type of Pharaoh in that he will level vicious attacks against the people of God in the tribulation. Yet the Antichrist will soon meet his match.

The preaching of the two witnesses will infuriate the Antichrist because they will expose his scheme and threaten his rule. In a fit of retaliation, he will display their dead bodies *in the street.* As they take their last breath, the world will erupt in jubilation. It is difficult to imagine a world so wicked that its citizens applaud as two of God's prophets die in agony.

I believe that 11:9 implies the existence of television. John wrote that the bodies of the witnesses will be seen by *the people and kindreds and tongues and nations* (11:9). John recorded these prophetic words in 95 A.D. It would have been physically possible only for the nations within traveling distance of Jerusalem to see these dead witnesses with their eyes. A global simultaneous viewing of events has become possible only in recent years. Our generation has the capability of broadcasting any world event into the four corners of the globe. As the two witnesses die at the hands of the wicked Antichrist, the world will be glued to broadcast screens in rapt attention.

Hell will have a holiday. Joy and jubilation will fill the earth to the extent that men and women will give gifts to one another in celebration of the death of the witnesses. At Christmas, we celebrate a birth. At this joyful holiday of the Antichrist, his followers will celebrate death. Only a spiritually blinded society could react in such a corrupt and degenerate manner.

An Astonishing Resurrection

Unbelievably, the two witnesses will spring to life and walk. God is a God of resurrection. Jesus died for our sins and rose again. As believers, we die to sin and are resurrected with a new life in Christ. John wrote of the two witnesses to resurrect in 11:11,

> *After three days and an half, the Spirit of life from God entered into them, and they stood upon their feet; and great fear fell upon them which saw them.*

The world will have witnessed the death and humiliation of these two witnesses on media screens for three and a half days. Men will scramble for a logical explanation. Were they in a state of coma? Were they medicated? Was it a psychologically induced state? What happened?

God is a God who breathes life into His children by His Spirit. The spirit of a believer never dies. At the moment of salvation, the Spirit breathes life into our spirits. The body may die yet the human spirit infused with God's Spirit never will.

These two witnesses will be supernaturally raised from death in a *triumphant resurrection.* The people of the world will gasp and wipe their eyes unable to believe what they see on the screen. These witnesses will be preserved by our Lord in a *triumphant rapture.* John wrote in 11:12,

> *They heard a great voice from heaven saying unto them, 'Come up hither.' And they ascended up to heaven in a cloud; and their enemies beheld them.*

This scene will be reminiscent of the ascension of Jesus on the Mount of Olives as the disciples stood with their mouths opened in shock.

This victory over the forces of the Antichrist will also serve as a *triumphant revenge.* At the departure to heaven of these two men, ten percent of the city will fall and seven thousand people will lose their lives. The *remnant,* comprised of those remaining alive after a devastating earthquake, will acknowledge the existence and power of our Lord.

The world will then know Who is in charge.

Chapter 26

THE CROWNING OF THE KING
Revelation 11: 14-19

Most of us go wherever we desire to celebrate Christmas. Palestinian leader Yasser Arafat has visited Bethlehem during the Christmas season since 1995 as a public display of his authority. In 2001, the Israeli government voted to deny him the privilege in light of the recent surge in fighting between the two countries. The Associated Press carried the headline, *Israel Tells Arafat to Arrest Assassins or Stay Home for Christmas.* Arafat vowed to walk to Bethlehem if required and quipped, "No one can humiliate the Palestinians or make them lose their determination" (AP, December 25, 2001). Time will tell.

The ongoing conflict has devastated the economy of Bethlehem, a city inhabited by some 30,000 Palestinians. Predictably, peace in the Middle East seems to be achieved for a time yet vanishes quickly.

A recent article in *Newsweek*, entitled "Does Peace Have a Prayer in Israel?" underscored the conflict between Jewish settlers and Palestinians over the West Bank in Israel. I cannot begin to express the significance of these peace negotiations between these two warring nations. Israel's willingness to discuss the concession of ownership of certain plots of land highlights the conflict within the nation of Israel between those willing to concede and the rigid Orthodox Jews who vow to never give up a single pinch of dirt.

The Antichrist will arrive on the scene as a charismatic man who will emerge from the European continent. His skill at negotiating a peace pact with Israel and at earning the admiration of the world will be breathtaking and unsurpassed.

After the two witnesses of the tribulation are killed by the Antichrist and then experience a miraculous resurrection, the last of the seven trumpets will sound precipitating the outpouring of the seven bowls of judgment of God's wrath.

In this passage, we are given a glimpse of the crowning of Jesus in heaven. The remaining inhabitants on earth will continue in stiff-necked opposition to the reign of Christ while heaven will shout for joy!

Greater intensity of divine judgment seems to result in greater expressions of resistance on earth. There will be rage on earth yet rejoicing in heaven. There will be cursing on earth yet crowning in heaven. John wrote in 11: 14-19,

> *The second woe is past; and, behold, the third woe cometh quickly. And the seventh angel sounded; and there were great voices in heaven, saying, 'The kingdoms of this world are become the kingdoms of our Lord, and of his Christ; and he shall reign for ever and ever'. And the four and twenty elders, which sat before God on their seats, fell upon their faces, and worshipped God, saying, 'We give thee thanks, O Lord God Almighty, which art, and wast, and art to come; because thou hast taken to thee thy great power, and has reigned.' And the nations were angry, and thy wrath is come, and the time of the dead, that they should be judged, and that thou shouldest give reward unto thy servants the prophets, and to the saints, and them that fear thy name, small and great; and shouldest destroy them which destroy the earth. And the temple of God was opened in heaven, and there was seen in his temple the ark of his testament; and there were lightnings, and voices, and thunderings, and an earthquake, and great hail.*

This prophetically significant passage refers to the third great war to impact the world. Jesus will make his dramatic entrance at the Battle of Armageddon (Revelation 19:11). Revelation chapters 12 and 19 are companion passages and describe the same events (see 19:11-21). This climatic moment will occur immediately prior to the return of Jesus on a white horse as depicted in Revelation 19.

The Rule of Satan Ends

The declaration of Christ's reign described in the regal language of 11:15 has found a second home in Handel's *Messiah* that continues to be sung across the hemisphere. This declaration of His rule will be *wonderful news* in heaven.

Prior to this momentous event, the kingdoms of this world will have not been in subjection to God except in the sense that God has always imposed predetermined limits on the activity of Satan. Scripture refers to Satan as the one in whose power the *"whole world lieth in wickedness"* (I John 5:19). One quick glance at the havoc and heartache in this world at any given moment indicates the evil hand of Satan steadily at work. His demonic beings influence governments to perpetrate evil upon mankind and to tempt men with a variety of sins. Yet God has a plan to obliterate any remaining vestiges of Satan's handiwork.

As Jesus is crowned in heaven in this scene, Satan will lose his fangs. Heaven will erupt in unending applause. Politicians have made valiant efforts to achieve peace and utopia on earth yet have failed miserably.

In many ways, education has produced smarter criminals. Prosperity has resulted only in a greater hunger for material possessions. When Jesus comes and is crowned as the ultimate Lord, all of our needs will be met. Satan is on a leash and his time is short.

The reign of Jesus will be perpetual. A favorite passage related to the Christmas season indicates that there will no end to His government and kingdom (Isaiah 9: 6-7). At His return, He will bind Satan for an initial period of one thousand years in order to demonstrate to man that peace will not occur unless divine shackles are clamped tightly binding Satan's hands. In the end, Satan ultimately will be tossed in the *lake of fire.*

Conversely, the crowning of Jesus will be *woeful news* on earth. Terrible judgments to occur in the time frame between the crowning of the king in heaven and the crowning of the king on earth will further enrage the inhabitants of the earth. Those judgments are discussed in Revelation 12-19.

The Rule of Jesus Begins

The hosts of heaven will *acknowledge His titles.* All focus will be upon the royalty and majesty of our Lord (11:17). Titles such as *"Almighty"* suggest his majesty and power. He has and always will define and sustain eternity.

They will also *acknowledge His triumphs.* John prophesied in 11:18 that the nations will be *"angry."* In our day, the nations of the world such as Bosnia, Iraq, and Ireland could certainly be viewed as angry. Yet the anger of the nations in the tribulation as the ultimate and final rule of Jesus commences will cause the current evil of international anger to pale in significance. The nature of man demands control and the loss of such control motivates internal resistance. The hardening of the heart makes a man deaf to the Spirit of God.

Heaven will also *acknowledge His timing.* The retribution or wrath of God will commence on His prophetic timetable. Two primary words for *wrath* are utilized in the Greek language. *Orge* refers to a sudden explosion of emotion. *Thumos*, the Greek root of our word thermometer, is used to describe an anger that is slow to develop. As the surging waters of anger reach the dam, they spill over with great force. The anger of God to be poured onto mankind is the latter type. God's wrath has accumulated through the ages. When it surfaces in the tribulation, it will do so with great force.

Renowned atheist Robert Ingersoll made a handsome sum of money in the nineteenth century giving lectures on the subject, *There is No God.* He was fond of challenging God to strike him dead and waited sixty seconds during his lectures for God to act. One brave fellow stood and noted that the patience of God could certainly not be exhausted in sixty seconds given His patience throughout history. Ingersoll, and all other rebels who have rejected the grace of God in their lifetimes, will experience the sure and sudden wrath of God.

Accompanying this time of retribution will be the judgment of the unsaved dead. This frightening scene of God's sure wrath is further described in 20:11-13 and is commonly known as the *Great*

White Throne Judgment. In contrast, a full reward to the servants of God will also be presented by the Lord to groups such as *"prophets, and to the saints, and them that fear thy name, small and great…"* (11:18b). No child of God who has given a cup of cold water in His name will be left with no reward.

Last, the inhabitants of heaven will *acknowledge His temple.* In this magnificent vision, John laid his eyes on the temple of heaven. As the final state of eternity begins and the new heavens and new earth make their appearance, no temple other than his heavenly one will be needed. The pattern of the tabernacle in the Old Testament delineated to Moses by God was a prototype of the original one existing throughout the ages in the chambers of heaven. John saw the temple opened and the ark appear.

It is important to note that in the Jewish temple on earth, the outer courts alone were open to the Jews. The high priest alone was allowed access in the inner chambers of the Holy of Holies. However, Christ eliminated that restriction with His death on the cross. As believers in heaven, we have full access to the presence of God and in heaven will be eyewitnesses to the full expression of His character and nature.

The Ark of the Covenant in Heaven

In John's vision, we read of the opening of this holy area in heaven. John caught an astonishing glimpse of the *"ark of his testament"* (11:19). I do not believe, however, that this ark in John's vision is the ark that Moses built for the Israelites of the Old Testament. The Ark of the Covenant of the Israelites preceded them in battle and gave spiritual guidance to them in their wilderness wanderings. It signified to them the presence of God.

The original Ark of the Covenant in heaven became visible to John's naked eye. John saw judgment emanating from it. To the Jews, the Ark of the Covenant represented the place where God met man. On top of the ark was the mercy seat on which the blood of the lamb was sprinkled as an act of atonement for the sins of man. In this scene to come, the people of this world who have rejected the blood of the Lamb as payment for sin will experience the awful and unrelenting wrath of God.

I believe that Jesus took His own precious blood and presented it in the Holy of Holies in heaven. This historical event is critical to God's plan of redemption for mankind. From that ark has come salvation, blessing, and forgiveness to those who believe and receive it. For those with hearts of stone and void of God's grace, John saw the wrath of God coming from the ark.

From this temple in heaven, John was eyewitness to the flashes of lightning that illuminated the skies, peals of thunder that rattled the heavens, and to a frightening and torrential hailstorm. Such cataclysmic events are symbolic of the judgment to be unleashed in full force (11:19).

To those who have rejected God's free gift of grace, there will be no place to hide!

Chapter 27

ISRAEL: THE RADIANT WOMAN
Revelation 12: 1-6

During the 2001 Christmas season, movie fans were treated to the first installment of the cinematic adaptation of J.R.R. Tolkien's classic series of novels, *The Lord of the Rings*. Rich with imagery and packed with battle scenes between the forces of good and evil, Tolkien's masterpiece is reminiscent of the imagery employed by John to describe the radiant woman and her adversary in Revelation 12.

Readers of this particular section of Revelation must be reminded that the Church will have vacated the earth in the rapture. John's writings refer to God's dealings with the nation of Israel and the covenant He established with the nation.

God had firmly promised that the One on the throne of David would rule throughout the ages. Isaiah 9: 6-7 indicates that there is One coming who will rule, and that His government and kingdom shall never end. God gave the Messiah through the medium of the Jews. This same Jesus will come again in power in the Battle of Armageddon.

Concerning the appearance of the radiant woman and her adversary Satan, John wrote these words in 12: 1-6,

> *And there appeared a great wonder in heaven; a woman clothed with the sun, and the moon under her feet, and upon her head a crown of twelve stars: And she being with child cried, travailing in birth, and pained to be delivered. And there appeared another wonder in heaven; and behold a great red dragon, having seven heads and ten horns, and seven crowns upon his heads. And his tail drew the third part of the stars of heaven, and did cast them to the earth: and the dragon stood before the woman which was ready to be delivered, for to devour her child as soon as it was born. And she brought forth a man child, who was to rule all nations with a rod of iron: and her*

> *child was caught up unto God, and to his throne. And the woman fled into the wilderness, where she hath a place prepared of God, that they should feed her there a thousand two hundred and threescore days.*

Who is this Woman?

Bible students through the ages have sought to identify this woman in John's vision. What is the message of this woman described as clothed with the sun and the moon at her feet? What is her relationship with the dragon?

Some conclude that she is the virgin Mary because she is seen as the mother of the man-child. This radiant woman, however, travels into the wilderness away *"from the face of the serpent"* to enjoy the supernatural protection of God (12:14b). The virgin Mary died a natural physical death and was taken to heaven. This radiant woman is not Mary. John is describing an event yet to occur.

Second, others believe the radiant woman represents the Church since the Church is known as the bride of Christ. This theory proposes that because the Church at the time of John's writing was suffering under the foot of the Roman government, the red dragon must assuredly be Rome. Yet this woman is not the Church since she is seen here giving birth to Christ. The Church did not give birth to Christ; Christ gave birth to the Church making this notion invalid.

Further, others propose that the radiant woman represents a false cult of which she is a leader. To be sure, many cult groups throughout history have had women as their leaders. In Revelation, women either symbolize that which is pure and wholesome or quite the opposite. Yet the radiant woman of chapter twelve is not a mere cult leader. This woman is pictured giving birth, traveling into the wilderness, and receiving divine protection. I believe that careful and studious study leads to a definite conclusion concerning her identity.

The Radiant Woman: The Nation of Israel

I believe that this radiant woman in John's vision is none other than the nation of Israel. The extensive use of symbols in this passage is amazingly similar to those used in the famous Old Testament story of Joseph who was sold into slavery in Egypt by his wicked brothers. Genesis 37:9 records, *"(Joseph) dreamed yet another dream, and told it to his brethren, and said, 'Behold, I have dreamed a dream more; and, behold, the sun and the moon and the eleven stars made obeisance to mw."* In his dream, Joseph envisioned eleven stars only. Joseph himself was the twelfth star. This vision represented God's promise that Joseph would one day occupy a position of national influence. After years of estrangement, his poverty-stricken brothers would find themselves in Joseph's presence in the royal court of Egypt and bow down to him in recognition of his authority.

Symbolically, the sun represents Jacob, the father of Joseph. The moon is representative of the mother of Joseph and the stars signify his brothers who were the progenitors of the twelve tribes of Israel.

Second, an additional reason this radiant woman represents Israel is due to the covenant of God with Abraham that He would create a great nation and would do so through the lineage of Abraham. In Genesis 15:5, God promised Abraham that his descendants would be like *"the stars"*, underscoring the glorious destiny of Israel. John wrote in 12:2 of this radiant woman, *"She being with child cried, travailing in birth."* I believe that this reference points to the suffering of Israel throughout history in order to become the nation through which the Messiah would be born.

The Suffering of Israel

Israel has suffered severely throughout her history. John wrote in 12:3a, *"There appeared another wonder."* In the Greek text, the word *wonder* refers to a sign or an absolute and unmistakable message from God. John described the cause of her suffering as, *"a great red dragon, having seven heads and ten horns, and seven crowns upon his heads"* (12:3b). This red dragon is wicked Satan himself. Satan's intense disdain for Israel throughout her history has been well documented. Graphically described in John's vision of these future tribulation events, Satan's hatred will surface once again.

This *"red dragon"* is sinister in nature. The color red denotes his heart of war and propensity for bloodshed. One of the four horsemen of the apocalypse that John saw in his vision was riding a red horse. This red dragon will declare war on the radiant woman, Israel. With seven heads, signifying completion, Satan is not of mere ordinary intelligence but rather is a superior being. The seven crowns on his head indicate great wisdom and significant power and authority.

The *"ten horns"* symbolize the Roman Empire that exercised full political control at the time of John's writing. The Jews suffered severely under the heel of Rome. They were obligated to pay both Jewish and Roman taxes placing them under severe financial distress.

At the outset of the tribulation era, the Antichrist will assume the leadership of a ten-nation confederacy uniting the most powerful nations of the hemisphere. From that vantage point, he will wield incredible power. Currently, the power of Satan is held in check by the presence of the Holy Spirit in the lives of believers. Yet when the Church is removed from the earth, that element of restraint will vanish giving full opportunity for Satan to rule and reign.

This red dragon identified as Satan also has surrogates to do his bidding. I believe that the stars of this passage represent angelic hosts. John wrote in 12:4, *"And his tail drew the third part of the stars of heaven, and did cast them to the earth."* A third of these angelic *"stars of heaven"* were entrapped by the tail of Satan and thrown to the earth. I believe that this incredible feat refers to the origination of Satan, called Lucifer meaning *light bearer* (Isaiah 14: 12), and to his demon emissaries who were fallen angels (II Peter 2:4). Satan is depicted as the most intelligent and shining angel of the hosts of heaven. Ezekiel 28: 12-17 indicates that he was incredibly beautiful and attracted the admiration of others with his charisma. Yet in his rebellion against God and under the intoxicating influence of self-love, Satan fell from his lofty perch.

John described the activity of the red dragon in 12:4, *"The dragon stood before the woman which was ready to be delivered, for to devour her child as soon as it was born."* The course of suffering began in Genesis 3:14-19. As soon as man sinned in the *garden*, God offered salvation to him. Pointing His finger at Satan, God said in Genesis 3: 15, *"I will put enmity between thee and the woman, and between thy seed and her seed; it shalt bruise thy head, and thou shalt bruise his heel."* This is a clear reference to the cross of Jesus. Jesus was the seed of woman. He had an earthly mother yet no human father. He was the seed of woman yet not the seed of man. The Holy Spirit was His supernatural father.

As Jesus breathed His last breath on the cross, He delivered an eternal deathblow to Satan. In so doing, Jesus crushed his head and was wounded for our transgressions and suffered the bruising of His heel.

Satan and Israel

Why does Satan possess such an intense hatred for Israel? Satan has known forever that to obliterate the nation of Israel would circumvent the birth of the Messiah. If successful in aborting the birth of Jesus through Israel, Satan would avoid his coming demise in the *lake of fire.*

Numerous examples of Satan's hatred for Israel decorate the pages of history. Israel suffered greatly under the tyrannical hand of Pharaoh for four hundred years. At the time of the birth of Moses, the wicked Pharaoh attempted to kill all of the male babies in Israel. In the book of Esther, the King of Persia was tricked into signing an edict ordering the extermination of the Jewish people. Had it not been for the bold intervention of Esther who was of Jewish origin, the nation of Israel would have been decimated. Again, Satan was the mastermind of this plot to destroy Israel.

In recent years, the Soviet Union has experienced a surge in anti-Semitism. More than seven hundred thousand Jews have vacated the former Soviet Union and returned home to their homelands of Israel during the 1990's. Jeremiah spoke of the time promised by God when Israel will speak not of their deliverance from Egypt but rather from the *north country*. I believe that this country from the north is the former Soviet Union.

The enemies of one of the most powerful leaders who served in the Soviet Parliament discovered that he was half Jewish in ethnicity. He had successfully concealed his Jewish origin knowing full well the persecution he would endure. Should he choose to do so, such a charismatic leader could become the savior of many Jews in Russia. Any serious bible student must consider the future prophetic role of such a powerful leader.

In addition, the Jews were savagely driven from Spain during the Inquisition of 1492. In World War II, German ruler Hitler instigated the obliteration of almost eight million Jews. Some political pundits doubt the existence of this Jewish holocaust and consider it to be a mere deception. Travel with me to Israel and I will escort you to the Holocaust museum featuring lampshades constructed from Jewish flesh and introduce you to the showers that housed huge masses of Jews who were annihilated with poisonous gasses. Any lingering hint of doubt as to the grim reality of the Holocaust will soon fade away. It is quite obvious that hatred for the Jews fuels this plot to deny the holocaust.

Satan hates Israel because the nation spells his doom. In spite of his powers, the doom to come for Satan will be swift and sure. His days are numbered and his leash will become more taunt as the horrifying days of the tribulation unfold.

Jesus: The Man-Child

This man-child born to the radiant woman in John's vision is the Lord Jesus Himself. Revelation 12: 4-5 is an accurate summary of the life of Jesus in capsule form.

This radiant woman of John's vision *"brought forth a man child"* (12:5). The seed mentioned in 12:17 is identical to the seed of Genesis 3:15 meaning Christ the Messiah. Satan could not harm Him yet throughout history his representatives have tried in vain to do so. As king of Judea, Herod issued an order to kill all male

Israelite babies two years of age and younger. He reacted with intense anger as he became painfully aware of the future rule of Jesus as the King of the Jews. To order such an atrocity in the death of thousands of babies certainly indicates the influence of Satan. Yet Satan could not *harm* Jesus as He was under divine protection.

Satan will forever be unable to *halt* the ministry of Jesus as well. John describes the baby born to the radiant woman as destined to rule with a *"rod of iron."* The Greek word *"rule"* in this context refers to the act of shepherding and indicates genuine tenderness and care for the needs of a flock.

In addition, Satan was unable and forever will be unable to *hinder* Jesus. In 12:6, John wrote, *"The woman fled into the wilderness, where she hath a place prepared of God, that they should feed her..."* This era of protection for Israel will span three and a half years, the last half of the tribulation period. This reference is to the activity of the tribulation when the Antichrist will abruptly turn against the nation of Israel. He will cast aside all reverence for the rebuilt temple and commit what Jesus referred to as the *abomination of desolation* (Matthew 24: 15). Essentially, the Antichrist will order the worship of himself.

Israel in the Tribulation

God will provide an impenetrable blanket of protection for Israel in the tribulation. He will have prepared a place of security for this *"radiant woman"* so that she will escape destruction at the hand of Satan, the red dragon. The location where Israel will be afforded this divine protection is undisclosed although much speculation abounds. Some claim that Petra, or modern Jordan, the city of the Edomites, will provide security for the Israelites. Petra is a city carved from stone and would provide unique protection. Whatever the place of protection for Israel may be, God has promised to *"feed her"* and meet her every need.

Today, most of Israel does not depend upon God but rather upon the United States or the United Nations to provide her protection. Today in Israel, it is not uncommon for an Israeli to refer to their nation as the fifty-first state of the union indicating deep admiration for the United States.

The merchants in Israel all accept personal checks and credit cards. Israel gladly welcomes the spending of American money since the economic viability of this tiny nation is dependent upon America to a significant degree. The day will come, however, when the United States will not exist to protect Israel. Israel will struggle under the domineering heavy hand of the Antichrist. In that day, Israel will be forced to trust God. One of the reasons that the Bible promised in the end that *all Israel shall be saved*, referring to the Jews of the last days, is that God will allow the degree of their desperation to escalate dramatically (Romans 11: 26). As a result, Israel will beg for a Savior.

Jesus will be ready and patiently waiting for that day.

Chapter 28

A BIOGRAPHY OF SATAN
Revelation 12: 7-17

The cable network known as C-SPAN recently featured an interview with a foreign dignity on the campus of Howard University. This guest was spitting hatred for the Jewish nation and blaming the Jews for the difficulties experienced by his native country. He detailed his version of Jewish crimes inflicted against his country throughout history.

The Jews have forever been the recipients of much hatred in the world. In recent years, Germany has experienced a surge in neo-Nazism and its accompanying hatred for the Jews. In America we have witnessed a recent rise in anti-Semitism and the proliferation of the Aryan Supremacy movement and other such bigoted groups. Hatred for the Jews, and others as well, continues to be in vogue.

The acts of murder committed and ridicule spewed against the Jews throughout history will pale in comparison to the onslaught of persecution to which they will be subjected when Satan unleashes another round of assault in the tribulation. Concerning this war in heaven John recorded these frightening yet consoling words in 12: 7-17,

> *And there was war in heaven: Michael and his angels fought against the dragon; and the dragon fought and his angels, And prevailed not; neither was their place found any more in heaven. And the great dragon was cast out, that old serpent, called the Devil, and Satan, which deceiveth the whole world; he was cast out into the earth, and his angels were cast out with him. And I heard a loud voice saying in heaven, 'Now is come salvation, and strength, and the kingdom of our God, and the power of his Christ: for the accuser of our brethren is cast down, which accused them before our God day and night.' And they overcame him by the blood of the Lamb, and by the word*

of their testimony; and they loved not their lives unto the death. Therefore, rejoice, ye heavens, and ye that dwell in them. Woe to the inhabitants of the earth and of the sea! for the devil is come down unto you, having great wrath, because he knoweth that he hath but a short time. And when the dragon saw that he was cast unto the earth, he persecuted the woman which brought forth the man child. And to the woman were given two wings of a great eagle, that she might fly into the wilderness, into her place, where she is nourished for a time, and times, and half a time, from the face of the serpent. And the serpent cast out of his mouth water as a flood after the woman, that he might cause her to be carried away of the flood. And the earth helped the woman, and the earth opened her mouth, and swallowed up the flood which the dragon cast out of his mouth. And the dragon was wroth with the woman, and went to make war with the remnant of her seed, which keep the commandments of God, and have the testimony of Jesus Christ.

War in Heaven

The players in this heavenly war will be Michael and his angels in conflict with the dragon and his demonic cohorts. Michael has been designated in the scriptures as Israel's guardian angel and the general of the armies of heaven (Daniel 10).

On numerous occasions throughout history, God has intervened on Israel's behalf. For example, as a pagan enemy advanced against King Jehoshaphat, the choir was sent to lead the battle with weapons of praise. God intervened and confused the enemy leading to a victory for the Israelites.

The phrase, *"the dragon… and his angels"*, refers to Satan and his angelic army (12:9). Originally, Satan the dragon had been cast out of heaven and away from the presence of God due to his desire for acclaim. In short, he loves to be loved. He claimed a third of the angelic hosts as his following when he departed the gates of heaven. He became the *"prince of the power of the air,"* the arena of his rule described as above the earth (Ephesians 2:2).

In this tribulation scene to come, Michael the archangel will do battle with the forces of the dragon. The conflict will be fierce yet Israel will be protected.

The Three Titles of Satan

Satan is described by John as that *"old serpent,"* referring to a being that radiates with brilliance and possesses the ability to transform himself into an angel of light by which to confuse others (II Corinthians 11:14). As an angel of light, Satan hoodwinked Eve in the Genesis story of the Garden of Eden. Satan is incomparably beautiful yet possesses the black heart of a serpent. Serpents move in a covert and subtle fashion by slithering and have the ability to see others in their path before they themselves are detected. Satan is equally clever and often unrecognizable yet his work in deceiving men is effective indeed.

Second, Satan is known as the *"Devil"* (12:9). Some biblical translators have capitalized his title to emphasize his diabolical and slanderous nature. He functions as the *"accuser of the brethren"* and did so in his harassment and punitive actions against a God-fearing man named Job (12:10). As Satan slandered the character of Job in accusing him of following God only for personal gain, Satan continues today to accuse, defraud, and tempt us to turn against our Lord. Unfortunately, his ploy is often effective.

Further, Satan is often seen in scripture as an adversary. The etymology of the name Satan is rooted in biblical language descriptive of an adversary. He delights in his adversarial role against God, the Church, the nation of Israel, and the purposes of God in the world in offering grace and redemption to fallen man.

The apostle Peter identified Satan very well as *"a roaring lion, walking about seeking whom he may devour"* (I Peter 5:8). He pounces upon weak or wounded prey in moments of weakness when our defenses are inadequate. He looks for vulnerable moments of weak links in our spiritual armor. He delights in heaping coals of condemnation upon the head of a Christian who continues to punish himself for sins already confessed and thrown into the sea of God's forgetfulness. He is the great deceiver, indeed.

Satan Banned

In this war in heaven in John's vision, a great proclamation concerning the banning of Satan from the presence of God was given (12:10). Before this episode in heaven occurs resulting in the banning of Satan, Satan will have enjoyed access before God and some level of ability to harass men such as Job. In this war described in John's vision, Satan will be eternally banned and completely lose his privileged position as the accuser of God's people.

In place of the former emphasis upon Satan's accusations and his acts of condemnation against the saints, God will refocus the emphasis to the victories in Christ that all believers possess. John wrote of this impending demise of Satan's influence, *"salvation, and strength, and the kingdom of our God, and the power of his Christ; for the accuser of our brethren is cast down…"* (12:10).

The Secret to Defeating Satan

One major intention of this passage regarding the ultimate defeat of Satan is to instruct us today as to how we may resist and repel Satan's advances toward us as believers. If this supernatural defense will be effective in that future day of increased satanic wrath, surely it will be effective in our day as well. As saints, we are able to *"overcome"* Satan by the blood of the Lamb on the cross (12:11). As Satan launches his attacks against us, we must learn to appropriate the blood of Jesus and remind Satan that he is a defeated foe on a short leash. We have been cleansed from the very sins by which Satan desires to enslave us once again.

Second, believers today may defeat Satan and thwart his advances by our *confession* (12:11). The *"word of their testimony"* is a phrase describing the sum total of the blessings of God given to believers who have received Him (12:11). To receive the grace of Christ is to simultaneously receive His promises of forgiveness and the power of the Spirit within. Satan must not be allowed to denigrate the blessings of God and convince us as believers that we are perpetually worthless as fallen men. One helpful practice is to substitute one's own name in scriptures that refer to God's promises to us. For example, *"I know whom I (Stan) have believed, and (I) am persuaded that He is able to keep that which I (Stan) have committed unto Him against that day"* (II Timothy 1:12). Are you a follower of Jesus? If so, the promises of God are in your spiritual portfolio to stay. Live life with that assurance!

In addition, believers today may defeat Satan by our *commitment.* John wrote in 12:11, *"They loved not their lives unto the death."* Individuals who are converted to faith in Christ during the painful days of the tribulation will refuse the *mark of the beast.* These new converts in the tribulation will lose their lives as martyrs due to their refusal to obey the demands of the Antichrist.

Those of us who are willing to lose our lives for Christ leave no arena of our lives for Satan to infiltrate. A committed believer is Satan's worst nightmare!

In our day, we may never be asked to give our lives for Jesus yet our Lord does expect His children to live for His glory. The question is whether we will stand for Him in this day of religious pluralism and amidst the proliferation of paganism in our society. For a person whose life is totally given to the things of God, Satan has no territory in which to stake a claim. The apostle Paul stated that he was *"crucified with Christ: nevertheless I live; yet not I, but Christ liveth in me: and the life I now live in the flesh, I live by the faith of the Son of God"* (Galatians 2:20). Essentially, we exchange the ownership of our lives for the experience of allowing Christ to live His life through us.

Satan's Swan Song

John wrote in 12:12, *"Woe to the inhabitants of the earth and of the sea! for the devil is come down unto you, having great wrath, because he knoweth that he hath but a short time."* Notice the *time* factor involved in these words. Even though Satan knows of his coming defeat, he will fight against the purposes of God all the more. He is well aware of the Battle of Armageddon and of his coming demise yet he is not thwarted in his efforts in the least.

In the climactic days of the tribulation, Satan will increase his efforts against the earth and against Israel. To draw a contrast of the fierce and unrelenting efforts of Satan with the feeble efforts of the Church of today is a convicting. As the Church, we are well aware that the window of opportunity to share Jesus with the world continues to close, yet we carry on like the Laodicean church in a state of mundane and often lifeless spirituality.

Satan will assemble all of the artillery of hell and launch a ferocious attack against the angel Michael and his heavenly forces. His ultimate target is Israel and he will spare no expense to achieve his evil goal. Then and now, Satan knows no boundaries except those imposed by his Master.

John also wrote of the *tribulation* to fall upon Satan as well. In 12:13 he wrote, *"The dragon saw that he was cast unto the earth."* Satan will be cast down and confined to the earth itself. In that moment, the tribulation era will be like no other era of time. Satan will rage against Israel, described in the scriptures as the radiant woman, and will attempt to afflict her with relentless pain and anguish yet his confinement will be near.

Satan will be thrown down and will hear the cold shackles of divine confinement snap into place. In a desperate flurry, Satan will unleash unprecedented attacks upon Israel. With unrelenting attacks and a heart full of hate, Satan will see his attempts ultimately fail.

The Destiny of Israel

Israel has perpetually been an object of God's admiration and love. The scriptures detail His unique love for Israel in a number of passages.

> *For the Lord's portion is his people; Jacob is the lot of his inheritance. He found him in a desert land, and in the waste howling wilderness; he led him about, he instructed him, he kept him as the apple of his eye* (Deuteronomy 32: 9-10).

> *As an eagle stirreth up her nest, fluttereth over her young, spreadeth abroad her wings, taketh them, beareth them on her wings: so the*

> *Lord alone did lead him, and there was no strange god with him* (Deuteronomy 32: 11).
>
> *To the woman were given two wings of a great eagle, that she might fly into the wilderness, into her place, where she is nourished for a time, and times, and half a time* (Revelation 12:14).

Notice the similarity of the symbolism utilized in these Old Testament passages written hundreds of years before John's vision was recorded during his stay on the Island of Patmos.

A supernatural cover of divine protection will blanket Israel during the last half of the tribulation. Satan will have incarnated himself as the ultimate one-world leader and will muster an unprecedented assault against Israel. In Matthew 24:22, Jesus informed us that this wicked assault will be limited or shortened in duration *"for the elect's sake,"* a reference to His love for Israel.

On numerous occasions, I have been asked questions concerning the role of the United States in these prophetic events to come. Some observers have noted that the symbol of America is the bald eagle, noting the strength and regal nature of our country. It has been well documented that America has been an eternal friend to Israel. The mighty wings of the United States have provided covering for Israel during times of great duress. I believe that to associate the symbol of America with John's words concerning the *"great eagle"* is a stretch and may overstep the bounds of acceptable hermeneutics yet God may choose to deploy the United States to provide protection to Israel during Satan's final assault against the Jews. By any and all means of His choosing, God will spread His wings of security over Israel. Satan will not be pleased.

In 12:15, John also wrote of the *triumph* of Israel. Satan will attempt to *"cause her (Israel) to be carried away."* Satan will use any and all means possible to obliterate Israel in a flood of persecution. In a miraculous display of protection, God will cause the earth to swallow these attacks keeping Israel out of harm's way. Some observers of these prophecies suggest that this reference to the opening of the earth implies an underground shelter to protect Israel, particularly designed for Jewish people converted to faith in Christ during the tribulation. Some bible students also propose that the location of this miraculous protection may be the ancient city of Petra, a city hewn from solid rock and seen as impenetrable. In any event, Israel will rest in security.

As the venom of Satan continues to spew against Israel, the Battle of Armageddon will loom near. The thunder of hoof prints announcing the coming war will increase in volume. John wrote, *"And the dragon was wroth with the woman, and went to make war with the remnant of her seed"* (12:17). Only the intervention of the Lord Himself will save Israel from certain destruction.

Satan is subtle and clever. His wrath never rests. Believers forgiven by the blood of Jesus on the cross and empowered by the Spirit have nothing to fear.

Satan roams about - but his leash is short!

Chapter 29

WHEN SATAN MONITORS THE WORLD
Revelation 13: 1-10

On the heels of the intense effort of Satan to destroy Israel will come the emergence of the Antichrist. His dramatic appearance will occur at the mid-point of the tribulation era and span the time commonly known as the *Great Tribulation.*

The Antichrist will emerge as a beast from the sea and will assume the unchallenged position as the last dictator of the world. His ability to persuade the masses with his charisma and oratorical ability will be reminiscent of Hitler's extended rallies in which he whipped his fanatical followers into a frenzied state and duped them into giving their very souls to pursue his evil goals.

Technological Wonders in Use

In 13:16-18, we read of the diabolical method of the Antichrist to control the world by monitoring human movement. Our current generation is the first to possess the necessary advanced technology to accomplish such a feat. Privacy during this intense period of global surveillance will be hard to find. The intrusive spirit of *big brother* will be hard at work.

Perhaps the watchful eye of the Antichrist will accomplish this global surveillance by use of a monstrous computer. The most advanced computer system in the world is reportedly in use in Brussels, Belgium. Many affectionately refer to it as *The Beast.* Technological wonders such as this are symbolic of the level of technology that will be necessary to accomplish the wicked and intrusive goals of the Antichrist. Many biblical observers believe that this process will involve the recording of a personal history and a number for each human being with the prefix *666.* Individuals not receiving such a number, the *mark of the beast*, may be unable to engage in trade, find employment, or enjoy healthcare. As a result of such isolation, many will die.

Concerning the sudden emergence of this beast, John wrote these terrifying words in 13: 1-10,

> *And I stood upon the sand of the sea, and saw a beast rise up out of the sea, having seven heads and ten horns, and upon his horns ten crowns, and upon his heads the name of blasphemy. And the beast which I saw was like unto a leopard, and his feet were as the feet of a bear, and his mouth as the mouth of a lion: and the dragon gave him his power, and his seat, and great authority. And I saw one of his heads as it were wounded to death; and his deadly wound was healed: and all the world wondered after the beast. And they worshipped the dragon which gave power unto the beast: and they worshipped the beast, saying, 'Who is like unto the beast? Who is able to make war with him?' And there was given unto him a mouth speaking great things and blasphemies; and power was given unto him to continue forty and two months. And he opened his mouth in blasphemy against God, to blaspheme his name, and his tabernacle, and them that dwell in heaven. And it was given unto him to make war with the saints, and to overcome them: and power was given him over all kindreds, and tongues, and nations. And all that dwell upon the earth shall worship him, whose names are not written in the book of life of the Lamb slain from the foundation of the world. If any man hath an ear, let him hear. He that leadeth into captivity shall go into captivity; he that killeth with the sword must be killed with the sword. Here is the patience and the faith of the saints.*

The Appearance of the Beast

In Revelation 5, we read of the little book in the hand of God that will be the title deed to the earth. No one was found capable of opening the book to reveal its contents except the Lamb, the Lord Himself.

The beast to arise from the waters of the ocean was portrayed by John in glaring contrast with the Lamb. The character and nature of the beast are the antithesis of our Lord. One is the man of salvation; the other is the man of sin. One is the deliverer while the other is the deceiver. Throughout history, Satan has attempted to duplicate the works of God and gain a personal following. Reformation leader Martin Luther referred to Satan as the *ape of God* due to Satan's desire to imitate God's work.

Antichrist the beast will emerge from the sea. The scriptures often picture the foreboding seas as symbolic of trouble. Isaiah uttered the phrase, *"the wicked are like the troubled seas"* (57:20). The movement of the oceans is often symbolic of unrest in the world. In this coming day of political corruption, turmoil, and emotional chaos, this global leader will emerge from the sea in dramatic fashion and will quickly gain a loyal following.

The Analogy of the Beast

The seas also represent the troubled nations and peoples of the world. In 17:15 John wrote, *"The waters which thou sawest, where the whore sitteth, are peoples, and multitudes, and nations, and tongues."*

This beast to appear will be a man with bodily form and appearance. John envisioned this man as possessing seven heads that represent the Roman Empire, according to many scholars. At the time of John's writing, the Roman Empire centered in Rome, a city whose landscape featured seven magnificent hills. Caesar was a historical figure similar in some ways to the Antichrist. Caesar demanded allegiance to his rule and was intoxicated with power. The Antichrist also will possess unsurpassed brilliance and knowledge yet his thirst for divine power will prove to be a deadly liability.

The *"ten horns"* of the beast are indicative of ten nations or ten kings. Revelation 17:12 predicts this coming seat of power, *"The ten horns which thou sawest are ten kings, which have received no kingdom as yet; but receive power as kings one hour with the beast."* The political skill of the Antichrist will enable him to assemble this ten-nation coalition from which he will govern the world. The horns of the beast signify power and authority while his *"ten crowns"* represent his unchallenged reign of terror. His global rule will be unprecedented in scope. The mouths of the adoring public will be agape in wonder and awe.

The Source of the AntiChrist's Authority

John wrote in 13:2b, *"The dragon gave him his power, and his seat."* The Greek word *seat* in this context refers to a throne or position of power. Recorded in Matthew 4 is an episode in which Satan tempted Jesus with the gift of the kingdoms of the world in return for Jesus' willingness to bow before Satan in an act of worship. In a similar manner, I believe that Satan will make an offer to the Antichrist that he cannot refuse. Jesus refused such an offer yet the Antichrist will leap at the chance to rule the kingdoms of this world.

The corrupted character of the beast and the dragon will be so intimately intertwined that their very beings will be merged into one. The beast will inculcate and personify evil in glaring contrast to the righteousness of our Lord. The peoples of this world will fall to him like willing prey volunteering for a snare.

The Strength of the AntiChrist's Authority

Characteristic of the entire book, John once again employed animal metaphors to describe the amazing strength of the Antichrist. The three animals of John's description are representative of the three great empires of the past that are also mentioned in Daniel 7.

First, the Antichrist will possess the *swiftness* of a leopard. The leopard has breathtaking speed and ability to pursue and overtake his prey. With leopard-like quickness, the Antichrist will emerge from the sea and seize control of the world. The leopard also is known as the symbol of the Grecian Empire. One of its leaders, Alexander the Great, conquered all of the known world at the young age of thirty-two. In short, the Antichrist will move swiftly into power.

John's analogy in this passage associates these past world empires with the coming empire of the Antichrist. He will embody all of the unique characteristics of these past empires that dominated the world in their day. John wrote in 13:2, *"His feet were as the feet of a bear."* Renown for his incredible *strength*, a bear is capable of subduing his adversary with one fell swoop of his paw.

This bear is representative of the Medes and the Persians, an empire that handily defeated the Babylonians.

The Antichrist will also possess the *superiority* of the lion. The roar of the Antichrist announcing his authority to the world will be unmistakable. This lion symbolizes Babylon of old and underscores the exalted status of the Antichrist when he assumes global rule.

The Adoration of the Beast

Human nature is easily swayed. Madison Avenue and Hollywood alike are adept in motivating an unsuspecting public to purchase any product or trend they choose to promote. I chuckle when I see the ongoing influence of President Ronald Reagan whose taste in dress suits is reflected in Congress even in our day. Even a few Democrats have followed suit, no pun intended! We flipped our hair like Elvis and expose our midsections like Britney Spears. Humans are a susceptible lot, indeed.

The oratorical and persuasive abilities of the Antichrist in the tribulation will cause the best techniques of the advertising world to pale in comparison. The apostle Paul wrote of this skill in II Thessalonians 2:9, *"Even him, whose coming is after the working of Satan with all power and signs and lying wonders."* All of us can readily name a politician or two with the ability to lie and smile simultaneously. As they do, the public often emits a collective yawn in disinterest.

The ability of the Antichrist to sell a bill of miraculous goods to the public in the form of supernatural *"signs"* will be breathtaking. The miracles that he performs before the adoring eyes of the world will be authentic yet demonic at their root.

Perhaps the Antichrist will claim to be virgin born in an attempt to duplicate Christ and therefore motivate the masses to bestow deity upon him instead. Nothing will please him more than to be viewed as the Messiah himself.

It appears that he will also attempt to duplicate the resurrection of Jesus Christ. John wrote in 13:3, *"And I saw one of his heads as it were wounded to death; and his deadly wound was healed: and all the world wondered after the beast."* The display of awe to be heaped upon the Antichrist will delight him to no end. Perhaps he will experience the wounding of one of his heads as a result of an assassination. He will appear dead yet will miraculously resurrect giving his credibility and status an enormous boost in the eyes of an adoring and sympathetic world.

The political platform on which the Antichrist will promote his cause will be world peace. Daniel 8:25a refers to this, *"And through his policy also he shall cause craft to prosper in his hand; and he shall magnify himself in his heart, and by peace (he) shall destroy many."* In that day, the hunger in the world for even a sliver of peace will cause the world to bow to the authority of the Antichrist. Coming under a guise of peace, he will bring death to many. In our day, any unrest in the world quickly captures the attention of the United Nations. These world rulers quickly attempt to snuff out any unrest that appears. Such a hunger for peace at any cost will naturally play into the deceiving hands of the Antichrist.

The Abomination of the Beast

The Antichrist will also emerge preaching a doctrine of change. Armed with amazing communication skills and charisma, he will offer security and hope to a degree never before imagined. John wrote in 13:5, *"There was given unto him a mouth speaking great things."* His ideas will be fresh and innovative. His rise to power will be swift and his rule will span three and a half years. A gullible public will follow his every whim and desire.

The Antichrist will display utter disdain for God and will *"blaspheme against God."* To blaspheme against our Lord is to mimic the act of Satan when he claimed before his fall from heaven that he would be *like the most high God.* He craved the worship reserved only for God Himself and therefore mounted a coup against God. The Antichrist will come to defy God and to claim the privileges of deity for his own personal benefit. He will arrogantly display himself in the temple in Jerusalem and proclaim himself as God. Matthew 24 and the prophet Daniel refer to this evil and dastardly act as the *abomination of desolation.*

Essentially, he will make Israel desolate and desperate and will persuade Israel to follow him by promising hope and security. He will completely defy the God of Israel with arrogance and contempt. In so doing, he will reveal his true identity.

In his wrath, the Antichrist will destroy the saints of the tribulation. John wrote in 13:7, *"[He will] make war with the saints, and to overcome them."* Further in John's vision we learn that people refusing to accept the *mark of the beast* will die as martyrs.

In addition, he will blaspheme and heap ridicule upon the tabernacle of God and all that God is. He also will hurl barbs of accusation and condemnation to the saints who are in heaven. All of his evil deeds will be performed in the name of religion. He will be the ultimate wolf in the clothing of a sheep.

The Antichrist will also dominate the nations of the world by wielding unrelenting power. In 13:7 we read, *"Power was given him over all kindreds, and tongues, and nations."* With ease he will delude the masses and blind them to the truth. All of the ones whose names are not written in the *book of life* will give fanatical allegiance to him. This book bears the names of every person who has been converted to faith in Christ and those who will do so in the future. It also records the names of those accepting Christ during the tribulation experience.

Ears That Hear?

In 13: 9 we read, *"If any man have an ear, let him hear."* Notice the deliberate distinction of these closing words with those that close the messages to the seven churches recorded in Revelation 2-3. I believe that the Spirit wants us to understand that the Church will not be present at the time the beast rises from the sea to establish his evil reign. In Revelation 2-3, John's words are directed *"unto the churches,"* a phrase strikingly absent from these words regarding the beast.

The phrase in 13:9, *"if any man have an ear"* surely refers to those who unwisely continue in rejection of God's grace and merely hope for the best in the world to come or who arrogantly deny the reality of any state of existence after their earthly deaths occur. Such a denial of any future state of existence is commonly known as *annihilation,* the notion that man merely reverts to the dust at his death. For some, the academic mindset prevalent in our day often leads to a denial of the reality of the supernatural, a major stumbling block to simple faith in Christ.

Revelation 13:10 is a simple prophecy concerning the coming demise of the Antichrist. John wrote, *"He that leadeth into captivity shall go into captivity."* With one short phrase, John reveals to us that the tables of destiny will turn and the Antichrist will experience imprisonment himself. In fact, Revelation 20 reminds us that he will be bound in the *bottomless pit* for a millennium, one thousand years.

Ultimately, Satan will meet his demise in the Battle of Armageddon looming on the horizon.

Take hope. I've read the last page. We win!

Chapter 30

WHEN YOUR MONEY FAILS YOU
Revelation 13: 11-18

Not only will one beast burst upon the prophetic scene but a second beast also will appear portrayed by John as arriving from *out of the earth*, signifying his demonic nature. Perhaps no prophetic event in all of John's writings strikes greater fear in the minds of readers than this event to come.

I recently read an interesting interpretation concerning these demonic beasts in light of current events. The prophet Daniel wrote about the Antichrist who will promise peace but deliver war to the world. Daniel 7: 3-6 records,

> *And four great beasts came up from the sea, diverse one from another. The first was like a lion, and had eagle's wings: I beheld till the wings thereof were plucked, and it was lifted up from the earth, and made stand upon the feet as a man, and a man's heart was given to it. And behold another beast, a second, like to a bear, and it raised up itself on one side, and it had three ribs in the mouth of it between the teeth of it; and they said thus unto it, 'Arise, devour much flesh.' After this I beheld, and lo another, like a leopard, which had upon the back of it four wings of a fowl; the beast had also four heads, and dominion was given to it.*

John's symbolic use of animals in Revelation 13 is very similar to these words of Daniel written hundreds of years prior to John's island exile. In this interesting interpretation, the lion represents Great Britain. The bear indicates Russia whose national symbol is the bear. The leopard is representative of the Greek Empire. This view also proposes that the ten-horned beast of Daniel 7:7 is the one-world government to be ruled by the Antichrist.

In Daniel 7:4, we read that the lion featured the wings of an eagle. Some interpret this passage intending to reflect the founding of the United States as it emerged from Great Britain. Is the United States mentioned in the Bible as involved in prophetic events? I believe that it is.

In any event, the beasts to invade the earth will whip the world into submission and may use modern advancements in technology to do so. Unlike the first beast who will arise from the sea, this second beast will emerge from the land. In 13: 11-18 John recorded this facet of his amazing vision,

> *And I beheld another beast coming up out of the earth; and he had two horns like a lamb, and he spake as a dragon. And he exerciseth all the power of the first beast before him, and causeth the earth and them which dwell therein to worship the first beast, whose deadly wound was healed. And he doeth great wonders, so that he maketh fire come down from heaven on the earth in the sight of men, and deceiveth them that dwell on the earth by the means of those miracles which he had power to do in the sight of the beast; saying to them that dwell on the earth, that they should make an image to the beast, which had the wound by a sword, and did live. And he had power to give life unto the image of the beast, that the image of the beast should both speak, and cause that as many as would not worship the image of the beast should be killed. And he causeth all, both small and great, rich and poor, free and bond, to receive a mark in their right hand, or in their foreheads; And that no man might buy or sell, save he that had the mark, or the name of the beast, or the number of his name. Here is wisdom. Let him that hath understanding count the number of the beast; for it is the number of a man; and his number is Six hundred threescore and six.*

A Second Beast: The False Prophet

Satan the dragon energized the first beast with power, thus enabling the Antichrist to pursue his wicked schemes. This second beast to appear from out of the earth will be empowered by precisely the same source, Satan himself. This second beast to appear will be the False Prophet whose purpose is to enforce the worship of the Antichrist.

In Revelation, we are introduced to the *unholy trinity*. In an effort to mimic God and claim a full measure of deity for himself, Satan will be disguised as a dragon, and later as the first and second beasts. This dragon is the evil counterpart of God the Father; the first beast is the counterpart to the Son; and the second beast is the antithesis of the Holy Spirit, an interesting concept we will pursue later in our study.

A Servant of Satan

The place of origin of the second beast, *"out of the earth,"* is seen by some scholars to refer to the land of Israel, the land of promise. Some biblical observers propose that he will be Jewish in origin and will abruptly turn against the God of his fathers.

Revelation 13:11 indicates that he will possess *"two horns like a lamb."* At first glance, a gentle lamb featuring two horns seems to be contradictory at best because lambs are known to be harmless, meek, and mild. Claiming to promote peace, this False Prophet will be a *goat* in disguise and will dupe the world into worshipping the Antichrist. Those failing to to worship him will be the recipients of his vicious wrath.

A Worker of Worship

In this terrible era of persecution to come, the False Prophet will work to ensure that the Antichrist receives his full measure of worship. At this juncture, the one-world church and one-world government will rule with an iron hand. At the outset of 2002, many nations of the world are heralding the acceptance of the euro, a measure of currency now readily used in a multitude of countries thus economically uniting many nations of the world.

This second beast will head the one-world church. In the Gospel of John, we read that the primary function of the Holy Spirit is to point attention to Jesus Himself (John 16: 13-14). The Spirit does not crave worship but rather deflects worship to the Lord. Believers in our day who focus their primary affections on the Holy Spirit to the detriment of God the Father and the Lord have distorted the biblical view of the Trinity. This second beast, the antithesis of the third person of the Trinity, will point to the Antichrist as the appropriate object of the world's worship. Forced worship will be employed to achieve the evil goals of the Antichrist.

Churches will continue to function in the tribulation. Satan has never been afraid of churches that are not comprised of Spirit-filled followers of Jesus Christ. He has cleverly manipulated religion throughout the ages to accomplish his diabolical schemes. Many cults and false creeds of our day have their root in Satan's world.

The intoxicating power of religion will organize the world into a one-world governing state. The church and the world system in this horrible day to come will be inseparable. The merger of church and state will be complete with no apparent distinction between the two establishments.

The church of the tribulation will promote the state in a manner reminiscent of the days of the Roman ruler Constantine who declared Christian baptism to be necessary and politically correct. Constantine issued such a degree to enhance his own rule. In a vision, he saw the words, *"In this sign, conquer."* Sadly, the masses submitted to the waters of baptism yet knew nothing of the power of Jesus within them. In a similar way, the False Prophet will manipulate the practice of worship for the personal gain of the Antichrist, Satan himself.

A Master of Magic

Revelation 13:13-14 predicts that the False Prophet will be gifted in working *"wonders."* These wonders to be performed will be yet another form of deception for a gullible world. In a dramatic show of power, he will make *"fire come down from heaven on the earth in the sight of men."*

In our day, many who claim to perform miracles do not lack for a crowd. It often appears that the offerings in the plate grow in proportion to the level of miraculous display. Human nature has forever had an insatiable hunger to experience the supernatural. Master showman P.T. Barnum of Barnum and Bailey Circus fame made a fortune tapping into the curious inner cravings of the heart of man. Please understand that our Lord is a God of miracles and does perform them in the lives of believers today yet God does not take pleasure at the manipulation of the supernatural for personal gain.

From the outset of creation, God has allowed Satan to operate within a certain realm of power. Not until Satan is shackled for a thousand years in the *bottomless pit* and cast into the *lake of fire* for eternity will his power be canceled. He operates only within God's allowable parameters.

The False Prophet will continue in that vein and will be allowed by God to send a strong and effective delusion to the remainder of mankind on the earth. Such a vivid display of demonic power impressive to the masses will further enable the False Prophet to enforce the worship of the Antichrist.

The False Prophet will cause the image of the beast to speak and will give *"life unto the image of the beast"* (13:15). One Greek word for life is *Zoë* from which we derive our English word zoology or to the act of birth. In this text, another word for life was employed by John to refer to the "animation" of the beast. Words will come from his mouth and give evidence of real life. I believe that this may indicate a prophecy of television considering that the scripture requires that all of the world see this event. How else will the world see?

An enormous worship gathering of unprecedented proportions will occur. John wrote in 13:15, *"and cause that as many as would not worship the image of the beast should be killed."* New technology in our day allows for two-way conversations including both audio and video communication. As we speak we may simultaneously watch one another, a sobering thought indeed. It seems safe to assume that such advancement may serve to motivate improvements in our personal hygiene and dress! I mean, who wants to be seen as sloppy?

It appears that the Antichrist will monitor this worship event and will see to the deaths of those who choose not to participate. Perhaps people coming to faith in Christ in the tribulation will be hunted down and destroyed by demonic patrols.

Such fine-tuned technology will allow for the monitoring of all individuals who will find no place to hide.

In the prophecy of Daniel, we read that the pagan king constructed an image and commanded the people to bow down before it in worship. Those refusing to bow the knee were tossed into a flaming furnace. This event in Daniel's day was a foreshadowing of the event to unfold at the command of the false prophet. Just as the Hebrew children Shadrach, Meshack, and Abednego were tossed into the flames to die, people refusing to worship the Antichrist will experience the fierce trials of the tribulation era. Yet as the Hebrew children escaped the fiery furnace, the hand of our Lord will safely lead children out of the tribulation and into the gates of heaven.

A Controller of Commerce

Revelation 13:16-18 describes the evil methods that the Antichrist will use to control the economy of the world. Money as we know it will not be in use. Only those in possession of a number will be allowed to engage in trade or commerce. The tribulation government may issue a number to each person on earth and thereby provide for all of the needs of men such as food, healthcare, and the means to conduct trade. This socialistic system will be forced upon the people causing those who attempt to circumvent the system to suffer greatly. Healthcare may be denied and those considered to be rebels may be told to return their groceries to the shelves, vacate the premises and never return.

In our day, we are witnesses to this type of system beginning to surface in the form of debit cards, bar codes, and other types of biometrics. The habits and actions of all men will be logged. No movement will go unnoticed under the watchful eyes of this wicked *big brother*.

The Number 666

Six is the number most commonly associated with man. Not by accident, God created man on the sixth day of creation. I am often amused to read of the various interpretations some men pursue in an effort to authoritatively unravel this mystery. Those who do so tend to miss the primary intention of God's use of this number, *666*.

II Thessalonians 2:7-8 teaches that the identity of the Antichrist will not be revealed until the Church has vacated the earth in the great snatching away of the saints. Paul also taught that the One who now restrains, the Holy Spirit in the life of every believer, will be taken out of the way allowing for the emergence of the evil one himself, the Antichrist. Any attempt to identify the Antichrist and remove all mystery is mere speculation. Perhaps he is alive and well today or at least is resting in the shadows of the world scene. Until the rapture of the Church, we will not fully know his identity.

John's phrase in 13:18, *"it is the number of a man"* gives some insight into its meaning. The number seven is the number of perfection. Six is one short of seven indicating that the number of the Antichrist is a reminder that he will never achieve a position of divine perfection and will never achieve his divine goal to steal the worship of God for himself. Try as he might, he will ultimately fail in his mission.

The three numbers, *"666"* also remind us of the *unholy trinity*. Readers should be alerted to John's words reminding us that Satan will disguise himself as a dragon, beast, and the False Prophet. This number represents the highest level of creation that man will ever achieve. Although rejecting this truth with all of his demonic power, Satan will never reach the position of deity he so desperately craves.

The number six also implies perfect imperfection. The Antichrist will be the epitome of the best that man has to offer in terms of human wisdom, strategy, and political skill, all wrapped in a cloak of evil intentions. His measure of wickedness will reach the pinnacle of evil. In that time, wickedness will have reached its ultimate expression.

I believe that this *mark* on the hand or forehead will be achieved by the use of a microchip implanted under the skin. This microchip will allow for scanning in order to monitor purchases and other human activity. Privacy will be no more.

The Bible indicates that the mark of the believer is the Holy Spirit who indwells every believer. We are sealed in security by the mark of the Holy Spirit in our hearts. The apostle Paul assured us, *"The foundation of God standeth sure, having this seal, The Lord knoweth those who are his"* (II Timothy 2:19). In that regard, every believer wears the number seven.

Folk musician Bob Dylan said it well with his tune, *You Gotta' Serve Somebody*. We either serve sin or we serve the Savior.

What about you?

Chapter 31

THE 144,000 IN HEAVEN
Revelation 14: 1-5

The evil deception and anguish to be doled out by the Antichrist and the False Prophet on the earth will grow in magnitude. After describing these awful events to occur upon the earth, the scene of John's vision reverts to heaven where we read of the 144,000 individuals first introduced to us in Revelation 7.

The escalation of evil upon the earth during this era of the tribulation will be in stark contrast to the pure character and faith of these 144,000 followers of Christ who are now in heaven at this point in John's vision. Their tireless efforts to share the gospel message on earth will have been completed.

Concerning this scene of praise in heaven John wrote these words in 14: 1-2,

> *And I looked, and, lo, a Lamb stood on the mount Zion, and with him an hundred forty and four thousand, having his Father's name written in their foreheads. And I heard a voice from heaven, as the voice of many waters, and as the voice of a great thunder: And I heard the voice of harpers harping with their harps: And they sung as it were a new song before the throne, and before the four beasts, and the elders: and no man could learn that song but the hundred and forty and four thousand, which were redeemed from the earth.*

The 144,000 in Praise

Evidently, the location of this scene is the Mount Zion in heaven. What a magnificent site to which John was an eyewitness in his vision. These special servants of God will stand before the throne of God as a vibrant congregation of Jesus' followers and offer their exuberant praises to Him. The sound of their praise will be thunderous. The melodious sound of harps will fill the air with the sweet aroma of praise.

These 144,000 special servants of God during the tribulation will be sealed by God and afforded divine protection. This multitude in John's vision was composed of twelve thousand people from each of the twelve tribes of Israel identified in the Old Testament. This extraordinary moment of praise will be a prelude to the final judgments to come. The praises erupt due in part to the promise of God to bring a swift end to the evil in the world and to establish eternal peace for His children. Wars will cease. Poverty will vanish. Marital heartache will be no more. These new residents of heaven will shout with joy because of God's promise to adjudicate the earth in fairness as well as in divine wrath.

An Exalted Group

John saw this multitude standing on the heavenly Mount Zion with the Lamb of God, our Lord Himself. The entire vision of Revelation is replete with numerous references to the Lamb. The lamb was chosen by God as a means to impart truth about the nature of Jesus and to demonstrate the necessity of a spotless sacrifice for our sins. As the lamb prepared for sacrifice was to have been spotless, Jesus Himself knew no sin and was therefore the spotless Lamb of God. In Revelation 5:6 we read of the crucified Lamb; in 5:8 we read of the glorified Lamb; Revelation 6 refers to the justified Lamb; and in Revelation 7 were are blessed to know of the magnified Lamb of God. Here in John's vision of the 144,000, the Lamb is seen as resurrected and secure on the throne of heaven.

The historical Mount Zion, in the City of David, was the home of the royal palaces occupied by a series of Israelite kings. The Mount Zion to which John referred in 14:1 is the heavenly one as Jesus is yet to descend to the earth once again. He came in the rapture to snatch away the Church yet his feet did not touch the earth. Seven years later at the end of the tribulation era he will descend to the Mount of Olives (cf. Acts 1).

The Mark of God

In his vision, John saw these 144,000 as safe and secure in heaven. Revelation 14:1 reminds us that they will have the *"Father's name written in their foreheads."* As if to counter the *mark of the beast* instituted by Satan, God's mark on these believers in heaven will have been placed on their foreheads for all to see. This divine mark will identify the emotions, cognitive abilities, and entire beings of these 144,000 believers as the property of God Himself.

This unique divine mark of God will protect its recipients from the terror of the Antichrist and enable them to share the claims of Christ for the world to hear during the tribulation era. Revelation 7 records the incredible spiritual revival that will occur as the message of these witnesses finds it mark and changes lives. The Antichrist will experience frustration each time he glares at any one of these believers and knows that the mark of God insulates them from his evil schemes.

In our day, we as believers are sealed with the mark of God, the Holy Spirit. As families *can* vegetables by tightening and sealing the lid of the jar, the Holy Spirit marks or seals the believer in an act of permanent preservation. Our secure state of preservation is not achieved on the basis of our relative measure of goodness but rather on the basis of the work of the Spirit within us.

An Exclusive Group

These Spirit-filled 144,000 worshippers in heaven are exclusive in their *song* in that they sing a new song not understood by others. Only those afforded divine protection will be capable of singing this song of praise. Men and women without the presence of Christ in their hearts simply do not know the *song of the redeemed.*

Psalm 137:4 posed the question, *"How shall we sing the Lord's song in a strange land?"* Those who are not dwelling in the land of the Spirit with Christ indwelling their hearts are simply unable to recognize and participate in the song of redemption. The notes and lyrics of this divine song of membership in the kingdom are foreign and meaningless to those who are without Christ.

Many of us today live with the fact that we are excluded from various clubs and organizations due to our lack of financial or societal qualification. As believers, we belong to the ultimate of all exclusive clubs, as it were, the fellowship of the redeemed. We are children of the King and citizens of heaven! To what other fellowship instead could we more desire to belong?

An Exemplary Group

The *conduct* of this group is a blessing to behold. John wrote in 14:4, *"These are they which were not defiled with women."* I believe that God intends to convey both spiritual and literal fidelity. In the midst of an evil and perverse world, these believers were accurate reflections of the holy God they served. Their images had not been tarnished nor their witness hampered by the stain of sinful living. The scriptures often utilize the metaphor of physical infidelity to portray spiritual unfaithfulness. Later in Revelation 17, we will read of *"Babylon, the mother of all harlots"* referring to the evil world system that has and will seduce the world into unfaithfulness to God. These believers will possess the sterling character that is derived only from the Spirit.

These 144,000 believers were exemplary in their *consecration* as well. John continued in 14:4, *"they which follow the Lamb whithersoever he goeth."* Those of us not following the life and example of Jesus should quickly take inventory of the passions and desires of our hearts. Intellectual ascent to the claims and existence of God falls short and is inadequate to become a devoted follower of Christ. These 144,000 individuals will live the faith without equivocation.

Amazing as well is the *calling* of the 144,000. John described them as *"redeemed from among men, being the firstfruits unto God and to the Lamb"* (14:4b). Although mere men like the rest of humanity, these 144,000 had experienced the full dose of the rejuvenating work of the Holy Spirit in their lives. Salvation is not merely an act of moral improvement but rather a re-creation of the heart in a new condition. John described these believers as *"firstfruits,"* with the prediction that many other converts will soon follow. The masses to be converted to Christ in the midst of the painful tribulation era will be too numerous to count with most, if not all, dying as martyrs during the wicked reign of the Antichrist.

The *conversation* of these 144,000 believers will be exemplary as well. John wrote in 14:5a, *"And in their mouth was found no guile."* John's use of the Greek word for *"guile"* indicates that these believers were not given to bitterness, lies, or harsh talk. James, one of the Jerusalem pastors in the early church, reminds us in his brief letter that the tongue is the most difficult part of the body to control. It has the capability for wickedness or for blessing and is capable of sparking the fires of controversy as a small spark ignited the enormous fires devastating California. In fact, James claimed that the tongue is not capable of being tamed. Only the Holy Spirit at work in us in full measure lassos the tongue for God's glory. In the Old Testament, Solomon reminded us that more personal power is required to control the tongue than to tame a city. These 144,000 believers will know the Holy Spirit in His fullness and speak only words of life and blessing.

Last, John wrote that these believers in his vision will be exemplary in their *character.* It has been well said that reputation is what people believe us to be; character is what God knows us to be. We are what we do in the dark. John wrote in 14:5b concerning these 144,000 believers, *"They are without fault before the throne of God."* Jude, the brother of James, wrote that God is perfectly capable to prevent us from falling away from God and has promised to do so. Further, God will present each of us as believers as faultless before Him. Such a faultless state is not earned by our good deeds or pure thoughts but rather by the blood of Jesus who stands in our place. The hymn writer expressed this promise well,

And when before the throne I stand in Him complete,
Jesus died my soul to save,
My lips shall still repeat,
'Jesus paid it all, all to Him I owe;
Sin had left a crimson stain
He washed it white as snow.

As one fellow quipped, "If we truly got what we deserved, we would all be dead." Our Lord is due all of our gratitude for His willingness to stand in our place.

Chapter 32

FIVE SECONDS AFTER DEATH
Revelation 14: 6-13

News reports often chronicle the graphic out-of-body experiences of individuals who temporarily ceased to exist in this life and traveled to the land beyond death. Descriptions of lights, tunnels, and vast spaces often characterize these vivid portrayals of the immediate moments after death.

Aside from the authenticity of these reports or the lack thereof, there is a land beyond for both believers and unbelievers. Such a supernatural claim is often not welcomed in our academically astute society, yet the scriptures declare this truth in unmistakable language.

In the opening words of Revelation 14, John described for us the blessing to await the 144,000 faithful believers in heaven. In glaring contrast, John's words turn dim as he describes the terrible fate of those who continue in stiff-necked rebellion against the offer of grace from our loving Lord. John wrote in 14: 6-13,

> *And I saw another angel fly in the midst of heaven, having the everlasting gospel to preach unto them that dwell on the earth, and to every nation, and kindred, and tongue, and people. Saying with a loud voice, 'Fear God, and give glory to him; for the hour of his judgment is come: and worship him that made heaven, and earth, and the sea, and the fountains of waters.' And there followed another angel, saying, 'Babylon is fallen, is fallen, that great city, because she made all nations drink of the wine of the wrath of her fornication'. And the third angel followed them, saying with a loud voice, 'If any man worship the beast and his image, and receive his mark in his forehead, or in his hand, the same shall drink of the wine of the wrath of God, which is poured out without mixture into the cup of his indignation; and he shall be tormented with fire and brimstone in the presence of the holy angels, and in the presence of the Lamb: And*

> *the smoke of their torment ascendeth up for ever and ever: and they have no rest day nor night, who worship the beast and his image, and whosoever receiveth the mark of his name.' Here is the patience of the saints: here are they that keep the commandments of God, and the faith of Jesus. And I heard a voice from heaven saying unto me, 'Write, Blessed are the dead which die in the Lord from henceforth: Yea, saith the Spirit, that they may rest from their labours; and their works do follow them.'*

Angelic Preachers

During this era of the tribulation, God will choose to utilize the unprecedented medium of angelic preaching. Throughout history, God has never left Himself without a witness. Even in the darkest of days and in the midst of a proliferation of evil, God has always provided a method to make His name known.

In the tribulation era, he will make full evangelistic use of the two witnesses earlier discussed, the 144,000 Jewish converts, and of these angelic preachers who will issue one last challenge to the rebels on earth to open their hearts to His grace. Deaf ears will respond in silence and with stubbornness of heart.

Heretofore, angels never preached the gospel. At the end of the prison stay of Paul and John, they were instructed by the angels to take the message of the cross into the Jewish temple. These powerful angels were quite capable of preaching yet reminded these men of their divine calling to do so. Perhaps the intense wickedness of this hour in the tribulation will necessitate the use of angelic preachers.

However, the *message* of the gospel delivered by the first angel to appear in this episode must be the correct one. John described the message of the angel as *"everlasting"* and continued to relate the truth of the eternal gospel in capsule form. Essentially, Jesus saves.

The *mandate* of the gospel message will be summarized well by the first angel to mount the pulpit. John wrote in 14:7, *"Fear God, and give glory to him; for the hour of His judgment is come: and worship him that made heaven, and earth, and the sea, and the fountains of waters."*

Essentially, the core of the gospel message requires a *choice* to live our lives in such a way as to communicate reverence to Him. Our lives should allow for God to be the sole recipient of all glory rather than craving attention for ourselves. Second, the gospel requires our *consecration* in that we must worship Him and live for Him under the controlling influence of the Holy Spirit. The spirit of Jesus within us should be our underlying motivation rather than external requirements imposed by man.

Babylon Will Fall

Faith in Christ will carry the believer safely into the courts of heaven. In an obvious contrast, John wrote that a second angel appeared in his vision proclaiming that *"Babylon is fallen, is fallen, that great city"* (14:8a). The biblical usage of the word Babylon is representative of the political, economic, and religious system to be imposed by the Antichrist. The worldview to which the followers of the Antichrist will adhere and give their lives is in diametric opposition to the nature of our Lord. To live for the benefit of self to the denigration and destruction of others is the fruit of Babylon as it invades and corrupts the human psyche. Such corruption is our inheritance from Adam and is only remedied by the cross of Christ alive in us.

Notice that the second angel proclaimed the fall of Babylon with double usage of the word *"fallen."* Perhaps the purpose of such duplication is indicative of the coming fall of religious Babylon depicted in Revelation 17, and of the coming demise of political and economic Babylon detailed in Revelation 18.

In Genesis, Babylon was renowned as the seat of cultic worship. The Tower of Babel was constructed on the geographic location now known as Baghdad, Iraq. Babylon was viewed by the Israelites without exceptional disfavor due to their seventy years of captivity there. Babylon had no concern or respect for Jewish values or beliefs and displayed great disdain for the Jews by destroying the crown jewel of Jewish life, the temple.

In our day, some prophetic observers predict that Babylon may be reconstructed in the same location as its origin and will become the tribulation center for world political and economic power. Regardless of what future location Babylon may assume, Babylon represents false religion and a system that the Antichrist will cleverly utilize in full measure to dupe the masses to follow him.

In Revelation 11, we read that Jerusalem will one day slide further into a state of sin and rebellion. Perhaps the coming epicenter of the rule of the Antichrist will be Jerusalem itself. In that day of full and complete deception, Jerusalem will be the hellish city, indeed. Perhaps the three great religions of the world (i.e. Islam, Judaism, and Christianity) will provide a global display of false unity. Perhaps this great religious conflagration on the area of the temple mound in Jerusalem will further intoxicate the masses with false promises of peace and hope.

The Sins of Babylon

John described the fall of Babylon in these verses in past tense. It is important to note that the predicative accuracy of John's vision is not in question. God promised it and revealed this coming event through the pen of John. Babylon will fall. For what reason will she fall? What are the specific sins of Babylon?

In 14:8b John wrote, *"She made all nations drink of the wine of the wrath of her fornication."* Characteristic of the common biblical use of metaphor, the marriage relationship is once again employed in this passage to discuss spiritual infidelity. The word *fornication* describes the act of emotional and spiritual infidelity that will prevent the nations of the world from receiving the truth of God. The false religion of Babylon will infiltrate the innermost chambers of the hearts of its adherents.

In their intoxication by the false promises of the world system, the masses of the tribulation era will perpetually reject God's offer of grace. Their faith in self-sufficiency will become so comprehensive and pervasive that their eyes and hearts will be blinded to the truth. This dastardly scheme will be the mother of all deceptions. Such blindness to the truth is alive and well in our day also. The spirit of spiritual immorality is an act of arrogance that repels the offer of God's grace in the hardened heart of man.

Revelation 13 is a clear warning that the effectiveness of the Antichrist to deceive the world will be so incredible that the response of the masses will be one of *wonder*. No charlatan in history possessed even a fraction of the deceptive skill the Antichrist will use with ease. The wrath of God will be applied in full force to those hardened by self-love and deceived by the Antichrist.

Punishment for Sinners

A third angel in John's vision appeared and provided for us a clear picture of the two distinct destinies facing all men. Revelation 14:9-10 unfolds the nature of these destinies for the reader.

> *And the third angel followed them, saying with a loud voice, 'If any man worship the beast and his image, and receive his mark in his forehead, or in his hand, The same shall drink of the wine of the wrath of God, which is poured out without mixture into the cup of his indignation; and he shall be tormented with fire and brimstone in the presence of the holy angels, and in the presence of the Lamb.'*

These rebels of the tribulation will continue in their rejection of God's *warning*. To take the *mark of the beast* in the tribulation era will cause evil men to inculcate Satan's evil ways and become his partners in crime. In essence, those so doing will adamantly reject the grace Christ offers. Such a bold and blatant refusal will be tantamount to the unpardonable sin of speaking against the testimony and word of the Spirit.

As a result, these hard-hearted rebels will become the unfortunate recipients of God's *wrath*, a wrath metaphorically described by John in 14:10 as *"wine."* As wine ages, its quality reaches full potential. In a similar manner, the wrath of God has been aging throughout history and will explode upon the scene in this tribulation episode. The *"cup of his indignation"* will pour out the full measure of His wrath upon evil men.

This divine wrath will also be applied *"without mixture"* (14:10). In our day of grace, God's compassion often results in an application of His grace in moments when our wicked behavior actually warrants a full dose of punishment. In the tribulation day to come, His wrath will not be tempered with any shred of grace whatsoever but rather will be composed of pure and unrestrained wrath. Hurricanes and other geological upheavals often mysteriously allow certain buildings to remain standing in an act of saving grace. In God's day of wrath to come, no one refusing His offer of grace will survive the storm.

John wrote that the recipients of His wrath will experience a torrential flood of fire and brimstone, a clear reference to their eternal confinement in the fires of hell. These evil men, dripping with self-love and arrogant rebellion, will not escape the coming pain of the tribulation and the everlasting flames of hell.

Hell is Real

Jesus provided for us a graphic description of hell as a place where fires are never quenched and the worm never dies. In 14:10-11, we are struck with fear and trembling as we realize that hell is a place of no *relief.* A foul-smelling and fiery torment awaits the unbeliever.

In addition, there will be no *rescue* from hell. John wrote that the Lamb and the holy angels were present in his vision of this incredible scene. Their purpose is not to rescue hardened sinners from the shackles of hell but rather to serve as a vivid reminder to all sinners of their eternal imprisonment in hell.

The parable concerning Lazarus in Luke 16 speaks of a rich rebel who died and entered the gates of hell. The rich unbeliever is pictured in hell as within eyesight of *Abraham's bosom* and fully aware of the divine blessing he had missed. One intention of the parable, and of John's words in 14:10-11, is to underscore the reality of hell. Those rejecting God's offer of grace will be well aware of the glory of the Lord they will never know.

Hell is also a destiny of no *reprieve.* John wrote in 14:11a, *"And the smoke of their torment ascendeth up for ever and ever."* This torment to afflict unbelievers will continue into eternity. The pain will never reach a conclusion. Similar terminology is employed in the scriptures to designate the length of our stay in heaven as well. Logically, let alone biblically, to believe in the unending duration of heaven also requires any thinking person to believe that hell also will span the same length of time. Neither destiny will ever come to an end.

The lowering of the physical body in the grave is not the final resting place of believers or unbelievers. Believers will rejoice for the rest of eternity in the fellowship of one another and in the presence of our Lord. The stay of unbelievers in hell will be filled with terror, *"they will have no rest day nor night"* (14:11). How could any thinking individual, aware of this astounding truth, reject God's grace?

Patience Rewarded

In contrast to the painful confinement of unbelievers, John wrote that believers will reap great blessings. Revelation 14:12 records, *"Here is the patience of the saints. Here are they that keep the commandments of God, and the faith of Jesus."* Faithful believers in our day realize that we are mere aliens living in this temporary world. The city of heaven in which we long to reside has a foundation whose builder and maker is God Himself. As the gospel hymn reminds us, we are *looking for that city.*

John's words do not imply that our ticket to heaven is earned or acquired by obeying the commandments of God. Conversely, those who truly know Christ in their hearts are possessed by an inner motivation to please our Lord by following His every wish and desire. John also wrote that the sheer knowledge that our earthly enemies will reap their just punishment ought to be further motivation for God's children to persevere.

People in Heaven

A familiar phrase often heard at the funeral service of a faithful Christian is taken from 14:13. The minister often encourages us with the words, *"Blessed are the dead which die in the Lord…"* (14:13). What do we know without a doubt about the state of Christians we love who pass away? What conscious experiences do dead believers have five seconds after death?

First, our fellow Christians who have died are *rejoicing.* John wrote in 14:13 that believers in heaven will be *"blessed",* indicating a position of high favor. Some cult groups, such as the Jehovah's Witnesses, propose that the body merely enters the grave at death and remains there. What kind of blessing is that? Annihilation, or the cessation of all existence, certainly is not a form of blessing! The truth is that believers who die with Christ residing in their hearts will erupt in heaven with continual joy. What a truth that is to value and share!

Believers in this heavenly state of existence will also enjoy a life of *resting.* John inscribed this incredible truth from the Holy Spirit and indicated that we will be at rest from *"our labours"* (14:13). This form of rest does not refer to the cessation of activity but rather indicates a state of welcomed rejuvenation.

After serving the Lord in the local church with the forty-year mark in sight, I will gladly welcome a bit of rest and rejuvenation! More than mere sleep, John wrote that our compassionate Lord has promised a perpetual state of euphoria and joy. What a day that will be when my Jesus I will see!

Last, believers in heaven will be handsomely *rewarded.* John wrote in 14:13, *"their works do follow them."* The memories of our love for Jesus, our acts of compassion, and our words of influence that have blessed others will continue to have an impact even after we pass away. In this regard, our deeds done for the glory of our Lord will continue to accrue eternal interest in the hearts of others in spite of our physical absence.

Death is both a bitter and sweet moment yet our Lord waits with open arms to welcome us into our eternal home.

Chapter 33

A PREVIEW OF ARMAGEDDON
Revelation 14: 14-20

Following closely on the heels of John's vision of the 144,000 Jewish converts and of a glimpse into heaven and hell alike, John also has provided for us a brief preview of the coming Battle of Armageddon. This unprecedented war will pit the forces of evil against the forces of Jesus Christ.

This portion of the vision details the coming harvest of judgment upon the earth. Throughout history, Satan has faithfully sown the seeds of evil in the hearts of mankind. Such a harvest one day will be subjected to the razor-sharp sickle of God's wrath.

Those who have sown seeds of rebellion against the grace of Jesus and who will accept the *mark of the beast* in the tribulation will face God's wrath in full force. Concerning this coming prophetic battle, John wrote these frightening words in 14:14-20,

> *And I looked, and behold a white cloud, and upon the cloud one sat like unto the Son of man, having on his head a golden crown, and in his hand a sharp sickle. And another angel came out of the temple, crying with a loud voice to him that sat on the cloud, 'Thrust in thy sickle, and reap: for the time is come for thee to reap; for the harvest of the earth is ripe.' And he that sat on the cloud thrust in his sickle on the earth; and the earth was reaped. And another angel came out of the temple which is in heaven, he also having a sharp sickle. And another angel came out from the altar, which had power over fire; and cried with a loud cry to him that had the sharp sickle, saying, 'Thrust in thy sharp sickle, and gather the clusters of the vine of the earth; for her grapes are fully ripe.' And the angel thrust in his sickle into the earth, and gathered the vine of the earth, and cast it into the great winepress of the wrath of God. And the winepress was trodden without the city, and blood came out of the winepress, even*

> *unto the horse bridles, by the space of a thousand and six hundred furlongs.*

This graphic description of the coming Battle of Armageddon speaks of carnage so intense that the blood will rise to the level of the horses' bridles. This river of blood will span the length and breadth of the land of Palestine estimated to be two hundred miles.

One of the more profound mysteries of the kingdom of God is the ongoing presence of evil. Why does God not simply erase all evil and allow for a world of complete purity and peaceful existence in all dimensions of our lives? Theologians continue to debate this gnawing issue. To be sure, God allows for the element of freedom of choice in our lives. A predetermined and guaranteed state of nirvana and total righteousness on the earth would eliminate the freedom to choose.

Jesus told a story concerning the coexistence of good and evil and did so with an analogy regarding an agricultural harvest. In this revealing parable in Matthew 13: 24-25 Jesus said,

> *The kingdom of heaven is likened unto a man which sowed good seed in his field: But while men slept, his enemy came and sowed tares among the wheat, and went his way.*

A *tare*, or a darnel is a plant that appears similar to genuine wheat yet is not distinguishable from wheat until the time of harvest. The harvest to which Jesus referred is the coming Battle of Armageddon during which those who have continued in their rejection of Jesus Christ will be gathered and cast into the fires of hell.

Just as tares in the field are gathered and burned, evil men will reap a similar fate. These evil men whose hearts have no room for Christ will suffer the worst of all calamities.

Discerning Wheat From Tares

The reaper of this harvest of judgment will be the Lord Jesus Himself. In his vision, John was an eyewitness to this coming judgment and the One who would adjudicate the deeds of men.

> *And I looked, and behold a white cloud, and upon the cloud one sat like unto the Son of man, having on his head a golden crown, and in his hand a sharp sickle* (14:14).

As Jesus fulfills His role as the *returning Christ*, He will also assume the role of the *reigning Christ.* Wearing a gold crown on His head and seated on a cloud, Jesus will come not as the suffering servant of His time on earth but rather as a mighty God to establish His eternal reign. He will preside as a judge over the harvest of the earth.

He will also come as the *reaping Christ* holding a sharp sickle in His hand. Jesus has existed as the One who has continued to sow the good seeds of righteousness in the hearts of man (Matthew 13:37). His work as a judge also will involve reaping a harvest of evil tares thereby punishing evil men who fully deserve it.

A Ripe Harvest

The events of judgment to come as recorded in Revelation 14 will fulfill the predictions concerning the harvest related by Jesus in the Matthew 13 parable. An angel will appear from the altar in heaven and encourage Jesus to swing his sickle in an act of judgment upon the earth.

> *Another angel came out of the temple, crying with a loud voice to him that sat on the cloud, 'Thrust in thy sickle, and reap; for the time is come for thee to reap; for the harvest of the earth is ripe* (14:15).'

Throughout the ages, the good seeds of Jesus have faithfully produced good fruit. Conversely, the evil seeds of Satan have consistently resulted in evil fruit in the corrupted hearts of evil men.

When the harvest is ripe, tares are gathered and burned in the harvest making way for the harvesting of healthy and pure wheat. Wheat turns darker in color as it ages. In a similar way, the corruption and evil sown in the world by the seeds of Satan are turning brown with sin. These seeds of evil take root and eventually reach full maturity.

Representing the followers of Satan, the tares of this world are progressively turning brown with corruption and will reach an advanced state of evil at which time Jesus will apply the sickle of judgment to them.

Tares grow in a different manner than wheat. Tares grow sturdy and in an upright position. They often develop a fungus that negatively affects the good wheat. In a similar manner, the evil men of this world often attempt to corrupt God's children. In addition, tares ultimately begin to blacken in appearance and become coarse as they age distinguishing them from the pure wheat.

As authentic wheat ripens, the head of its stalk gradually bows toward the ground. At the time of its harvest, it rests in a fully bent position weighted from the fruit of its stalk. Biblically, this ripened stalk is symbolic of the righteous character filling the heart of every genuine believer in Jesus Christ. In addition, wheat dies as it ripens, a process representative of the truth that as a believer matures in his faith he is filled with a growing love for Christ rather than a love for himself. In that regard, young believers are not yet prepared for heaven as the process of maturing has yet to reach its end. God's desire is that we mature and actively express our faith until the time of our harvest into the Master's arms.

A Quick Harvest

This coming harvest of judgment accomplished by the application of God's sickle will occur rapidly. God will separate the chaff from the wheat, bind it into bundles, and burn the worthless chaff of evil men in the perpetual and unquenchable fires of hell. With a few swift swipes of his heavenly sickle, judgment will be handed down in a just and awesome display of His wrath.

The glaring contrast between evil men without Christ and the authentic believers who have righteous hearts, represented by the pure wheat, will be obvious. In this coming day of judgment, the cries of evil men for leniency and reprieve will go unheard. The sickle of God's wrath will be swift and sure.

The Valley of Armageddon

In the first century, wine was made by allowing the grapes of the trees to age for a considerable length of time before harvesting. The grapes were placed in a winepress where workers lifted their robes and stomped on the grapes with their bare feet. A scarlet river of grape juice would result giving us a vivid word picture of the coming judgment.

Another angel will come out of the temple and cry out to the One holding the sickle to *"gather the clusters of the vine,"* again signifying the judgment to be enacted by our Lord (14:18). This judgment will feature a bloody war in which the wounds of men and women will cause blood to flow freely.

The Valley of Armageddon is the most fertile of the lands of Israel. While under Arab and British control, the Valley was essentially swampland. The Israelis discovered that the planting of eucalyptus trees would allow the waters of the valley to be drained thus allowing for full use of the land. Israel planted trees in the valley and discovered the incredible fertility of this land.

Israel's natural resources have blossomed in recent years. Gardens now decorate the landscape and feature golden wheat crops, fields of white cotton, a variety of vegetable plants, and groves of citrus fruits. As Jesus spoke of the harvest in his day, all of his hearers were well aware of the analogy he utilized in his message to them.

The reference of Jesus to vineyards underscoring the coming Battle of Armageddon is quite appropriate as Israel is certainly a nation of healthy vineyards. One of the nation's wines was recently recognized internationally for its excellence.

As the Lord brings evil to judgment in the Battle of Armageddon, the grapes of the vine, representing evil men and the

Antichrist, will be subjected to the winepress of God's wrath. These grapes of evil will have reached a fully ripened state prepared for judgment. The Valley will be transformed into a place of judgment as the armies of the world will assemble and fight against the nation of Israel. This event will truly be a harvest of destruction for evil men.

A Harvest of Evil

In this coming period of judgment, God will gather the *"vine of the earth,"* referring to a gathering of all the evil in the world (14:18). Satan is not a being gifted with original thoughts. He is a mere duplicator of the works of God. God gave to the world the gift of Jesus to reveal Himself and to save man from his inherited sin; Satan will give the Antichrist to the world. God presents the authentic Church comprised of Jesus worshippers; Satan offers a false religion that will produce nothing more than the one-world church comprised of tares posing as pure wheat who worship themselves. God gave the Holy Spirit; Satan will give the False Prophet in another feeble effort to duplicate and counteract the works of God.

This coming judgment by our Lord at the Battle of Armageddon will appropriately punish and expose the false religion established by Satan and will reveal the corrupt nature of all of his claims. At that time, the world will have fully nourished itself on the strength and power of the false vine, Satan himself.

We must be absolutely certain that the vine from which we drink is the true vine of Jesus Christ. It is from the root of that vine that we as believers draw our strength and supernatural power to discern evil and share the gospel. Jesus said in John 15:5, *"I am the vine, ye are the branches; He that abideth in me, and I in him, the same bringeth forth much fruit."* Fruit bearers know where true power may be found.

The Demise of Evil

The presence and mystery of evil in the world will continue to haunt all of us this side of heaven. Evil does exist and even appears to run unabated at times in our world.

Taliban leader Osama bin Laden appeared to accomplish his deadly goals without suffering a commensurate punishment. Innocent children die of cancer. Where is God in all of that? Why do these things occur? Is God retaliating? Is He unconcerned?

The scriptures indicate that when the grapes of the vines of evil are fully ripe, God will intervene and settle the score. This harvesting of evil will occur in the Valley of Megiddo. Demonic forces will gather in the northern reaches of the Valley. Through that same valley have marched a number of the major armies and conquerors of the world such as Napoleon, Charlemagne, Alexander the Great, the Romans, the Syrians, and the fierce Babylonians. In these last days to come, the armies of the Antichrist will assemble in that same region to war against the forces of Jesus Christ (16:14).

Napoleon commented that the Valley of Armageddon is the single most suitable geographical location for battle in the world. Approximately twenty civilizations of yesteryear rested upon this land and met their demise there. Layers of destroyed civilizations are stacked on top of one another in this area.

It is to this Valley that demon spirits will draw the kings of the earth to engage in this final battle. Anticipating this event, our minds often attempt to envision this incredible assembling of missiles, artillery, and millions of soldiers to war against our Lord. Novelists Jerry B. Jenkins and Tim LaHaye have whetted our appetites for these events to come in their blockbuster series of prophetic novels, *Left Behind.*

Changes in Israel

Israel has advanced in recent years in several facets of its existence. The population has swelled to more than four million compared to a population of approximately two million in the late 1980's. More than a million Jews have returned to their homeland from the former Soviet Union. At the moment that immigration was allowed, Jews began returning to Israel in unprecedented numbers and are continuing to do so today.

The prophet Jeremiah foretold of the day that Israel would not speak of her deliverance from bondage in Egypt but rather will talk of her return from the *north country,* identified by scholars as Russia (Jeremiah 23:8, 31:8). That prophecy continues to experience fulfillment in our day.

The continuing struggle with the Arabs concerning ownership of certain tracts of land has exhausted many Israelis who desperately crave an end to the struggle. News of peace treaties between the Israelis and the Palestinians continue to dominate world news reports. In recent years, we were witness to the astonishing handshake between former President Clinton, Palestinian Yasser Arafat, and then Prime Minister Rabin of Israel.

Such overtures of peace will be short-lived, however. At the beginning of 2002, Arafat's headquarters and other Palestinian properties were destroyed by Israeli gunfire as a response to the deaths of many Jewish citizens. Peace between the two nations will continue to be elusive.

Israelis disagree among themselves regarding the current efforts to achieve peace with the Palestinians. I know of a thirty-four year old tour guide, a graduate of Hebrew University in Jerusalem, who is a Jewish patriot. He served in the Israeli armed services as a member of the Special Forces. He worked covertly as an undercover spy in Lebanon, Syria, and Egypt in an effort to gain intelligence information. He is adamantly opposed to the current movement toward peace with Palestine and strongly believes that peaceful coexistence will never be possible.

The Temple Institute in Jerusalem features facsimiles of garments, made according to biblical instructions, for priests to wear in the new Temple yet to be constructed in Jerusalem. This Institute also features many of the artifacts and paraphernalia to be utilized in the reinstitution of the Jewish sacrificial system. The director of the Temple Institute observed that when the Israelis vacated Gaza, over five hundred thousand Jewish citizens protested the move and the treaty with Arafat. News reports listing the crowd at only twenty thousand were inaccurate, according to the Institute director. According to most reports, the Palestinians are unable to control their own countrymen and are certainly not to be considered trustworthy to obey the dictates of a treaty of any kind.

In the Tribulation, the Antichrist will forge a treaty with Israel that will remain in force for three and a half years and then be broken by the Antichrist himself. Current efforts to achieve peace for Israel merely foreshadow this false treaty to be signed during the Tribulation.

Territories previously occupied by Israel have experienced enormous unrest in recent years. Numerous occurrences of pandemonium among Palestinians have led news anchors to predict that no peace treaty will ever be obeyed. In recent years, the Palestinians have experienced severe financial shortages making peace and internal order even more elusive. Unrest seems to be the only predictable forecast for the future.

Syria and Lebanon border Israel on the north. The control of the Golan Heights currently under Israeli rule continues to ignite unrest. This region sports some of the best farmlands Israel has to offer. Residents in this region are in grave danger. Should Syria move in, long-time Israeli settlers will have enemies in their backyards. An Israeli military station on a northern mountain allows Israel to monitor the movement of Syria and Lebanon.

In the middle 1990's, Israel conducted an air raid against Lebanon and successfully destroyed many terrorist camps. The terrorists responded by launching several missiles into the lap of the Golan Heights forcing Israeli residents to scramble into their bomb shelters. Such conflict continues to be a common occurrence for Israel. The control of the Golan Heights is critical for Israel's ongoing security.

Many Jews are much closer today to a belief in Jesus Christ as the Messiah than in recent years. On all of the biblical sites in Israel, the scriptures are read from both the Old and New Testaments. I firmly believe that God is preparing the 144,000 Jewish converts in the land of Israel today to preach during the tribulation. Israeli school curriculum now includes material concerning the life of Jesus Christ as historical fact. Whether they are aware of it or not, to expose individuals to the Word of God is to plant seeds that one day will take root in their hearts.

Our prayer must be that the seeds of the Word of God will take root and lead many in Israel and around the world to faith in Christ. The Battle of Armageddon looms on the horizon.

We must be ready.

Chapter 34

THE CALM BEFORE THE STORM
Revelation 15: 1-8

The far reaches of the Panhandle of Texas and its surrounding flatlands are renowned for the sudden appearance of tornados. Residents often greet one another in the street or front yards of their homes and together look for funnel clouds gathering in the blackened skies. Those of us with tornado experience are well aware that the surroundings become eerie and breathtakingly still during the moments preceding the unleashed fury of a tornado. When quietness grips the skies, head for shelter!

Revelation 15 describes a lull before the final storm of judgment. These final seven judgments, depicted by John as bowl judgments, will underscore the severity of God's wrath that will be unleashed upon mankind in the Great Tribulation. As these judgments unfold in John's vision, we are provided with deeper glimpses into the character and nature of our Lord, and further understand why such retribution must occur. Additionally, the tribulation must occur to allow for the completion of God's dealings with Israel.

In his vision, John looked into heaven and saw another sign; seven angels held the seven plagues in their hands. In Revelation 15: 1-8 John wrote,

> *And I saw another sign in heaven, great and marvelous, seven angels having the seven last plagues: for in them is filled up the wrath of God. And I saw as it were a sea of glass mingled with fire: and them that had gotten the victory over the beast, and over his image, and over his mark, and over the number of his name, stand on the sea of glass, having the harps of God. And they sing the song of Moses the servant of God, and the song of the Lamb, saying, 'Great and marvelous are thy works, Lord God Almighty; just and true are thy ways, thou King of saints. Who shall not fear thee, O Lord,*

> *and glorify thy name? for thou only art holy: for all nations shall come and worship before thee; for thy judgments are made manifest.' And after that I looked, and, behold, the temple of the tabernacle of the testimony in heaven was opened; And the seven angels came out of the temple, having the seven plagues, clothed in pure and white linen, and having their breasts girded with golden girdles. And one of the four beasts gave unto the seven angels seven golden vials full of the wrath of God, who liveth for ever and ever. And the temple was filled with smoke from the glory of God, and from his power; and no man was able to enter into the temple, till the seven plagues of the seven angels were fulfilled.*

Seven Angels and Seven Bowls of Judgment

What an incredible sight! John was introduced to seven mighty and shining angels standing before our Lord who were holding the bowls of the seven last judgments to come. John described this scene as *"great and marvelous"* indicating that this episode to come will be unprecedented in scope and magnitude (15:1).

Both the temple built under Solomon's rule and the tabernacle built by Moses in the wilderness were patterned after the true temple in heaven. The earthly tabernacle housed the revered Ark of the Covenant that spoke of God's covenant and promise to the nation of Israel to bless them. However, such blessings were predicated upon their willingness to obey Him.

John's vision, and the judgments that will ensue ushering in the final Battle of Armageddon, relate to the nation of Israel. As the temple of Solomon was dedicated, the *shekinah* glory of God filled the temple prohibiting the priests from ministering. In response, they fell on their faces before God in an act of humble adoration (I Kings 8:11).

Reminiscent of that scene in Solomon's temple, this moment in John's vision will be unprecedented in the magnitude of its holiness and awesomeness. Revelation 15 and 16 describe two aspects of the same event of judgment to come. Revelation 15 is a mere prelude of the actual events described in Revelation 16. These judgments will occur during the three and a half year era of the Great Tribulation and will produce an unmistakable sense of finality.

The scriptures predict that at the time of His second coming, holy angels will accompany Him in this moment of vengeance. In II Thessalonians 1:7-8 Paul wrote that the angels will come with Jesus Christ *"in flaming fire, taking vengeance on them who know not God...."*

The Finality of the Seven Plagues

Again underscoring the number seven as one of completion, John counted seven plagues in the possession of the angels. At this juncture during the tribulation era, severe punishment and great anguish will have afflicted man. Earthquakes will have shaken the globe, and mountains and islands will have been ripped asunder. Billions of people will have perished due to war, famine, and a variety of diseases. Such carnage will make the debris of nuclear explosions pale in comparison.

These seven plagues to inflict mankind will be the full and complete measure of vengeance delivered by the hands of our Lord. These plagues will involve a variety of physical and geological calamities that will descend upon the earth.

Fifteen hundred years before the time of John's writing, the wicked Egyptian ruler Pharaoh steadfastly refused to allow for the release of the Israelites from forced captivity and labor. God responded by afflicting the Egyptians with terrible plagues. During the tribulation, God's people will once again be the recipients of a great deliverance from persecution. The Antichrist will refuse to cease his retaliation and persecution of God's people resulting in God's retaliation as these seven plagues unfold.

John referred to these plagues to come as the *"last"* to afflict mankind. The word "*last*" is derived from the Greek word *eschatache*, meaning last things and the word for our English theological term eschatology, the study of last things.

The Fullness of the Seven Plagues

As the seven horrendous plagues begin to take effect, the wrath of God will be *"filled,"* meaning fully unleashed (15:1b). As the Holy Spirit continues to fill the heart of the believer, we experience the maturing of our faith. We are to strive for that sense of completion by fully yielding to the Spirit. These plagues will not lack in any dimension. They will accomplish a full and complete exhibition of the wrath of God unleashed upon those who fully deserve it.

Jesus' death on the cross was an act of completion. In his last gasps of breath, he uttered the phrase, *"It is finished."* At that very moment, His plan for redemption was completed. No act of man or additional work of heaven would ever be required for man to enter into fellowship with our Lord other than by His shed blood. The severity of these plagues will leave no room for more. God's wrath will be completely and finally revealed.

God's Limited Patience

The finality and severity of these judgment events to come also suggests that our patient God is a God of limited patience. Obviously, the patience of our Lord significantly exceeds that of our own. No doubt, if any of us were God for a day, many people in this world would suddenly disappear! In contrast, the apostle Peter reminds us that our Lord is *"longsuffering to us-ward, not willing that any should perish"* (II Peter 3:9).

In an honest moment, most of us would be forced to admit that we secretly hope for the demise of some people. Yet even the patience of a patient God has a point of no return.

God truly loved the rebellious people in the day of Noah yet He sent a flood when His patience wore thin. Jesus promised that the judgment of the tribulation would be similar to that which occurred in the days of Noah. His patience reached its end in Noah's day and will do so in the tribulation as well. Consistent with His promise of just wrath, those who deserve the wrath will certainly receive a full dose.

In Revelation 15:2-4 we see a beautiful picture of the saints of God standing in His presence on a sea of glass, reminiscent of a similar scene in 4:6. In reality, this sea of glass may be clear, reflecting still waters. The implication is that our Lord has always been faithful to provide a sense of serenity in our lives even in the moments of greatest chaos. The hymn writer well described this sense of quiet rest for our souls,

There is a place of quiet rest
Near to the heart of God,
A place where sin cannot molest
Near to the heart of God.

At the time of the end of His patience with wicked mankind, our Lord will continue to provide a place of quiet solitude and rest for His children. Safely at rest in His presence, we will continually sing our songs of praise.

The Saints at Rest

John saw the saints of God in heaven standing victoriously on these serene waters. John envisioned the saints of God in heaven standing on a *"sea of glass."* The sea was mingled with fiery flames. The saints are pictured as reveling in their victory over the *"beast"*, the Antichrist himself. The Antichrist believes that he will claim a victory against the saints of God by their death, yet the death of the saints will produce precisely the opposite effect. We will stand in heaven in a state of victory undeterred by physical death.

In earlier chapters, we learned that individuals not accepting the *mark of the beast* will be savagely killed. However, the Antichrist will soon discover that our physical resurrection and our eternal life with Christ will never be subjected to the sting of death.

The victory of the saints over their resistance to the *"mark"* will also be celebrated (15:2). The mark of the Antichrist is one of damnation signifying his desire to take all men to the place of his own eternal damnation. In utter frustration, his last stab at forcing men into eternal damnation will miserably fail. Consistent with his evil nature, Satan will never give up but will suffer permanent confinement in the lake of fire where he will have nothing to sing about!

The Saints Will Sing

Singing has long been the primary choice and method of the saints whereby we worship. It releases the accumulation of joy welled up within our souls. The exuberance in our hearts finds physical expression in song.

These saints in heaven in John's vision will sing a two-fold song. In 15:3 John wrote, *"They sing the song of Moses the servant of God, and the song of the Lamb."* The Red Sea, an integral facet of the exodus from Egypt under the leadership of the reluctant Moses, is a classical example of Old Testament typology. The Red Sea, although a literal body of water, represents a type of judgment and tribulation upon the world. The armies of Pharaoh were destroyed by the encompassing waters of the Red Sea abruptly ending their pursuit of the Israelites. God's people were spared and they erupted into a song of deliverance from their bondage in Egypt. In like manner, the saints of God resting on this sea of glass in heaven will sing a song of praise for their deliverance from the clutches of the Antichrist.

Their successful victory over the schemes of the Antichrist will be secured by the *blood of the Lamb.* Their song of praise will contain phrases similar to our stalwart tune, *"How Great Thou Art"*. In the midst of this service of praise, the saints will not question the Lord regarding His lack of intervention in the painful moments of our lives while on earth. Our sole purpose will be to shower the Lord with continual praise. They will readily admit, *"just and true are thy ways"* (15:3b).

The reasons motivating the saints to sing praises to the Lord will include His indescribable *virtue.* They will continually say concerning the Lord, *"Thou only art holy"* (15:4). The prime attribute of God is His inherent holiness and in Him is no flaw of any kind. His justice is based upon His unsurpassed perfection and holy character. In that regard, sin must be punished and hell is a necessary destiny for those who stand in direct opposition to His holy nature.

These heavenly saints will also lift up praises due to God's *victory.* A host of nations will be represented in the New Jerusalem, the heavenly city. In that day, every knee will bow in humble recognition that Jesus truly is the Lord. The Antichrist will attempt to steal that title and its accompanying recognition yet will fail miserably in the end. In spite of his global success in duping the masses to pledge support of his dastardly schemes, he will fall in defeat. At this moment in the tribulation, the sum totality of the things of the earth will recognize the final and ultimate Lordship of Jesus Christ over all things.

The praises of the saints will also be motivated by the application of God's *vengeance.* John wrote, *"thy judgments are made manifest,"* indicating the actual fulfillment of His promise to apply harsh judgment upon the unbelieving world (15:46). If for a moment, any of us could be exposed to the comprehensive nature of evil in its fully developed state, we would better understand God's decision to respond with a full measure of wrath.

These heavenly saints will have been eyewitnesses to much evil, including their own deaths at the vicious hand of the Antichrist, and will praise God that the Antichrist soon will be eternally bound. Evil will be overthrown. The Battle of Armageddon will be Custer's Last Stand for the Antichrist as he will be bound for one thousand years before mounting one final unsuccessful revolt. The arrows of God's wrath will find their intended target.

In a concluding thought, John wrote in 15:7, *"One of the four beasts gave unto the seven angels seven golden vials full of the wrath of God."* These four beasts are indicative of all of creation. The creation continues to yearn for redemption in anticipation of its final restoration and the reclaiming of the earth for the glory of God.

As if silenced by the announcement of these coming plagues, the temple in heaven will be temporarily closed, so to speak. Concerning this heavenly suspension of activity, John wrote in 15:8, *"No man was able to enter into the temple till the seven plagues of the seven angels were fulfilled."*

All of the inhabitants of heaven will watch in stone-faced silence and with great anticipation as the final seven judgments invade the earth with blinding speed.

Children of God, rejoice. Unbelievers, beware!

Chapter 35

THE WAR OF ALL WARS
Revelation 16: 1-11

The surprise attack by the nation of Japan on Pearl Harbor, Hawaii on December 7, 1941 left an indelible legacy of carnage in its wake. The war was brought to an abrupt conclusion by the dropping of an American atomic bomb on Hiroshima leaving indescribable destruction in its path. The leveling of the Twin Towers in New York City by al Qaeda terrorists on September 11, 2001 took the lives of thousands of people and cost billions of dollars to remove the rubble and compensate the families of the victims.

As devastating as were these international tragedies, the coming Battle of Armageddon and its accompanying plagues will wreak even greater havoc in an unprecedented fashion. No man alive in that day will question the divine source of this painful judgment.

The ongoing instability within our world and constant pleas for peace remind us of the biblical predictions that the end of this age will occur in a moment of presumed peace. The republics that emerged from the fall of the former Soviet Union continue to operate with unstable economies and leaders inexperienced in capitalism and democratic rule. North Korea continues to pursue nuclear weaponry and is a country held firmly in the grip of Communism and totalitarianism.

When the Iron Curtain fell in Germany, many former Communist countries adopted democratic forms of government motivating world leaders to hail the emergence of world peace. As the world clamors for peace, the last great battle upon the face of the earth continues to loom on the horizon.

As the Bible unveils the intense and devastating nature of the last seven bowls of judgment to come, we are struck with the fact that the scriptures are not always palatable to our modern tastes. Such an outpouring of wrath causes many modern readers to question the true character of a loving God who would afflict such pain. Yet to underscore His holiness, His divine wrath upon sin must be applied.

Revelation 16 focuses upon the suffering of individuals as these bowl judgments are applied. Dominion over the world, a privilege lost by man and captured by the clever schemes of Satan, will be returned to our Lord in this climactic episode. Seven bowl judgments will precede this final battle. Concerning these horrendous judgments John wrote in 16: 1-11,

> *And I heard a great voice out of the temple saying to the seven angels, 'Go your ways, and pour out the vials of the wrath of God upon the earth.' And the first went, and poured out his vial upon the earth; and there fell a noisome and grievous sore upon the men which had the mark of the beast, and upon them which worshipped his image. And the second angel poured out his vial upon the sea; and it became as the blood of a dead man: and every living soul died in the sea. And the third angel poured out his vial upon the rivers and fountains of waters; and they became blood. And I heard the angel of the waters say, 'Thou art righteous, O Lord, which art, and wast, and shalt be, because thou hast judged thus. For they have shed the blood of saints and prophets, and thou hast given them blood to drink; for they are worthy.' And I heard another out of the altar say, 'Even so, Lord God Almighty, true and righteous are thy judgments.' And the fourth angel poured out his vial upon the sun; and power was given unto him to scorch men with fire. And men were scorched with great heat, and blasphemed the name of God, which hath power over these plagues: and they repented not to give him glory. And the fifth angel poured out his vial upon the seat of the beast; and his kingdom was full of darkness; and they gnawed their tongues for pain, And blasphemed the God of heaven because of their pains and their sores, and repented not of their deeds.*

At this climactic moment, the remaining inhabitants of the earth will have steadfastly rejected the mercy of God leaving no alternative except for wrath to occur. The wrath of God will be applied in appropriate measure. The saints of God who refuse the *mark of the beast* will be savagely murdered at the hands of the Antichrist. Their innocent blood will have flowed freely in the streets. Evil men contaminated by the Antichrist will be worthy to drink from the cup of God's wrath.

These seven angels will serve as the emissaries of God to distribute His wrath. The plagues to come are reminiscent of the plagues by which God punished the Egyptian ruler Pharaoh and his people for their abuses against God's chosen people. This similarity in punishment is not accidental. Pharaoh of Egypt, representative of the enemies of God, is a type of Antichrist.

These events of the tribulation will focus again on the nation of Israel in an attempt to direct her attention to the authenticity of Jesus as the promised Messiah. Pharaoh stubbornly hardened his heart as the plagues attacked his people. As the tribulation plagues find their mark, the Antichrist and his cohorts will respond in like manner with stiff-necked rebellion. God once again will deliver His people to safety by the Red Sea of His grace.

First Bowl Judgment: Cancerous Sores

As the first vial of judgment pours from the container held by the angel, evil men will be stricken with cancerous sores so filled with infection that onlookers will have to turn away. John described them as *"noisome,"* or putrid in smell (16:2).

The *mark of the beast* will be placed upon the hands or foreheads of willing individuals and will indicate their allegiance to the one-world government under the autocratic rule of the Antichrist. Perhaps these cancerous sores will appear on the identical location of the *mark* as an indication of God's superior rule in comparison to that of the Antichrist.

Due to the economic devastation of the tribulation, medicines will be scarce. These bodily afflictions will have no cure and will continually punish their victims with agonizing pain.

The afflictions will be visible on the bodies of evil men. The grotesque display of these plagues will underscore the necessity of

God's punishment on those who willingly submitted to the demands of the Antichrist and received his *mark*. The world will fully understand the justification for such severe punishment.

Second Bowl Judgment: Contaminated Seas

A second angel appeared in John's vision and *"poured out his vial upon the sea"* (16:3). The healthy condition of the seas is critical to the survival of man because food and livelihood are derived from the sea to a significant extent. The seas will be strewn with carnage due to the death of every living thing existing in their waters.

The waters of the sea will turn to blood. The death of all that lives in the sea will produce a putrid smell making all who are exposed to it recoil and flee. Severe shortages of food will occur as a result.

In a similar episode, the Israelite leader Moses was used by God to convert the waters of the Nile River in Egypt to blood. The Egyptians worshipped the Nile River because it provided for their sustenance and the irrigation of their crops. In its corrupted and bloody condition, it could no longer sustain life. As a result of this second plague in the tribulation, the seas will become lifeless and of little use.

Perhaps the waters will be contaminated by the detonation of thermonuclear weaponry or by the intense warfare between battleships and aircraft carriers. In any regard, the waters of the sea will lose their lives and become man's enemy.

In the 1990's, we were horrified to watch news reports chronicling the mass genocide of the people of Rwanda as their bodies were tossed into the waters of Lake Victoria. Dead bodies rolled like forest logs into the murky waters. Perhaps that scene is a precursor of the coming devastation and poisoning of the seas.

Third Bowl Judgment: Contaminated Waters

The judgment in the hands of the third angel will corrupt the fresh waters of the rivers and fountains. These fresh springs of water, necessary for the ongoing health and life of man, also will turn to blood as they did in the time of the persecution of Israel by the Egyptians. In our day, it is not uncommon to gaze at the glistening waters of a beautiful lake or stream on whose bank has been posted a sign reading, *Do Not Drink the Water.* The prospect of ecological disaster is well on its way in our day given our propensity to abuse natural resources.

In the former Soviet Union, little or no control by the governing authorities has been established to protect the supply of drinking water. The result of such neglect has been the exposure of the people to water contaminated with bacteria and other harmful parasites. To an extent, the contamination is due to the infiltration of the supply by radioactive nuclear waste but human abuse takes its toll as well.

This judgment upon evil men, although painful and devastating, will be righteous in nature. The angel commented, *"O Lord, which art, and wast, and shalt be, because thou hast judged thus"* (16:5). The age of grace will have concluded; the age of wrath will seek its ultimate purpose of just punishment upon evil men. Jesus desires to serve as the defense attorney for men yet will willingly serve as their judge in perfectly executing the law should men refuse to receive His gift of grace.

Revelation 16:6 stands as one of the most startling verses in all of scripture. Of the deeds of evil men John wrote, *"They have shed the blood of saints and prophets, and thou hast given them blood to drink; for they are worthy."* Few Sunday morning gatherings in the churches of our day are ever exposed to this dimension of our Lord's character. In our salvation, we are worthy on the basis of His worthiness rather than upon our own innate goodness. Men who thrive and exist on the basis of their own self-worth will be worthy candidates of God's terrible wrath. Further, evil men without Christ will be exceptionally worthy of judgment due to their vicious slaughtering of innocent believers and sprinkling the earth with their blood. Evil men will drink the blood of slain believers in retribution for their evil deeds. What a gruesome sight!

Fourth Bowl Judgment: Catastrophic Sun

It appears that the fourth angel carries in his hands a judgment upon the sun and the magnetosphere surrounding the earth. The earth is shielded from the devastating effects of ultraviolet rays. If the axis of the earth were to be disturbed forcing it closer to the sun, the earth would burn from intense heat.

The judgment of God will result in the alteration of the magnetosphere causing the sun to *"scorch men with fire"* (16:8). Perhaps God may accomplish this goal by the destruction of the ozone layer as a result of man's abuse or by intense warfare that could result in exposing man to the ultraviolet rays of the sun. In any event, evil men will scream from bodily sores and from the intense heat covering his flesh like flaming gasoline.

Jesus gave warning of this unusual use of the sun to punish evil men. In Luke 21:26, He promised that the powers of heaven would be shaken. In Matthew 24:29, He warned that *signs* in the sun, moon, and stars would accompany the end of time. The sun, heretofore the friend of man, one day will become his worst nightmare.

One might rightly assume that such severe punishment would cause men to cry out for mercy and grace. Yet these evil men of the tribulation with their hearts captured by the intoxicating charisma and deception of the Antichrist will angrily curse God. They will display no hesitancy whatsoever to *"blaspheme the name of God"* (16:9).

Fifth Bowl Judgment: Concentrated Darkness

To lose the ability to see must be a frightening experience. In addition to the horrifying experience of burning flesh, darkness will penetrate the earth as the fifth angel pours further judgment from his vial. Evidently, this event will involve a total eclipse of the sun. To fully understand the method God will employ to accomplish this task is not really possible but we may speculate at least.

During the Gulf War of 1991, huge oil well fires resulted in such billowing black smoke and pollution that the face of the sun was temporarily hidden. High noon appeared to be midnight. Perhaps the blinding smoke of global warfare will hide the sun when this plague afflicts mankind.

This severe darkness to permeate the earth in the tribulation will be a literal occurrence having symbolic meaning as well. Jesus spoke of hell as *outer darkness.* When Jesus hung on the cross and experienced hell in our place, darkness blanketed the earth. In that horrendous moment, Jesus cried aloud and asked why God had forsaken Him. God had not forsaken His son, yet for a fleeting moment, it must have felt that way to our Lord.

Darkness suggests separation from God. This darkness to envelope the earth in this fifth plague will center on the *"seat"* of the beast, referring to Jerusalem, the command center of the Antichrist during the tribulation. In our day, Jerusalem is well on its way to assuming the role as capital of the *New World Order* in fulfillment of biblical prophecy.

The *fullness* of the darkness to cover the earth will be obvious. The city of Jerusalem and the entire kingdom of the Antichrist will be subjected to this darkness. The prophet Joel also wrote of this astrological event in predicting that the sun would turn dark.

The *futility* of this eerie darkness will be seen in the agonizing response of evil men who are subjected to it. John wrote in 16:10b, *"They gnawed their tongues for pain."* Fully aware of the judgment of God and suffering severely, evil men will recoil and angrily refuse to acknowledge the one true God. This intense moment of the tribulation will be *hell on earth* as these evil companions of the Antichrist wallow in their pain and gnaw their tongues in hope of relief.

As the rumblings of the coming Battle of Armageddon begin to be detected, the world will be fully aware of the opponents set to do final battle. As Jesus warned, be ready!

Will Communist China be involved? Will the army of North Korea sporting more than one million soldiers play a role as the tribulation unfolds? The scriptures foretell that a huge army will descend from the east into the land of Palestine to engage in the last great battle.

The tension continues to mount. Redemption draws nigh!

Are you ready?

Chapter 36

DIRECTIVES FOR THE BATTLE
Revelation 16: 12-21

No athletic team and coaching staff ever engage in an athletic contest without a battle plan. Napoleon would have met an early demise had he failed to plan and execute a battle plan to capture large chunks of the world. Our Lord also has a plan for the greatest of all battles to come.

The story that continues to unfold in Revelation reveals a systematic plan in the mind of our Lord to bring history as we know it to a dramatic close. The Antichrist will be given enough slack in his divine leash to dupe the masses left behind in the rapture into selling their souls to him. Yet his days are numbered, a fact he knows all to well. God will arrange for a climactic moment as the nations of the world gather sixty miles north of the city of Jerusalem for the mother of all battles, the Battle of Armageddon.

Sixth Bowl Judgment: Drying of the Euphrates River

The mighty Euphrates winds its way from Mt. Arafat along a route of eighteen hundred miles to the Persian Gulf. A main segment of this river is located in the lands of Turkey, Iran, and Iraq in particular. The movement of the river has been under the control of Turkey. A dam has been constructed in that country allowing for the flow of the river to be halted at any moment.

At the outpouring of God's wrath from the judgment bowl of the sixth angel, the bed of this river will miraculously dry up allowing for the passage of masses of men and artillery. Revelation 16:12 predicts that an army from the east will make use of this miraculous drying of the river in order to invade the land of Palestine. Concerning the directives for the coming battle John wrote in 16:12-16,

> *And the sixth angel poured out his vial upon the great river Euphrates; and the water thereof was dried up, that the way of the kings of the east might be prepared. And I saw three unclean spirits like frogs come out of the mouth of the dragon, and out of the mouth of the beast, and out of the mouth of the false prophet. For they are the spirits of devils, working miracles, which go forth unto the kings of the earth and of the whole world, to gather them to the battle of that great day of God Almighty. Behold, I come as a thief. Blessed is he that watcheth, and keepeth his garments, lest he walk naked, and they see his shame. And he gathered them together into a place called in the Hebrew tongue Armageddon.*

The Unholy Trinity

In reality, the dragon, the beast, and the false prophet will be Satan, the Antichrist, and the religious companion of the Antichrist, respectively. This evil band will preside over the one-world system of religion during the tribulation. John described these three *"unclean spirits"* as emerging from the mouth of the Antichrist *"like frogs"* (16:13).

Frogs were considered by Old Testament custom as unclean and to be avoided. The imagery of frogs reminds the reader of one of the plagues by which God afflicted the rebellious Egyptians under the command of Pharaoh. The frog was one of the many pagan gods of the Egyptians. Archaeological digs have confirmed the significance of the frog to the Egyptians and its association with the Nile River. The river was an icon to be worshipped in their culture since it provided a major source of life for the people in terms of water and food and had religious significance as well.

Seductive Spirits

These evil *"spirits of devils"* to be at work in the tribulation are actually spirits of demons that have the ability and power, when permitted by God, to be workers of miracles (16:14). The supernatural demonic ability of these emissaries of Satan is further reason the scriptures sternly warn believers today to *test the spirits* in order to discern their true nature and intention. In our day, not every man who performs alleged *miracles* is pure in heart. Seducing spirits are also alive and well today. Unfortunately, men and women who are less than ethical coupled with a desire to dabble in the supernatural world are often handsomely rewarded in so doing. The things of the Spirit have become a marketable commodity subject to much abuse, a sad trend to say the least. For every true work of God, a counterfeit lurks nearby.

In the tribulation era, these demon spirits will be permitted to display their evil powers. The apostle Paul also warned of this phenomenon in his letter to young Timothy. One accomplishment of these demon forces in the tribulation will be seen in a mass gathering of the leaders of the nations to engage in the *"battle of that great day of God Almighty"* (16:14).

The prophet Joel spoke of a time in the last days when God's spirit would be poured out upon all flesh. He also wrote of a coming battle to occur in the Valley of Jezreel, also known as Armageddon.

God promised that a supernatural evil will afflict and influence the kings of the earth during the tribulation. The Antichrist will work to unite the political powers of Europe creating a new alliance of the Roman Empire. The Antichrist will then reside over this global assembly.

The deceitful methods of these demonic spirits will infiltrate the minds of political leaders and sway their decisions to accomplish the will of the Antichrist. In our day as well, we regularly witness skirmishes between the forces of darkness and people of the Light.

American idealism has come to worship the mushy middle of any particular view and is rabidly intolerant of any and all who hold to moral absolutes. Some idealists in our day are simply intolerant of those whom they charge to be intolerant, a sad inconsistency, indeed!

A Call to Armageddon

Within the permissive will of our Lord, these demonic forces will be allowed to call for the mass assembly of the armies of the rulers of the earth to engage in this final climactic battle. John wrote of the promise of Jesus to appear unexpectedly and allow for this mass gathering in the Valley of Megiddo (16:15). As always, Satan will be allowed to pursue his schemes yet will be confined within the sphere of God's permissive will.

This breathtaking Valley of Megiddo was also the site of the victory of Gideon over the forces of the pagan Midianites hundreds of years before the time of Christ on earth. World leaders have consistently commented on the unique suitability of this valley for war.

The Seventh Bowl Judgment: Mass Destruction

I firmly believe that this awesome description of the last of the seven bowl judgments is consistent with thermonuclear war. Of the incredible scene yet to occur John wrote in 16: 17-21,

> *And the seventh angel poured out his vial into the air; and there came a great voice out of the temple of heaven, from the throne, saying, 'It is done.' And there were voices, and thunders, and lightnings; and there was a great earthquake, such as was not since men were upon the earth, so mighty an earthquake, and so great. And the great city was divided into three parts, and the cities of the nations fell: and great Babylon came in remembrance before God, to give unto her the cup of the wine of the fierceness of his wrath. And every island fled away, and the mountains were not found. And there fell upon men a great hail out of heaven, every stone about the weight of a talent: and men blasphemed God because of the plague of the hail, for the plague thereof was exceeding great.*

With this seventh and final judgment involving mass destruction, geological upheaval, and personal pain and death, the wrath of God will have reached a climax. This final moment of judgment will be punctuated by the sounds of an earthquake so enormous it will shake the heavens.

The *"great city"* of Jerusalem will be splintered into three parts followed by the fall of the *"cities of the nations"* (16:19). Zechariah 14: 4-5 also predicted that the Mount of Olives one day will be divided by an enormous earthquake. This cleavage and upheaval of the land will occur as our Lord descends, not to halt His descent in the air as in the rapture episode, but rather to touch His feet to the ground on the Mount of Olives seven years after the rapture. This sudden upheaval will also serve as preparation for the unique role of the city of Jerusalem in the millennial kingdom.

The Final Battle

John wrote that the *"great Babylon"* will be specifically targeted by our Lord in this great unleashing of His wrath (16:19). The spirit of Babylon is representative of the world system of government and religion that serves primarily to exalt man who believes he has no need of God. This evil system will reach its full expression in the tribulation.

The builders of the Tower of Babel in Old Testament history attempted to reach and connect with God in their construction efforts. In essence, they constructed a tower of worship that was occultist in nature. In our day, the proliferation of the need to consult horoscopes and to seek astrological advice originates from this same deceptive spirit of Babylon.

Babylon also represents the false religious system that is abhorrent to our Lord in that it denies His very name and power. The apostle Paul also wrote of this subtle form of evil and deception in saying that some in the last days will have a *"form of godliness, but denying the power thereof"* (II Timothy 3:5). This deceptive form of religion will be a primary recipient of God's fierce judgment.

In addition, enormous upheaval of the topography will uproot the islands and mountains from their longstanding locations. Such radical alteration of the landscape will further prepare the world for the millennial kingdom.

Evil men will experience the pounding of huge hailstones weighing as much as a talent, or approximately seventy-five pounds. This thunderous storm will result in indescribable anguish, death, and unparalleled atmospheric convulsions.

The world will unmistakably see and recognize God, the Lord of all things.

Chapter 37

THE ONE-WORLD CHURCH
Revelation 17: 1-6

After the horrifying destruction of the Twin Towers in New York City on September 11, 2001, a popular religious broadcaster featured a Muslim religious leader in his televised evangelical worship service. Apparently, the broadcast was an attempt to display compassion and a common bond of fellowship between Christian and Muslims. Whether intentional or not, this deceptive message heard around the globe by the viewers, essentially equates Islam and Christianity. We must realize that cries for tolerance in our society often require that doctrinal issues be relegated to secondary status in order to achieve this false show of unity. Acquiescence to this unhealthy trend will lead to greater apostasy within the Christian community as we know it. Sadly, such tolerance is alive and well today.

The blending of religions will play into the hands of the Antichrist forming the one-world church, identified in Revelation 17 as *"MYSTERY, BABYLON THE GREAT."* The origin of this religious apostasy dates to the building of the Tower of Babel when the builders attempted to reach heaven, as it were, in an attempt to understand the meanings of the stars and the movement of the planets (Genesis 11). Astrological folklore and the ongoing hunger for purpose and direction from horoscopes have their root in the infamous Tower of Babel. Our modern appetite for the occult and demon worship finds its predecessor in the same brand of falsehood and perversion that motivated the building of the Tower of Babel.

False cults such as the Church of Jesus Christ of Latter Day Saints and the Jehovah's Witnesses, and even Christian churches, who have perverted the message of Jesus, play into the hands of *Babylon,* the false religious system that will exert unprecedented influence during the tribulation.

A God-Shaped Vacuum

The church father Augustine once commented, *"We are restless until we find our rest in thee, O God."* The soul of every man longs for that which only God is capable of providing. Man was created for fellowship with our loving Lord. All men yearn for God and search for Him along many paths with the hope of finding meaning and purpose. In a moment of honesty, even a staunch atheist will acknowledge the existence of a supreme being. It has been said that the worst day in the life of an atheist is the day he finds himself full of thankfulness yet has no one to thank.

Man is incurably religious. Fully aware of that fact, the Antichrist will take full advantage of the religious system at work during the tribulation and capture the heart of the world. In that day, church and state will unite merging the power and wealth of the church with the governing authority. Individuals who refuse such a union and deny allegiance to the Antichrist will meet sudden death.

A Great Apostasy

The scriptures are quite clear that a falling away from the faith of our fathers will occur in the last days. The essential fabric of Christianity will degenerate and be absorbed into the false religions of the world in favor of global unity.

In our day, some non-denominational and mainline churches have allowed for false doctrine to creep into their faith systems in order to attract the masses. The absence of biblical doctrine in establishing the truth of God's word in a church will lead to certain apostasy. To dilute the truth of the Word in order to build the crowd will guarantee failure. Such blurring of the distinctive beliefs of our faith will be the methodology the Antichrist will employ to capture the hearts of the masses.

Such apostasy in our day is seen in the moral degeneration of our culture. Many individuals and religious groups willingly give ascent to the claims of Christ yet without acknowledging a need for behavioral change. Many people today simply want to be Christian without the ethical requirements that display the authenticity of our faith.

Furthermore, our modern apostasy shows itself in spiritual lethargy in which there is often little or no anointing of the Holy Spirit at work in some churches. John wrote in Revelation 3:16 that some churches are spiritually *lukewarm*, meaning that the minds of some people are filled with correct doctrine yet their hearts are often lifeless and void of the Holy Spirit. Spiritual deadness is difficult to self-diagnose.

Apostasy will reach its climax as the Antichrist dupes the world into a false system of religious unity. The cancer of spiritual deadness will have reached an advanced stage and essentially be undetected by its victims.

The One-World Church: The Great Whore

To describe a person in our day as a *whore* is intended to denigrate and expose the dirty character of the individual. John described this coming one-world church of the tribulation as *"the great whore"* (17:1). Such a nasty description is intended to reveal the true nature and intention of the Antichrist. He will employ religious seduction to achieve his goals.

The names of women were often employed by the biblical writers to depict good and evil. For example, Mary portrays spiritual goodness and faithfulness. The Church is known as the *bride of Christ.* In contrast, the Old Testament character of Jezebel, an early feminist, personifies evil, false religion and idol worship.

In this passage of Revelation, John seized the opportunity under the inspiration of the Holy Spirit to depict false religion as a female whore. In 17:1-2 and in 17:15 John wrote,

> *And there came one of the seven angels which had the seven vials, and talked with me, saying unto me, 'Come hither; I will shew unto thee the judgment of the great whore that sitteth upon many waters: with whom the kings of the earth have committed fornication, and the inhabitants of the earth have been made drunk with the wine of her fornication.'*

> *And he saith unto me, 'The waters which thou sawest, where the whore sitteth, are peoples, and multitudes, and nations, and tongues.'*

The latter verse, Revelation 17:15, is an explanation of the earlier phrase concerning the one who *"sitteth upon many waters"* (17:1). Essentially, the union of the empire of the Antichrist including the nations, multitudes left behind on the earth from all people groups, and the global political system, will comprise the one-world church.

After the Antichrist captures the allegiance of the masses in the net of his one-world religion, he will proclaim himself to be God and then destroy the very religious system that catapulted him to power. He will not share the glory with any other person or entity.

The Seductive Power of False Religion

In both the Old and New Testaments, the behavior of the nation of Israel was compared to that of an unfaithful wife such as in the Hosea narrative. Gomer, the unfaithful wife of Hosea, forever remained covered by his love in the same manner by which our Lord perpetually loves His bride, the Church.

The prophets wrote in graphic terms of the unfaithful behavior of Israel. The nation was guilty of spiritual adultery and the worship of idols. Biblical fornication refers to any form of sexual expression that extends beyond the confines of marriage. In Revelation 17:2 John wrote, *"the kings of the earth have committed fornication (with her),"* indicating the seductive power of this system of false religion to entice and intoxicate the masses. The leaders of the world will be smitten by the temptations of the *whore* and will gladly eat her evil fruit.

The rulers of the earth, in love with the world system and intoxicated by self-love as well, will embrace the *"great whore"* who will lure unsuspecting men and women into her grasp. This false brand of religion will create euphoria among the masses caught in her web of deception and unable to see the Truth.

Babylon: Her Unique Position

John wrote that he was an eyewitness in his vision to this seductive system at work personified as *Babylon.* In 17:3 John records, "*....I saw a woman sit upon a scarlet coloured beast, full of names of blasphemy, having seven heads and ten horns.*" John saw this *Babylon* as dry and barren in the wilderness yet mounted upon a scarlet beast, representative of the Antichrist (c.f. Revelation 13:1). This picture of the horse and rider is the false religious system that will be empowered by the Antichrist to imprison the minds and hearts of the people.

The *"beast"* is scarlet in color underscoring her bloodthirsty nature. The religious system of the tribulation will blaspheme and denigrate the name of God in every conceivable manner.

The *"seven heads"* of the Antichrist refer to the city of Rome, again reminding the reader of the coming revival of a Roman Empire form of rule during the tribulation. The *"ten horns"* of the Antichrist are symbolic of the ten kingdoms comprising the political coalition over which the Antichrist will rule. John recorded these words indicating that this global power will sweep throughout the world exercising total control.

Babylon: Her Unlimited Prosperity

Christian martyrs in the tribulation era will rest comfortably in heaven no longer affected by the pains of hunger, thirst, or persecution. The vicious attack on believers converted during the tribulation by the forces of the Antichrist will cause widespread pain and poverty. Such persecution will stand in glaring contrast to the financial prosperity of the false religion system of *Babylon.* Concerning the appearance of *Babylon*, John wrote that she will be clothed in the finest of linens and adorned with precious jewels. *Babylon* will be the epitome of wealth and royalty in her day and will proudly display and make use of her wealth to control the masses.

The *"golden cup in her hand full of abominations and filthiness of her fornication"* will serve to magnify her prosperity and corrupt character (17:4). Certain eras of church history have produced a corruption within the churches similar to that of *Babylon* in the tribulation era. During the Dark Ages, priests were known to manipulate the religious system of the day and line their own pockets in so doing. The seductive powers of this religious system will entice the masses, actions that will cause no concern or sense of guilt in the mind of the Antichrist. The *"great whore"* will wipe the pleasure from her mouth and look for her next victim.

Many scholars predict that the employment earnings of the people will merely flow into the treasuries of this wicked religious system. In essence, the masses will be taxed by *Babylon* creating enormous wealth and further allowing the one-world church to exert unchallenged authority. Perversion will be rampant and will corrupt every facet of society.

Babylon: Her Unholy Perversion

It was customary for Roman prostitutes who roamed the streets to wear headbands displaying their names in an act of proud defiance. John saw upon the forehead of *Babylon* the inscription, *"MYSTERY, BABYLON THE GREAT, THE MOTHER OF HARLOTS AND ABOMINATIONS OF THE EARTH"* (17:5). In glaring contrast to Jesus, this religious harlot will come to be served rather than to serve. The Church of our Lord exists to introduce the grace of Jesus to a lost and dying world. The spirit of this religious harlot will exist to legitimize evil and will be self-serving in so doing.

Perversion and immorality were two of the tools of Branch Davidian leader David Koresh who established his religious stronghold in Waco, Texas in the early 1990's. He convinced his willing followers to believe that he was the Lamb of God incarnate and that a sexual relationship with him was the divine privilege of a select few. He also taught that the women of the cult group were possessions of his and his alone. What was holy and sacred was made unholy and filthy in the eyes of God and done so under the guise of religion, a common deception as old as the world itself.

In biblical days, pagan rituals often included sexual acts as vital components of their worship. The imprisonment of the emotions and passions of men in the tribulation will be a primary means whereby the Antichrist will fortify his stronghold of power and reign. The religious system of *Babylon* will arrogantly deny that Jesus Christ in the only path to a relationship with God and to eternal life. The blood of the saints dripping from the mouth of this religious system will stand in stark contrast to the blood of Jesus spilled for all men.

In recent years, Pope John Paul met with the leaders of Israel to bless their efforts as a nation. In addition, there has been a movement to unite Catholics and several evangelical Christian groups in an alliance to fight against abortion and other societal evils. Such alliances may appear healthy and productive on the surface yet have theological corruption beneath. The scriptures warn us that even a small quantity of leaven will spoil the entire loaf.

The attitude and mentality of the one-world church to come is alive and well in our day and is a foreshadowing of the wicked scheme of the Antichrist to blend all religions for his own personal benefit.

The current movement toward globalism and a *New World Order* to unify all facets of our lives could spell disaster for the purity of our faith and is a trend that we must oppose. Thank God that not all believers are willing to accept this blurring of the fundamentals of our faith! Judge Roy Moore of Alabama is to be commended for his stand for the gospel in the midst of the hot fires of persecution by the ACLU and other liberal groups. He defiantly held to his decision to post the Ten Commandments on his courtroom wall and displayed a second empty frame on the wall for the benefit of those who *believe in nothing!* In our quest for unity, we must not cast aside the purity and distinctive tenets of our faith!

Babylon: Her Unparalleled Persecution

In 17:6 John wrote that he was struck with awe and *"great admiration"* (translated in New American Standard as *"I wondered greatly"*) when he saw the harlot of *Babylon* intoxicated with the *"blood of the saints."* John was awestruck with the bold and unrelenting passion of the Antichrist to claim the role of Christ for himself and to kill all true followers of the Lord.

By the persecution of the one-world church, Christians of the tribulation will meet their deaths in a cruel and painful manner. They will be hunted and killed in the streets without remorse.

This system of false religion has persecuted the people of God throughout history and has attempted to silence and annihilate all true believers. This system of one-world religion in the tribulation will not rest until it achieves dominion over the world and its inhabitants. In this thirst for peace and unity, the world will be imprisoned in the clutches of the Antichrist with nowhere to turn.

In recent years, I have given my full support to the conservative resurgence within my Southern Baptist denomination. The goal of the movement has been to return our community of faith to the absolute trustworthiness and inerrancy of the scriptures as the Word of God. The scriptures *are* the Word of God rather than merely *contain* the Word of God, as some contend. Verbal gymnastics and semantic ploys are intended to create a theological loophole for some who are uncomfortable with certain passages of scripture. In the course of this movement, critics have pointedly asked whether I had any desire for peace at all. The insinuation of the question is that theological war is the real goal of our movement rather than peace among friends. My response is that peace at any price is no peace at all. Peace achieved on the altar of doctrinal falsehood is an achievement that our Lord will never honor.

The motto, *peace at any price,* will infiltrate the mindset of the masses, all of whom will gladly adopt any and all policies the Antichrist desires to impose. The persecutors of the true followers of Jesus Christ in the tribulation will be thoroughly convinced that their actions are worthy and justified. Saul of Tarsus, before his heart-opening experience with the Lord, thought the same. He terrorized believers and found a sense of nobility and purity in so doing.

The writer John must have reacted in stunned disbelief that mankind one day will reach such an advanced state of corruption. In Jeremiah 17: 9, the prophet wrote that the heart is deceitful and wicked and difficult to understand.

He was right.

Chapter 38

BABYLON: MOTHER OF ALL HARLOTS
Revelation 17: 7-18

Few societies place value upon blatant harlotry yet the acceptability of sexual freedom continues to gain support in our own country. The motto of the 1970's, *Make Love Not War,* continues to find energetic support in the twenty-first century.

The motivating factor of such an outcry for freedom is to rid man of all inhibitions and moral restrictions and to disengage himself from any system of moral accountability. In essence, man resists being held accountable and often views religion a barrier to his freedom.

The evil nature of the Antichrist during the tribulation will lure man into a web of deceit and promise a state of nirvana free from the shackles of divine intervention. The false system of religion, identified by John as *Babylon,* will deceive men and entrap them in this world system. Devised by the Antichrist, this ploy will achieve world dominion and claim the glory for himself.

The symbol of Babylon as a harlot stands in glaring contrast to the purity of the bride of Christ, the Church. With amazing charm and allure, the harlot of Babylon will enslave men and women in the tribulation with ease. This system of false religion will be comprised of all the false religions of the world that deny the divinity of Jesus Christ and reject His absolute rule.

The church of the tribulation era will be composed of all peoples, nations, and dialects of the world (17:15b). Seizing this moment of counterfeit unity among the masses, the Antichrist will amass enormous power and acclaim. In a predicted turn of events, he will suddenly revolt against the one-world church, plunder her goods as spoil, and further capture the affections of the world for himself.

Concerning the harlot who appears riding on the back of the beast, John wrote in 17:7-8,

> *And the angel said unto me, 'Wherefore didst thou marvel? I will tell thee the mystery of the woman, and of the beast that carrieth her, which hath the seven heads and ten horns. The beast that thou sawest was, and is not; and shall ascend out of the bottomless pit, and go into perdition: and they that dwell on the earth shall wonder, whose names were not written in the book of life from the foundation of the world, when they behold the beast that was, and is not, and yet is.'*

Curiously, this beast is identified as existing in the past, not presently in existence at any given moment, yet as one who will appear again in his ascent from the *bottomless pit.*

Who is the Beast?

I certainly count myself among the hosts of bible students who recognize that this passage is fraught with difficulty. We will proceed through these murky prophetic waters with caution.

Some commentators identify the beast as the Roman Empire that was doling out persecution to the Church with reckless abandon at the time John penned these inspired words. Proponents of this view contend that the empire *was*, does not now exist and therefore *is not,* yet will experience a revival in the future and therefore *shall ascend.* Although this logical analysis is clear, the scriptures seem to be more centered upon the Antichrist himself than upon the empire that he will lead. The one-world government to seize control during the tribulation will exist as a revival of the old Roman Empire united by the Antichrist.

This beast does feature *seven heads* and *ten horns*, representing his intellect and wisdom and a coalition of kingdoms under the rule of the Antichrist, respectively (17:9, 12). Staunch proponents of this view believe that the beast is the Roman Empire, an interesting yet inadequate proposal.

Others believe that the beast will be Judas Iscariot risen from the pit and inhabiting the person of the Antichrist. In essence, the claim is that Judas will infiltrate the body of the Antichrist. Judas is known in the scriptures as the *"son of perdition"* (John 17:12) and the Antichrist is given the identical title (II Thessalonians 2:3). Further, the scriptures say of Judas what is said of no other person in that Satan, and not merely demons, entered into him (Luke 22:3). Judas was not alive at the time of John's writing and therefore *was not.* It is an interesting proposal, yet not accurate.

The best interpretation, however, is that the beast will be none other than the Antichrist himself. Due to the fact that his *"deadly wound"* will result in a miraculous resurrection, the admiration and affection of the world will focus upon him in fulfillment of his lifetime dream (13:3). As the beast bursts upon the scene as a world leader, he will do so with great credibility and authority.

The Antichrist *was* in that his evil nature was personified in the reign of world leaders such as Nebuchadnezzar, Caesar, and others. He *is not* in that he will experience a temporary death, or at least the appearance of death, during the tribulation. Finally, he *shall ascend* from the *bottomless pit* to establish his evil reign.

As the Antichrist ascends to the earth, Satan will incarnate him in an act enabling the fulfillment of Satan's eternal desire to be worshipped. In short, Satan loves to be loved.

Why Will the Beast Appear?

Antichrist the beast will bask in the affections of his global following. The breathtaking resurrection from his mortal wound will drop the jaw of mankind in amazement. Those whose *"names were not written in the book of life from the foundation of the world"* will be eyewitnesses to his wounds and to his recovery from death.

What conceivable event would engender more acclaim than resurrection from death? If Russian leaders Gorbachev or Putin were assassinated only to resurrect, the throngs of the world would respond with undying love and obedience. The world loves heroes and is all too willing to heap praise and admiration upon anyone who performs an extraordinary feat. At this resurrection, the Antichrist will manipulate the masses capture a loyal global following.

The wicked Antichrist will be religiously astute and fully aware of what skills will be necessary to earn the adoration of the masses. However, during the height of his reign he will be allowed to operate only within the purview of God's sovereign will.

The Antichrist: The Center of His Power

Although the beast will establish a global reign, his primary arena of power will be centered in Rome. John wrote in 17:9, *"And here is the mind which hath wisdom. The seven heads are seven mountains, on which the woman sitteth."* Rome was renowned as the city of seven hills yet other cities are known to feature seven mountains as well. However, Rome was the center of world power at the time of John's writing in the first century and will become so once again. Rome will serve as the headquarters of a unified Europe, a movement well on its way in our day of unified global economies and an insatiable appetite among world leaders for a coalition capable of ensuring world peace.

In addition, Rome will serve as the command center of the one-world church. The Antichrist will appear invincible yet the time of his demise will draw near.

The Antichrist: The Eighth Ruler

John hints at the timing of the appearance of the Antichrist and recorded these words in 17:10-11,

> *And there are seven kings; five are fallen, and one is, and the other is not yet come; and when he cometh, he must continue a short space. And the beast that was, and is not, even he is the eighth, and is of the seven, and goeth into perdition.*

Admittedly, this is a difficult passage to understand. Of the seven kings, five have fallen. A number of world kingdoms are mentioned in Daniel 7. Five of them, Egypt, Assyria, Babylonia, Persia, and

Greece, have been blotted from the pages of world history. Rome, the sixth kingdom, existed in power at the time of John's writing and evidently is the kingdom in fulfillment of the words, *"one is"* (17:10).

The seventh kingdom referenced in 17:10 is described as *"not yet come."* This kingdom is the empire of the beast, the world ruler yet to appear. In essence, the *"eighth"* ruler will arise from the midst of the seven kings. His initial form will be that of a beast emerging from the seas, signifying the masses of humanity that will give to him their undying and fanatical allegiance.

Identifying these world empires is fundamental in understanding the forward motion of history and how biblical prophecy predicts this movement. The vision of King Nebuchadnezzar regarding gold, representative of the coming world kingdoms, also included a vision of the coming kingdom of the Antichrist and its predictable demise at the hands of our Lord (Daniel 7).

The Antichrist: His Charismatic Rule

The leaders of the nations in the tribulation will gravitate to the Antichrist and acknowledge him as the supreme and undisputed leader. In Revelation 17: 12-18 we read,

> *And the ten horns which thou sawest are ten kings, which have received no kingdom as yet; but receive power as kings one hour with the beast. These have one mind, and shall give their power and strength unto the beast. These shall make war with the Lamb, and the Lamb shall overcome them; for He is Lord of lords, and King of kings: and they that are with him are called, and chosen, and faithful. And he saith unto me, 'The waters which thou sawest, where the whore sitteth, are peoples, and multitudes, and nations, and tongues. And the ten horns which thou sawest upon the beast, these shall hate the whore, and shall make her desolate and naked, and shall eat her flesh, and burn her with fire. For God hath put in their hearts to fulfill his will, and to agree, and give their kingdom unto the beast, until the words of God shall be fulfilled. And the*

> *woman which thou sawest is that great city, which reigneth over the kings of the earth.'*

The nations will hail the rule of the Babylonian monster and will unite in submission to his evil ways. After a brief moment of shared reign, these *"ten horns"*, representing the ten powerful leaders in the tribulation era, will step aside and allow the beast to assume full and unchallenged rule.

A curious experience will follow in the wake of the establishment of the full reign of the Antichrist. John wrote in 17:2 that the kings of the earth will commit fornication with the beast in the form of spiritual and political cohabitation. Seducing spirits inhabiting the minds of deceived people will create an atmosphere of joyful euphoria at the creation of the one-world church. Politicians will applaud this one-world religious system and gladly lend their support and allegiance to it. Any endorsement of this religious system will be politically expedient and find immediate approval from the masses. The intoxicating power of false religion will raise its ugly head yet another time.

In the middle 1990's, Palestinian Liberation Organization leader Yasser Arafat defiantly presented himself in the land of Israel. His bold appearance represented hope to the Arab nations that they one day will overcome the Jews and capture their lands. That war for control will never cease. However, a day will come when Jews, Muslims, and Christians will unite in support of the one-world church. Joining their merry band will be all of the false religious systems of the world including worshippers of the occult. Churches that proclaim themselves as Christian, yet deify man as the center of his own universe will be in this assembly as well. This melting pot of humanity, assembled under the guise of religion, will meet a sudden demise at the hands of the Antichrist who will be unable to share even a single sliver of glory.

The one-world church will achieve fame, success, and will amass incredible wealth. The rulers of the earth will fall at her feet. I am certain that the writer John stood in amazement at the vast holdings of the one-world church in comparison to the church of his day that owned no buildings or properties whatsoever. The church at Jerusalem was powerful yet poor, which may explain its power!

The kings of the earth, *"drunk with the wine of her fornication,"* and under the heavy hand of the Antichrist, will grow resentful against the church and viciously destroy her. Essentially, the evil government controlled by the Antichrist will destroy the very religious system they will have worked so feverishly to construct.

The Antichrist and his minions will hate this false system for *practical* reasons, confiscate its wealth, and expose its corruption to the public. Perhaps the Antichrist will publicly accuse this false church of hording its wealth and showing unconcern at the sight of the hollow faces of starving men and women.

This intense hatred of the false church by the kings of the earth and the Antichrist will be motivated for *providential* reasons as well. John wrote in 17:17, *"God hath put in their hearts to fulfill his (Antichrist) will......"* When necessary, God reserves the right to change the hearts of evil men and to accomplish his will in so doing. In the story of Joseph who was enslaved by the wicked Egyptian king, God intervened and turned the heart of the king in support of Joseph in order to proclaim His name. As the nation of Israel adopted idolatrous ways, God used the wicked Assyrians to teach the Israelites a harsh and necessary lesson. He will do the same for you and me if necessary.

Satan the Loser

Satan strives with all his might yet remains the epitome of all losers. He will create the one-world religion yet will seek to destroy it in hatred for the competition it will give him.

The angel reminded John that the *"woman,"* the system of deception and the one-world church in place in the coming tribulation episode, will establish headquarters in the city of Rome (17:18). The iron-fisted rule of Caesar in the early days of Rome will pale in comparison to the terror to be imposed by the Antichrist.

Believe me; you do not want to be present for this experience.

Chapter 39

WHEN THE ECONOMY CRUMBLES
Revelation 18: 1-10

The fall of the one-world religious system and the ruling political and economic system will signal the end of the seven-year tribulation on earth. The Church will not be present for the frightening events of the tribulation yet the rest of the world will continue in arrogance and self-sufficiency and in support of the Antichrist and his false promises of hope.

Revelation 17 records the coming collapse of religious *Babylon* that will have served to unite the religions of the world. Our current outcry for *tolerance* and our social and political habit of discarding any sense of moral absolutes as relics of yesteryear will pave the way for the Antichrist to assume full power. So effective and powerful will be the one-world church, the Antichrist will suddenly turn against the church like a traitor and seek her swift destruction.

Revelation 18 focuses upon the fall of economic and political *Babylon.* In 14:8, John wrote that Babylon *"is fallen, is fallen,"* indicating two phases or aspects of the fall that I believe is a reference both to the religious and economic systems of the last days. Concerning this fall John wrote in 18:1-10,

> *And after these things I saw another angel come down from heaven, having great power; and the earth was lightened with his glory. And he cried mightily with a strong voice, saying, 'Babylon the great is fallen, is fallen, and is become the habitation of devils, and the hold of every foul spirit, and a cage of every unclean and hateful bird. For all nations have drunk of the wine of the wrath of her fornication, and the kings of the earth have committed fornication with her, and the merchants of the earth are waxed rich through abundance of her delicacies.' And I heard another voice from heaven, saying, 'Come out of her, my people, that ye be not partakers of her sins, and that ye*

> *receive not of her plagues. For her sins have reached unto heaven, and God hath remembered her iniquities. Reward her even as she rewarded you, and double unto her double according to her works: in the cup which she hath filled fill to her double. How much she hath glorified herself, and lived deliciously, so much torment and sorrow give her: for she saith in her heart, 'I sit a queen, and am no widow, and shall see no sorrow. Therefore shall her plagues come in one day, death, and mourning, and famine; and she shall be utterly burned with fire: for strong is the Lord God who judgeth her. And the kings of the earth, who have committed fornication and lived deliciously with her, shall bewail her, and lament for her, when they shall see the smoke of her burning, Standing afar off for the fear of her torment, saying, 'Alas, alas that great city Babylon, that mighty city! for in one hour is thy judgment come.'*

John penned these sobering words against the backdrop of the mighty Roman Empire that existed in the lap of luxury and enslaved approximately a third of the population of the world at that time. John's description of the coming destruction of political and religious *Babylon* is amazingly reminiscent of the corrupt Roman Empire of the first century.

Signs in our Times

As I began to teach Revelation in the 1970's, news reports made few references to terms such as *one-world order* or *global economy.* In our day, such talk is quickly becoming reality. Events such as the introduction of the *euro* as a form of money in early 2002 have quickly found ready acceptance from several nations further uniting our global economies.

The economies of Japan and Europe and others make headlines in our day. The American dollar is often compared in value with the currency of these major economic players of the world. Nations are no longer isolated from one another. The North American Free Trade Agreement, commonly known as NAFTA and viciously opposed by presidential contender Ross Perot, broadened the scope of trade in North America. The Common

Market in Europe, as it was formally known, has become the European Economic Community. On numerous occasions, Israeli leader Simon Perez urged his fellow countrymen to understand that they must peacefully coexist with their neighbors. He referred to this international partnership as the *New Middle East.* Peace treaties that Israel continually pursues are born primarily from economic necessity. Presidents of the United States have encouraged us to educate our young people to deal with a rapidly changing global economy. Governmental and economic change will reach a climax in the Tribulation. As quickly as the Iron Curtain fell in a heap, a consolidated world government will emerge on the scene after the Church is swept away into heaven at the outset of the Tribulation.

Israel in Need

In the middle 1990's, a fierce riot broke out in Gaza and many lives were lost in a bloody skirmish. Israel moved out of the region leaving it under the control of the Palestinians and Yasser Arafat. As Israel began to vacate the area, too few Palestinian police officers were available to maintain the peace. The crack of gunfire rang out resulting in the death of many Israelis and Palestinians. Israel quickly responded to stop the violence and protect themselves.

In March 2002, some Palestinians detonated explosives hidden on their bodies killing many Israelis in the process. Israel responded by trapping Arafat in his own headquarters and severing electrical service to the building. Arafat cried for help. Israel will always be suspicious of any and all who offer promises of peace on their behalf.

I predict that we will see the United Nations assume a more active and influential role in future Israeli peace efforts by intensifying peace-keeping efforts in Israel. The day may come when the Israelis, Palestinians, Jordanians, Saudis, and others will engage in such fierce conflict that the United Nations will feel compelled to intervene.

A dictator one day will arise who will befriend Israel and sign a significant peace agreement with the nation. Such an agreement will have never been forged in the life of Israel until this deceptive treaty in enacted.

Such occurrences forecast the coming false global unity that will further entrench the Antichrist. Yet the intervention of our Lord at the climax of the seven-year tribulation will result in the destruction of this evil system of economy enslaving the world.

Two Systems in Conflict

The economic system of our Lord is diametrically opposed to that of man. God's plan is that His children be rewarded for their labors in order to give generously of their resources. In contrast, the inner urges and desires of man compel him to live for the almighty dollar and to keep every cent! God's system assumes that God Himself is the source of all that we have; the system imposed by man insists that man himself serves as the sole source of whatever he may want or need.

Such a conflict is a fierce one, indeed. Revelation 18 is a graphic portrayal of the worldly system that will meet its sudden and painful demise. Essentially, these colliding worlds are those of true spirituality versus humanism.

Where is Babylon?

The name *Babylon* is symbolic, of course. The word Babylon indicates the coming capitol of the world. Religious Babylon will be centered in Rome. Perhaps the headquarters of political Babylon will be located elsewhere such as in the geographic location of Babylon on the Euphrates River. The word *Babylon* is also highly significant as well. There is much speculation in our day that the United States, due to its unchallenged reputation as the world's superpower, may play a role in the establishment of the great Babylon of the last days. Babylon was the center of power in the world in earlier days as is our great country today.

Babylon was the epicenter from which the evil King Nebuchadnezzar, a type of Antichrist in his day, maintained rule over the world. There is some indication that Jerusalem, the *holy city* will become the stronghold of the Antichrist in the tribulation.

Why is God so adamantly opposed to *Babylon?* To clarify the reasons for His fierce opposition and wrath, we must understand the history of man in relation to Babylon of old. The quest for unity is increasingly becoming the central focus of the world. Former President George H.W. Bush refused to confront Iraq in order to liberate the tiny nation of Kuwait until a large coalition of nations gave consent and support. Many in our day cry for the elimination of nationalism and patriotism in favor of unity and under a guise of world peace. Few countries act alone and in political isolation. Global unity is upon us as never before!

Soon after the creation of man, the world was unified and communicated with one language. Genesis 11:1-4 records that story,

> *The whole earth was of one language, and of one speech. And it came to pass, as they journeyed from the east, that they found a plain in the land of Shinar; and they dwelt there. And they said to one another, 'Go to, let us make brick, and burn them thoroughly.' And they had brick for stone, and slime they had for mortar. And they said, 'Go to, let us build us a city and a tower, whose top may reach unto heaven; and let us make us a name, lest we be scattered abroad upon the face of the whole earth.'*

The tower that the people so desperately desired to construct was meant to reach *"unto heaven,"* indicating a hunger to comprehend the supernatural world and provide meaning and purpose for them. The intelligence of the people was sufficient to allow them to understand that they would never physically reach heaven. They simply wanted a place of worship and a better understanding of the cosmos. The meaning of the movement of the stars forever has been elusive and continues to hold a powerful allure for many. Archaeologists have uncovered towers in ancient Mesopotamia, the location of the tower of this Genesis story, and have found evidence of the horoscope, the means whereby man believes that he may study the stars and thereby direct the affairs of his life.

However, such activities are deceptive and mere substitutes for a true relationship with our Lord.

People in our day readily call psychic hotlines and various other astrologers for advice. Singer Dionne Warwick endorsed such a hotline in recent years. Why any educated individual would place confidence in her advice remains a mystery to me - she does not even know the way to San Jose!

Our current infatuation with the promises of humanism is deadly. It implies that man possesses within himself all he will ever need for success simply by discovering and releasing his talent. This notion runs counter to a relationship with our Lord who is our true source of power. Humanism crowns man as lord of himself; Christianity recognizes Jesus as the only Lord.

New Age religions continue to appear and capture the appeal of the masses. The sales volume of New Age literature often eclipses that of all other religions combined. During a recent visit to Albuquerque, New Mexico, a city in which I formerly lived, a pastor commented that the dominant religious affiliation was no longer Catholic but rather New Age. New Age philosophy insists that man himself is God. New Age proponents believe that as we gaze at a man, we see God. Shades of naturalism and deadly religious pluralism are resident within this false religious system.

The Tower of Babel of the Genesis 11 story is rooted in that same humanistic notion. Man either *is* God or creates his own god by the power of his intellect, according to this false religious system.

God took no pleasure in this arrogant act by man to get to God. In Genesis 11: 6-9 we read,

> *And the Lord said, 'Behold, the people is one, and they have all one language; and this they begin to do; and now nothing will be restrained from them, which they have imagined to do. Go to, let us go down, and there confound their language, that they may not understand one another's speech.' So the Lord scattered them abroad from thence upon the face of all the earth: and they left off to build the city. Therefore is the name of it called Babel; because the Lord*

did there confound the language of all the earth; and from thence did the Lord scatter them abroad upon the face of all the earth.

The use of the plural *"let us go down"* is a reference to the three persons of the Trinity. God confused and scattered the people due to their intense desire to discover meaning and purpose apart from Him.

In the days of the apostle John in the first century, Greek was the universal language and the language of the New Testament. The empire of Rome was a Babylonian type of empire in that it united the world in its use of a single language. The people were expected to bow to the political entity of Rome or risk certain retaliation or death.

In our day, English is the universally accepted language and often taught to elementary children in many of the major countries of the world. The unifying of political, economic and educational systems of our planet points to the coming activity of the Antichrist that also will be global in scope. It appears that the United Nations is a forerunner of the sweeping rule and power of the Antichrist to come.

The potential use of nuclear warheads will necessitate the emergence of a world leader capable of unifying the masses and offering promises of peace. Any country that resists this movement toward unity initiated by the Antichrist may feel the sting of retaliation at the hands of the United Nations.

A recent headline in *Newsweek* magazine entitled, *"The Headless Beast,"* detailed the death of the long-time dictator of North Korea. He was responsible for the Korean War and enjoyed taunting the United States by refusing to comply with the United Nations policy regarding the development of nuclear power. Now dead, and described as headless, many political pundits fear that his son will rule with even greater ruthlessness. His son was secluded for more than thirty years and is less knowledgeable concerning the political climate of the world.

A beast will arise with seven heads from the coalition of European nations. The political climate of our world, increasingly unified by our global economies, will pave the way for the conniving ways of the Antichrist.

A Crumbling Economy

Revelation 18 is an announcement of judgment upon the economic system ruled by the Antichrist. The coming economic system will be judged largely due to the *magnitude* of its sins. This evil system will be the home of demons, *"habitation of devils and the hold of every foul spirit, and a cage of every unclean and hateful bird"* (18:2).

All of the cults of Satanism, witchcraft, the occult, New Age, followers of astrology, and other groups will have gravitated toward the promises of *Babylon.* Even in our day, the blending of a variety of world religions is rapidly unifying the world and offering a false state of nirvana.

This false system will give evidence of the spirit of the world (I Corinthians 2:12), the spirit of disobedience (Ephesians 2:2), the spirit of error (I John 4:6), the spirit of bondage (Romans 8:15), and the spirit of fear (II Timothy 1:7). These evil and demonic spirits are alive and well in our day and will become the enslaving forces in the last days to which the peoples and leaders of the world will willingly submit themselves. In short, *Babylon* is descriptive of the sum total of the coming depravity that will enslave the world.

The nations and peoples of the world left behind in the tribulation will sell their very souls for membership in this evil system. Promises of wealth and prestige will find little resistance among the people. John wrote in 18:3,

> *For all nations have drunk of the wine of the wrath of her fornication, and the kings of the earth have committed fornication with her, and the merchants of the earth are waxed rich through the abundance of her delicacies.*

The first half of the tribulation will feature unbelievable prosperity. Throughout the history of mankind, man has been most willing to submit to the system of rule in his life promising the greatest level of prosperity. Money and prestige are tempting stimulants that man struggles to resist. All such stimulants are mere substitutes for the filling of the Holy Spirit. To be *drunk* with the Spirit eliminates the need for any other form of intoxication, a truth few people ever learn.

This world system also will reap divine wrath and certain destruction due to the sense of *enticement* it will offer. In the tribulation, man will face the decision to take or to resist the *mark of the beast* with which he may buy and sell, reap the benefits of the Antichrist, and be afforded economic and political protection. In that day, God strictly commands that His people *"come out of her"* indicating the absolute necessity to separate oneself from the world system and be counted among God's people (18:4). Unfortunately, many believers today simply blend with the culture rather than confront the culture with Godly lifestyles and verbal witness.

In 18:5 John also wrote of the *enormity* of the sins of the world system in that coming day, *"For her sins have reached unto heaven, and God hath remembered her iniquities."* The construction of the Tower of Babel was also an effort to reach into the heavens for purpose and direction apart from the one true God. The sins of mankind will have reached heaven resulting in intense judgment upon *Babylon* and her followers. The mercy and patience of God will have run its course with only judgment remaining in His hand.

God will apply a double judgment in that the angel instructed that the judgment to fall upon *Babylon* will fall with twice the intensity and magnitude of her sins (18:6). This false system of the world, guilty of duping and betraying man, will fall in a heap of ruins.

The sins of *Babylon* in enslaving mankind in the tribulation will be obvious. Such luxuriance and opulence in the tribulation era will be unsurpassed yet the demise of that world system will be swift and painful. John wrote in 18:8,

> *Therefore shall her plagues come in one day, death, and mourning, and famine; and she shall be utterly burned with fire: for strong is the Lord God who judgeth her.*

In the stock market crash of 1929 panic struck our nation and world. On Black Monday in 1987, the trustworthiness of our economy was shrouded in doubt as stock values plummeted to record lows. At the beginning of 2002, Enron, a Houston-based company, saw its stock value fall into oblivion in a freefall of near 99%. The evil religious and political systems of the tribulation will fall even harder and leave even greater destruction in their wake.

Accept our Lord.

Today.

Chapter 40

THE COLLASPE OF WORLD COMMERCE
Revelation 18: 11-24

A familiar sound bite of a recent United States presidential campaign was, *It's the economy, stupid.* Although riding a wave of wartime popularity, former President George H.W. Bush lost the 1992 election largely due to a weakened economy and a perceived lack of a plan to strengthen it. The security of people today largely depends upon the size of the lump of cash in our wallets, so it seems.

After the annihilation of the one-world religious system detailed in Revelation 17, the economy, political life, and the wealth of the world will be centered in the one-world government ruled by the Antichrist. To an extent, we are witnessing a surge of economic instability even in our day, an instability that will reach full throttle in the tribulation. The tragedy of untold suffering in Rwanda in the middle 1990's and the poverty and bloodshed in Haiti motivated the United Nations to step up its role to relieve suffering and police the activities of the world. Fierce factional infighting and various wars are further driving the continent of Africa into a state of advanced poverty.

Jesus predicted an escalation of famine as a sign of the last days, a prophecy of the end times continuing to be fulfilled before our very eyes (Matthew 24). Stories of mass poverty dominate news reports today as never before.

During the tribulation, millions of refugees will flee in despair and countless masses will die horrible deaths and be flung into makeshift graves or merely shoved aside in unconcern. The tragedies in Rwanda and other such suffering in our day will pale in comparison to the carnage of the tribulation.

The evil economic and political systems headed by the Antichrist will benefit only a select few who will hold tenaciously to power. God's judgment will be unleashed upon those who are guilty of oppressing the masses, stealing from the poor, and abusing humanity in order to line their own pockets, all activities resulting from the evil in their hearts and their rejection of God's gift of grace.

The fierce judgment of God will have a devastating effect on the system of trade and the economy. John recorded that prediction in 18: 11-18,

> *And the merchants of the earth shall weep and mourn over her; for no man buyeth their merchandise any more: The merchandise of gold, and silver, and precious stones, and of pearls, and fine linen, and purple, and silk and scarlet, and all thine wood, and all manner vessels of ivory, and all manner vessels of most precious wood, and of brass, and iron, and marble, and cinnamon, and odours, and ointments, and frankincense, and wine, and oil, and fine flour, and wheat, and beasts, and sheep, and horses, and chariots, and slaves, and souls of men. And the fruits that thy soul lusted after are departed from thee, and all things which were dainty and goodly are departed from thee, and thou shalt find them no more at all. The merchants of these things, which were made rich by her, shall stand afar off for the fear of her torment, weeping and wailing, and saying, 'Alas, alas, that great city, that was clothed in fine linen, and purple, and scarlet, and decked with gold, and precious stones, and pearls! For in one hour so great riches is come to nought'. And every shipmaster, and all the company in ships, and sailors, and as many as trade by sea, stood afar off, And cried when they saw the smoke of her burning, saying, 'What city is like unto this great city!'*

The *"her"* of 18:11 refers to *Babylon*, the wicked system of rule established by the Antichrist involving the government, economy, and political system of the tribulation era.

The name Babylon is mentioned continually in the scriptures and refers not only to the city but also to the governmental system in place in the tribulation. In a similar manner, Wall Street refers to a geological locale yet also to a system. The Babylon of this passage is not the Babylon of the Old

Testament but rather the wicked ruling elite to which God will direct His fierce scorn and wrath. The arrogant display of evil and deception shown by this system, and those who endorse it, will not escape God's intense wrath.

Two Different Reactions

The coming destruction of this evil governmental system will draw two distinct reactions. In 18:19-20 John wrote,

> *And they cast dust on their heads, and cried, weeping and wailing, saying, 'Alas, alas that great city, wherein were made rich all that had ships in the sea by reason of her costliness! for in one hour is she made desolate. Rejoice over her, thou heaven, and ye holy apostles and prophets; for God hath avenged you on her.'*

The scriptures consistently draw a distinction between those who spend their lives for the kingdom of God and those who merely live as servants of themselves. The martyrs of Revelation, those converted to Christ in the tribulation and then paid for that decision with their lives, will erupt in heaven will shouts of praise for this judgment as it unfolds.

In glaring contrast, evil men of the tribulation will wail in agony as their wealth and business ventures go up in flames. Insurance policies and all other forms of security will be unable to salvage the carnage. The evil empire of the Antichrist will meet its end. God's judgment will be applied to each and every sinner.

The Collapse of the Marketplace

No segment of the economy will go unscathed by the sharp sword of our Lord's wrath. In 18: 21-22 John wrote,

> *And a mighty angel took up a stone like a great millstone, and cast it into the sea, saying, 'Thus with violence shall that great city Babylon be thrown down, and shall be found no more at all. And the voice of harpers, and musicians, and of pipers, and trumpeters, shall be heard no more at all in thee; and no craftsman, of*

> *whatsoever craft he be, shall be found any more in thee; and the sound of a millstone shall be heard no more at all in thee.'*

Silence will fill the factories and workers will stare in stunned disbelief. All facets of the economic system in which men have placed their hope will cease to function. Such eerie silence is reminiscent of the gospel tune by Bill Gaither entitled *The King is Coming* that reads in part,

> *No more traffic in the streets*
> *All the builders tools are silent*
> *No more time to harvest wheat.*

The freeways will lack for traffic. World commerce will come to a screeching halt. The roar of activity in the stock market will grow strangely quiet. The sudden collapse of all that evil men and women hold dear will underscore what is truly eternal.

What has eternal value will become very clear. When boys and girls find Christ in a Vacation Bible School setting, eternity takes notice. When a marriage is dedicated to the Lordship of Christ and is restored to vitality, eternity smiles. When interest rates climb a fraction of a point, do the residents of heaven erupt in applause? I doubt it.

All of the great plans and schemes of men to chart their respective paths of success in the tribulation will utterly fail. As the familiar saying indicates, "only one life will soon be past; only what is done for Christ will last."

To be sure, we must live and carve out our existence within the economic system of our day yet we are not to be consumed by it nor place our hope within it. We are to manage the assets of this world divinely entrusted to us for the benefit of the kingdom of God. In a real sense, we are managers rather than owners of the goods God assigns to us.

The End of Happiness

The Antichrist will have been enormously successful in his efforts to dupe the masses and intoxicate his loyal followers with the hollow promises of the world system. Music will have faded from the scene. Instrumentalists will no longer stroke their harps and craftsmen will have designed their last piece of work.

A dark cloud of heaviness will drape humanity with no place to turn for relief. In 18: 23-24 John wrote,

> *And the light of a candle shall shine no more at all in thee; and the voice of the bridegroom and of the bride shall be heard no more at all in thee: for thy merchants were the great men of the earth; for by thy sorceries were all nations deceived. And in her was found the blood of the prophets, and of saints, and of all that were slain upon the earth.*

Such personal and economic heartache will be the fruit of the *"sorceries"* at work in the lives of the people. This term finds its etymological origin in the Greek word *pharmakeia* from which the English word *pharmacy* is derived. In essence, the Antichrist will cleverly use the false promises of his world system to intoxicate the masses and entrap their minds and hearts as effectively as if powerful drugs were injected into their bodies. This evil stupor induced by the Antichrist will blind men and women to the Truth and ultimately will send them to a sinner's hell. The hearts of men will be so incredibly evil they will gladly kill the prophets and saints of God yet will pay dearly for having done so.

The End of Wealth

At least three distinct groups will wail in agony at the destruction of *Babylon*: kings, merchants, and mariners with each description preceded by the words, *"alas, alas"* (18: 10,16,19). The kings of the earth will suddenly be dethroned and will lose all of their wealth. Merchants will no longer have the option of entrusting their financial security to the hollow promises of *Babylon.* Mariners will have no seas to sail and their goods will suddenly disappear.

All forms of support and security will be cut from beneath them as the sword of the Lord swings with unrelenting precision. Evil men will appear naked and void of all hope with no place to turn. Their unshakeable belief that the system and rule of the Antichrist is impregnable will suddenly shatter. Their pockets will be empty. Wealth will become no more than a fleeting hope.

The textile industries, fine linens, financial markets, the furniture and building business, industries of ivory, brass, iron, wine, flour, wheat, cattle, petroleum, gambling and drugs, and people who abuse others for financial gain, all will suffer under the ferocious wrath of God. In our day, the value of a human life continues to plummet as man continues to see himself as the ultimate good. The wicked system of the lottery, the gambling industry, and the proliferation of drug use continue to appeal to the carnal nature of man. To a significant extent, we have lost our way and no longer see any significant purpose for which we have been created except to gratify ourselves. The ultimate conclusion to such self-love will be the loss of all man holds as dear when God's wrath finds its target.

The onslaught of this fierce judgment will motivate a spontaneous burst of joy from believers now in heaven (18:20). John wrote in 18:21 that he envisioned an angel heaving a giant millstone into the sea that I believe is a graphic depiction of the violent overthrow of *Babylon.* Whether this violent expression of God's wrath will take the form of thermonuclear war, meteors from space, or will be realized in another form, remains a mystery. In any event, Satan and his minions, and the evil men of the tribulation will lose all hope and the means to survive.

The End of Satan

A cursory glance at our world today reveals the unmistakable handprint of Satan as the master instigator of all sin and carnage. Yet in the end, he will lose. Although he charts victories along the pathway of life, his cause will ultimately fail. Former President Woodrow Wilson once commented, "I would rather temporarily fail with a cause that will ultimately succeed than to temporarily succeed with a cause that will ultimately fail."

Satan will fail. Invest in the kingdom of our Lord. The returns on the investment are out of this world.

Chapter 41

THE MARRIAGE SUPPER OF THE LAMB
Revelation 19: 1-10

Did you hear the story about the police officer who stopped a man in a car that had reached speeds in excess of one hundred miles per hour? The officer bolted out of the car and snidely challenged the speeder to offer an excuse he had never heard before. The fellow sheepishly replied, "My wife ran off with a policeman and I thought you were bringing her back!"

It has been said that at marriage, two become one – and after the honeymoon they discover which one! Weddings are a beautiful sight to behold yet life after the wedding often includes a few moments less than beautiful. When Jesus returns to usher in the millennial reign with the marriage supper of the Lamb, no distress will accompany the Bride and Groom on this happy occasion.

This passage fits appropriately within the context of the coming Battle of Armageddon. This climactic battle will burst upon the world scene immediately prior to the glorious appearing of our Lord and seven years after the snatching away of the Church in the rapture episode.

To summarize the chronology of events, the Church will be raptured at the outset of the seven-year tribulation era. The horrifying events of the tribulation will climax at the Battle of Armageddon introducing the millennial reign of Christ into the world scene. This battle of all battles will be won solely because of the appearance of Jesus Christ to fight on behalf of the nation of Israel.

A Series of Contrasts

Revelation is filled with contrasts depicting good and evil. The marriage supper of the Lamb is set in glaring contrast with the supper of the vultures as God calls upon them to devour the flesh of human bodies massacred at the Battle of Armageddon. Second, as the judgments are unleashed upon the earth, the saints in heaven will erupt in spontaneous praise while evil men utter blasphemous words and bullets of war fly in every direction. Third, two types of rewards will be realized. The saints of God will be adorned with the dazzling white linens of purity. In contrast, evil men without Christ will be draped in the darkness of God's judgment due to their lifetime of defiance of our Lord.

At the very least, Armageddon remains seven years in the future as it will not occur until the climax of the tribulation events. Believers will accompany our Lord to the Battle of Armageddon and be numbered within His holy army. The site of this coming war is the spacious Valley of Megiddo, said to be fifteen miles in breadth, and twenty miles in length, and with numerous other valley areas on its circumference.

The Preparations for Battle

Extensive preparations for this mother of all battles will include the invasion of the land of Israel by a massive army of two hundred million troops arriving from the east and motivated by demonic spirits. Interestingly, former Chinese leader Mao Tse-Tung announced in his diary that China was capable of fielding troops of this magnitude. An army of this size would equal roughly eighty percent of the population of the United States. The evil leaders of the nations of the world will publicly admit that their enemy is the Lord Himself with whom they will contend for control of the world.

The hosts of heaven are preparing for this final battle even now. The wedding supper of the Lamb and His bride, the Church will precede this final battle episode. In 19: 1-10 John wrote,

> *And after these things I heard a great voice of much people in heaven, saying, 'Alleluia; Salvation, and glory, and honour, and power, unto the Lord our God: For true and righteous are his judgments: for he hath judged the great whore, which did corrupt the earth with her fornication, and hath avenged the blood of his servants*

at her hand.' And again they said, 'Alleluia.' And her smoke rose up for ever and ever. And the four and twenty elders and the four beasts fell down and worshipped God that sat on the throne, saying, 'Amen; Alleluia.' And a voice came out of the throne, saying, 'Praise our God, all ye his servants, and ye that fear him, both small and great.' And I heard as it were the voice of a great multitude, and as the voice of many waters, and as the voice of mighty thunderings, saying, 'Alleluia: for the Lord God omnipotent reigneth. Let us be glad and rejoice, and give honour to him: for the marriage of the Lamb is come, and his wife hath made herself ready.' And to her was granted that she should be arrayed in fine linen, clean and white: for the fine linen is the righteousness of saints.' And he saith unto me, 'Write, Blessed are they which are called unto the marriage supper of the Lamb.' And he saith unto me, 'These are the true sayings of God. And I fell at his feet to worship him. And he said unto me, 'See thou do it not: I am thy fellowservant, and of thy brethren that have the testimony of Jesus: worship God: for the testimony of Jesus is the spirit of prophecy.'

The appearance of the bride of Christ, the Church, clothed in the fine linens of purity and preparing to join her Bridegroom, will be an incredible sight to behold.

The Pronouncement of the Wedding

The analogy of a wedding is most appropriate to describe this scene to come. Before the day of a wedding in our culture, printed announcements invite others to the ceremony, indicate the parties to be honored and the date of the event, and provide other appropriate information. In a similar manner, God will announce this holy union between Jesus and His bride.

We are unaware of the exact time of this marriage supper yet to occur but it will follow closely on the heels of the snatching away of the Church and the judgment seat of Christ at which all the deeds of all believers will be scrutinized and rewards distributed accordingly. Immediately preceding the final battle, this wedding of all weddings will be held.

The Place of the Wedding

This wedding of the Church and the Bridegroom will occur in heaven. In 19:1 John wrote that he heard *"a great voice of much people in heaven, saying, 'Alleluia.'* " Perhaps our Lord has preserved this event as the climactic expression of all praise. The use of the word *"alleluia"* occurs only here in the entire New Testament (19:1,3,4,6). John heard the roar of the praise reverberate throughout the halls of heaven as the *"great harlot"* will be finally dethroned, judgment secured, and the great wedding feast of the Lamb set to commence.

During His time on earth, Jesus spoke of Himself as a bridegroom in one of His parables, *"at midnight there was a cry made, 'Behold, the bridegroom cometh; go ye out to meet Him,'* " a prediction of the coming rapture of the Church (Matthew 25:6). The great supper will follow the heavenly wedding ceremony uniting Jesus with His Church.

Knowing that it was *"not good that man should be alone,"* God arranged for the marriage of Adam and Eve. From the wounded side of Adam came his bride whom God intended to be an integral part of her husband. In a similar manner, Jesus died on the cross and demonstrated that His love for us is full and complete, shown is His willingness to die for His bride. A burly Roman soldier pierced His side spilling water and blood, another indication that Jesus died of a broken heart full of love for His Church. From the open side of Adam came Eve, and from the open wound in the side of Jesus came the birth of the Church, His bride.

When Jesus comes to claim His bride we will reign with Him as His bride. No event or evil power will spoil or interfere with the relationship of Christ with His bride. Both bride and Bridegroom will be enamored with one another.

A Pure Bride

Many critics in our day attempt to make a case for the insignificance of the church in society. Yet in the scriptures, we read of the incredible value of the bride of Christ to Him. Betrothed to Jesus, the Church will be presented to Him *pure* in nature. Ephesians 5:26-27 indicates that the Church will be sanctified and cleansed,

> … *with the washing of the water by the word, That he might present it to himself a glorious church, not having spot, or wrinkle, or any such thing; but that it should be holy and without blemish.*

The moment we come to faith in Christ we experience His complete and full cleansing from the stain of sin and therefore are seen in His eyes as pure. Far from living perfect lives, when we do engage in sin we experience the continual correction and purifying effects of His word. This daily *washing* by His word removes the dirty effects of our sin and keeps us secure by the application of His blood shed on the cross. The process of maturing and *washing* with His word will be repeated continually until He comes. Salvation is really three-dimensional; we are saved; we are being saved; and, we will be saved. Salvation is secured once and for all by His death on the cross in which we place our faith and hope yet the ongoing process of maturing in Him will reach its conclusion only in heaven.

Before we stand at the wedding altar with the Bridegroom, we will be purified by evaluation as well. At the judgment seat of Christ, we will give *"an account"* of the activities of our lives and be rewarded in proportion (I Corinthians 3:3, II Corinthians 5:10, Romans 14:12). Frivolous or self-centered behavior will be burned away like chaff burning in a harvest. Eternal investments made by the use of our gifts and talents will stand the test of time and be valued like pure gold in the eyes of our Lord. This evaluation of our behavior will occur before the marriage supper of the Lamb and the Battle of Armageddon.

A Prepared Bride

John wrote in 19:7b, *"his wife hath made herself ready."* The betrothed Church will be seen adorned with fine linens, sparkling clean and gorgeous as a result of the effects of the purity and righteousness of the Lord deposited into the lives of His people. In glaring contrast, the false religious system of the day incarnated by the deceitful immoral woman riding upon the beast, will be seen *"arrayed in purple and scarlet"* (17:4). This evil *woman* will be the antithesis to the holy bride of the Lord.

As the bride of Christ, we are now at work preparing our wedding garment with the lives that we live. The quality of our living reveals itself in acts of service for our Lord and further enhances the beauty of the wedding garment we will wear when we join our Bridegroom at this great marriage supper.

The Wedding Music

The music featured at this magnificent wedding will be masterful and breathtaking (19:1-6). It will feature the *Hallelujah Chorus* in that four significant expressions of hallelujah will be offered.

The hallelujah of *redemption* will be heard. In 19:1b John wrote, *"Salvation, and glory, and honour, and power, unto the Lord our God."* God's salvation will be fully vindicated when evil is dramatically overthrown. The Battle of Armageddon must occur in order for Israel to recognize her utter dependence upon the Messiah and for the forces of evil to meet their demise.

This scene will also feature a hallelujah of *retribution* in that God's vengeance will be swift and sure. In 19:2 John wrote, *"He.........hath avenged the blood of his servants at her (the great whore's) hand."* Such a fierce display of judgment seems inconsistent with the acts of a loving God yet God's nature also demands justice. Vengeance balances mercy in the sovereign scheme of life. Wrath applied against evil counterbalances the rewards given to those who have received the purity of Christ within their hearts and who have been faithful to avoid the temptations of evil.

There will also come a hallelujah of *realization* in that the final acts of vengeance against evil men will lead to their eternal demise. The *"smoke"* of the fires of vengeance will continually rise to the heavens, perhaps both figuratively and literally due to the physical incineration of large portions of the earth (19:3).

The result of this climactic display of vengeance applied by our Lord will be glorious and unrestrained worship of our Lord Jesus. The *"four and twenty elders and the four beasts"*, representing all of the saints of God collectively and the whole of creation, will fall on their faces in humble worship. The Old Testament saints will not be numbered with the bride at this juncture yet will be an integral part of the chorus of praise to be focused upon our Lord.

Last, we will witness the hallelujah of God's *reign.* John described the roar of the voices of praise in heaven as *"the voice of many waters, and as the voice of mighty thunderings"* (19:6). The powerful rumble of rushing waters reveals their deep and grandeur character. The breathtaking force of the tumbling waters of Niagara Falls reminds onlookers that no natural force is capable of restricting its movement or silencing its roaring voice. John heard praises in heaven that will never be silenced. These voices of praise, rejoicing at the demise of evil and the reappearance of the Lord Jesus, no longer will be hindered by sin or physical inadequacies. The waters of praise will gush forth unbridled by any force.

A Happy Occasion

Noting the exuberant atmosphere of this wedding to come, John wrote in 19:9, *"He saith unto me, 'Write, Blessed are they which are called unto the marriage supper of the Lamb.'"* The biblical word *blessed* indicates a position of being highly congratulated, favored, or in essence, happy. Evidently, some friends of the Bridegroom will be in attendance at the wedding. John the Baptist referred to himself as the *"friend of the bridegroom,"* perhaps aware that he also would be in attendance at this wedding in the distant future. He was not of the Old or New Testament dispensations but rather was a forerunner assigned the task of announcing the coming of Christ and His kingdom. In a sense, John the Baptist existed between the two dispensations. The Old Testament saints will be guests at the wedding ceremony and not part of the bride as the Church. This was not a new thought in the mind of God. The apostle Paul wrote that God would redeem a people for Himself as His bride and would do so from among the Gentiles. Paul referred to this concept as the *"mystery of the church."*

The people of Israel are God's chosen people divinely assigned the role of physically representing God upon the earth. The Church is identified as God's chosen people to represent Him spiritually on the earth. Israel and the Church are significantly different in that Israel found salvation by looking forward to the coming of the Messiah. The saints of the Old Testament never saw the cross event, yet each time that they obeyed God in believing in the blood of the sacrificial lambs slain on the Day of Atonement, they placed their faith in Him.

Those in attendance at this wedding of the bride and Bridegroom will erupt will hearts full of praise. The collection of all praises growing in our hearts throughout history will erupt like a huge geyser shouting its contents.

A Beautiful Banquet

This breathtaking and unprecedented banquet, the marriage supper of the Lamb, will be unsurpassed in its scope and beauty. Jesus spoke of the new wine of the kingdom of God as He instructed the disciples regarding the institution of the last supper. In Matthew 26:28-29 Jesus said,

> *For this is my blood of the new testament, which is shed for many for the remission of sins. But I say unto you, I will not drink henceforth of this fruit of the vine, until that day when I drink it new with you in my Father's kingdom.*

Each time that we partake of the elements of the Lord's Supper we anticipate the moment when we will be fully united with our Bridegroom at the wedding supper of the Lamb.

Jesus once told a prophetic parable concerning a great supper. The master of a great house prepared a magnificent supper and sent his servants to invite the guests. They were to say, *"Come, for all things are now ready"* (Luke 14:17b). If we have accepted the invitation to come to faith in Christ, our names are included among the guests to be invited to the marriage supper of the Lamb. Every dish of blessing in the mind of the Father will adorn the table. Some interpreters view this passage as indicating that the saints will eat food in heaven! Perhaps this is true yet we may be fully assured that the Father will spare no expense in providing all that is required to please those whom He loves.

An Eternal Future

After returning with our Lord from the Battle of Armageddon, the Church will reign with Him on the earth for a period of one thousand years, a millennium. Believers will assist Him in the details of this coming reign.

Many believers today are unaware that we will exist in glorified bodies during the millennial reign while others will remain in physical human bodies (Revelation 20). The new home of the bride and Bridegroom will be none other than the New Jerusalem to descend from heaven (Revelation 21).

The Supper will come soon.

PART 4

THE MAGNIFICENT RETURN OF CHRIST

Chapter 42

THE REENTRY OF JESUS TO THE EARTH
Revelation 19: 11-13

The movie *Apollo 13,* starring popular Hollywood actor Tom Hanks, portrayed the true story of the intense panic that gripped the crew of the space shuttle as they encountered severe mechanical failure while in space. In communicating the trouble with NASA, they muttered that memorable phrase, "Houston, we've got a problem!" In spite of the difficulties, they successfully touched down in the blue waters of the ocean safe and sound.

When Jesus Christ touches down on the surface of the earth, He will experience no hindrance of any kind. His reappearance will occur with breathtaking fanfare and in a display of unsurpassed power.

The ruthless reign of the Antichrist, spanning the seven years of the tribulation, will meet its sudden demise as the evil armies of the world clash with the forces of our Lord. The dark and corrupted hearts of the followers of the Antichrist will be exposed for all to see when they war against the tiny nation of Israel and against our Lord Himself.

The writer John witnessed the opening of the courts of heaven and the appearance of Jesus seated upon a magnificent white horse. In 19: 11-13 he recorded that event to come,

> *And I saw heaven opened, and behold a white horse; and he that sat upon him was called Faithful and True, and in righteousness he doth judge and make war. His eyes were as a flame of fire, and on his head were many crowns; and he had a name written, that no man knew, but he himself. And he was clothed with a vesture dipped in blood: and his name is called The Word of God.*

In Revelation 19, John recorded three times the phrase, *"I saw."* The first indicates his vision of heaven; the second instance details his vision of an angel who called for the birds to consume the flesh of the dead in the Battle of Armageddon; the third reference is to the beasts and kings who make war against *"him that sat upon the throne"* (19:11,17,19).

This language concerning the opening of heaven is similar to that also used in 4:1 at which time John was summoned to heaven to receive this revelation. The rapture of John into heaven is a precursor to the coming rapture of all believers in Christ who will be *"...caught up together with them in the clouds"* (I Thessalonians 4: 16-17).

From the moment of the vanishing of the Church into heaven, the *age of grace* will no longer be at work. In Revelation, no mention of the Church is to be found from chapters four and beyond because the universal Church will be residing comfortably in heaven during the tribulation era.

The rapture of the Church will occur as a clandestine event in stark contrast to the public reappearance of Jesus at His second coming. Jesus will plant His feet on the earth in a global display of world dominion for the multitudes of the earth to see and marvel.

The Manner of His Descent

This second coming of Jesus will also serve as a means to inflict arrogant sinners with the retribution they will so richly deserve. In the first coming of Jesus at the beginning of the first century, He came clothed in human flesh, humbled Himself as a servant, and gave Himself as a sacrifice on the cross in the manner reserved only for the most despised of all criminals.

In glaring contrast, His second coming in the Armageddon episode pictures Him bursting upon the scene as the *commanding* Christ. In His coming as the Christ-man in the first century, He rode into Jerusalem on a borrowed donkey in an act of utter humility and willing service. In His second coming, He will arrive on a magnificent white horse with unquestioned power and as the only One who is worthy of all worship.

He will also return as the *confirming* Christ. Jesus was seen in John's vision as One who is *"Faithful and True,"* a reference to His unchanging nature (19:11). The Holy Spirit must have inspired John to pen these words as an encouragement to the churches of his day that Jesus one day will fulfill every single promise that He made. Fierce attacks upon the churches at the hands of the Roman governing authorities must have taken a severe toll on the morale of the early Christians. With words of hope, John wrote that our faithful Lord Jesus eventually will settle the score.

Our Lord will return as the *conquering* Christ as well. He will not return as a babe born in a poverty-stricken manger in an unpopular neighborhood but rather as a global King who will boldly *"judge and make war"* (19:11b). The victims in this war to go down in utter defeat will be Satan, the Antichrist, the False Prophet, and all of their minions who willingly submitted to the *mark of the beast,* identifying them as rebellious objectors to the grace offered by our Lord.

John also wrote that Jesus will come again as the *comprehending* Christ in that the Jesus of John's vision had penetrating eyes *"as a flame of fire"* (19:12). Such a startling appearance underscores the omniscience of Jesus who will return as a judge. With searing insight, Jesus will be privy to all of the innermost facts concerning mankind. The secret works and the true nature of men heretofore hidden from the eyes of the public will be fully known by our Lord. Hebrews 4: 13b records, *"All things are naked and opened unto the eyes of him with whom we have to do."* Every intimate detail concerning mankind will be exposed for swift and sure divine judgment.

Last, Jesus will arrive as the *consuming* Christ as well. John wrote in 19:13a, *"He was clothed with a vesture dipped in blood."* In Isaiah 63, Jesus is portrayed as one who tramps out the vintage, the grapes of the wrath of God. In biblical days, wine presses often featured a top section in which the grapes were crushed. The lower section served to catch the juice from the trampled grapes. The Battle of Armageddon is depicted in Revelation as an event in which Jesus will stamp out the grapes of the wrath of God in His winepress. Just as juice flows from crushed grapes, the blood of Armageddon will flow so abundantly that it will reach the bridle of the horses

(14:20). Such a bloody battle is difficult to comprehend as occurring in ancient days, yet Revelation 16 predicts that a massive army of two hundred million soldiers will appear on the prophetic scene and invade the land of Israel. The carnage of strewn carcasses will be unprecedented in magnitude and blood will flow like a river.

In the days of Isaiah the prophet of Israel, the Jews would not accept the notion of a Messiah born to suffer but rather looked for a warlike messiah who would rule by conquest. Isaiah 63: 1-4 says,

> *Who is this that cometh from Edom, with dyed garments from Bozrah? This that is glorious in his apparel, traveling in the greatness of his strength? I that speak in righteousness, mighty to save. Wherefore art thou red in thine apparel, and thy garments like him that treadeth in the winevat? I have trodden the winepress alone; and of the people there was none with me: for I will tread them in mine anger, and trample them in my fury; and their blood shall be sprinkled upon my garments, and I will stain all my raiment. For the day of vengeance is in mine heart, and the year of my redeemed is come.*

The Salvation of Israel

The Armageddon war will focus upon the salvation of Israel. The apostle Paul wrote that *"all Israel will be saved,"* not indicating that every single Israelite will experience salvation but rather that the nation itself will be spared in the final battle (Romans 11:26a). Another holocaust of the Jews will occur during the tribulation making the Nazi persecution of the Jews of World War II pale in comparison. After these deadly events of the tribulation, only a remnant of Israel will remain.

The Antichrist and his evil followers will launch relentless attacks upon Israel and will attempt to occupy her land by force. The salvation of Israel will come in the arrival of Jesus Christ, ironically the One *"whom they pierced"* (John 19:37). He will arrive with the nail prints of love still embedded in His hands. All of Israel will look to Him for help and survival.

The Names of Jesus

In picturesque language, John described the many facets of our Lord. In 19:12 John wrote, *"He had a name written, that no man knew, but he himself,"*, indicating the *mystery* of His nature. Essentially, God knows what we know and He is fully cognizant of the vast chasm of knowledge that we are unable to grasp. Nothing is hidden from His eyes.

John also wrote, *"His name is called The Word of God"* signifying the supernatural relationship between God and His word (19:13b). In our day, there is an effort to drive a wedge of discontinuity between the words of the scriptures and the spirit of our Lord. Some wrongfully content that if the scriptures appear overly harsh or unsettling, we should look for the spirit of Jesus to properly understand the scriptures in light of cultural considerations. In reality, such an effort is heretical in nature. In short, Jesus is *The Word of God.*

In 19:13b, John also intended to magnify and identify God as *"The Word of God"*. The Greek word *logos* is utilized to identify God Himself as the *Word*, *"In the beginning was the Word, and the Word was with God, and the Word was God"* (John 1:1). There is no doubt that Jesus Christ was God in human flesh, contrary to the heretical position cult groups in our day choose to take. Most cult groups propose that Jesus was relegated to the role of a gifted prophet akin in nature and significance to that of their respective founders. No question about it - that is sheer heresy!

A word in its most basic and simple form is an expression of thought. The most significant thought Jesus had of Himself was that His very nature is identical to, and in reality, *is* the Word of God.

When Jesus returns to conquer evil and usher in the millennial reign, He will do so as the *logos* of God, the vivid display of the God-man through the medium of human flesh. At His triumphant return at the Battle of Armageddon, this same Jesus will dole out retribution and judgment consistent with His character as just and fair.

His name is also one of incredible *majesty.* He will reign as the *"KING OF KINGS, AND LORD OF LORDS"* (19:16). The awesome display of His power will be unmistakable in the eyes of the watching world. Israel will see and recognize His authority and divinity and be spared from destruction in the battle to come.

The reign of Jesus will have only begun.

Chapter 43

THE SIGNS OF ARMAGEDDON
Revelation 19: 14-21

Hollywood actor Bruce Willis starred in *Armageddon*, a blockbuster movie in which he portrayed the rugged head of a motley crew assigned the monumental task of thwarting the coming collision of a giant meteor with the earth. The epic is a bit far-fetched, of course, yet Willis and his brave crew saved the earth from certain destruction causing the world to sigh in relief.

When Jesus makes His final entrance upon the earth to set His feet on the Mount of Olives and encounter the forces of the evil, nothing will prevent the destruction of the Antichrist and the nations that will have aligned themselves with him. In this dramatic appearance, Christ will not be coming *for* His saints in order to claim and remove them from the earth but rather *with* His saints as members of His divine army.

In Zechariah 7:14, the prophet predicted this event hundreds of years before John received an identical vision to be recorded during his island exile. Jesus will return in honor rather than in humility, not to a cross but rather to a coronation, and not merely as a resident but to rule as the divine president.

Jesus will arrive in a cloud of glory mounted upon a white horse, crowned with the many crowns of glory and honor, his vesture dipped in blood, and with the name written on His robe, *King of Kings, and Lord of Lords.* As He approaches the final battle in the Valley of Armageddon, the army of the saints and the hosts of heaven will ride with Him into victory with their heads held high.

Scripture predicts that the Mount of Olives will split into halves allowing for the passage of Christ and His army. Jesus will enter the temple mound where He will announce His global rule as the Lord of all lords. Notable seismologists have confirmed the presence of a geological fault in Israel that will allow for such an earth-rending event. Even without the presence of a geological fault, our Lord possesses the power to create geological turbulence of any dimension. He will require no geological assistance when he bursts into the Valley of Megiddo.

Concerning His coming entrance into northern Israel, John wrote these victorious words,

> *And the armies which were in heaven followed him upon white horses, clothed in fine linen, white and clean. And out of his mouth goeth a sharp sword, that with it he should smite the nations: and he shall rule them with a rod of iron: and he treadeth the winepress of the fierceness and wrath of Almighty God. And he hath on his vesture and on his thigh a name written, KING OF KINGS, AND LORD OF LORDS. And I saw an angel standing in the sun; and he cried with a loud voice, saying to all the fowls that fly in the midst of heaven, 'Come and gather yourselves together unto the supper of the great God'* (19: 14-17).

A Second Great Supper

In Luke 14, Jesus related the story of a wealthy gentleman who made preparations for a great feast with invitations to attend given to a vast assortment of people. Yet when the time for the meal arrived, the banquet chairs were empty. In response, the wealthy fellow gave instructions for those in the *highways and hedges* to be invited and compelled to attend. This second invitation focused upon the blind, lame, poor, and all others willing to admit their need.

The parable is a vivid picture of the gospel supper, the menu of which is comprised of the bread of life and the food of salvation. God has prepared this spiritual feast with His death on the cross and invites *any one who will* to come and enjoy the great supper of salvation.

In 19: 14-18, John wrote of a second great supper, the supper of the Lord's judgment. In 19:18 he wrote,

> *That ye may eat of the flesh of kings, and the flesh of captains, and the flesh of mighty men, and the flesh of horses, and of them that sit*

> *on them, and the flesh of all men, both free and bond, both small and great.*

This clash of divine and demonic forces will be the final showdown of history as we know it, the Gunfight at OK Corral, as it were. Once and for all, the identity of the head of the universe will be cast in stone. Satan will lose.

The Composition of Heaven's Armies

Distinct from the rapture event, this second coming of Christ will be accompanied by a breathtaking array of mighty angels. In II Thessalonians 1:7-9 Paul wrote,

> *And to you who are troubled rest with us, when the Lord Jesus shall be revealed from heaven with his mighty angels. In flaming fire taking vengeance on them that know not God, and that obey not the gospel of our Lord Jesus Christ: Who shall be punished with everlasting destruction from the presence of the Lord, and from the glory of his power.*

These piercing words reveal a horrible eternity without God and an everlasting destruction to afflict evil men. The two words, everlasting destruction, appear at first glance to be mutually exclusive yet life lived apart from God will result in evil men existing in a state of unending destruction.

The scriptures also inform us concerning the past activities of God's angels. As Jesus was taken prisoner in the Garden of Gethsemane, Peter attempted to forcefully defend his Lord by taking a swipe with his sword at one of the Roman soldiers. Thankfully, Peter missed his intended target area yet sliced the ear of the soldier. Jesus promptly scolded Peter and reminded him that He could employ the assistance of legions of angels at any moment to deliver Him from harm if He so chose. These angels, who once stood nearby as Jesus was hauled away to captivity, one day will release a full measure of vengeance on those who have rejected our Lord. No display of military power in history will even begin to compare with that of our Lord and His angels in the day of Armageddon.

Joining the angels in the army of God will be those of us who are His followers. Paul wrote in II Thessalonians 1:10a, *"When he shall come to be glorified in his saints, and to be admired in all them that believe."* Biblically, those of us who are followers of our Lord also are soldiers who wear God's armor (Ephesians 6). As a rule, we do not contend in physical battles in this *age of grace* but rather we wrestle with spiritual and demonic forces in the heavenly realm.

The Battle of Armageddon will involve both spiritual and physical realms of existence. This divine army to win the final battle will be composed of angels, saints of God who comprise the Church, saints of the old and new testament periods, and the saints who will be savagely martyred in the tribulation era.

This army of the Lord will be outfitted and clothed quite differently than the average army. John described the army as sporting *"fine linen, white and clean."* This attire essentially is a robe of righteousness draped over the army of the Lord. Side arms, rifles, and various other instruments of war will not be necessary.

Our weapons of righteousness, secured by God in the death of Jesus on the cross, will suffice and will lead to a decisive victory over God's enemies. Our uniforms of righteousness will radiate the glory of God and will thwart any and all plans of evil men.

The Sole Weapon of Warfare

John vividly described in 19:15 the sole weapon of our Lord in this final climactic battle scene as a *"sharp sword."* The intended emphasis here is not on military might but rather upon the unsurpassed power of the Word of God. The writer of Hebrews described the world as having been framed with the Word of God. At the moment God was prepared to redeem the world, He accomplished the task by means of the Word of God. Jesus Christ *is* the Word of God made flesh and by the Word, He has the capability of cutting into the innermost chambers of man's heart (John 1:14).

In this final battle, John envisioned the *"sword of the spirit, which is the word of God"* as protruding from His mouth (Ephesians 6: 17). With His word as His weapon, God will destroy all of the sophisticated weaponry and strategies of evil men. Those to fall under His unyielding control at the final battle scene will be ruled by His divine *"rod of iron,"* indicating a forced and involuntary submission.

During the millennial reign, full submission to the rule of Christ by the entire creation will be in effect until the time when God allows for the temporary parole of Satan from the bottomless prison to engage in a final and unsuccessful revolt. Even in this final rebellion, Satan will exist on God's leash. This episode will further underscore the fact that unredeemed men inherently fall under the evil spell of Satan when given an opportunity. Sinners do love to sin.

The Wrath of His Warfare

John returned once again to the metaphor of the *"winepress,"* a device utilized in the crushing of grapes, to depict the fierceness of His wrath to come (19:15b). In the messianic Psalm 2, God prophesied that the heathen one day will be presented to the people of God as spoil in the battle. The Psalmist further promised that Jesus Christ will continue His reign until His enemies become like a footstool under His feet, indicating the full submission of the enemies to Him (Psalm 110:1).

As grapes were crushed under the stomping feet of the harvesters, the armies of the Antichrist will fall under the feet of God's army. The wounds of the Antichrist and his evil followers will flow with blood and reveal the horrendous nature of God's wrath.

Stricken with the temptations of human nature, we often enjoy extracting revenge from others who have wronged us. We enjoy claiming a pound or two of flesh from those we dislike. Yet to do so is to venture into a territory reserved for God alone. He clearly has said, *"Vengeance is mine; I will repay, saith the Lord"* (Romans 12: 19).

Rest assured, Jesus will be the avenger of all that is wrong. Those who fall under His wrath will be consumed in the end by the birds of prey summoned by our Lord in a grim act depicting the end of the earthly existence of evil men.

In Matthew 24: 27-28, Jesus described this gruesome scene,

> *For as the lightning cometh out of the east, and shineth even unto the west; so shall also the coming of the Son of man be. For wheresoever the carcass is, there will the eagles be gathered together.*

In glaring contrast to the delightful marriage supper of the Lamb, vultures will remove any remaining signs of the existence of evil men. Evil itself and evil men will vanish from the scene.

The Lure: Hatred for the Jews

The forces of Satan will be not only *doomed* at the final battle but will also be *drawn* to this event by their intense ongoing hatred for the Jewish people. In addition to the lust for power burning in the heart of the Antichrist and other such temptations, the Antichrist will possess an insatiable appetite to annihilate the Jews from the earth and thereby remove his primary obstacle to world dominion.

In ancient times, the Jews were an irritant to the Romans and once again will be a stumbling block to the revival of the new Roman Empire headed by the Antichrist. The focal point of contention will be Jerusalem. It appears strange that powerful nations of the world will fight against our Lord Himself until we understand the full intent of Psalm 2. King David existed in the lineage of Jesus Christ and also served as a forerunner of Jesus. David wrote in Psalm 2:1-3 concerning the armies of the world that will position themselves as enemies of God,

> *'Why do the heathen rage, and the people imagine a vain thing?' the kings of the earth set themselves, and the rulers take counsel together, against the Lord, and against his anointed, saying, 'Let us break their bands asunder, and cast away their cords from us.'*

Heathen men often live in a perpetual state of anger because the darkness of their hearts compels them to rebel against the laws of God that they consider restrictive. In the core of their hearts, evil men reject God in favor of wickedness. Evidently, evil loves evil.

The nations of the earth failed in their valiant attempt to destroy King David and his kingdom. David led the nation to victory and to the establishment of Israel as the greatest world power of his day. In like manner, God will establish Jesus Christ, a King greater than David, upon the throne of David to rule forever and ever. Psalm 2: 4-9 records this prophecy yet to be fulfilled in the millennial reign,

> *He that sitteth in the heavens shall laugh: the Lord shall have them in derision. Then shall he speak unto them in his wrath, and vex them in his sore displeasure. Yet have I set my king upon my holy hill of Zion. I will declare the decree: the Lord hath said unto me, 'Thou are my Son; this day have I begotten thee. Ask of me, and I shall give thee the heathen for thine inheritance, and the uttermost parts of the earth for thy possession. Thou shalt break them with a rod of iron; thou shalt dash them in pieces like a potter's vessel.'*

God will laugh at the bold audacity of those who oppose Him in the battle. The scripture indicates that a day will soon come when the knees of every demon, every political power, and every creature will bow at the feet of our Lord and be forced to acknowledge His unchallenged claim to the throne of the universe. Every knee will bow yet not every knee will accept the Lordship of Jesus Christ in their hearts (Philippians 2:10). Evil men will walk into hell cursing the very Lord they have chosen to reject.

Satan's Armies Destroyed

Fight as they may, the armies of Satan will go down in utter defeat. John wrote of this defeat to come in 19: 19-20,

> *And I saw the beast, and the kings of the earth, and their armies, gathered together to make war against him that sat on the horse, and*

> *against his army. And the beast was taken, and with him the false prophet that wrought miracles before him, with which he deceived them that had received the mark of the beast, and them that worshipped his image. These both were cast alive into a lake of fire burning with brimstone.*

Jesus clearly taught that hell is a place where the fires are never doused. Torment will inflict its captives and will not allow for a single moment of rest. The frightening words *"cast alive"* indicate that people in hell will exist in a state of dying yet never die. Screams for relief and for the alternative of physical death will go unheard.

The coworkers of evil in our day include proponents of the occult who may have been duped by a false display of healings and other such alleged supernatural phenomenon. The one-world church, personified and led by the False Prophet, will see a sudden surge of interest in the last days. One lure to prove enormously effective in capturing the hearts of evil men will be counterfeit displays of the miraculous. The scriptures give a clear and stern warning that believers must *try the spirits* to ascertain their divine or satanic origin (I John 4: 1a).

The battle of all battles looms on the horizon of history. Join the army of the Lord while there is yet time. The outcome of the battle has been predetermined. We win.

PART 5

THE MILLENIAL REIGN OF CHRIST

Chapter 44

THE MILLENIUM: EARTH'S GOLDEN AGE
Revelation 20: 1-6

Actress Jodi Foster starred in a very innovative movie entitled *Contact* in which scientists attempted to establish communication with extraterrestrial life. The character portrayed by Ms. Foster was transported through time and space into a beautiful and undisturbed meadow in which the surroundings were untarnished by human hands. This life-changing journey tempted the character played by Ms. Foster to remain in this land of nirvana rather than return to face the harsh realities of life on earth.

Philosophers have perpetually longed for a state of peaceful existence upon the earth in which nations might dwell together without strife and conflict. Such a state of peace, forever elusive in our creaturely existence, will be established in the millennial kingdom spanning one thousand years. This peaceful state of living will be established by our Lord as the smoke clears from the Battle of Armageddon.

Concerning this coming golden age, John wrote these words of hope in 20: 1-10,

> *And I saw an angel come down from heaven, having the key of the bottomless pit and a great chain in his hand. And he laid hold on the dragon, that old serpent, which is the Devil, and Satan, and bound him a thousand years. And cast him into the bottomless pit, and shut him up, and set a seal upon him, that he should deceive the nations no more, till the thousand years should be fulfilled: and after that he must be loosed a little season. And I saw thrones, and they sat upon them, and judgment was given unto them: and I saw the souls of them that were beheaded for the witness of Jesus, and for the word of God, and which had not worshipped the beast, neither his image, neither had received his mark upon their foreheads, or in their hands; and they lived and reigned with Christ a thousand years. But*

the rest of the dead lived not again until the thousand years were finished. This is the first resurrection. Blessed and holy is he that hath part in the first resurrection: on such the second death hath no power, but they shall be priests of God and of Christ, and shall reign with him a thousand years.

Perhaps more biblical material exists concerning the subject of the coming *kingdom of God* than concerning any other subject. Cries for unity and peace continue to echo from governments circling the globe. In our day of modern technology, no nation successfully exists in isolation from the rest of the world community. In spite of breathtaking accomplishments unifying the economic world, the quality of the peace achieved by man is less than lasting and will always be limited in quality and scope. Several years ago, a United States senator announced that more than thirty wars were in progress at the very moment his words were spoken in the chambers in Congress. Peace will forever be a fleeting fancy.

Those of us who are Christ's followers will experience the fulfillment of our dreams and hopes in the millennial kingdom. The term *millennial* is not found in the pages of scripture but is a derivative of the expression, *a thousand years* referenced in Revelation 20: 2-4. Several primary views concerning this era of time have developed in theological circles in recent years.

Amillennialism

The negative particle *a* in the term amillennialism indicates that proponents of this view believe that a literal one- thousand year reign will not occur. This perspective, rejected and unpopular in conservative circles, is not found in church historical documents or in the earliest writings of the church fathers. Proponents do accept the coming literal and physical return of Jesus to the earth. Unfortunately, they also spiritualize the millennium as a mere state of mind.

This position has been propagated to some extent by most mainline theological schools in the last fifty years. Popular bible students such as Charles Stanley, W.A. Criswell, Billy Graham, and

John McArthur, Jr. firmly reject this position as do others who contend for a literal interpretation of the scriptures. I gladly join their ranks.

Postmillennialism

Postmillennialists contend that Christ will return to a literal kingdom of God on earth yet inaccurately assume that Christ will return only at the conclusion of the one-thousand year reign. Proponents contend that Christ will return when the Church has successfully evangelized the world, resolved the social dilemmas we all face, and has created effective educational programs resulting in the readiness of society to welcome the return of Jesus.

This view, overly optimistic concerning the potential for good in society, was quite popular at the beginning of the twentieth century yet is currently lacking in credibility due to the World Wars, Korean conflict, and the obvious deterioration of the moral fabric of our society. Any astute observer will readily admit that the church will never usher in a state of societal nirvana and cure all that ails mankind.

Birth rates in the world outpace the rate of Christian conversions seen by the church. Many observers estimate that only two percent of the world population will be classified as born-again Christians in the near future. Jesus clearly taught that the road to heaven is indeed a narrow one. The world wanders in spiritual lostness oblivious to the road leading to heaven or at least unwilling to follow its path.

Premillennialism

I gladly join the massive chorus of adherents to the premillennial method of interpretation and believe that the scriptures clearly indicate the one thousand-year reign of Jesus will be a literal event to encompass one thousand chronological years (Revelation 20). In this view, Jesus will triumphantly return to the earth a second time at the close of the prophet Daniel's *seventieth week*, a reference to the seven years of the tribulation era.

This literal view of prophetic scripture is most consistent with the biblical teachings concerning the nature of man, salvation, and Satan and his rule on the earth. Satan has recruited the kingdoms of this world as coworkers in his dastardly scheme to enslave the world. He has been known by names such as the *god of this world* and the *great deceiver* (II Corinthians 4:4, Revelation 12:9). In a moment of temptation, he offered to Jesus the kingdoms of this world indicating that such kingdoms were Satan's to offer. He rules indeed, yet does so with a divine leash and well within the limitations of God's sovereign permission.

Jesus will pursue His reign until He has placed all of His enemies *under His feet.* When Jesus taught the disciples that the kingdom of God was *within them*, He was indicating that the kingdom is composed of those who have willingly surrendered their own will to that of Christ. Yet Satan continues to run amuck in this world enslaving willing followers. The millennial reign will clearly differentiate between the world as governed by Satan and the world under the rule of Jesus Christ.

Satan Bound

At the outset of the millennial period, Satan will be unceremoniously removed and imprisoned with a life sentence. In 20: 1-3a John wrote,

> *And I saw an angel come down from heaven, having the key of the bottomless pit and a great chain in his hand. And he laid hold on the dragon, that old serpent, which is the Devil, and Satan, and bound him a thousand years, And cast him into the bottomless pit.*

This episode to come is literal. John employed the phrase *"And I saw"* indicating the details of his eyewitness account as revealed in the vision God gave him. In my view, no adequate reason has been put forth indicating that the binding of Satan to come is merely figurative in nature.

Other biblical references do exist underscoring the binding of demon spirits as suggested in 20:2. Jude 6 records, *"the angels which kept not their first estate, but left their own habitation."* The *"first estate"* indicates God's original design for His angels to praise Him and perpetuate His divine plan for the universe. One-third of the angelic hosts failed to follow God's plan resulting in their captivity in chains under darkness until the time of judgment. The *abyss*, the location of demonic confinement, is mentioned seven times in Revelation. The precise meaning of the phrase *"chains of darkness"* is unknown but it does suggest a dungeon or pit. This *abyss* is not the final hell but rather a prison house in which spirit beings await God's judgment.

In the Mark 5:1-13 episode concerning demonic influence, a man was empowered with supernatural strength and often snapped his iron chains due to the demonic presence within him. He was unaware of his nakedness and often heard emitting bone-chilling screams in the night.

Demons held in bondage are tormented and are fully aware that eternal torment in the bottomless pit and lake of fire awaits them. According to God's sovereign plan, some of Satan's minions evidently are released from the pit to spread heartache on the earth. Other demons, however, are imprisoned in the *"chains of darkness"* for eternity with no possibility of parole.

The binding of Satan will span the full one thousand years. The purpose of this captivity is *"that he should deceive the nations no more, till the thousand years should be fulfilled"* (20:3b). For the prophecies concerning peace on earth, the restoration of the ecology, and a world without sickness or death to be fulfilled, Satan must be removed from the scene. The Garden of Eden existed in a state of perfection until Satan reared his ugly head and poisoned man with temptation thereby introducing sin into the world. He lives and breathes to enslave mankind.

The ability of Satan to deceive the nations and present himself as an *angel of light* is well documented. Satan convinces man that strengthening his financial portfolio will solve all of the problems men face and will fulfill his every need. In convincing fashion, Satan blinds men to the truth of the gospel and enslaves the passions and desires of men for his own evil schemes. His evil deeds will come to a screeching halt as he hears the clank of slamming doors in his bottomless prison.

The Reign of the Saints

As the saints of the old and new covenant periods and the martyrs of the tribulation join with Jesus in the millennial reign, we will experience a magnificent coronation. In 20:4 John wrote,

> *And I saw thrones, and they sat upon them, and judgment was given unto them: and I saw the souls of them that were beheaded for the witness of Jesus, and for the word of God....and they lived and reigned with Christ a thousand years.*

In II Timothy 2:12, Paul wrote that suffering saints one day will become reigning saints. Faithful believers have taken up the cross of Jesus but one day will wear a crown.

Biblically, Jesus best modeled the experience of suffering followed by reigning. The letter to the Philippians records the *kenosis* or self-emptying of Christ as He *"humbled himself"* as a man and suffered for mankind. As a result, God *"exalted Him"* and gave to Him the undisputed right to rule and reign. In essence, He descended before He ascended. In a similar manner, we must humble ourselves as believers and identify with Jesus and His sufferings if we are to reign with Him one day (Philippians 2: 1-5).

John also witnessed on the throne those who had been *"beheaded"* due to their faith in Christ. These souls were seen under the altar at the time of the breaking of the fifth seal in John's vision (6:9-11). This group may also include some who will be martyred during the first segment of the tribulation. If we were alive during the fierce persecution instigated by the Roman Empire, these words would offer greater meaning and consolation to us. Many faithful believers were killed during that horrible era merely for sport and in an effort to obliterate Christianity. Martyred believers in that day, and those to be killed in the tribulation era, will be handsomely rewarded by our Lord with an exalted place on the throne of God.

Such persecution, followed by blessing and the privilege of ruling, is further exemplified in the Genesis character of Joseph. Joseph experienced an undeserved confinement for years yet later was rewarded by God with a position of enormous influence in the nation of Egypt. Joseph exemplified a type of Christ in that he was punished for a crime he did not commit. He suffered unjustly yet was rewarded with the privilege of ruling.

The book, *Destined for the Throne* by Bill Heimer has been affectionately described as training for reigning. Heimer clearly articulates the maturing process of the character of believers who will join the millennial reign. We will be *joint heirs with Christ* and will sit with Him in the chair of global authority. Even now, we are in preparation for that day.

In the scriptures, we are introduced to a story in which the mother of two of the disciples of Jesus wished for her two sons to be seated on the right and left sides of our Lord when He reigns on the earth. This concept has been deeply embedded in Jewish thought throughout their history. The Jews believed that their messiah would come as a powerful conqueror defeating the enemies of Israel and that He would share his reign with those who were faithful. This image of Christ is consistent with that of the Old Testament and Revelation 19, yet the Jews did not recognize or accept the Messiah of the first century. They recognized the prophecy of the future unchallenged rule of Jesus yet are confused regarding the time sequence.

Jews today continue to reject the gentle shepherd of the first century as the savior of the world. His rule by love clashes with their desire for rule by might.

The First Resurrection

The various facets of the biblical concept of resurrection are primarily rooted in Christ as the first person to actually resurrect. In I Corinthians 15:20 Paul wrote, *"[Christ is] the firstfruits of them that slept."* This concept of *firstfruits* is symbolic in the scriptures. The first portion of the grain given to God indicated an abundant harvest to follow. The waving of the grain before the

Lord signified their acknowledgement that God was the giver of the harvest and therefore deserved the first portion of the harvest.

Jesus bodily arose from the grave with both personality and identity. The nature of His resurrection serves as a type of things to come. In 20: 6 John wrote,

> *Blessed and holy is he that hath part in the first resurrection: on such the second death hath no power, but they shall be priests of God and of Christ, and shall reign with him a thousand years.*

This first resurrection will involve believers who are *"blessed and holy,"* referring to the entire personhood of tri-dimensional man: the salvation of the spirit, the soul, and the body. A full measure of happiness and peace will accompany this marvelous experience for every believer.

This first resurrection will also involve believers who will be snatched away at the outset of the tribulation era. As Christ returns with His saints at the Battle of Armageddon, martyred tribulation saints will be resurrected as well. No longer existing as flesh and blood, we will enjoy our glorified heavenly bodies never again to be subjected to the frailties of mankind. All of our creaks and groans will vanish!

The saints of God will enjoy enormous confidence due to these gifts of God to His children. The first resurrection will occur in stages: the resurrection of Christ from the tomb; the snatching away of the saints at the rapture; the resurrection of the two witnesses in Revelation 11; and the resurrection of martyred saints in the tribulation.

The second resurrection of John's vision involved the opening of the *"books"* which will record the deeds of men without Christ (20:12). This frightening event will occur at the end of the one thousand-year reign of Jesus with His saints on earth.

The second death, the death that will span eternity and involve perpetual punishment for evil men, will have no effect upon believers in Jesus Christ. Jesus once warned, *"Fear not them which kill the body, but are not able to kill the soul: but rather fear him which is able to destroy both body and soul in hell"* (Matthew 10: 28).

It has been well said that to be born only once is to die twice, both physically and spiritually. Conversely, to be born twice, both physically and spiritually, is to die only once.

A man with Jesus in his heart will die - and live forever.

Chapter 45

POLITICS AND SOCIETY IN THE MILLENIUM
Revelation 20: 1-6

As citizens of the United States, we are well aware of the combative nature of the American political system and watch in awe as elected officials square off and challenge one another with less than endearing words. Given the rugged nature of politics, one wonders if any good will ever be accomplished. Many citizens simply ignore the entire process only to be awakened from their slumber when their pocketbooks are negatively affected.

Universal Peace and Justice

In glaring contrast, the political and societal atmosphere of the millennial reign will be one of universal peace and justice. Conflict and the deterioration of society will suddenly disappear.

In His earthly tour of duty, Jesus was pictured as a suffering servant as depicted in Isaiah 53:5-6, *"He was wounded for our transgressions, he was bruised for our iniquities….All we like sheep have gone astray; we have turned every one to his own way; and the Lord hath laid on him the iniquity of us all."* However, a facet of the reign of the branch of Jesse (the father of David) yet to come also will be righteous and comprehensive in the unlimited scope of its rule.

In part, the reason for the coming kingdom of Christ on earth in the millennium is to fulfill the prophecy concerning the throne of David. Isaiah 11: 1 records,

> *There shall come forth a rod out of the stem of Jesse, and a Branch shall grow out of his roots.*

Isaiah is herein referring to the human, physical earthly lineage of the Messiah from the tribe of Jesse. The gospel writer Matthew meticulously presented the truth that the tribe of

Judah and the family of Jesse are within the genealogy of Jesus. Isaiah also prophesied concerning our Lord in 11: 2-11a,

> *And the spirit of the Lord shall rest upon him, the spirit of wisdom and understanding, the spirit of counsel and might, the spirit of knowledge and of the fear of the Lord; And shall make him of quick understanding in the fear of the Lord: and he shall not judge after the sight of his eyes, neither reprove after the hearing of his ears: But with righteousness shall he judge the poor, and reprove with equity for the meek of the earth: and he shall smite the earth: with the rod of his mouth, and with the breath of his lips shall he slay the wicked. And righteousness shall be the girdle of his loins, and faithfulness the girdle of his reins. The wolf also shall dwell with the lamb, and the leopard shall lie down with the kid; and the calf and the young lion and the fatling together; and a little child shall lead them. And the cow and the bear shall feed; their young ones shall lie down together: and the lion shall eat straw like the ox. And the sucking child shall play on the hole of the asp, and the weaned child shall put his hand on the cockatrice' den. They shall not hurt nor destroy in all my holy mountain: for the earth shall be full of the knowledge of the Lord, as the waters cover the sea. And in that day there shall be a root of Jesse, which shall stand for an ensign of the people; to it shall the Gentiles seek: and his rest shall be glorious. And it shall come to pass in that day, that the Lord shall set his hand again the second time to recover the remnant of his people, which shall be left.*

The society and economic order of the millennial period will not be fraught with the same unrest and instability we now experience. Men have forever longed for a perfect society. That day will finally arrive in the millennial reign.

How will this state of perfect peace and tranquility which will extend even to the animal kingdom, be established? Hosea 2:18 predicts this event as well,

> *And in that day will I make a covenant for them with the beasts of the field, and with the fowls of heaven, and with the creeping things of the ground: and I will break the bow and the sword and the battle out of the earth, and will make them to lie down safely.*

No era of total peace has existed on the earth since before the fall of man in the Garden of Eden when Satan interfered and usurped the rule of the earth. However, our Lord will reclaim that rule from the clutches of Satan and blanket the earth with universal peace and justice for one thousand years.

A Christian Majority

Committed believers are no longer in the majority in our nation in our day of religious pluralism and cries for tolerance for any and all forms of behavior. Voices of dissent continue to pound away at every vestige of moral absolute in favor of situational truth or no truth at all. Today, to believe nothing is considered a virtue.

In the millennium, believers will be struck with awe as we see and hear Jesus in person. His knowledge and supremacy will cover the hemisphere as waters cover the seas. The earth will reverberate with the *"knowledge of the Lord"* (Isaiah 11: 9b).

Evidently, all of the unconverted individuals who survive the Battle of Armageddon will experience death at the outset of the millennium. Two of the major parables told by our Lord deal with the methods by which God will judge the world at the second coming of Christ and with the Battle to occur seven years after the rapture.

The Parable of the Wheat and Tares relates the story of the coming of Jesus with His holy angels to separate the wheat from the tares, representative of believers and non-believers, respectively. Concerning this coming harvest of the souls of men, Jesus said in Matthew 13:30,

> *Let both grow together until the harvest: and in the time of harvest I will say to the reapers, 'Gather ye together first the tares, and bind them in bundles to burn them: but gather the wheat into my barn.'*

The apostle John also wrote of this sin-ripened harvest in Revelation 14:18b, *"Thrust in thy sharp sickle, and gather the clusters of the vine of the earth: for her grapes are fully ripe."* This harvest refers to a major component of the last judgments of God upon the earth.

An additional harvest story utilizes the metaphor of the harvesting of fish in which God predicted the coming kingdom of heaven (Matthew 13: 47-50). The kingdom of heaven is a spiritual one for which Jesus explained was *within you.* This spiritual kingdom of the heart continues to be established in our hearts in this *age of grace.* The coming kingdom of the millennial reign will exist physically before our very eyes yet will be spiritual in nature as well.

The millennium will be launched with a clean slate as wicked men will be removed from the earth leaving a generation of God's children to rule and reign. It is difficult for our finite minds to fathom such a magnificent state of divine tranquility. Jesus said in Matthew 13: 47-50,

> *Again, the kingdom of heaven is like unto a net that was cast into the sea, and gathered of every kind: Which, when it was full, they drew to shore, and sat down, and gathered the good into vessels, but cast the bad away. So shall it be at the end of the world: the angels shall come forth, and sever the wicked from among the just, And shall cast them into the furnace of fire: there shall be wailing and gnashing of teeth.*

I believe that people in the millennium existing physically will bear children. In fact, a tremendous explosion of the population may occur given the perfected state of health and healing that Jesus will establish.

Satan will be temporarily loosed from confinement at the end of the millennium and proceed to deceive the nations once again (20:7). An enormous rebellion against God will be instigated yet short-lived (20:9).

Even when blessed with a perfect environment, a sinless society, and faultless parents, men still have hearts that are deceitful, victims of the sinful curse inherited from Adam. In the millennium, many will obey Christ solely out of necessity fully aware that He will rule with a *rod of iron.* When Satan is paroled from his prison abyss, men who are not genuine believers in our Lord will leap at the chance to join Satan's rebellious army. Essentially, sin is an issue of power, a struggle to determine the controlling authority in our lives. God once again will demonstrate that men will choose evil when given the opportunity.

We live in a society in which the guilty present themselves as mere victims. Some point the finger of blame at an unfortunate childhood or unfair treatment rather than toward themselves. Man seldom enjoys admitting his sinfulness.

The dirtiness and residue of sinful living will be fully washed away during the millennium. Drugs will vanish and immorality will lack for victims. Yet when Satan is freed for a time, men and women posing as believers will display their true colors and gladly join in his rebellion. However, this uprising will meet a quick and final demise.

A Suspended Curse

The curse that has inflicted the earth since the *fall of man* will be partially lifted in the millennium. The final removal of the curse will occur at the appearance of the new heavens and earth. The earth will become a productive environment in which unproductive lands, such as the barren Sahara Desert, will produce luscious greenery in unprecedented fashion. Droughts will disappear allowing for bumper crops. Isaiah 35: 1-2 records this event,

> *The wilderness and the solitary place shall be glad for them; and the desert shall rejoice, and blossom as the rose. It shall blossom abundantly, and rejoice even with joy and singing: the glory of Lebanon shall be given unto it, the excellency of Carmel and Sharon, they shall see the glory of the Lord, and the excellency of our God.*

Torrential rains will bless the earth as well. Isaiah 30:23 predicts the rains of the millennium, *"Then shall he give the rain of thy seed, that thou shalt sow the ground withal; and bread of the increase of the earth, and it shall be fat and plenteous: in that day shall thy cattle feed in large pastures."* These words were penned after the Babylonians destroyed the nation of Israel in a rout. These fierce enemies of Israel polluted the lands in order to destroy their productivity. Israel has experienced many droughts in its history, some which were divinely instigated to discipline the nation, yet in the millennium the floodgates will open and blessings of every dimension will flow.

Food will be in abundance. Isaiah 30:24 predicts, *"The oxen likewise and the young asses that ear the ground shall eat clean provender, which hath been winnowed with the shovel and with the fan."* The cattle will eat to their heart's content.

However, death will continue to occur in the millennium. Yet those reaching old age will be children simultaneously because the curse of aging will be held at bay. Men will live to ages comparable to the advanced ages of men in early Old Testament history. The curse of sin has continued to effect each successive generation throughout history shortening life spans. This aspect of the curse, and other such creature limitations, will be suspended during the millennial reign ushering in an era of prosperity too magnificent to imagine. The prophet Jeremiah wrote of this fruitful era as well,

> *Therefore they shall come and sing in the height of Zion, and shall low together to the goodness of the Lord, for wheat, and for wine, and for oil, and for the young of the flock and of the herd: and their soul shall be as a watered garden; and they shall not sorrow any more at all* (Jeremiah 31:12).

Millennial Prosperity

The prophet Malachi wrote words of chastisement to the people of Israel who had grown lax in their worship and giving practices. He reminded the people of the prosperity that would accompany their repentance and obedience. Malachi 3: 10-11 reads in part, *"Bring ye all the tithes into the storehouse...prove me now herewith... if I will not open the windows of heaven and pour you out a blessing...And ... will rebuke the devourer for your sakes..."*

Life in the millennium will feature such magnificent harvests that the *"plowman shall overtake the reaper"* (Amos 9:13a). The abundance and quality of the harvest will fill containers to overflowing. God has promised this time of great harvest and prosperity, a time upon the earth involving the future restoration of Israel as well.

Politicians in our day promise prosperity yet voters seldom expect to see the fruit of such promises. God's promises of unfathomable prosperity will flood His faithful children with blessings too abundant to contain. These blessings will also demonstrate to mankind what might have occurred on earth prior to the rapture had man not fallen into sin and instead chosen to obey God. This era of millennial prosperity will be representative of God's original and ultimate intention for the world and for His children.

Workers in the millennium will receive just compensation for their labor leaving no further need for strikes or union workers to quibble with management. Jesus will provide full and equal rights for all. No system of unfair treatment will be in existence.

The kingdom of animals will exist in utter harmony. Children will play with untamed beasts and do so without fear or harm because the essential nature of animals will be affected by millennial tranquility as well. The curse hovering over creation since the Garden episode will be lifted never again afflicting God's people.

Hospitals will close with empty beds and no further need for medical assistance. Bottles of medication will lie dormant on the shelves. Isaiah 33: 24 reads,

> *The inhabitants shall not say, 'I am sick': the people that dwell therein shall be forgiven their iniquity.*

In part, the sicknesses of mankind are due to the gnawing presence of our sin nature. When Jesus establishes the millennial reign, an outpouring of physical and spiritual healing will occur. Isaiah 29:18 predicts this unprecedented event, *"And in that day shall the deaf hear the words of the book, and the eyes of the blind shall see out of obscurity, and out of darkness."* Disability will disappear. The brokenhearted will receive ultimate comfort, captives will be released, and people bound in prisons will walk away in freedom (Isaiah 61: 1-2).

Men who have lived in mourning will receive the soothing grace offered by our loving Lord. Isaiah penned these beautiful words,

> *To appoint unto them that mourn in Zion, to give unto them beauty for ashes, the oil of joy for mourning, the garment of praise for the spirit of heaviness; that they might be called trees of righteousness, the planting of the Lord, that He might be glorified* (Isaiah 61:3).

Short Memories

The painful experiences of our past will fade from view as God erases them from our minds and hearts. Praise will replace heartache. Joy will sooth all sorrow. Ultimately, this state of perfect tranquility and peace will find its fulfillment in the establishment of the new heavens and new earth.

No words to describe this moment compare with those of our Lord given through the prophet Isaiah,

> *But be ye glad and rejoice for ever in that which I create: for, behold, I create Jerusalem a rejoicing, and her people a joy. And I will rejoice in Jerusalem, and joy in my people: and the voice of weeping shall be no more heard in her, nor the voice of crying. There shall be no more thence an infant of days, nor an old man that hath not filled his days: for the child shall die an hundred years old; but the sinner being an hundred years old shall be accursed* (Isaiah 65: 18-20).

Chapter 46

A RIGHTEOUS MILLENNIAL GOVERNMENT
Revelation 20: 1-6

When governmental corruption occurs, American eyes are riveted to television screens like fans at the racetrack hoping for a collision. Conflict and carnality in high places tends to capture the fancy of most of us for some curious reason. We are well aware that money corrupts yet we seem to enjoy watching the process. Concerning the political arena, one fellow quipped, "A fool and his money are soon elected!" However, government does provide a necessary and biblical service to its constituency even when mired in partisan battles.

In the coming millennial reign, also biblically known as one facet of the kingdom of God, no such distress or corruption will be found. To summarize, Satan will be bound in the pit for one thousand years at the outset of the millennial period. Unable to concede defeat, Satan will be loosed temporarily at the conclusion of that era for a last ditch effort to reestablish himself. Faithful believers who refused the *mark of the beast* and chose not to worship his image will come to life as part of the first resurrection and reign with Christ. Evil men will not live again until the end of the millennium when they face the *Great White Throne Judgment* (20:11-15).

Faithful Christians will spring to life and will reign *"with Christ a thousand years"* (20:4b). Ask yourself whether this passage has come to fruition. If not, then when will this era of time occur? Psalm 2: 2-3 informs us,

> *The kings of the earth set themselves, and the rulers take counsel together, against the Lord, and against his anointed, saying, 'Let us break their bands asunder, and cast away their cords from us.'*

This passage depicts the time of the reign of the Antichrist when the kings of the earth will assemble to mount a rebellion against Jesus Christ. It further describes the events of the Battle of Armageddon when Jesus will annihilate the armies headed by the Antichrist.

The geological location of this *"Zion"* will be the city of Jerusalem. Psalm 2:4-6 clarifies the coming reign of our Lord and records the Father speaking to the Son. The Psalmist refers to this literal reign of Jesus on the earth,

> *He that sitteth in the heavens shall laugh: the Lord shall have them in derision. Then shall he speak unto them in his wrath, and vex them in his sore displeasure. Yet have I set my king upon my holy hill of Zion* (Psalm 2: 4-6).

> *I will declare the decree: the Lord hath said to me, 'Thou art my Son; this day have I begotten thee. Ask of me, and I shall give thee the heathen for thine inheritance, and the uttermost parts of the earth for thy possession. Thou shalt break them with a rod of iron: thou shalt dash them in pieces like a potter's vessel. Be wise now therefore, O ye kings; be instructed, ye judges of the earth. Serve the Lord with fear, and rejoice with trembling'* (Psalm 2: 7-11).

God the Father promised that the coming reign of His Son would extend to the ends of the earth. Identifying the precise meaning of the phrase *kingdom of God* is a real challenge and calls for a brief review of the major theological perspectives and definitions of this concept. As a rule, shreds of truth exist in all of these viewpoints.

The Kingdom as Heavenly or Spiritual

Some bible students view the kingdom of God as synonymous with the eternal state of the earth and our residency in heaven. However, we enter the kingdom of God after the moment of death. When we comment that our loved ones are *with the Lord*, the inference is that they have gained entrance into the kingdom of God.

Those that reject the literal one thousand-year reign of Jesus on the earth believe that the promises of the kingdom of God essentially will be fulfilled when Jesus comes again. In this view, one great judgment and resurrection event will occur with the kingdom of God coming to fruition at that same moment.

Proponents of this view contend that no kingdom of God on earth will ever be in existence and further propose that the kingdom is nonmaterial and merely spiritual in nature. Jesus did say that the kingdom of God would be *within* us and does establish residence in the heart of every true believer, to be sure, yet this definition is limited in scope.

In this perspective, the kingdom relates only to the present age and will not find fulfillment in a future reign on the earth. This view also holds that the spiritual kingdom of the heart now residing in every believer will find its ultimate fulfillment in our eternal stay in heaven.

The Earthly Kingdom

In contrast, others contend that the kingdom of God will be ushered into existence on the earth by human skill, economic success, and by the efforts of social programs. The ultimate goal of these diligent efforts of man is to create an atmosphere on earth of peace, righteousness, and complete justice for all men. Equality for all will blanket the earth as this goal is achieved thereby paving the way for the earthly reign.

Essentially, the method to achieve this earthly kingdom is humanistic in origin. Humanists see no limit to their abilities in achieving nirvana and perfection and believe that man is fully capable of fulfilling any and all desires he will ever have.

A related facet of this view involves Israel. Some see Israel as the sole mechanism through which God will establish His kingdom. The nation of Israel is certainly an integral element in biblical prophecy, yet the kingdom of God extends beyond the nationalism of Israel. Israel has become a viable nation yet Israel is not synonymous with the kingdom as her people continue to live with the blinders of unbelief covering the eyes of their hearts.

The Church as the Kingdom

An additional view sees the visible organized church of today as synonymous with the kingdom of God. Proponents contend that the church is fully capable of transforming society by means of political, economic, and societal involvement. In that regard, the church *is* the kingdom.

To be sure, the church of today composed of true believers is a vital element within God's kingdom yet the kingdom is even more comprehensive in nature and scope. The church age is defined as extending from the time of the ascension of Jesus into heaven, leaving the Holy Spirit as a gift to the church, to the time Jesus returns in the rapture to claim His bride and sweep her away into heaven. Understood comprehensively, the kingdom of God transcends this era.

The Kingdom as Sovereign Intervention

Others propose that the kingdom of God must be viewed as an intervention of the universal sovereignty of God into the affairs of men. Some bible students contend that as men are affected by God's intervention in daily living, the kingdom of God has come upon them.

As believers, we do live and exist in the kingdom of God and develop an intimacy with Him as He intervenes in our lives. Yet the kingdom reaches far beyond God's involvement at the level of our daily living.

Present and Future Kingdoms of God

God does rule in this present age although the visible evidence of His rule often appears to hide at inopportune times in our lives. His rule focuses upon our hearts underscoring the truth that the condition of our hearts determines our behavior.

In addition, He rules within and through the church yet these facets of His rule do not encompass all of the biblical prophecies concerning the kingdom. The earthly rule to come in the millennium will find literal and physical fulfillment as well.

In the Sermon on the Mount, Jesus taught, *"Blessed are the meek, for they shall inherit the earth"* (Matthew 5:5). Should bible students merely spiritualize a beatitude such as this? I do not think so. Those of us who are *"meek"* are under the authority of Jesus Christ as He invades and occupies our human hearts.

In biblical language, a wild stallion that is tamed is described as *meeked.* In Matthew 5:5, Jesus attempted to convey that believers under His authority one day will rule and inherit the earth, an era involving a physical reign as well.

To summarize, the scriptures reflect both spiritual and earthly aspects of the kingdom in the here and now and in the future millennial reign as well. He rules in our hearts, yet will rule on the earth as well.

Justice in the Earth

The prophet Isaiah wrote of the coming One who one day will govern the earth with righteousness, fairness, and with much severity of judgment. Isaiah 11: 1-4 predicts,

> *And there shall come forth a rod out of the stem of Jesse, and a Branch shall grow out of his roots: And the spirit of the Lord shall rest upon him, the spirit of wisdom and understanding, the spirit of counsel and might, the spirit of knowledge and of the fear of the Lord; And shall make him of quick understanding in the fear of the Lord: and he shall not judge after the sight of his eyes, neither reprove after the hearing of his ears: But with righteousness shall he judge the poor, and reprove with equity for the meek of the earth: and he shall smite the earth with the rod of his mouth, and with the breath of his lips shall he slay the wicked.*

Jesus will strike the earth with the *rod of his mouth* at the Battle of Armageddon thereby adjudicating judgment upon evil men who fully deserve it.

Concerning this physical and earthly reign on the earth, Isaiah 42: 1 sheds much light.

> *Behold my servant, whom I uphold; mine elect, in whom my soul delighteth; I have put my spirit upon him: he shall bring forth judgment to the Gentiles.*

In part, the ministry of Jesus fulfilled this prophecy with His first coming yet a portion of the prophecy awaits reality in the millennial reign. Isaiah 42: 4 records,

> *He shall not fail nor be discouraged, till he have set judgment in the earth: and the isles shall wait for his law.*

Where will this system of justice center? In the millennium, the location of such rule will be the earth itself. Jesus will not throw in the towel of defeat in the face of the enormous carnage left by the Antichrist. His rule will be undeniable.

Jesus will establish justice on the earth without any delay. What is unfair and unjust in our world will be made right. Jesus will rule with full authority and will blanket the world with His purity and justice.

In the days of Jesus on the earth, two-thirds of the world population existed as slaves. Palestine suffered under the Roman yoke causing the people to long for a Messiah to relieve their distress. In that day, a system of fairness and equity would have been more valued than a cool drink of water in the Sahara Desert.

Jesus came to serve but He is also coming to rule. His rule will be sovereign and unchallenged as predicted by Zechariah 14:9, *"And the Lord shall be king over all the earth; in that day shall there be one Lord, and his name one."*

The reign of Jesus on the earth is also necessary to confirm the covenants of God with Abraham and David and to fulfill His promise regarding the re-gathering and restoration of Israel in the land. Isaiah 42 refers to *isles* or specific territories.

The scriptures indicate specific locations that will fall under His coming rule and also intend to underscore the comprehensive territory of His kingdom. In short, the whole earth will be full of His glory and rule.

Jesus the King

No global king will exist in the millennium other than our Lord. He was born a king as indicated by the wise men who inquired of the whereabouts of the birth of the *king of the Jews.* He was, is, and forever will be the King of all kings.

God promised King David long ago that an heir would sit upon his throne and his kingdom would never end. God spoke to David concerning the kingdom that had been ripped out of the hands of Saul. God desired that this perpetual kingdom be propagated by David rather than Saul and that the house of David would rule and reign forever. Nathan the prophet confirmed God's desire in II Samuel 7:16 in these words to David,

> *And thine house and thy kingdom shall be established for ever before thee: thy throne shall be established for ever.*

For this prophecy to find fulfillment, Jesus must reign as king upon the throne of David. We often fail to comprehend the importance of the precise words regarding the birth of Jesus and their significance in the fulfillment of prophecy. Look carefully at what the angel spoke to Mary in Luke 1: 31-32,

> *Thou shalt conceive in thy womb, and bring forth a son, and shalt call his name JESUS. He shall be great, and shall be called the Son of the Highest; and the Lord God shall give unto him the throne of his father David.*

This enduring kingdom found fulfillment in the birth of Jesus. Jesus was given the *"throne of his father David"* (Luke 1:32). David is within the earthly lineage of Jesus; Jesus descended from the family of Jesse, the father of David. David's throne is not located in heaven or within our hearts but rather is seen in scripture as in Jerusalem on the hill of Mount Zion. It is in and from that earthly location that David's descendent will reign forever.

Jesus was rejected as a king and mocked as the King of the Jews. The Roman ruler Pilot questioned Jesus concerning His kingdom during their encounter and later was nailed to the cross in humiliation as the King of the Jews, a term used by the authorities in derision. None of this occurred by accident or without prophetic importance. The nature of Jesus' death serves as further biblical indication that the King who suffered and died is identical to the One who will flourish and live forever.

The Nature of His Reign

The angel of the Luke account also referred to the coming earthly reign of Jesus in 1:33, *"He shall reign over the house of Jacob for ever; and of his kingdom there shall be no end."* The kingdom of God began with the earthly arrival of Jesus, continues with the rule of Christ in our hearts, and will continue in the second coming of our Lord at the Battle of Armageddon and millennial reign. It will have no end.

This kingdom will be universal in scope. Romans 5 details the origin of sin and the failures of Adam. It is through Adam that all men will die in their sins yet through Christ all men may be made alive with the gift of life ever after. In this magnificent passage, Paul contrasted the failure of Adam in succumbing to temptation with the victory that we have in Christ Jesus. When Adam sinned, the effects of the sin were thereby transferred into the entire human race in a sentence of death. Jesus, the second Adam, was to restore what mankind had lost in the sin of the first Adam. In His original design, man was to subdue and reign in the earth. Satan duped man into sin thereby thwarting this perfect plan and usurping God's authority. Jesus came to atone for the failures of Adam and to subdue the earth, an act finding fulfillment spiritually, yet also to be realized physically in the millennium.

The millennial reign of Jesus also will be fraught with enormous *severity* in God's wrathful response. His power will be absolute and comprehensive in scope, demonstrated by the destruction of those who oppose Him. Children will be born to the survivors of Armageddon and to the tribulation saints and will be reared with an awareness of Jesus yet some will not give their hearts to Him. Their rebellion against the Lord will be quickly squelched.

At the time of Satan's short parole from the bottomless pit and final rebellion, many of the lost men and women of this era will leap at the chance to join him. Psalm 72:11-12 details His coming reign,

> *All kings shall fall down before him: all nations shall serve him. For he shall deliver the needy when he crieth; the poor also, and him that hath no helper.*

Jesus also will rule with hands of compassion, especially toward those having suffered for their faith in Him. The poor will find their riches in Him and people who have been persecuted will find loving comfort.

The *subjects* of His reign will include the wicked and evil survivors of Armageddon who will be put to death quickly and decisively (Psalm 2: 9-12). No person will experience persecution or oppression at the hands of any one who is more powerful or influential. God will right all wrongs and settle all scores. The scales of justice will weigh with precise purity and holiness.

Only the saints of God will enter the millennial kingdom. This redeemed assembly will be comprised of those of us raptured to be with the Lord in our glorified bodies, and those believers killed in the tribulation era and then resurrected. The millennial reign will be one of holiness and divine integrity. Survivors of the tribulation who are born again saints of God will also be present yet will exist in their physical bodies.

Israel Purged

All rebels will be purged from the nation of Israel. Children born to the tribulation saints will be quickly put to death if they rebel against God. This may appear as cruel and unusual punishment but the holy nature of the millennial reign demands such action in order to preserve its pure state.

If sin were not dealt with decisively, man would gravitate toward sinfulness thereby destroying the peace won at

Armageddon. Man's evil tendencies without Christ would surface once again.

In Zechariah 14:16, the prophet promised that Jesus will strike at the nations that fail to celebrate the feast of tabernacles, referring to the enforcement of the worship of our Lord. During the millennial period, saints will actually journey to Jerusalem to worship the King on His throne. Zechariah wrote,

> *And it shall come to pass, that every one that is left of all the nations which came against Jerusalem shall even go up from year to year to worship the King, the Lord of hosts, and to keep the feast of tabernacles.*

Israel Blessed

Israel has been miraculously reunited as a nation. In the millennium, once again Israel will exist in a holy union with The Messiah. Israel's exalted position will actually exceed that of the Gentiles. Israel will be made holy and righteous as a nation and the people of Israel will serve as flaming testimonies of the promises of Christ. The blessings to come to the Israelites will be seen as visible and tangible expressions of God's promises.

In a lesser role, Gentiles will enjoy all of the economic and spiritual benefits of the millennium yet in a subordinate position in comparison to Israel. The Old Testament prophets made this unique arrangement quite clear. Saints, such as you and I comprising the Church of God, will exist in a different category. We will not exist as Jews or Gentiles but rather as redeemed saints blessed with glorified bodies.

The saints of all ages will breathe a collective sigh of relief as the blessings of the millennium unfold.

Are you ready?

Chapter 47

THE SECOND COMING OF SATAN
Revelation 20: 7-10

Given our academic mindset that demands either logic or natural means to consider the validity of any claim, the concept of a literal one thousand year millennial reign is often rejected in our day. Yet the scriptures treat this coming era as a literal reality.

Many Jewish scholars from ancient times have held the view that the seven days of the week are analogous to the time of man upon the earth. They contend, as the scriptures indicate, that a day with the Lord is as thousand years, and vice versa (II Peter 3:8). Many of these scholars propose that God has granted man seven thousand years on the earth, six thousand representing the work of creation and the seventh thousand representing the millennial era of Christ's reign on the earth. It is an interesting observation.

During the millennium, every person will have his every need met and will enjoy a perfect state of health and harmony. The scripture employs poetic language to describe this coming era with phrases such as, the desert will *blossom as a rose*, the lion and the lamb will *lie down together*, and a *little child shall lead them.*

Science continues to propose that man has existed for millions of years and that the earth is billions of years old. There is significant evidence, however, that man has been in existence for approximately six thousand years.

It appears that God dramatically intervenes in a major way in biblical prophecy every two thousand years. After the creation of Adam and Eve, Abraham was born two thousand years later and was the recipient of God's covenant to bless his descendents. Two thousand years beyond the time of Abraham, Jesus Christ appeared on the earth. Two thousand years after the time of Christ, we find ourselves living in the *last days.* Soon to come are seven years of tribulation on the earth after the Church vanishes into heaven, followed by the one thousand year millennial reign.

Without the millennial reign on earth, the words of the model prayer given by Jesus, *"Thy kingdom come, Thy will be done on earth, as it is in heaven"*, would not see fulfillment. Given our era of widespread carnality, famine, and war, we have yet to experience the material and spiritual promises of the coming millennium.

Satan Loosed

At the conclusion of the millennium, a strange episode will occur. John wrote in 20:7-10,

> *And when the thousand years are expired, Satan shall be loosed out of his prison. And shall go out to deceive the nations which are in the four quarters of the earth, Gog and Magog, to gather them together to battle: the number of whom is as the sand of the sea. And they went up on the breadth of the earth, and compassed the camp of the saints about, and the beloved city: and fire came down from God out of heaven, and devoured them. And the devil that deceived them was cast into the lake of fire and brimstone, where the beast and the false prophet are, and shall be tormented day and night for ever and ever.*

The prison to hold Satan in confinement is also referenced in other New Testament passages. This bottomless pit is the dark place of incarceration for evil angels and demonic spirits.

Of necessity, Satan will be detained in this prison for one thousand years. Should his confinement not occur, the promises of peace and prosperity of the millennium will not come to fruition. Should Satan be allowed to run loose in the millennium, the same havoc that afflicted the Garden of Eden, when Satan successfully tempted man with sin, would occur once again. Lawless mayhem and perpetual heartache would again afflict every segment of society.

Perhaps in another futile effort to mimic the life of Christ, Satan will be loosed as if eager for his own second coming. The scriptures emphasize that Satan *must* be loosed (20:3). This identical Greek word for *must* was also utilized in John 3 when Jesus commented about the serpent in the Israelite wilderness being lifted up by Moses, *"even so must the Son of man be lifted up."* An additional use of this identical term concerns the travel of Jesus through Samaria about which he said that He *"must needs go through Samaria."* Revelation 20:3 records one of the mandatory *musts* of our Lord. The question as to why Satan needs to be loosed begs for an answer?

To Demonstrate the Reliability of Scripture

The presence of sin, inherent in the heart of every man, instigates his rebellion against God. Sin may take the form of active disobedience against the Lord or passive resistance to His will. Man simply prefers to design his own life without divine intervention.

The wisdom of man, apart from the Spirit of God, essentially is sin. The loosing of Satan and his efforts to mount one last coup against the Lord will serve to demonstrate again the carnality in the heart of all unregenerate men.

During the millennium, not all of the children born will turn their hearts to the Lordship of Christ. With the blood of Adam running through their veins, some will leap at the chance to sell their souls to Satan. They will be ideal prey for the claws of Satan and will be willing subjects for him to enslave for his evil scheme. The scriptures once again will be shown to be authentic and trustworthy in that the heart of man truly is deceitful at its core. Many people will gladly join the forces of Satan although guaranteed defeat will be imminent.

To Demonstrate Man's Inability to Save Himself

In our day of advanced education and technological advancement, many continue to believe that the needs of man may be met by adequate education. Some observers further propose that effective educational and social programs are capable of altering the basic character and heart of man, a faulty notion that is essentially humanistic at its root.

Some segments of the church of today have adopted social work as the primary method by which the church strives to achieve its goals. Ardent proponents of this false notion offer programs such as voter registration, self-esteem classes, and vocational training thereby suggesting that self-improvement is synonymous with a meaningful experience with Jesus Christ. To be sure, such programs have their validity yet the government has expended billions of dollars with only meager success in raising man from the slums and placing him on higher ground. The truth is, we can take man out of the slums yet are unable to take the slums out of man.

Man will never achieve a changed heart by his own efforts. Only Jesus is capable of recreating our hearts in His image.

The Work of the Church

The foundational assignment of the church is to proclaim the gospel of Jesus Christ and in so doing, proclaim good news to the poor. The good news, even the best news, is that the heart of man may be changed only by the work of Jesus in man's heart and by the regenerating work of His Spirit.

In the millennium, man will exist in a perfect environment void of slum conditions, disease, and starving children. Yet when Satan mounts his final rebellion, multitudes of men and women with evil hearts will gladly join his ranks again demonstrating the validity of God's word regarding the corrupted nature of the heart of man.

As the Church, indeed we are assigned a responsibility to care for the poor. In that regard, social ministry has merit and must not be neglected. However, the danger inherent in social programs is that we often end our efforts when the food is distributed and job counseling is offered. We must remind ourselves that men dressed in fine clothing with food in their stomachs yet without Christ in their hearts still go to hell!

When Jesus encountered the sinful woman at the well, a story recorded in the gospel of John 4: 13-14, he demonstrated the priority of living water as her primary need.

> *Whosoever drinketh of this water shall thirst again: but whosoever drinketh of the water that I shall give him shall never thirst; but the*

> *water that I shall give him shall be in him a well of water springing up into everlasting life.*

Bread feeds the stomach but the bread of life feeds the soul. To the extent that the giving of bread enhances our ability to offer the bread of life, such social ministry plays a vital role in our mission.

Satan's Appeal

Considering the magnificent life that man will lead in the millennium, it is appalling that many men will be so willing to join Satan in his last ditch effort to reclaim the world. Men will beat their swords into plowshares and exchange their weapons of warfare for those of peace. No battles will occur, and no starvation in Somalia or other needy countries will appear in the news yet many men will allow Satan to dupe them once again. The heart truly is deceitful and difficult to understand.

Satan will proceed to *"deceive the nations"* and gather any and all men who are willing to battle righteousness once again (20:8a). The true colors of the heart of men will be on display for all to see.

Many in the church today contend that some men and women who profess their faith in Christ do so only because of the gift of food or other help. To be sure, some deception takes place and always has in the history of the gospel. Yet those who do not genuinely give their hearts to Christ will demonstrate their lack of sincerity by the absence of behavioral change and a fading interest in the things of Christ.

The outward appearance of religion without an inward change of the heart is faulty and less than genuine. Such a religious façade underscores the old expression, *a faith that fizzles at the finish was faulty from the first.*

In the millennium and at the time of Satan's final uprising, the true nature of the heart of man will be exposed once again. The great challenge of the church today is to produce hearts that are truly changed by the power of the gospel, an experience that transcends mere lip service or moral improvement.

Satan's Design and Plan

Satan's final rebellion will be global in scope. People born during the millennium will have birthed children and repopulated the earth.

Rebels joining Satan's forces will include *"Gog and Magog"*, previously mentioned in Ezekiel 38 and 39 and referring also to the great country from the north that will invade the land of Israel. That great nation from the north is destined to experience destruction on the mountains of Israel in the Battle. *"Gog and Magog"* are representative of the enemies of Israel.

The scheme of Satan will be predictable and similar to his evil work in the tribulation era. He will work feverishly to capture the minds of world leaders and seductively convince them of his worthiness and credibility.

Concerning the plan of Satan, John wrote in 20:9, *"(Satan) compassed the camp of the saints about, and the beloved city."* The Old Testament saints and the tribulation saints will be saved in the first resurrection. Satan will employ weapons of warfare to war against the saints of God who will exist in glorified bodies and will possess perfect knowledge as co-heirs in the reign of Jesus on earth.

Satan's plan also will include attacking the authority of Jesus. The intensity of evil and jealousy in the heart of Satan may not be overstated. Satan's greatest nightmare is to be dethroned. He craves power and will stop at nothing to achieve his desires.

Satan will surround the beloved city of Jerusalem, the capitol of the nations of the world. However, his revolt will be short-lived. Revelation 20: 9b-10 predicts his final demise,

> *Fire came down from God out of heaven, and devoured them. And the devil that deceived them was cast into the lake of fire and brimstone, where the beast and the false prophet are, and shall be tormented day and night for ever and ever.*

God will allow such evil to rear its ugly head for this final episode to expose the works of darkness and point to the need for a Savior.

The massive armies, assembled against our Lord and deceived by Satan's evil powers of persuasion, will be unceremoniously annihilated. We do contend with Satan and his wicked schemes in our day, yet such daily battles for us are mere skirmishes since the ultimate battle against sin was won on the cross.

The Doom of the Devil

The vivid description of the *"lake of fire and brimstone"* housing the false prophet and the beast, should be understood literally (20:10). Some false cults and others contend that no literal hell exists. This graphic passage transcends mere figurative language. The language employed by John under the inspiration of the Holy Spirit is in present tense indicating that hell is where they *are*. This evil duo will be banned to this eternal dungeon for a period of one thousand years. John wrote that the beast and false prophet ultimately will be confined in the *"lake of fire"*.

This frightening passage is vital in understanding our eternal destiny apart from faith in Jesus Christ. Satan hates the book of Revelation in that it prophesies his doom and eternal prison. In his final abode, Satan's anger and furor will continue to intensify. He will continue to spurt vile words of hatred and contempt and will do so for all of eternity.

Hell, created for Satan and his emissaries and those who reject Christ, eventually will find fulfillment as it achieves the reason for its existence.

Chapter 48

THE GREAT WHITE THRONE JUDGMENT
Revelation 20: 11-15

The eyes of the world were riveted on television screens as the trial of former professional athlete O.J. Simpson took center stage in the middle 1990's. Simpson was accused of murdering his ex-wife Nicole in a fit of jealous rage. He was acquitted of the charge yet the majority of observers believed that he was guilty. He walked away without a prison sentence although a black cloud of suspicion will hover over him the rest of his life.

In the coming *Great White Throne Judgment*, all unbelievers will receive a harsh and swift punishment for their failure to receive the grace of Jesus Christ. The defendants in this divine courtroom will be unbelievers only of whom none will be found innocent. Believers will be present yet only as members of Christ's reigning assembly and as witnesses to the adjudication and punishment to be handed down by our Lord.

Concerning this divine moment of judgment, John wrote in 20: 11-15,

> *And I saw a great white throne, and him that sat on it, from whose face the earth and the heaven fled away: and there was found no place for them. And I saw the dead, small and great, stand before God; and the books were opened: and another book was opened, which is the book of life: and the dead were judged out of those things which were written in the books, according to their works. And the sea gave up the dead which were in it; and death and hell delivered up the dead which were in them: and they were judged every man according to their works. And death and hell were cast into the lake of fire. This is the second death. And whosoever was not found written in the book of life was cast into the lake of fire.*

This throne will be one of judgment rather than mercy, a prophecy that causes consternation for some who are unable to rationalize this facet of God's nature with His nature of love and grace.

The unbelieving dead will be judged from the *"books"* on the basis of the deeds performed during their lives (20:12). This divine judgment will be so awesome and permanent that surely no thinking person will want to face it. Yet unbelievers will stand before our holy God in fulfillment of this divine prophecy.

One of the clever ploys utilized by Satan is to convince man that an all-loving God would never cast anyone into a *"lake of fire"* and thereby contradict His loving nature. To make such an assumption is to ignore the clear teachings of both the Old and New Testaments. Consistent with His holy and just character, he will apply a full measure of judgment.

God did not hesitate to judge sinning angels. He vigorously judged Lucifer, His archangel of praise, and cast him out of His presence in the third heaven. When Israel sinned and rebelled, God sent discipline and judgment to them. He judged cities that adopted heathen practices. Individuals in the New Testament, such as Ananias and Saphira who lied to the Holy Spirit, felt the sting of God's judgment as well.

This ultimate judgment for the unbeliever is reserved for the courtroom event known as the *Great White Throne Judgment.* All unbelieving defendants will receive a life sentence in hell with no possibility of parole.

God's Courtroom

John's words, *"earth and heaven fled away,"* indicate that no single person will elude this judgment. No unbeliever will avoid this courtroom scene or escape certain punishment.

The trial judge will be none other than Jesus Christ Himself. John 5:22 also indicates this promise, *"The Father judgeth no man, but hath committed all judgment unto the Son."* The resurrected Jesus, spurned and rejected while on earth, will assume the role of divine judge.

Prophetically, we do not live in an age of judgment but rather in an age of grace. We live and exist in an era in which *whosoever will may come.* People do not find hell in their paths because they reject God the Father but rather for their rejection of God the Son, Jesus Christ. Jesus once encouraged some curious people who were skeptical of Him, *"Ye believe in God, believe also in me"* (John 14:1b). We must realize that to reject the Son ultimately is to reject the Father as well, for the Son is the perfect image of His Father.

A pointed story is told of a young boy who was saved from certain death by a neighbor who reacted quickly and whisked him away from the danger in the middle of a highway. The young boy grew into manhood and adopted a dangerous and rebellious lifestyle. Brought into a courtroom on felony charges, the rebel recognized the judge as the neighbor who had saved his life years ago. The young man breathed a sigh of relief at the thought of receiving a light sentence or perhaps none at all. However, the judge issued the maximum sentence possible, a verdict stunning the guilty young man. He shouted, "But sir, do you not recognize me? I was your neighbor. Remember, you saved me!" The judge replied, "Yes, son, I remember. That day I was your savior; today I am your judge."

Men and women who reject Christ often assume that He is out of the picture and removed from their lives forever. Although they may sense the conviction of the Holy Spirit, many people fail to respond to God's gentle nudge. However, all unbelievers will again face Jesus Christ in this courtroom scene. No unbeliever receiving this divine punishment will enjoy the experience.

The Defendants

John identified the defendants at this coming trial as *"the dead, small and great"* (20:12). Dead souls will be united with resurrected bodies of corruption to stand before our holy God and receive the harshest of all punishments known to mankind.

This literal resurrection of the bodies of Christians is known as the first resurrection (20:6). The first phase of this first resurrection will occur at the rapture of the Church. As believers, we will be the *firstfruits* to come after the resurrection of Jesus Christ. This first resurrection will also involve the resurrection of tribulation saints at the beginning of the millennial reign.

In contrast, this second resurrection will involve unbelievers only. John wrote in 20:13a, *"The sea gave up the dead which were in it; and death and hell delivered up the dead which were in them."* The defendants at this trial will be left on the earth when Satan is released at the end of the millennium to deceive the masses once again. The souls of those who have died without Christ and gone to hell will be physically returned to stand trial. For example, Pontius Pilot is in hell today, not because he served as the judge at the trial of Jesus, but rather due to his rejection of Jesus as Messiah and Lord.

Unbelievers buried in the earth and in the sea, or residing anywhere in the world will be paraded into the divine courtroom of our Lord. No sinner will avoid this moment.

The Purpose of the Trial

Some may question why people in hell need to appear for further punishment. Is not hell itself adequate punishment? First, the *Great White Throne Judgment* must occur to demonstrate to unbelievers that they are permanently condemned because of their rejection of God's way of salvation through Christ. Those who have spent their lives on the wrong road in search of salvation and those who have deliberately and arrogantly rejected the grace of Jesus will be present to see the Truth one final time.

Second, this final judgment will occur to signify the end of all things. This judgment will commence at the beginning of the new heaven and earth, and at the beginning of the eternal state for believers in heaven. The rest of humanity will suffer in a sinner's hell.

The ongoing influence of men who lived in sin will come to an abrupt end. The influence of our lives, for good or for evil, continues long after our death. In the former Soviet Union during the days of the Bolshevik Revolution and at other times in its history, the evil teachings of Karl Marx and Vladimir Lenin concerning atheism hung like a dark cloud over the nation and spread throughout the world. God will hold accountable men like these and others for the evil they have passed along to others

In this regard, I firmly believe that degrees of punishment in hell will be assigned. The evil deeds of some men are far greater in magnitude than others. In the final eternal state in the *"lake of fire,"* hell will be significantly worse than any hell on earth that men will have previously known.

This judgment at the hands of our Lord will also occur to fulfill prophecy. Many scriptures underscore the certainty of this judgment.

> *In the day when God shall judge the secrets of men by Jesus Christ according to my gospel* (Romans 2:16).

> *Nothing is secret, that shall not be made manifest* (Luke 8:17a).

> *The Lord knoweth how....... to reserve the unjust unto the day of judgment to be punished* (II Peter 2:9).

God will leave no prophecy unfulfilled. This divine trial will be of such a harsh and unrelenting nature that men in hell will prefer to stay in their eternal dungeons than to stand before our Lord clothed with nothing other than their sins.

The Evidence Against Unbelievers

John wrote in 20:12, *"the books were opened"*, indicating more than one book will exist at this trial. Bible students may only speculate as to the exact identity of these books yet surely one of them must be the Word of God. The Word reveals and identifies our sin and points to the need for a Savior.

Throughout history, men and women have thrown caution to the wind and lived lives of ease and personal pleasure apart from God and with the hope that their good deeds one day will outweigh their sins. It must be said that attempting to gain heaven on the basis of our personal goodness is futile at best. To break even a single law of God by committing a single sin is to violate the entire law of God (James 2:10). Measuring goodness in comparison to evil will gain nothing for the unbeliever. The scriptures indicate that our righteousness has the same value as *filthy rags* (Isaiah 64:6).

In this day to come, every single deed and word of unbelieving men will be displayed and judged. In contrast, the sins of believers will have been covered and atoned by the blood of Jesus on the cross. In a sense, God is unable to see our sins while looking at them through His blood.

Unbelievers will attempt to offer no excuses or rational explanations for their sins. God will so clearly and graphically display the sin that unbelievers will have nothing to say.

I am certainly thankful that my sins are covered by the cross of Jesus Christ! Who would want his every word and mistake on display in God's courtroom? How humiliating this moment will be for men who are *"without excuse"* (Romans 1:20)!

The Book of Opportunity

How will God determine degrees of punishment? Jesus taught that the severity of punishment will be commensurate with the opportunity evil men will have been given to receive Him (Luke 12:47).

These degrees of punishment will be determined by the quality and nature of the influence resulting from our lives. We do sow what we reap, a principle God also will also apply in His courtroom. Determined by degree of evil, the seeds of evil planted in the heart of society by evil men will reap varying degrees of punishment.

Those who have received significant exposure to the gospel will reap a more harsh punishment for their rejection of Christ. Jesus said of certain rebellious cities in Galilee, *"It shall be more tolerable for the land of Sodom and Gomorrah in the day of judgment, than for that city* (Matthew 10:15). Only God truly knows who will repent when given the opportunity to realize the serious nature of his or her sins. However, men who are well aware of their sins and unconcerned about them will reap a harsher punishment in the judgment.

Jesus performed his most significant and mighty works in Capernaum yet the people of that city received his harshest rebuke. In spite of the obvious display of the miraculous in their midst, these stiff-necked rebels of Capernaum still refused to repent. The more serious the rebellion against our Lord the greater the punishment will be.

The Book of Life

The ultimate question is whether our name appears in the *"book of life"* (20:12, 21:27). In Revelation 3:5 John wrote, *"He that overcometh, the same shall be clothed in white raiment; and I will not blot out his name out of the book of life."* This concept has splintered friendships and established and identified denominations to a significant degree.

If it is possible to *"blot out"* one's name, may salvation be lost and if so, by what means? The scriptures clearly teach that salvation may not be lost. The Bible does not teach that as a man is converted to faith in Christ his name is entered into the divine ledger of all believers, a concept I will later explain.

When Jesus died, He did so for all men. The scriptures teach, *"For as in Adam all die, even so in Christ shall all be made alive"* (I Corinthians 15:22). When Jesus died, He became the propitiation for the sins of the entire world (I John 2:2). Yet not every person in the world will be saved.

I remember reading of a Southern Baptist seminary professor who taught that all people exist in a state of salvation and that our responsibility is to inform them of their regenerated condition. Thankfully, the new school president sent the professor and her false doctrine of universal salvation to greener pastures. Others contend for the doctrine of limited atonement meaning that Jesus died only for the *elect* and also suggesting that the *non-elect* have no chance of heaven since Jesus did not die for the *non-elect.* This notion flies in the face of the scriptural promise, *"whosoever will, let him take the water of life freely"* (22:17b).

When Adam sinned, he passed the sentence of death to all of us. When Jesus came, lived a sinless and perfect life and died for our sins, He paved the way for the salvation of every person. All men may be saved yet not all men will be saved. To be sure, only God foreknows who will accept Him and who will not.

As a man rejects Christ, his name is blotted from the book of life. Essentially, the name of every man and woman in history once appeared in the *"book of life."* Yet as men and women fully and finally reject the grace of Christ, die without Christ in their hearts, or commit the unpardonable sin so that they are unable to receive Christ, their names are blotted from the book. Ultimately, the *"book of life"* will list and retain the names of only those born into the family of God. Those who reject him have their names removed. Their names are not removed by their sinful deeds but rather by a personal decision to reject the grace He so lovingly offers.

Men who do not know Christ essentially have one destiny that awaits them, *"the lake of fire"* (20:15).

Hell was created as an eternal prison for Satan and his angels. Yet hell has ample room for those who reject him.

Now is the time. Receive Him today.

PART 6

A NEW HEAVEN AND A NEW EARTH

Chapter 49

DEATH: PROMOTION TO HAPPINESS
Revelation 21: 1-8

We live in a vacuum of worry and stress. To be sure, some stress is external in origin yet much of it is self-imposed and unwarranted. The story is told of an older lady named Madge who had an incurable hearing deficiency. Her family informed her that a new surgical procedure would quickly correct the problem. She shot back, "Sorry, not interested! I am ninety years old and I have heard enough!"

The scriptures are quite clear that when the new heaven and earth appear all pain and distress will quickly vanish from our lives (21:1). We will be ushered in to a perpetual state of divine bliss and tranquility. Such a magnificent blessing is certainly ample reason to wipe away the tears from our eyes today, hence the title of this book. Concerning this coming new heaven and earth, John wrote in 21: 1-8,

> *And I saw a new heaven and a new earth: for the first heaven and the first earth were passed away; and there was no more sea. And I John saw the holy city, new Jerusalem, coming down from God out of heaven, prepared as a bride adorned for her husband. And I heard a great voice out of heaven saying, 'Behold, the tabernacle of God is with men, and he will dwell with them, and they shall be his people, and God himself shall be with them, and be their God. And God shall wipe away all tears from their eyes; and there shall be no more death, neither sorrow, nor crying, neither shall there be any more pain: for the former things are passed away.' And he that sat upon the throne said, 'Behold, I make all things new.' And he said unto me, 'Write: for these words are true and faithful.' And he said unto me, 'It is done. I am Alpha and Omega, the beginning and the end. I will give unto him that is athirst of the fountain of the water of life freely. He that overcometh shall inherit all things; and I will be his*

> *God, and he shall be my son. But the fearful, and unbelieving, and the abominable, and murderers, and whoremongers, and sorcerers, and idolaters, and all liars, shall have their part in the lake which burneth with fire and brimstone which is the second death.*

Three Heavens

After the rapture of the Church, the seven-year tribulation episode, the Battle, the judgment seat of Christ, the marriage supper of the Lamb for all believers, the temporary revolt of Satan, and the conclusion of Great White Throne judgment scene for evil men, we will be blessed with the descent and establishment of a new heaven and earth. Such a monumental event strains our finite abilities to fathom.

The scriptures speak of three heavens. The firmament, declaring the glory of God in the creation, is the atmospheric heaven in which birds fly in the highway of the skies. Second, heaven also includes the planetary and astrological systems and galaxies. Third, the heaven into which Paul was *caught up* is paradise, the current dwelling of Jesus who also is unrestricted by time and space (II Corinthians 12:4). John wrote that the first heaven will *"pass away"* in favor of its new replacement (21:1).

The Earth Passes Away

The physical earth as we know it will be burned with fire and vanish from our very eyes. In its place, God will present a new heaven and earth for His people. This amazing event will continue God's plan of judgment on the earth and its evil inhabitants. The apostle Peter predicted this event to come. In the first century, he penned these words in II Peter 3:7, 10-13,

> *But the heavens and the earth, which are now, by the same word are kept in store, reserved unto fire against the day of judgment and perdition of ungodly men.*

> *But the day of the Lord will come as a thief in the night; in the which the heavens shall pass away with a great noise, and the*

> *elements shall melt with fervent heat, the earth also and the works that are therein shall be burned up. Seeing then that all these things shall be dissolved, what manner of persons ought ye to be in all holy conversation and godliness, looking for and hasting unto the coming of the day of the God, wherein the heavens being on fire shall be dissolved, and the elements shall melt with fervent heat? Nevertheless, we, according to his promise, look for new heaven and a new earth, wherein dwelleth righteousness.*

The ecology has been adversely affected by the sins and negligence of mankind. The curse upon the earth originating at the time of Adam fell upon mankind as well. The ravages of sin have penetrated every facet of our existence. Sin is no respecter of persons or things and gladly tarnishes or destroys individuals and all things it touches.

A primary assignment to the believer is to live alert to His imminent return and be aware that one day we will dwell *in righteousness.* As the hymn writer wrote, "what a day that will be when my Jesus I shall see!"

A Brand New World

The sea represents isolation and separation. John penned these eternal words while seated on the beach of the isolated island of Patmos. The extent of his view with the naked eye did not reach beyond the horizon of the sea. He was separated by force from his family and friends and all that he held dear.

His vision of things to come and the descent of the *"holy city, new Jerusalem"* must have been a welcomed sight for the sore eyes of this aging warrior (21:2). John wrote that this new heaven and earth will be *"prepared as a bride adorned for her husband"* (21:2).

The beauty of this new bride and the sense of blessing derived from the fulfillment of these prophecies will envelope God's people with indescribable euphoria. God's people will be ushered into an arena of blessings and joy that finite minds are unable to fathom.

A New Kingdom

It is critical for us to understand the meaning of the phrase, *"the tabernacle of God is with men"* (21:3a). The term *tabernacle* refers to a dwelling place. The scriptures indicate that our bodies are the dwelling place of the Holy Spirit (I Corinthians 6:19).

As God *tabernacles* with us as believers, He *dwells* within us. This concept is rooted in the teachings of the tabernacle that God revealed to Moses during the Israelite wilderness wanderings. The physical tabernacle housed the Holy of Holies and the revered Ark of the Covenant. It served to remind the people that God dwelt with them and camped in their midst in the wilderness. The Ark represented to them His perpetual presence. At each successive camp location, the Israelites erected the tabernacle as a reminder of His presence.

Reminiscent of that Old Testament imagery, one day God will *camp* with His people in the new heaven and earth to descend. This new world now on the way will feature breathtaking *perfection.* John wrote that our tears of sorrow, death, and pain will vanish away with the physical earth as we now know it (21:4).

Surely these comforting words were precious to early church believers who were suffering greatly for their faith in Christ. Family members lost their lives at the hand of the Roman government and homes were lost in unemployment. Fraudulent activities and oppression by the government continually afflicted the early believers who cried out for relief.

Every parent knows of the compassion that is communicated when he or she comes to the aid of a child with a bloody knee or a damaged ego. God will come to the aid of every believer in this day and will wipe away all tears and bandage all wounds.

The Psalms indicate that our compassionate Lord stores our tears *in a bottle* (cf. Psalm 56:8). Perhaps the accumulation of the tears of His children will be wiped away with His compassionate intervention in the New Jerusalem. In addition, death will no longer exist in our eternal vocabulary. Life with Jesus will be unending and pain non-existent.

Until that day, we must look beyond the pain and anguish of our daily experiences with an eye on the Hope to come. When He comes, all of our cares will melt away in the arms of our loving Lord who will truly wipe away every tear from our eyes.

Our Faithful Lord

When John penned the first few words of the Revelation, he saw Jesus Christ seated upon the throne. At the fulfillment of all of the prophetic events in John's vision, Christ still will be on the throne as the One who is *"true and faithful"* (21:5). Jesus reminded us that He is the *"Alpha and Omega,"* the A and Z of the Greek alphabet, signifying the beginning and end of all things. He initiated the events of history and will conclude them as well. God is not subject to history; He *is* history.

As He offered to the sinful woman He encountered at the well, Jesus once again will offer the *"fountain of the water of life freely"* (21:6b). His living water quenches the thirst of our hearts never to thirst again for meaning and purpose apart from Him. Salvation is never earned. God never assigns our spiritual grade regarding salvation *on the curve.* It is a gift freely given and fully undeserved.

The blessings and promises of this perfected state of existence will be awarded to those *"that overcometh"* (21:7). It is critical to note that John does not indicate that it is our responsibility to grit our ethical teeth and thereby *overcome* as believers. Quite the opposite, our faith in Jesus Christ establishes us as overcomers. We have overcome the effects of sin and the schemes of Satan on the basis of our faith rather than upon the basis of our personal strength to achieve such an exalted spiritual position. As it has been said, we do not fight *for* victory but rather *from* victory since Jesus won the victory over the penalty of sin by His death on the cross.

Eight Groups Not in Heaven

Those who promote the false notion of universal salvation for all men will be sadly disappointed in that day. In bold and unmistakable language, John provided a laundry list of the types of individuals who may have hoped for heaven yet who will be tossed into a sinner's hell.

To summarize, hell will be populated with those who do not confess Jesus as Lord, those who refuse to believe in the Son of God as the Christ, people polluted with evil hearts, those with murderous hearts and no regard for the value of life, sexual predators, those involved in spiritism and the occult, people in love with other gods, and liars who deny truth while simultaneously claiming a relationship with God. Hell will be filled with men and women who believe they do not deserve this final destination (21:8).

Former sinners, however, will be in heaven. The apostle Paul wrote, *"such were some of you, but ye are washed, but ye are justified in the name of the Lord Jesus, and by the Spirit of our God"* (I Corinthians 6:11).

In which category are you?

Chapter 50

AN EYEWITNESS VIEW OF HEAVEN
Revelation 21: 9 – 22:5

I heard a humorous story about a reluctant groom who showed up at the altar for his wedding carrying his golf clubs. He set them down on the front pew, looked at the wedding party and then asked the minister, "This won't take too long, will it?" Needless to say, his bride was not amused.

When Jesus comes back, establishes the millennial reign with His children, and then presents the new heaven and earth as the bride or the *"Lamb's wife,"* no one will want to rush through this event (21:9). One of the seven angels accompanied John to a high mountain and introduced him to the heaven that will descend some day. John wrote of this experience in 21: 9-14,

> *And there came unto me one of the seven angels which had the seven vials full of the seven last plagues, and talked with me, saying, 'Come hither, I will shew thee the bride, the Lamb's wife.' And he carried me away in the spirit to a great and high mountain, and shewed me that great city, the holy Jerusalem, descending out of heaven from God, having the glory of God: and her light was like unto a stone most precious, even like a jasper stone clear as crystal. And had a wall great and high, and had twelve gates, and at the gates twelve angels, and names written thereon, which are the names of the twelve tribes of the children of Israel: On the east three gates; on the north three gates, on the south three gates; and on the west three gates. And the wall of the city had twelve foundations, and in them the names of the twelve apostles of the Lamb.*

This magnificent heavenly city to come transcends human imagination and will become a physical reality. This new heaven and earth also will have measurable dimensions.

Heaven's Inhabitants

John saw twelve angels at the gates of heaven symbolizing the presence of the twelve tribes representing the Old Testament saints. Three gates will be featured on each of the four sides of heaven. These gates will exist for those persons who were not considered part of the Old Testament saints or the Church. For example, Naaman the Syrian leper who was cleansed in the days of Elijah as he was dipped in the Jordan River, will be present. Noah also will be present although he lived in an era prior to the time of the covenant of God with Abraham, the progenitor of the Israelite nation (Genesis 12).

The fact that the twelve tribes of Israel and the twelve apostles of the New Testament, representing the New Testaments believers, will be residents in heaven indicates that heaven and its benefits rest upon the Word of God. All of God's children throughout the ages will be permanent residents there.

Heaven's Size

The enormous magnitude and dimensions of heaven as described in John's vision are breathtaking. John wrote in 21: 15-18,

> *And he that talked with me had a golden reed to measure the city, and the gates thereof, and the wall thereof. And the city lieth foursquare, and the length is as large as the breadth: and he measured the city with the reed, twelve thousand furlongs. The length and the breadth and the height of it are equal. And he measured the wall thereof, an hundred and forty and four cubits, according to the measure of a man, that is, of the angel. And the building of the wall of it was of jasper: and the city was pure gold, like unto clear glass.*

The dimensions of our heavenly city are described as fifteen hundred miles foursquare and fifteen hundred miles in height. This holy city will be the capitol of the heaven, so to speak. According to mathematical calculations, billions of God's children could live in comfort and with adequate space within its walls. These dimensions also indicate the unfathomable majesty and glory of God that will illuminate the atmosphere and focus all attention and praise on God.

The city also will feature a great wall spanning two hundred sixteen feet. The wall will consist of jasper, a clear stone similar to a diamond but with different shades of color. The composition of the walls of the city signifies that entrance into the city will be via the gates. Jesus clearly said that He himself is the *door*, and those who enter through Him are granted entrance into a life of salvation and eternal bliss.

Heaven's Beauty

This heavenly city is made of gold with a transparent appearance like that of clear glass. John also described the foundations of the walls of the city as *"garnished with all manner of precious stones"* (21:19a).

The heavenly city will feature twelve foundations representing the twelve apostles from whose pens the Holy Spirit has given us the scriptures. In our day, even a small quantity of any of these precious stones is worth a fortune. In heaven, entire foundations will be comprised of these precious stones signifying the inestimable value and glory of heaven.

These exquisite and radiant stones also signify the mosaic of humanity to which God's grace has been offered. They also symbolize the multifaceted dimensions of God's grace and His unending love.

The twelve gates will also feature pearls large enough to serve as a gate. Rich symbolism accompanies John's description of these gates and I see significant theological truth within John's description as well. Pearls are derived from wounded oysters that have experienced the irritation of sand or other foreign matter. In time, the secretion within the oyster shell, due to the irritation, forms the pearl. Jesus spoke in the gospels concerning the *pearl of great price* (Matthew 13:46). Believers, although wounded and harassed by the cares of this life and by the enemies of the cross, will be afforded honor like that of a pearl upon their arrival in heaven. Aware of our affliction on earth as believers, Jesus will heap lavish honor upon us as we walk into the gates of heaven.

As John viewed heaven, he noted that he saw *"no temple"* since the Lord Himself will adequately serve as the temple His followers will ever desire or need (21:22). The Lord will dominate our thoughts and the entire atmosphere of our existence. We will never again be interrupted or disturbed by earthly concerns with which now afflict us. Our sole purpose will be to offer unending praises to our Lord.

Heaven's Light

Darkness quickly will fade away when illuminated by the glory of the Lord shining in heaven. Artificial light now produced by man or the light produced by the sun no longer will be necessary because heaven will radiate with the glory of God.

Moses experienced this *"light"* in the wilderness at Mt. Sinai. The Israelites experienced it in the pillar of clouds in the day and in the pillar of fire by night leading them in their wandering journeys. This same light will penetrate the streets of heaven never to fade away. In addition, no darkness of night will be experienced in heaven. Sorrow and sin will no longer cause distress or separation from our Lord or from our fellow believers.

The nations comprised of believers and the kings of the earth who have followed Jesus Christ will *"walk in the light of it,"* meaning that all of God's children will relish in the light of God's eternal glory. Satan's influence will have vanished because he will remain shackled in his bottomless pit unable to respond.

Heaven's Prosperity

John's vision of a river suggests the unending prosperity that believers will experience in heaven (22:1). Coming from the throne of God, this literal river also will afford us the blessing of drinking real water, the purity and beauty of which will be unsurpassed!

In addition, this water will be a welcomed reminder of the *"water of life"* Jesus offered to the sinful woman at the well, a gift offered to us as well. Water also symbolizes the Holy Spirit that Jesus promised to deposit within us resulting in waters of overflowing joy in our innermost beings. This heavenly river will contain no impurities or pollution signifying the pristine and untarnished nature of God's love and heaven itself.

John also wrote of the tree of life and its fruit in 22:2,

> *In the midst of the street of it, and on either side of the river, was there the tree of life, which bare twelve manner of fruits, and yielded her fruit every month: and the leaves of the tree were for the healing of the nations.*

This tree symbolizes a guarantee of all the nourishment we will ever need. The fruit of the tree signifies the incredible health we will experience. The leaves of this heavenly tree will serve to heal the *"nations,"* or peoples of the world. Essentially, Jesus will provide perfect health to all of His children.

As prosperous people rich with the love of God, we will serve Him forever. In 22: 3-5 John wrote,

> *And there shall be no more curse: but the throne of God and of the Lamb shall be in it; and his servants shall serve him: And they shall see his face; and his name shall be in their foreheads. And there shall be no night there; and they need no candle, neither light of the sun; for the Lord God giveth them light: and they shall reign for ever and ever.*

All of the hosts and inhabitants of heaven will praise the Lamb in an atmosphere of unending worship. Our love and passion for the Lord today will be fully unleashed in that day showering our Lord will loving praise. Hymn writer Fanny Crosby, blinded as a child but gifted with heavenly vision, captured this coming time with her pen in the familiar tune, *I Shall Know Him,*

> *When my life's work is ended,*
> *And I cross the swelling tide,*

Then the light of His glory I shall see.
I shall know my Redeemer
When I reach the other side,
For His smile will be the first to welcome me.

I shall know Him, I shall know Him,
And redeemed by His side I shall stand.
I shall know Him, yes, I shall know Him,
By the prints of the nails in His hands.

Heaven's Joy

Jesus will have permanently sealed the ownership and destiny of our lives resulting in the overflowing of our joy. The name of Jesus will be *"in their foreheads,"* referring to believers in heaven (22:4). Throughout eternity, Jesus has reserved a special place in his heart for those who love Him.

In the absence of night, not a sliver of evil will find its way into heaven (22:5). All sorrow will fade into oblivion and will be replaced with the praises of the Lamb. We will bask each day in the light of His glory.

As we reign with Him, He will entrust us with the management of the affairs of the universe. All questions will have answers. Tears will never again well up in our eyes.

Are you ready to go?

Chapter 51

LAST THINGS IN THE BIBLE
Revelation 22: 6-21

The last words spoken by famous men in history seem to be the most memorable. Martin Luther King Jr. is remembered for his oratorical phrase, *I have a dream.* Former President Richard Nixon declared, *I am not a crook.* Former President George H.W. Bush muttered the shaky promise, *Read my lips, no new taxes.*

The apostle John was the last of the New Testament writers to complete his work and did so at the instruction of and under the inspiration of the Holy Spirit. He penned these memorable and prophetic words in approximately 95-99 A.D. Revelation was the last book of the New Testament to be accepted into the canon of scripture. These concluding words underscore the accuracy and importance of the scriptures and serve as a vivid reminder of the solemn nature of God's word.

The Value of the Word

The angel who carried the bowl judgments took John on a guided tour of heaven and communicated words of comfort to John as well as to believers of all ages. The angel communicated the *accuracy* of the scriptures in 22:6 in saying that they are *"faithful and true."* This passage clearly underscores the inerrancy or infallibility of God's word. It truly is truth without any mixture of error. Not only does the Bible contain the Word of God, it *is* the Word of God.

Unfortunately, there are those who attempt to differentiate between certain words or passages of scripture as to their accuracy and validity as God's word. I firmly believe that all scripture, every syllable and word of it, is the Word of God. As one fellow quipped, I might even agree that the maps are inspired as well! No clear reading of John's last words renders any other conclusion than the scriptures, all of them, are God's word.

Jesus also spoke of the *assurance* of God's Word as well. He assured His readers that those who read and heed the Word will be spiritually rewarded in so doing. John wrote in 22:7,

> *Behold, I come quickly: Blessed is he that keepeth the sayings of the prophecy of this book.*

The initial words of Revelation promise a similar result for those who obey the instructions of the book. The book concludes with a similar promise. Promises obeyed must first be understood. Serious bible students will allow these prophetic words to penetrate their hearts and result in behavioral change. Faithful readers will also feel the warm encouragement to be derived from a close relationship with the scriptures and consequently, with their Author as well.

In addition, the *authority* of the Word must not be underestimated or neglected. In the days of the New Testament, a significant desire to worship angels became such a dangerous doctrinal error that the apostle Paul and others sensed the need to offer a correction.

Underscoring the need to center all focus upon Jesus alone, John wrote in 22: 8-9,

> *And I John saw these things, and heard them. And when I had heard and seen, I fell down to worship before the feet of the angel which shewed me these things. Then saith he unto me, 'See thou do it not: for I am thy fellowservant, and of thy brethren the prophets, and of them which keep the sayings of this book: worship God.'*

John fell at the feet of the angel in an act of worship only to be quickly rebuked by the angel for doing so. The angel was a mere messenger and reminded John that only God was worthy of worship. In our day of celebrity worship, such a reminder is vitally important. The gospel lends itself to the abuses of men who are tempted to manipulate it for personal gain. For some men who are lacking in integrity, the commercialization of the gospel pays well.

Jesus is not an angel but rather the Son of God. He is God and was revealed in human flesh. Angels, or any other member of the creation, do not deserve our worship. Jesus alone is worthy of our praise.

The Word also offers to us an uncanny *accessibility*. The angel instructed John to *"seal not the sayings of the prophecy of this book: for the time is at hand"* (22:10). Believers in our day who question the essential importance of Revelation or who doubt the possibility of gaining an understanding of its contents deny themselves a great blessing.

In contrast to the prophecy of Revelation given to John, Daniel was instructed to seal tightly the contents of the book *until the end of time* (Daniel 12:4). Revelation is the key that opens the door of the mysteries of Daniel. Only after Christ comes and the revelation given could the vagueness of Daniel's prophecies be clarified. The writings of Daniel shed much light on the events of our world today, i.e. the New World Order, the rise and reestablishment of Europe as a world power, Communism, and events in the Middle East. The old adage is accurate, *The New Testament is in the Old Testament concealed; the Old Testament is in the New Testament revealed.*

Destiny Set

The work of Christ and His blood on the cross of Calvary set in stone the heavenly destiny of all believers. Conversely, the rejection of the grace of Christ by unbelievers has established their eternal destiny in hell. Heaven and hell are of equal duration. John wrote in 22:11,

> *He that is unjust, let him be unjust still: and he which is filthy, let him be filthy still: and he that is righteous, let him be righteous still: and he that is holy, let him be holy still.*

Believers in Jesus Christ are set apart, sanctified, and declared as righteous in His eyes. Such security does not result from our individual performance or from inherited goodness. In other words, Jesus has no grandchildren! No level of goodness passed along to us from our parents ever earns our salvation. Christ alone became our sacrifice and the payment for sins with His death on the cross. He alone sets us apart as holy in the eyes of God, a position we receive when we place our faith in Him.

Conversely, those who continue with rebellion in their hearts and in arrogant refusal of the grace of God will remain forever lost in the wilderness of their sins. Ultimately, their destination will land them in the fires of a sinner's hell, a destiny of their own choosing. At this juncture in the prophetic timetable, destinies will have been set with no possibility for change.

Grace and Works

The doctrine of salvation by grace alone, taught in the scriptures and the precepts of which were nailed onto the Wittenberg Door by Martin Luther, is further authenticated by this passage. Some men and women who are misinformed have attempted to require a combination of grace and works in order to achieve salvation and do so by misinterpreting John's words in 22:12-14,

> *And, behold, I come quickly; and my reward is with me, to give every man according as his work shall be. I am Alpha and Omega, the beginning and the end, the first and the last. Blessed are they that do his commandments, that they may have right to the tree of life, and may enter in through the gates into the city.*

Our works and good deeds result from the inner workings of grace in our hearts. The apostle Paul posed the argument in Romans that salvation must be received either by works or by grace and not a combination of the two. In his day, and ours as well, some religious legalists attempted to require both. Of course, salvation is never earned or lost on the basis of our deeds. Salvation is not about what we do, but rather about what He did!

To illustrate, salvation is viewed by some like a rowboat with one oar of faith and another oar of works. To row with the single oar of faith or with the single oar of works causes the boat to move in a circular motion and make no real progress. Of course, good works do result from pure faith yet the rowboat analogy is inaccurate in that we do not earn our place in heaven on the basis of personal effort in tandem with our faith in God. As Martin Luther so forcefully said, faith plus nothing is what God expects.

To be sure, good works do result from the inner character of the heart yet absolutely are not the means whereby we gain entrance into heaven. Works are the *fruit* rather than the *root* of our salvation. In essence, Jesus rows the boat to heaven and does so by the power of the cross. Our duty is to believe in His ability to do the job.

Degrees of Reward

Jesus clearly declared that those who have been given great opportunity must acknowledge their great responsibility. In the parable of the talents, Jesus communicated that we will be rewarded on the basis of the manner in which we capitalize upon our opportunities in the kingdom rather than on the magnitude of talents we may possess. To whom much have been given, much is required.

Some Christians today are in error in assuming that heaven will be a place of inactivity and mundane predictability. The rewarding of believers will be an incredible experience for all to see and enjoy and will create a buzz of activity in heaven. Rewards will be distributed to those who were obedient to the Word, suffered great persecution for their faith, lived exceptionally holy lives, and to those who took evangelism seriously.

These promised rewards serve as encouragement to us and as motivation to remain strong and determined in our ongoing commitment to Christ and His kingdom. For many of us, the rewards of today seem few and far between yet Jesus clearly promised that our day of reward will certainly come. He is the One who watches our behavior *in secret* and will heap blessings upon us as His children at the appropriate moment. Men may cast aspersions and hurl insults at our faith yet our loving Lord will wipe away every tear with His hand of blessings.

The Lord Himself will guarantee our eternal rewards. He is the One who is the *"Alpha and Omega, the beginning and the end, the first and the last"* (22:13). This phrase makes reference to the beginning and ending letters of the Greek alphabet signifying that God is the One who initiated all things and will bring human history to its final conclusion as well.

John also wrote in 22: 14 that those who *"do his commandments"* will experience His blessings and *"enter in through the gates into the city."* The gates of the heavenly city in John's vision were fashioned with pearl. Pearls are formed in the wound of a living organism. In like manner, the living person of Jesus Christ was wounded and by His wounds the Church, described as the *pearl of great price*, was formed.

It is only through the finished work of Christ that we may enter into the heavenly kingdom. We obey His commandments because we *have* been redeemed rather than *in order to* be redeemed. As our faith matures through the years, we experience a greater understanding of the work of grace within us. As this work of grace has its effect within us, behavioral change results. People do not miss heaven because their works or deeds are sub-par and unworthy. The truth is, inadequate or self-centered works are the result of unchanged hearts.

A heart that is void of the love of Christ lacks the necessary motivation to experience a fruitful lifestyle. As Jesus said, *"ye shall know them by their fruits* (Matthew 7:16).

Lost Forever

John employed graphic language to depict the kinds of people who will reside in hell never to see the gates of heaven. In 22:15 he wrote,

> *For without are dogs, and sorcerers, and whoremongers, and murderers, and idolaters, and whosoever loveth and maketh a lie.*

Jews often chided Gentiles as *dogs* to indicate that the Gentiles were banned from the covenant of God as unworthy and underprivileged. *Sorcerers*, from the root word for pharmacy indicating drug usage, Satanism, and the occult, will not inherit God's kingdom. Those who live their lives in pursuit of sexual gratification, who have the spirit of murder in their hearts, who create their own gods in place of the one true God, and other sinners have no right in the *"tree of life"* as believers do (22:14). However, redeemed murderers and other sinners, exemplified best by Paul as the chief of all sinners, will walk the streets of gold.

Our Identity

As believers, we are securely positioned in the body of Christ, the Church. We arrive at that spiritual position by means of spirit baptism, the work of the Holy Spirit sweeping us into the arms of God in an unmerited display of His grace.

Jesus Himself is the root and offspring of David in fulfillment of biblical prophecy. John wrote of this concept in 22:16,

> *I Jesus have sent mine angel to testify unto you these things in the churches. I am the root and the offspring of David, and the bright and morning star.*

God promised King David that his offspring would rule the kingdom perpetually. Jesus was human in that He was of the *"root of David"* and was divine in that He was the *"bright and morning star"* (22:16). Mary, the mother of Jesus was in the lineage of David further underscoring the humanity of Jesus. This speaks of the mystery of the incarnation and of His nature as simultaneously human and divine. In what manner could Jesus be both the father of David and the son of David? Only Jesus Himself is capable of fulfilling this prophecy. David descended from Christ in that Christ is the creator yet He was also born into the family of David as the infant child of Mary. As famous black preacher quipped, "He is older than His mother and the same age as His father!" These truths concerning the God-man are mysterious, indeed.

Our Mission

John reminded His readers of their ultimate mission, the communication of the message of salvation given to men by our loving Lord. John wrote in 22:17,

> *And the Spirit and the bride say, 'Come.' And let him that heareth say, 'Come'. 'And let him that is athirst come. And whosoever will, let him take the water of life freely.*

No clearer invitation to present to the world could have been written. The church must take care to erect no artificial barriers that communicate exclusivity to a needy world. The Holy Spirit offers to all men the privilege of coming to faith in God and finding forgiveness and salvation.

This invitation to a lost world is to be offered both by the Church and by individual Christians who understand the urgency of our message. Men and women who come to Christ must thirst for the living water only Jesus offers. To be saved, men must know that they are lost.

No legion of angels in heaven or hosts of demons in hell are capable of preventing the salvation of any individual who truly calls upon the Lord for a cup of His grace. The full scope of the doctrines of election and predestination are for God only to comprehend. How many of us truly know the identity of the elect? We may be assured, however, that those of us who have accepted the free gift of eternal life have been elected. The doctrine of election is for the assurance of those who already believe in Christ and is not meant to categorize those who have not yet believed. Our loving Lord has granted the freedom of choice to us. As the Holy Spirit does His work of conviction in the human heart, salvation becomes a matter of the will.

Essentially, we must share the good news with every man. As one man quipped, "It seems to me that every person I nominate, He elects." When the Holy Spirit convicts the heart, men find Christ.

A Serious Warning

The biblical story begins in Genesis with a warning for man to avoid a particular tree. In a similar vein, Revelation ends with a warning not to tamper with the scriptures. The communication of Revelation by the Holy Spirit to man as the last book of the Bible was not accidental. This prophetic revelation closed the pages of the canon of scripture. God's final words to man have been given.

Cult groups such as the Mormons make a serious error in their addition of the Book of Mormon to the scriptures. Cult groups such as the Mormons and others exist under the judgment of God for such unwise activity. John's warning 22:18-19 strictly forbids tampering with the Word,

> *For I testify unto every man that heareth the words of the prophecy of this book, If any man shall add unto these things, God shall add unto him the plagues that are written in this book: And if any man shall take away from the words of the book of this prophecy, God shall take away his part out of the book of life, and out of the holy city, and from the things which are written in this book.*

Others assume that adopting a monastic lifestyle removed from earthly concerns is the proper way to prepare and wait for the return of Christ. In essence, such an assumption is adding to the Word and therefore subjects those who foolishly behave in this manner to the judgment of God. Those who sense the liberty to add to the Word are not genuine believers and will reap the *"plagues"* of this prophetic book for so doing.

In addition to those who add to the scriptures, others foolishly attempt to deny the miraculous element in the Bible and to denigrate the reliability and authority of the scriptures. John's words plainly teach that men who live in such arrogance and rebellion are not genuine believers. Men who teach such heresy should be muted and those who receive compensation for doing so should be unceremoniously dismissed from their classrooms.

John's words do not teach that a man may lose his salvation as a result of tampering with the Bible but rather indicate that men who engage in such foolishness have never truly met Christ. Lost men and women such as these will never have a part in the *"book of life"* (22:19). Of course, I am not insinuating that questions of interpretation will never arise because they do and will continue to do so. Holy curiosity has its merit. Men without Christ, however, who maliciously and willfully tamper with the Word of God fly their true spiritual colors and will reap a just compensation in hell for so doing.

Even So, Come

John wrote in 22:20, *"He which testifieth these things saith, 'Surely I come quickly'. Amen. Even so, come, Lord Jesus."* This climatic promise of our Lord to come again is the last of numerous references to His soon return. In the New Testament, this promise to return occurs at least three hundred and eighteen times. His promise to return "*quickly*" refers to the sudden, unexpected nature of His return.

Some people might note that two thousand years have passed into the annals of history since these words were penned yet Jesus is yet to return. We must remember that a day and a thousand years essentially are the same in the mind of the Lord.

He will return.

Will it be today?

Chapter 52

REVELATION IN A NUTSHELL

To summarize the myriad of prophetic details in Revelation is a daunting task. Perhaps this brief summary will capture the essence of the book.

I am reminded of the story of the salty lady named Mrs. Brown who walked into the offices of the local newspaper and stated that she wanted to place an advertisement to sell a pickup. She was informed that the cost of the notice would be fifty cents per word. She scribbled on a piece of paper and handed it to the clerk. Her request read, "Pickup for sale. Cheap." The lady was informed that a seven-word minimum charge was in effect. She paused, grabbed the note and added, "Fred Brown died. Pickup for sale. Cheap."

Revelation is full of words, to say the least, and rich with symbolism and metaphors. The book itself promises a blessing to the reader who also obeys its implications. Perhaps a brief summary and commentary of the entire book will plant its precepts and chronology deep in our hearts as we draw this work to a close.

Revelation 1: The Revelation of Jesus

A revelation, from the Greek *apakulupto*, is an unveiling or removal of the veil. The writer John identified the meaning of the Revelation by graphic and extensive use of signs and symbols. He recorded the vision given to him by the Spirit and carefully avoided personal opinion and interpretation (1:1).

John provided a vivid photograph of Jesus in 1:9-20. This passage clearly reveals his glory as the resurrected Christ.

Revelation 2-3: Review of the Churches

John wrote of the condition of seven actual churches in existence at that time of his writing in the late 90's A.D. The church at Laodicea, the last of the churches, was known to be lukewarm and spiritually lethargic. This brand of lethargy will be prevalent during the last days. Indifference will infiltrate the churches of the end times, a condition already finding a home in many churches.

A study of these seven churches reveals valuable lessons for the church of today.

Revelation 4: Rapture of the Church

The Church is not mentioned after 4:1 indicating that believers will not be present for the tribulation episode to come. John heard a voice like that of a *"trumpet"* in heaven. This sound is reminiscent of the one to which Paul referred in I Thessalonians 4:16a describing the coming of the Lord to gather His children and whisk us away into His eternal home.

The love of God for us will protect us from the ravages of the seven-year tribulation.

Revelation 5: The Redemption of the World

The Lord Jesus Himself is the One who is solely capable of taking the little book of redemption from the One who sits on the throne of heaven and redeeming the world for God. Our fallen world, abused and tarnished by Satan, will be reclaimed and redeemed by Jesus Christ.

Revelation 6: Four Horsemen of the Apocalypse

Each horseman represents a distinct phase of the terrifying tribulation era following on the heels of the sudden disappearance of the Church. Chapter six provides a summary of the coming destruction of the earth.

Panic will grip the entire world and men without Christ will beg for rocks to fall upon them rather than face the painful judgments of the tribulation. The tribulation will climax and end at the Battle of Armageddon.

Revelation 7: The 144,000 Jewish Remnant

A select group of Jewish converts to Christ will serve as evangelists in the tribulation period and will point the masses toward the Messiah. Countless numbers of Jews and Gentiles will turn to Christ ushering in a great revival.

People converted during the tribulation will have never previously heard the gospel. They will respond to Christ and steadfastly refuse the *mark of the beast* imposed upon mankind by Satan.

Revelation 8: Retribution on the World

In this breathtaking episode of judgment, a fourth of the earth will incinerate, a third of the creatures of the sea will die, a third of the ships will be destroyed, waters will be poisoned rendering them useless, and other enormous upheavals will alter the earth. The impurity and lead contamination of our water in America is a precursor to the poisoning of the waters, both sea and fresh, that will occur in this judgment. Mankind will suffer tremendously.

As the *"star"* falls from heaven, the waters will become *"wormwood"* or poisoned (8:11).

Revelation 9: Revenge of the Demons

The bottomless pit, the prison home of demons, will open and legions of demonic locusts will swarm from its depths. These demons will be held in captivity until their day of judgment and be released to attack the minds and souls of men.

Severe persecution will come to the nation of Israel as Satan unleashes his evil forces upon it.

Revelation 10: An Interlude

Chapter ten describes a time of reaffirmation of the sovereignty of God. An angel will descend from heaven and plant one foot on the land and the other foot on the sea, raise his hand to the heavens, and announce that time will be no more (10: 2, 6).

God will assume full control and will draw human history to a close.

Revelation 11: Prediction of the Rebuilding of the Temple

The rebuilding of the revered Jewish temple is currently in its initial stage. Funds are being collected in Israel and preparations have been made for the reinstitution of temple sacrifices.

The vestments of the high priests and all of the instruments utilized in the sacrifice of animals are currently being gathered. Priests now are receiving training to reestablish the sacrificial system of the Old Testament (11:1-2).

The appearance of the two witnesses is detailed in 11:3-12. God will send two prophets like those who ministered during the days of the Old Testament who will possess the power to call down fire from heaven and turn water into blood. Their miracles will be numerous. These two witnesses will lose their lives yet miraculously rise from the dead. Their bodies will lie in the streets of Jerusalem and be exposed for the entire world to view with astonishment, presumably via television or internet.

Only with the technological advancement prevalent in our day could a prophecy such as this find fulfillment.

Revelation 12: Satan and Israel

The *"radiant woman"* is Israel who receives the hatred and vile attacks of Satan, the *"red dragon."* The life of Jesus Christ is depicted in the initial verses of the chapter beginning with His birth and Satan's attempt to devour Him at the time of His birth via Herod's unsuccessful plot to find and destroy Him.

However, a remnant of Israel will be kept safe and be airlifted to a wilderness location removed from the effects of the tribulation (12:6). Many bible students in our day believe that the United States will play a pivotal role in enabling the safety of Israel.

Satan will make an additional attempt to destroy Israel yet will fail.

Revelation 13: The Antichrist and the False Prophet

Two beasts will emerge, one from the sea representing the Antichrist, and the other from the land representative of the False

Prophet. The false prophet will head the one-world government and ultimately the one-world church as well. He will lend support to the Antichrist by insisting that the masses of the world worship the Antichrist as the undisputed god of the universe.

The evil and seductive powers of these two individuals will dupe the masses and intensify the evil of this era.

Revelation 14: Reaping Judgment

God's word provides for us the symbolism of the vineyard and details the trampling of grapes under foot metaphorically describing the judgment to be unleashed. The Son of Man will return with a full measure of judgment to afflict evil men. The harvest of evil in the earth will have ripened. Judgment upon evil men will be fully deserved.

Jesus spoke of this coming judgment. He said that one day God will send His angels to gather all of the evil that offends Him. He will gather all of the genuine wheat into the barn signifying believers kept in safety away from judgment, and He will burn the tares with fire.

In our day, tares biblically represent evil men who continue to live and grow among the pure wheat, representative of genuine believers. These tares, representing evil men posing as believers, sit in the pews of many churches today and are largely undetected by genuine believers who lack discernment.

Revelation 15: Completion of God's Judgment

Chapter fifteen details the last of the seven plagues or seven bowls of judgment to inflict evil men. Angels will make full preparations for the outpouring of God's judgment on the earth to occur in the last half of the seven-year tribulation.

Revelation 16: The Road to Armageddon

As the judgments are fully unleashed upon mankind, the pathway to the Battle of Armageddon will become clear. The waters of the great Euphrates River will be *"dried up"* preparing a passageway for the kings of the east to enter the land of battle

(16:12). As if underscoring the potentiality of this feat, Turkey constructed a dam in 1990 temporarily stopping the flow of the Euphrates.

John envisioned a huge army of some two hundred million soldiers. Red China once boasted of its capability to mount such an incredible offensive.

Demonic spirits will work feverously behind the scenes to prepare the nations of the world for the Battle (16:14). Temporary peace will calm tensions in the Middle East. Yet terrorism and global unrest will continue even in the midst of peace talks.

The prophet Daniel, the writings of Paul in Thessalonians, and Revelation all indicate that the Antichrist will arrive proclaiming a platform of peace. Discussions of global peace in United Nations assemblies are more common in our day than ever before.

Ongoing discussions concerning peace are consistent with biblical prophecy. Yet any semblance of peace to be realized will be short-lived at best and will yield to the demands for war.

Demonic forces will initiate and orchestrate the final Battle of Armageddon. When peace treaties ultimately fail, the attention of the nations will be riveted upon the location of the Battle, the land of Israel.

Revelation 17: Judgment of False Religion

Satan's pride and joy, the one-world religious system, is detailed in chapter seventeen. In the tribulation era, the church will be comprised of a myriad of cults, followers of witchcraft, occult worshippers, and all false religions in total.

This false religion is depicted in scripture as a scarlet prostituted woman who will wallow in her wealth and human power yet be completely void of the Holy Spirit.

God will unleash full judgment upon this false system and quickly destroy it.

Revelation 18: The Fall of the One-World Government and Economic and Political Systems

The tribulation era will feature unprecedented world trade. The merchants of the world will become partners in crime with this system, headed by the Antichrist, and will experience enormous prosperity in so doing.

A prelude to this event began in the late 1990's as Europe experienced the fall of communism and the United States began to move into these countries with the goal of strengthening their economies thereby enabling trade. Political advances such as these serve to prepare the world for a single one-world economic system. The popularity and acceptance of the *euro* in early 2002 further underscores this prophecy. This deceptive system of the tribulation will reap God's certain judgment.

Revelation 19: The Reward of Believers

As the tribulation terror afflicts evil men on earth, God's children will enjoy the marriage supper of the Lamb. Such an incredible celebration will fill believers with indescribable joy and euphoria.

Revelation 19:1-10 also deals with our preparations in heaven for Armageddon. Revelation 19:11 portrays the dramatic reentry of Jesus to the earth and His coming in power on a cloud of incredible glory.

As the nations of the earth gather for battle in the Valley of Megiddo, Jesus will burst onto the scene. He will defeat the forces of the Antichrist and will accomplish a dramatic rescue of the remnant of Israel who will have turned to Christ.

Revelation 20: The Millennium

As the Battle of Armageddon draws to a close, Jesus will establish the one thousand-year millennial reign with His children. This chapter also details the final judgment upon the world.

Satan will mount a temporary and unsuccessful revolt and will be summarily bound in the pit for a thousand years and ultimately cast into the lake of fire, hell itself.

Revelation 21: The New Heaven and Earth

Descending from the heavens will be the new heavens and new earth. Specific measurements further describe the breathtaking nature of these new heavens and earth.

Righteous men in love with Jesus Christ will experience God's best rewards.

Revelation 22: Eternal Rejoicing

With evil adjudicated and the hands of Satan bound forever in the lake of fire, the saints of heaven will bask in unending joy and praise of the Lord of the universe.

John closed the vision with final promises and the last prophecy recorded in written scripture. Jesus promised to *"come quickly"* (22:20). Believers should live with a delicate balance between remaining on earth in order to lead others to faith in Christ and longing for His immediate return.

My friend Dr. Jerry Vines of First Baptist Church, Jacksonville, Florida, tells the story of a school for mentally challenged children located in the hills of Kentucky. The teachers have faithfully taught the children that Jesus one day will dramatically appear in the skies to take us home. These precious children are so eager for His return that the teachers continually wipe away the smudges from the windowpanes left by the children who press their shining faces to the glass looking for His return.

We must diligently search the scriptures with a heart in love with Him and with an eye to live for His glory rather than for our own. An academic grasp of the concepts and chronological events in Revelation without a heart of love for our Lord Jesus entirely misses the point of John's vision. If this book has enhanced your love for Jesus and motivated your heart to long for His return, my goal for recording these thoughts has been reached.

Read the scriptures. Obey their implications. Love your church.

And wipe away the tears.

He is on the way!

OTHER BOOKS BY DR. STAN COFFEY

Building the Greatest Churches Since Pentecost

America, Armageddon and End Times Prophecy

Comfort, Peace and Hope: Help for Hurting Hearts in Times of Grief

Eternal Life: How to Know for Sure

Possessing the Promises of God

What to Do When You Feel Like Giving Up